This book is based on NCERT syllabus prescribed by the Central Board of Secondary Education (CBSE) for Class IX

Science for Ninth Class

(Part – 1)

Physics

As per NCERT/CBSE Syllabus

Containing answers to NCERT book questions and value-based questions

LAKHMIR SINGH

And

MANJIT KAUR

This Book Belongs to:

Name...

Roll No. ....

Class .... Section ....

School ....

S CHAND SCHOOL BOOKS
(An imprint of S Chand Publishing)
A Division of S Chand And Company Limited
(An ISO 9001 Certified Company)
Head Office : B-1/D-1, Ground Floor, Mohan Co-operative Industrial Estate (MCIE), Mathura Road, New Delhi–110 044
Phone : 011–6667 2000, **e-mail :** info@schandpublishing.com
Registered Office : A-27, 2nd Floor, Mohan Co-operative Industrial Estate, New Delhi–110 044
www.schandpublishing.com; **e-mail :** helpdesk@schandpublishing.com

Branches :

Chennai	:	Ph: 044-2363 2120, chennai@schandpublishing.com
Guwahati	:	Ph: 0361-2738 811, 2735 640, guwahati@schandpublishing.com
Hyderabad	:	Ph: 040-4018 6018, hyderabad@schandpublishing.com
Jalandhar	:	Ph: 0181-4645 630, jalandhar@schandpublishing.com
Kolkata	:	Ph: 033-2335 7458, 2335 3914, kolkata@schandpublishing.com
Lucknow	:	Ph: 0522-4003 633, lucknow@schandpublishing.com
Mumbai	:	Ph: 022-2500 0297, mumbai@schandpublishing.com
Patna	:	Ph: 0612-2260 011, patna@schandpublishing.com

First Published in 1982
Revised Edition 2014, 2016, 2017, 2018, 2020
Reprints 1983, 84, 85, 86, 87, 88, 89, 90, 91, 92, 93, 94, 95, 96, 97, 98, 99, 2000, 2001, 2002, 2003, 2004, 2005, 2006, 2007, 2008, 2009, 2010, 2011, 2012, 2013, 2015, 2016, 2017, 2018, 2019 (twice), 2020 (twice), 2021 (twice)

ISBN : 978-93-52837-92-2 **Product Code :** SCS3LKS090PHYAE19CBN

PRINTED IN INDIA
By Vikas Publishing House Private Limited, Plot 20/4, Site-IV, Industrial Area Sahibabad, Ghaziabad–201 010
and Published by S Chand And Company Limited, A-27, 2nd Floor, Mohan Co-operative Industrial Estate, New Delhi–110 044.

ABOUT THE AUTHORS

LAKHMIR SINGH did his M.Sc. from Delhi University in 1969. Since then he has been teaching in Dyal Singh College of Delhi University, Delhi. He started writing books in 1980. Lakhmir Singh believes that book writing is just like classroom teaching. Though a book can never replace a teacher but it should make the student feel the presence of a teacher. Keeping this in view, he writes books in such a style that students never get bored reading his books. Lakhmir Singh has written more than 15 books so far on all the science subjects: Physics, Chemistry and Biology. He believes in writing quality books. He does not believe in quantity.

MANJIT KAUR did her B.Sc., B.Ed. from Delhi University in 1970. Since then she has been teaching in a reputed school of Directorate of Education, Delhi. Manjit Kaur is such a popular science teacher that all the students want to join those classes which she teaches in the school. She has a vast experience of teaching science to school children, and she knows the problems faced by the children in the study of science. Manjit Kaur has put all her teaching experience into the writing of science books. She has co-authored more than 15 books alongwith her husband, Lakhmir Singh.

It is the team-work of Lakhmir Singh and Manjit Kaur which has given some of the most popular books in the history of science education in India. Lakhmir Singh and Manjit Kaur both write exclusively for the most reputed, respected and largest publishing house of India : S.Chand And Company Limited.

An Open Letter

Dear Friend,

We would like to talk to you for a few minutes, just to give you an idea of some of the special features of this book. Before we go further, let us tell you that this book has been revised according to the NCERT syllabus prescribed by the Central Board of Secondary Education (CBSE). Just like our earlier books, we have written this book in such a simple style that even the weak students will be able to understand physics very easily. Believe us, while writing this book, we have considered ourselves to be the students of Class IX and tried to make things as simple as possible.

The most important feature of this revised edition of the book is that we have included a large variety of different types of questions to assess the learning abilities of the students. This book contains :

(i) Very short answer type questions (including true-false type questions and fill in the blanks type questions),
(ii) Short answer type questions,
(iii) Long answer type questions (or Essay type questions),
(iv) Multiple choice questions (MCQs) based on theory,
(v) Questions based on high order thinking skills (HOTS),
(vi) Multiple choice questions (MCQs) based on practical skills in science,
(vii) NCERT book questions and exercises (with answers), and
(viii) Value based questions (with answers).

Please note that answers have also been given for the various types of questions, wherever required. All these features will make this book even more useful to the students as well as the teachers. "A picture can say a thousand words". Keeping this in mind, a large number of coloured pictures and sketches of various scientific processes, procedures, appliances, manufacturing plants and everyday situations involving principles of physics have been given in this revised edition of the book. This will help the students to understand the various concepts of physics clearly. It will also tell them how physics is applied in the real situations in homes, transport and industry.

Books by Lakhmir Singh and Manjit Kaur

1. Lakhmir Singh's Science for Class 1
2. Lakhmir Singh's Science for Class 2
3. Lakhmir Singh's Science for Class 3
4. Lakhmir Singh's Science for Class 4
5. Lakhmir Singh's Science for Class 5
6. Lakhmir Singh's Science for Class 6
7. Lakhmir Singh's Science for Class 7
8. Lakhmir Singh's Science for Class 8
9. Science for Ninth Class (Part 1) PHYSICS
10. Science for Ninth Class (Part 2) CHEMISTRY
11. Science for Tenth Class (Part 1) PHYSICS
12. Science for Tenth Class (Part 2) CHEMISTRY
13. Science for Tenth Class (Part 3) BIOLOGY
14. Science for Ninth Class (J & K Edition)
15. Science for Tenth Class (J & K Edition)
16. Science for Ninth Class (Hindi Edition) : PHYSICS and CHEMISTRY
17. Science for Tenth Class (Hindi Edition): PHYSICS, CHEMISTRY and BIOLOGY
18. Self-Practice Book for Science for Ninth Class Part-1 Physics
19. Self-Practice Book for Science for Ninth Class Part-2 Chemistry
20. Self-Practice Book for Science for Tenth Class Part-1 Physics
21. Self-Practice Book for Science for Tenth Class Part-2 Chemistry
22. Self-Practice Book for Science for Tenth Class Part-3 Biology

We are sure you will agree with us that the facts and formulae of physics are just the same in all the books, the difference lies in the method of presenting these facts to the students. In this book, the various topics of physics have been explained in such a simple way that while reading this book, a student will feel as if a teacher is sitting by his side and explaining the various things to him. We are sure that after reading this book, the students will develop a special interest in physics and they would like to study physics in higher classes as well.

We think that the real judges of a book are the teachers concerned and the students for whom it is meant. So, we request our teacher friends as well as the students to point out our mistakes, if any, and send their comments and suggestions for the further improvement of this book.

Wishing you a great success,

Yours sincerely,

Lakhmir Singh
Manjit Kaur

396, Nilgiri Apartments,
Alaknanda, New Delhi-110019
E-mail : singhlakhmir@hotmail.com

CONTENTS

Reflection of Sound ; Laws of Reflection of Sound ; Applications of Reflection of Sound : Megaphone, Bulb Horn, Stethoscope and Soundboard ; Echo : A Reflected Sound ; Calculation of Minimum Distance to Hear an Echo ; Reverberations ; Methods of Reducing Excessive Reverberations in Big Halls and Auditoriums ; The Frequency Range of Hearing in Humans ; Audible Sound, Infrasonic Sound and Ultrasonic Sound ; Applications of Ultrasound ; Sonar ; Finding the Depth of Sea and Locating Shoal of Fish, Shipwrecks and Enemy Submarines by Using Sonar; Characteristics of Sound : Loudness, Pitch and Quality (or Timbre) ; The Human Ear : Construction and Working ; Care of Ears

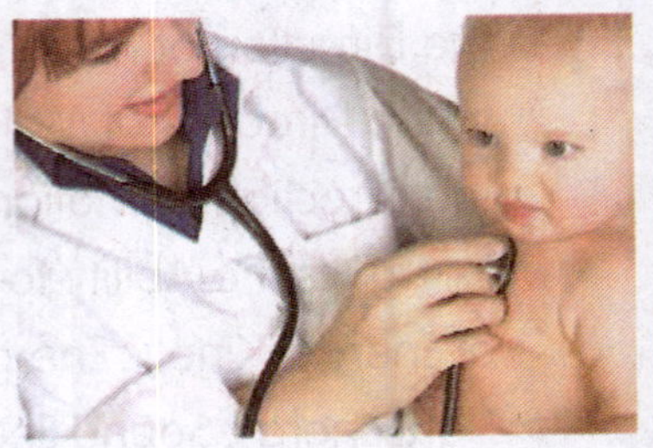

LATEST CBSE SYLLABUS CLASS 9 SCIENCE

(PHYSICS PART – 1)

Motion : Distance and displacement ; Velocity ; Uniform and non-uniform motion along a straight line ; Acceleration ; Distance-time and velocity-time graphs for uniform motion and uniformly accelerated motion ; Equations of motion by graphical method ; Elementary idea of uniform circular motion

Force and Newton's Laws : Force and motion ; Newton's laws of motion ; Inertia of a body ; Inertia and mass ; Momentum ; Force and acceleration ; Elementary idea of conservation of momentum ; Action and reaction forces

Gravitation : Gravitation ; Universal law of gravitation ; Force of gravitation of the earth (gravity); Acceleration due to gravity ; Mass and Weight ; Free fall

Flotation : Thrust and pressure ; Archimedes' principle; Buoyancy; Elementary idea of relative density

Work, energy and power : Work done by a force ; Energy ; Power ; Kinetic energy and potential energy ; Law of conservation of energy

Sound : Nature of sound and its propagation in various media ; Speed of sound ; Range of hearing in humans ; Ultrasound ; Reflection of sound ; Echo and SONAR ; Structure of the human ear (auditory aspect only)

MOTION

A tree is fixed at a place, so we say that it is stationary. Similarly, a house, a school, a factory, electric poles and telephone poles are all stationary objects which remain fixed at a place. On the other hand, a man, animals, birds, cars, buses, trains, ships and aeroplanes, etc., do not remain stationary all the time. They can move from one place to another. For example, a man moves when he walks along a road, a bird moves when it flies in the sky, a cheetah moves when it runs in the jungle, and a fish moves when it swims in water. Similarly, a car or bus moves on a road, a train moves on the track, a ship moves

Figure 1. All the vehicles seen in this photograph are moving on the road. They are in motion.

in water and an aeroplane moves when it flies in air from one place to another. The movement of a body (or object) is called motion. **A common characteristic of all the moving bodies is that they change their position with time**. We can now define motion as follows :

A body is said to be in motion (or moving) when its position changes continuously with respect to a stationary object taken as reference point. For example, when the position of a car changes continuously with respect to stationary objects like houses and trees, etc., we say that the car is moving or that the car is in motion. Let us take an example to understand the meaning of motion more clearly.

In Figure 2 we see a car at position *A* in front of a house and a tree at a particular time (In this case, the house and tree are the stationary objects which are taken as a reference point). Now, after 5 seconds, we see the same car at position *B* which is quite far away from the house and the tree (see Figure 2). This means

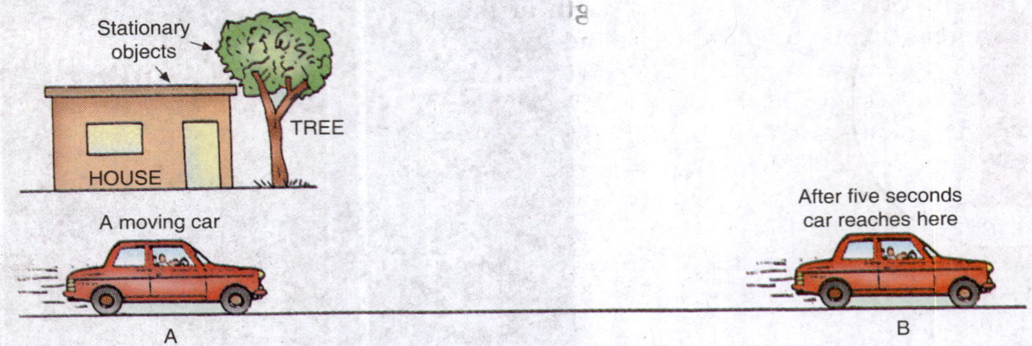

Figure 2. The position of moving car changes with time. So, the car is in motion.

that the position of this car is changing continuously with respect to a stationary object, house or tree. So, we say that this car is moving or that this car is in motion. Some other bodies (or objects) around us which show different kinds of motion are : swing (*jhoola*), merry-go-round, pendulum of a clock, and hands of a watch.

If a body moves fairly fast, then its movement (or motion) can be observed easily. But if a body moves very slowly, then it becomes difficult to observe its movement immediately. For example, a wrist watch has three hands : a seconds' hand, a minutes' hand and an hours' hand, which move round and round on the dial of the watch. Now, the seconds' hand of a watch moves quite fast, so we can observe the movement (or motion) of the seconds' hand of the watch very easily. But the minutes' hand and hours' hand of a watch move quite slow, so their movement cannot be observed easily. We will have to keep on observing the position of minutes' hand and hours' hand for quite some time to find out whether they are moving or not. This is because when a body moves, its position changes with time.

In order to study the motion of bodies (or objects), we should first know the meanings of two terms : **distance** and **displacement**. These are discussed below. Another point to be noted is that in the study of motion, whether we use the term 'body' 'or 'object', it means the same thing.

DISTANCE TRAVELLED AND DISPLACEMENT

In everyday language, the words distance and displacement are used in the same sense but in physics these two words have different meanings. Let us understand this difference by taking an example.

Suppose a man lives at place *A* (Figure 3) and he has to reach another place *C*, but first he has to meet his friend living at place *B*. Now, the man starts from point *A* and travels a distance of 5 km to reach *B*, and then travels another 3 km from *B* to reach *C*. Thus, the man goes along the path *ABC* (shown by dotted lines). Length of the path *ABC* gives us the actual distance travelled by the man. Thus, **the distance travelled by a body is the actual length of the path covered by a moving body irrespective of the direction in which the body travels.** For example, in this case, the actual length of the path covered by the man is 5 km + 3 km = 8 km, so the distance travelled by the man is 8 km.

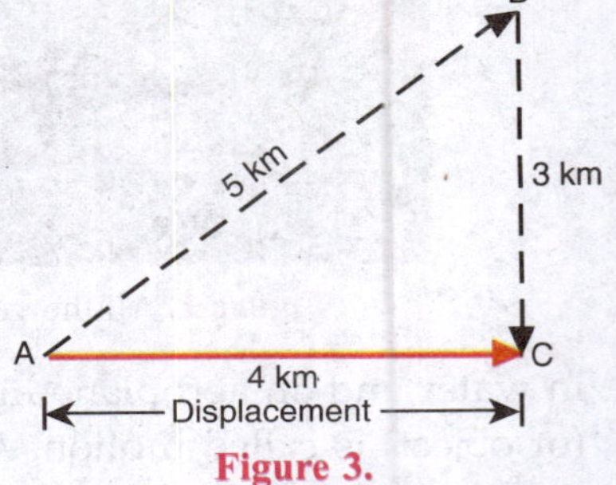

Figure 3.
Distance travelled = 5 + 3 = 8 km
Displacement = 4 km towards East.

We will now discuss this problem in a different way. When the man has reached point *C*, we want to know how far he is now from the starting point *A*, that is, we want to know the shortest distance between point *A* and point *C*. Let us draw a straight line *AC* between *A* and *C*. The length of the straight line path *AC* (which is 4 km here) is the displacement of the man from point *A*, that is, on reaching C, the man is only 4 km away from the starting point A. This displacement is in the East direction. Thus, **when a body moves from one point to another, the distance travelled refers to the actual length of the indirect path whereas displacement refers to the straight line path between the initial and the final positions.** So, whatever be the actual length of the path followed by a moving body, displacement of the body is always represented by the shortest distance between the initial and final positions of the body. Thus : **When a body moves from one position to another, the shortest (straight line) distance between the initial position and final position of the body, alongwith direction, is known as its displacement.** In the above example, the shortest distance between the initial position A and final position C of the man is 4 km, so the displacement of man is 4 km in the East direction. It is clear that **the distance travelled has only magnitude whereas displacement has magnitude as well as direction.**

Figure 4. If a vehicle goes from Town A to Town B by travelling on road over the hill, it will have to travel a distance of 25 kilometres. But if a vehicle goes from Town A to Town B on a straight road made through a tunnel in the hill, it will have to travel only 10 kilometres. So, in this case, the distance travelled is 25 km whereas the displacement is only 10 km.

The quantities like distance, displacement, etc., are known as physical quantities (or quantities of physics). The *magnitude* of a physical quantity means *size* of the physical quantity. A physical quantity having only magnitude (or size) is known as a scalar quantity. A scalar quantity has no direction. On the other hand, a physical quantity having magnitude as well as direction is known as a vector quantity.

(*i*) **Distance is a scalar quantity** (because it has magnitude only, it has no specified direction).

(*ii*) **Displacement is a vector quantity** (because it has magnitude as well as a direction).

For example, if a car travels a distance of 50 km, then **the expression "50 km" is the distance travelled,** and if the car is travelling in a straight line in the East direction (or any other direction), then **the expression "50 km towards East" is the displacement** of the car.

The distance travelled by a moving body cannot be zero but the final displacement of a moving body can be zero. The displacement of a moving body will be zero if, after travelling a certain distance, the moving body finally comes back to its starting point (or starting position). This will become clear from the following examples. Suppose a man starts from place A and travels a distance of 5 km to reach place B [see Figure 5(*a*)]. From place B he travels another 3 km and reaches place C. And finally the man travels 4 km from place C to reach back to the starting point A [see Figure 5(*a*)]. In this case, though the man has travelled a distance of 5 km + 3 km + 4 km = 12 km, but the final displacement of the man is zero.

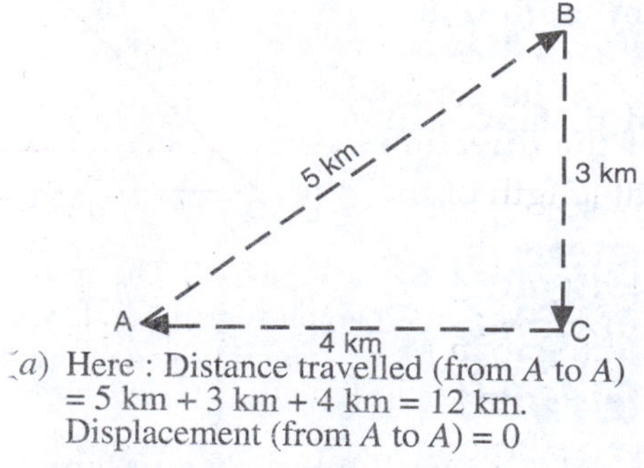

(*a*) Here : Distance travelled (from A to A) = 5 km + 3 km + 4 km = 12 km.
Displacement (from A to A) = 0

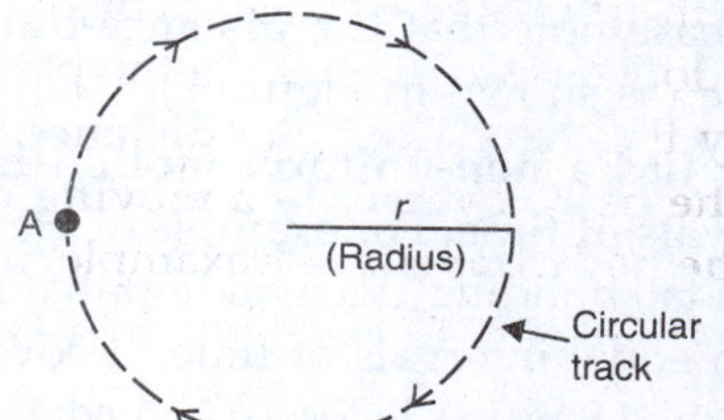

(*b*) Here : Distance travelled (from A to A) = $2\pi r$ (where r is radius of the circular track).
Displacement (from A to A) = 0

Figure 5. Two examples where a body travels a certain distance but the final displacement of the body is zero.

This is because the man has reached back at the starting point *A* and the straight line distance between the initial position *A* and final position *A* is zero. Thus, **if we take a round trip and reach back at the starting point then, though we have travelled some distance, our final displacement will be zero. This is because the straight line distance between the initial and final positions will be zero**. For example, if we travel along a circular track of radius *r* and reach back at the starting point *A* [see Figure 5(*b*)], then though we have travelled a distance $2\pi r$ (equal to circumference of track) but our final displacement will be zero. We will now solve a problem based on distance and displacement.

Sample Problem. A man travels a distance of 1.5 m towards East, then 2.0 m towards South and finally 4.5 m towards East.

(*i*) What is the total distance travelled ?

(*ii*) What is his resultant displacement ?

Solution. (*i*) Total distance travelled $= 1.5 + 2.0 + 4.5$

$= 8.0$ m

(*ii*) To find the resultant displacement we should draw a map of the man's movements by choosing a convenient scale. Let 1 cm represent 1 m. Then 1.5 m can be represented by 1.5 cm long line, 2.0 m by 2.0 cm line and 4.5 m by a 4.5 cm long line.

We draw a 1.5 cm long line *AB* from West to East to represent 1.5 m towards East (see Figure 6). Then we draw a 2.0 cm long line *BC* towards South to represent 2.0 m towards South. And finally we draw a third line *CD*, 4.5 cm long, towards East to represent a distance of 4.5 m towards East. Now, the resultant displacement can be found by joining the starting point *A* with the finishing point *D*. Thus, the line *AD* represents the final displacement of the man. Let us measure the length of line *AD*. It is found to be 6.3 cm.

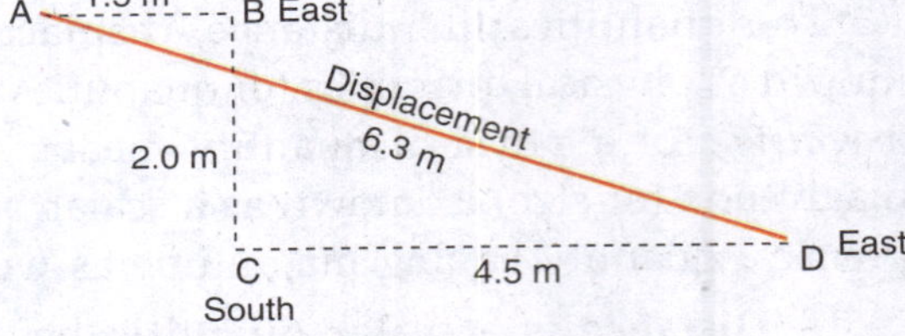

Figure 6. Diagram for sample problem (Scale : 1 cm = 1 m)

Now, 1 cm = 1 m

So, 6.3 cm = 6.3 m

Thus, the final displacement as represented by *AD* is 6.3 metres.

Please note that **whenever a body travels along a zig-zag path, the final displacement is obtained by joining the starting point and the finishing point of the body by a straight line.**

UNIFORM MOTION AND NON-UNIFORM MOTION

A body has a uniform motion if it travels equal distances in equal intervals of time, no matter how small these time intervals may be. For example, a car running at a constant speed of say, 10 metres per second, will cover equal distances of 10 metres, every second, so its motion will be uniform. Please note that **the distance-time graph for uniform motion is a straight line** (as shown in Figure 7).

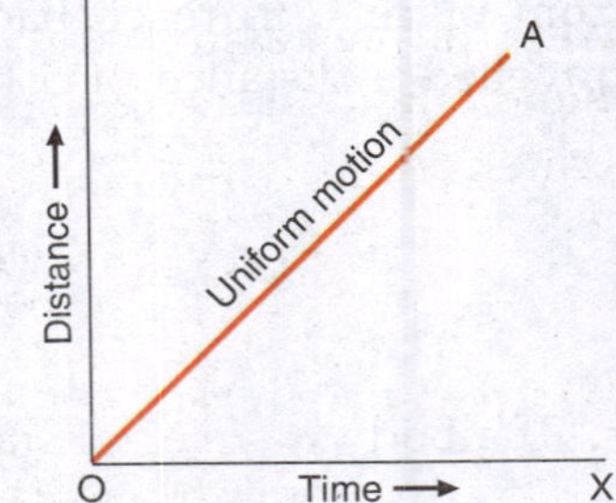

Figure 7. The distance-time graph for a body having uniform motion is a straight line.

A body has a non-uniform motion if it travels unequal distances in equal intervals of time. For example, if we drop a ball from the roof of a tall building, we will find that it covers unequal distances in equal intervals of time. It covers :

4.9 metres in the 1st second,

14.7 metres in the 2nd second,

24.5 metres in the 3rd second, and so on.

Thus, a freely falling ball covers smaller distances in the initial '1 second' intervals and larger distances in the later '1 second' intervals (see Figure 8). From this discussion we conclude that **the motion of a freely**

falling body is an example of non-uniform motion. The motion of a train starting from the Railway Station is also an example of non-uniform motion. This is because when the train starts from a Station, it moves a very small distance in the 'first' second. The train moves a little more distance in the '2nd' second, and so on. And when the train approaches the next Station, the distance travelled by it per second decreases. Please note that **the distance-time graph for a body having non-uniform motion is a curved line** (as shown in Figure 9). Thus, in order to find out whether a body has uniform motion or non-uniform motion, we should draw the distance-time graph for it. ***If the distance-time graph is a straight line, the motion will be uniform and if the distance-time graph is a curved line, the motion will be non-uniform***. It should be noted that **non-uniform motion is also called accelerated motion.**

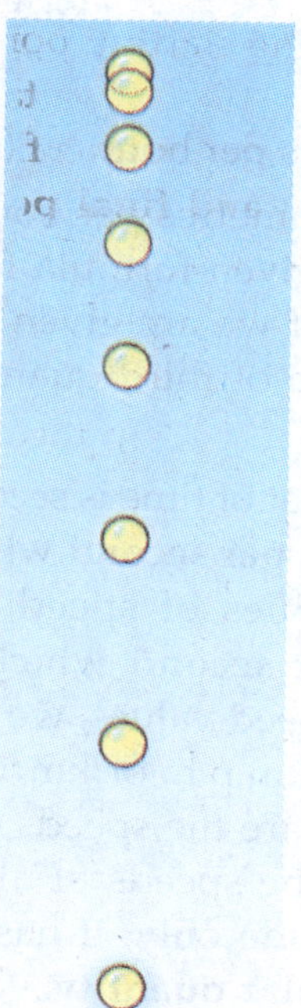

Figure 8. A ball dropped from the roof of a tall building travels unequal distances in equal intervals of time. So, it has non-uniform motion.

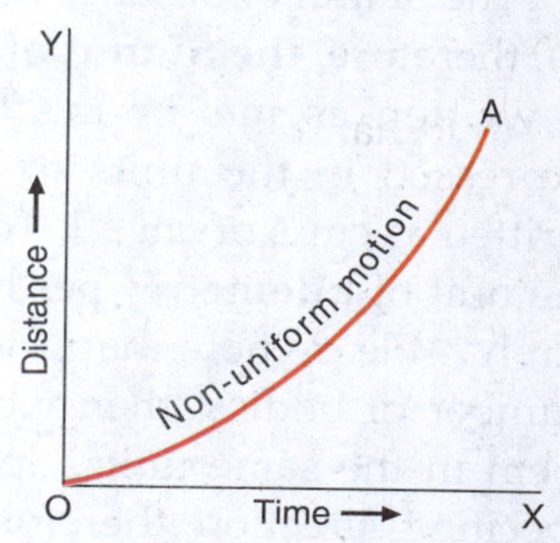

Figure 9. The distance-time graph for a body having non-uniform motion is a curved line.

Speed, Velocity and Acceleration

The motion of a body can be described by three terms : Speed, Velocity and Acceleration. Let us study them in detail, one by one.

SPEED

If a car is running slow, we say that its speed is low. And if a car is running fast, then we say that its speed is high. Thus, **the speed of a body gives us an idea of how slow or fast that body is moving.** We can now define the speed of a moving body as follows : **Speed of a body is the distance travelled by it per unit time**. The speed of a body can be calculated by dividing the '**Distance travelled**' by the '**Time taken**' to travel this distance. So, the formula for speed can be written as :

Figure 10. This bus is running fast. So, its speed is high.

$$\textbf{Speed} = \frac{\textbf{Distance travelled}}{\textbf{Time taken}}$$

If a body travels a distance s in time t, then its speed v is given by :

$$v = \frac{s}{t}$$

where v = speed

s = distance travelled

and t = time taken (to travel that distance)

Suppose a car travels a distance of 100 kilometres in 4 hours, then the speed of this car is given by :

$$\text{Speed} = \frac{100 \text{ kilometres}}{4 \text{ hours}}$$

or Speed = 25 kilometres per hour (or 25 km/h)

Thus, the speed of this car will be 25 kilometres per hour. This means that the car travels a distance of 25 kilometres 'every one hour'. The above given formula for calculating speed has three quantities in it : Speed, Distance travelled and Time taken. If we are given the values of any two quantities, then the value of third quantity can be calculated by using this formula.

The SI unit of distance is metre (m) and that of time is second (s), therefore, **the SI unit of speed is metres per second** which is written as m/s or m s^{-1}. The small values of speed are expressed in the units of **centimetres per second** which is written as cm/s or cm s^{-1}. To express high speed values, we use the unit of **kilometres per hour**, written as km.p.h. or km/h or km h^{-1}. Please note that if we have to compare the speeds of a number of bodies, then we must express the speeds of all of them in the same units. Speed has magnitude only, it has no specified direction, therefore, **speed is a scalar quantity.**

Figure 11. Speedometer and odometer of a car. This speedometer shows a speed of 85 km/h and odometer shows a reading of 2.0 km for the distance travelled by the car so far. The distance travelled suggests that it is a brand new car.

The speed of a running car at any instant of time is shown by an instrument called '**speedometer**' which is fixed in the car. The speedometer gives the speed in kilometres per hour. The distance travelled by a car is measured by another instrument called '**odometer**' which is also installed in the car. It records the distance in kilometres.

Average Speed

The average speed of a body is the total distance travelled divided by the total time taken to cover this distance. While travelling in a car (or a bus) we have noticed that it is very difficult to keep the speed of the car at a constant or uniform value because at many places the brakes are to be applied to slow down or stop the car due to various reasons. Thus, the speed of a body is usually not constant and the distance travelled divided by time gives us the average speed during that time. For example, for a car which travels a distance of 100 km in 4 hours, the average speed is $\frac{100}{4} = 25$ km per hour. Although the average speed of this car is 25 km per hour, it does not mean that the car is moving at this speed all the time. When the road is straight, flat and free, the speed may be much more than 25 km per hour but on bends (curved road), hills or in a crowded area, the speed may fall well below this average value. We should remember that :

$$\text{Average speed} = \frac{\text{Total distance travelled}}{\text{Total time taken}}$$

We will use this formula for solving numerical problems after a while. The average speeds of some of the moving objects are given below.

Moving object	*Average speed*		
1. Tortoise	0.06 m/s	or	0.216 km/h
2. Human walking	2 m/s	or	7.2 km/h
3. Human running (sprinter)	10 m/s	or	36 km/h
4. Birds	5 to 15 m/s	or	18 to 54 km/h
5. Cheetah	27 m/s	or	97.2 km/h
6. Fast car	30 m/s	or	108 km/h
7. Racing car	60 m/s	or	216 km/h
8. Sound in air (at 20°C)	344 m/s	or	1238.4 km/h
9. Jet aeroplane	500 m/s	or	1800 km/h
10. Light (in vacuum)	3×10^8 m/s	or	1.08×10^9 km/h

(a) A sprinter (fast runner) can have a speed of about 10 m/s (which is 36 km/h)

(b) A cheetah can have a speed of up to about 27 m/s (which is more than 97 km/h)

(c) A military jet aircraft can have a speed of about 500 m/s (which is 1800 km/h)

Figure 12. The moving things can have many different speeds.

Uniform Speed (or Constant Speed)

A body has a uniform speed if it travels equal distances in equal intervals of time, no matter how small these time intervals may be. For example, a car is said to have uniform speed of say, 60 km per hour, if it travels 30 km every half hour, 15 km every quarter of an hour, 1 km every minute, and $\frac{1}{60}$ km every second. As we have already discussed above, in actual practice the speed of a body rarely remains uniform (or constant) for a long time. If, however, the speed of a body is known to be constant, we can find out exactly how much distance it will travel in a given time or if we know the distance travelled by the body, we can calculate the time taken to travel that distance. We will now solve some numerical problems based on speed.

Sample Problem 1. A scooterist covers a distance of 3 kilometres in 5 minutes. Calculate his speed in :

(a) centimetres per second (cm/s)

(b) metres per second (m/s)

(c) kilometres per hour (km/h)

Solution. (a) In order to calculate the speed in centimetres per second we should convert the given distance of 3 kilometres into centimetres and the given time of 5 minutes into seconds. Please note that 1 kilometre has 1000 metres and 1 metre has 100 centimetres. Now,

$$\begin{aligned}\text{Distance travelled} &= 3 \text{ km}\\ &= 3 \times 1000 \text{ m}\\ &= 3 \times 1000 \times 100 \text{ cm}\\ &= 300{,}000 \text{ cm} \qquad \text{.... (1)}\end{aligned}$$

$$\begin{aligned}\text{Time taken} &= 5 \text{ minutes}\\ &= 5 \times 60 \text{ seconds}\\ &= 300 \text{ s} \qquad \text{.... (2)}\end{aligned}$$

We know that,

$$\begin{aligned}\text{Speed} &= \frac{\text{Distance travelled}}{\text{Time taken}}\\ &= \frac{300{,}000 \text{ cm}}{300 \text{ s}}\\ &= 1000 \text{ cm/s} \qquad \text{.... (3)}\end{aligned}$$

Thus, the speed of scooterist is 1000 centimetres per second.

(b) In order to express the speed in metres per second we should convert the given distance of 3 kilometres into metres and the given time of 5 minutes into seconds. Thus, in this case :

$$\begin{aligned}\text{Distance travelled} &= 3 \text{ km}\\ &= 3 \times 1000 \text{ m}\\ &= 3000 \text{ m} \qquad \text{.... (4)}\end{aligned}$$

$$\text{Time taken} = 5 \text{ minutes}$$
$$= 5 \times 60 \text{ seconds}$$
$$= 300 \text{ s} \quad \text{.... (5)}$$

Now,
$$\text{Speed} = \frac{\text{Distance travelled}}{\text{Time taken}}$$
$$= \frac{3000 \text{ m}}{300 \text{ s}}$$
$$= 10 \text{ m/s} \quad \text{.... (6)}$$

So, the speed of scooterist is 10 metres per second.

(*c*) And finally, in order to calculate the speed in kilometres per hour, we should express the given distance in kilometres (which is already so), and the given time in hours. So, in this case :

$$\text{Distance travelled} = 3 \text{ km} \quad \text{.... (7)}$$
$$\text{Time taken} = 5 \text{ minutes}$$
$$= \frac{5}{60} \text{ hours}$$
$$= 0.083 \text{ h} \quad \text{.... (8)}$$

We know that,
$$\text{Speed} = \frac{\text{Distance travelled}}{\text{Time taken}}$$
$$= \frac{3 \text{ km}}{0.083 \text{ h}}$$
$$= 36 \text{ km/h} \quad \text{.... (9)}$$

Thus, the speed of scooterist is 36 kilometres per hour.

Figure 13. This road sign shows the speed limit of 40 km/h in a particular area of a city. All of us should drive vehicles within the specified speed limit. This will keep us as well as other road users safe.

Figure 14. This photograph shows a traffic police officer using the speed gun (or radar gun) to determine a running car's speed. The overspeeding drivers are fined heavily.

Sample Problem 2. The train *'A'* travelled a distance of 120 km in 3 hours whereas another train *'B'* travelled a distance of 180 km in 4 hours. Which train travelled faster ?

Solution. In order to solve this problem, we have to calculate the speeds of both the trains separately. The train having higher speed will have travelled faster.

(*i*) We know that :
$$\text{Speed} = \frac{\text{Distance travelled}}{\text{Time taken}}$$

Now, Distance travelled by train A = 120 km
And, Time taken by train A = 3 h

So, $$\text{Speed of train } A = \frac{120 \text{ km}}{3 \text{ h}}$$
$$= 40 \text{ km/h} \quad ...(1)$$

Thus, the speed of train A is 40 kilometres per hour.

(*ii*) Again, $$\text{Speed} = \frac{\text{Distance travelled}}{\text{Time taken}}$$

Now, Distance travelled by train B = 180 km
And, Time taken by train B = 4 h

So, $$\text{Speed of train } B = \frac{180 \text{ km}}{4 \text{ h}}$$
$$= 45 \text{ km/h} \quad ...(2)$$

Thus, the speed of train B is 45 kilometres per hour.

From the above calculations we find that the train A travels a distance of 40 kilometres in one hour whereas the train B travels a distance of 45 kilometres in one hour. Since the speed of train B is higher, therefore, train B has travelled faster.

Sample Problem 3. A car travels 30 km at a uniform speed of 40 km/h and the next 30 km at a uniform speed of 20 km/h. Find its average speed.

Solution. (*i*) First the car travels a distance of 30 kilometres at a speed of 40 kilometres per hour. Let us find out the time taken by the car to travel this distance.

Here, Speed = 40 km/h
Distance = 30 km
And, Time = ? (To be calculated)

We know that, $$\text{Speed} = \frac{\text{Distance}}{\text{Time}}$$

So, $$40 = \frac{30}{\text{Time}}$$

And, $$\text{Time} = \frac{30}{40} \text{ hours}$$

Or $$\text{Time } (t_1) = \frac{3}{4} \text{ hours} \quad .... (1)$$

(*ii*) Next the car travels a distance of 30 km at a speed of 20 km/h. We will also find out the time taken by the car to travel this distance. In this case :

Speed = 20 km/h
Distance = 30 km
And, Time = ? (To be calculated)

Again, $$\text{Speed} = \frac{\text{Distance}}{\text{Time}}$$

So, $$20 = \frac{30}{\text{Time}}$$

And, $$\text{Time} = \frac{30}{20} \text{ hours}$$

Or $$\text{Time } (t_2) = \frac{3}{2} \text{ hours} \quad .... (2)$$

We can get the total time taken by the car for the whole journey by adding the above two time values t_1 and t_2. Thus,

$$\text{Total time taken} = \frac{3}{4} + \frac{3}{2} \text{ hours}$$

$$= \frac{3+6}{4} \text{ hours}$$

$$= \frac{9}{4} \text{ hours} \quad \text{.... (3)}$$

And, $$\text{Total distance travelled} = 30 \text{ km} + 30 \text{ km}$$

$$= 60 \text{ km} \quad \text{.... (4)}$$

Now, $$\text{Average speed} = \frac{\text{Total distance travelled}}{\text{Total time taken}}$$

$$= \frac{60 \times 4}{9}$$

$$= \frac{240}{9}$$

$$= 26.6 \text{ km/h}$$

Thus, the average speed of the car for the whole journey is 26.6 kilometres per hour.

Figure 15. This road accident has occurred due to the over speeding by the drivers of the bus and the car. We should never drive a vehicle (car, motorbike, etc.) too fast. Motor accident may injure a person seriously, it may paralyse a person for the whole life or it may kill a person instantly. Life is too precious. Don't waste it. Remember : speed thrills but kills !

Figure 16. Look at this woman who is talking on mobile phone while driving a car. This is a very dangerous practice. It has resulted in many serious road accidents. If it is absolutely necessary to talk on mobile phone, first stop the car (or motorbike) and then talk. Life is short. Don't make it shorter !

Sample Problem 4. On a 120 km track, a train travels the first 30 km at a uniform speed of 30 km/h. How fast must the train travel the next 90 km so as to average 60 km/h for the entire trip ?

Solution. In this numerical problem we have been given the total distance travelled by the train (which is 120 km), and the average speed of the train for the whole journey (which is 60 km/h). From these two values we can calculate the total time taken by the train for the entire journey. This can be done as follows :

We know that, $$\text{Average speed} = \frac{\text{Total distance travelled}}{\text{Total time taken}}$$

So, $$60 = \frac{120}{\text{Total time taken}}$$

And, $$\text{Total time taken} = \frac{120}{60} \text{ hours}$$

$$= 2 \text{ hours} \quad \text{.... (1)}$$

We will now calculate the time taken by the train for the first 30 km journey, and the next 90 km journey, separately (see Figure 17).

(*i*) For the first part of the train journey, we have :

$$\text{Speed} = 30 \text{ km/h}$$
$$\text{Distance} = 30 \text{ km}$$

And, $\text{Time} = ?$ (To be calculated)

Now, $$\text{Speed} = \frac{\text{Distance travelled}}{\text{Time taken}}$$

So, $$30 = \frac{30}{\text{Time taken}}$$

And, $$\text{Time taken} = \frac{30}{30} \text{ hours}$$
$$= 1 \text{ hour} \quad \text{.... (2)}$$

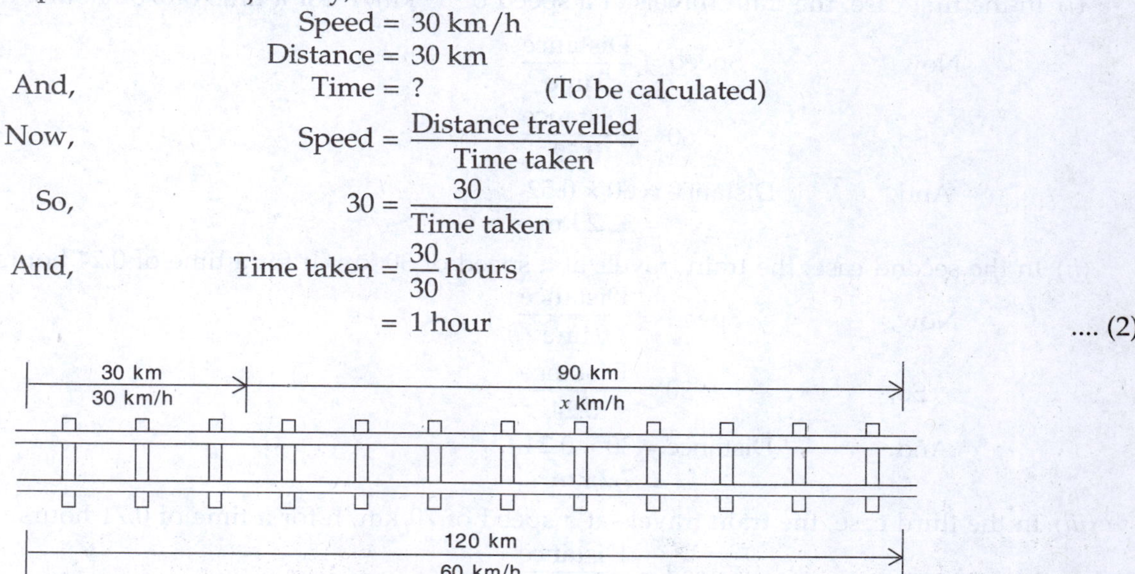

Figure 17. Diagram for sample problem 4.

(*ii*) For the second part of the train journey, let us suppose that the speed of the train is x km/h. So, for the second part of the train journey, we have :

$$\text{Speed} = x \text{ km/h} \quad \text{(Supposed)}$$
$$\text{Distance} = 90 \text{ km}$$

And, $\text{Time} = ?$ (To be calculated)

Now, $$\text{Speed} = \frac{\text{Distance travelled}}{\text{Time taken}}$$

So, $$x = \frac{90}{\text{Time taken}}$$

And, $$\text{Time taken} = \frac{90}{x} \text{ hours} \quad \text{.... (3)}$$

Now, adding equations (2) and (3), we get the total time taken for the entire trip :

$$\text{Total time taken} = 1 + \frac{90}{x} \text{ hours} \quad \text{.... (4)}$$

We already know from equation (1) that the total time taken for the entire trip is 2 hours. So, comparing equations (4) and (1), we get :

$$1 + \frac{90}{x} = 2$$
$$\frac{90}{x} = 2 - 1$$
$$\frac{90}{x} = 1$$

And $$x = 90 \text{ km/h}$$

Thus, the train should travel the next 90 km distance at a speed of 90 km/h.

Sample Problem 5. A train travels at a speed of 60 km/h for 0.52 h, at 30 km/h for the next 0.24 h and then at 70 km/h for the next 0.71 h. What is the average speed of the train ?

Solution. In this problem, first of all we have to calculate the distances travelled by the train under three different conditions of speed and time.

(*i*) In the first case, the train travels at a speed of 60 km/h for a time of 0.52 hours.

Now, $\text{Speed} = \dfrac{\text{Distance}}{\text{Time}}$

So, $60 = \dfrac{\text{Distance}}{0.52}$

And, $\text{Distance} = 60 \times 0.52$

$= 31.2 \text{ km}$ .... (1)

(*ii*) In the second case, the train travels at a speed of 30 km/h for a time of 0.24 hours.

Now, $\text{Speed} = \dfrac{\text{Distance}}{\text{Time}}$

So, $30 = \dfrac{\text{Distance}}{0.24}$

And, $\text{Distance} = 30 \times 0.24$

$= 7.2 \text{ km}$ .... (2)

(*iii*) In the third case, the train travels at a speed of 70 km/h for a time of 0.71 hours.

Again, $\text{Speed} = \dfrac{\text{Distance}}{\text{Time}}$

So, $70 = \dfrac{\text{Distance}}{0.71}$

And, $\text{Distance} = 70 \times 0.71$

$= 49.7 \text{ km}$ .... (3)

Now, from the equations (1), (2) and (3), we get :

Total distance travelled $= 31.2 + 7.2 + 49.7$

$= 88.1 \text{ km}$ .... (4)

And, Total time taken $= 0.52 + 0.24 + 0.71$

$= 1.47 \text{ h}$ .... (5)

We know that : $\text{Average speed} = \dfrac{\text{Total distance travelled}}{\text{Total time taken}}$

$= \dfrac{88.1}{1.47}$

$= 59.9 \text{ km/h}$

VELOCITY

The speed of a car (or any other body) gives us an idea of how fast the car is moving but it does not tell us the direction in which the car is moving. Thus, to know the exact position of a moving car we should also know the direction in which the car is moving. In other words, we should know the speed of the car as well as the direction of speed. This gives us another term known as velocity which can be defined as follows : **Velocity of a body is the distance travelled by it per unit time in a given direction.** That is :

$$\textbf{Velocity} = \frac{\textbf{Distance travelled in a given direction}}{\textbf{Time taken}}$$

If a body travels a distance '*s*' in time '*t*' in a given direction, then its velocity '*v*' is given by :

$$v = \frac{s}{t}$$

where v = velocity of the body

s = distance travelled (in the given direction)

and t = time taken (to travel that distance)

We know that the '**Distance travelled in a given direction**' is known as '**Displacement**'. So, we can also write the definition of velocity in terms of '**Displacement**'. We can now say that : **Velocity of a body is the displacement produced per unit time**. We can obtain the velocity of a body by dividing the 'Displacement' by 'Time taken' for the displacement. Thus, we can write another formula for velocity as follows :

$$\textbf{Velocity} = \frac{\textbf{Displacement}}{\textbf{Time taken}}$$

$$v = \frac{s}{t}$$

where v = velocity of the body

s = displacement of the body

and t = time taken (for displacement)

The SI unit of velocity is the same as that of speed, namely, metres per second (m/s or m s^{-1}). We can use the bigger unit of **kilometres per hour** to express the bigger values of velocities and **centimetres per second** to express the small values of velocities. It should be noted that both, speed as well as velocity, are represented by the same symbol v.

Figure 18. This car is travelling on a straight road at a speed of 25 km/h in the 'North' direction, so the velocity of this car is 25 km/h directed towards 'North'.

The difference between speed and velocity is that speed has only magnitude (or size), it has no specific direction, but velocity has magnitude as well as direction. In fact, velocity of a body is its speed in a specified direction (in a single straight line). **Speed is a scalar quantity** (because it has magnitude only). **Velocity is a vector quantity** (because it has magnitude as well as direction). For example, **the expression '25 km per hour' is the speed** (because it has magnitude only), but **the expression '25 km per hour towards North' (or any other direction) is velocity** (because it has both magnitude as well as a specified direction). To be strictly accurate, whenever velocity is expressed, it should be given as speed in a 'certain direction'. *Usually, however, velocities are expressed without mentioning direction for the sake of convenience.* The direction is assumed without being stated. **The direction of velocity is the same as the direction of displacement of the body.**

The 'Distance travelled' by a body in a given direction divided by 'Time' gives us average velocity. For example, if a car travels a distance of 100 km in 4 hours in the North direction, then its average velocity is $\frac{100}{4}$ = 25 km per hour, due North.

We have just seen that, $v = \frac{s}{t}$

So, $s = v \times t$

Thus, **Distance travelled = Average velocity × Time**

This formula should be memorized because it will be used in solving numerical problems.

Uniform Velocity (or Constant Velocity)

If an object travels in a specified direction in a straight line and moves the same distance every second, we say that its velocity is uniform. Thus, **A body has a uniform velocity if it travels in a specified direction**

in a straight line and moves over equal distances in equal intervals of time, no matter how small these time intervals may be.

The velocity of a body can be changed in two ways :

(*i*) **by changing the speed of the body,** and

(*ii*) **by keeping the speed constant but by changing the direction.**

When a body does not cover equal distances in equal intervals of time, the velocity is said to be variable or non-uniform velocity. In this case the speed of the body is not constant. Even if the speed of a body is constant but the direction is changing, the velocity will not be uniform. Suppose a car is moving on a circular road with constant speed. Now, though the speed of the car is constant, its velocity is not constant because the direction of car is changing continuously.

Figure 19. This car is running on a circular road with a constant speed. Now, since the direction of motion of car is changing continuosly (due to circular road), its velocity is also changing (though the speed is constant). The motion of car in this case is said to be accelerated.

Speed and Velocity are Not Always Equal in Magnitude

In most of the cases, the magnitude of speed and velocity of a moving body is equal. This will become clear from the following example. Suppose a boy runs a distance of 100 metres in 50 seconds in going from his home to a shop in the East direction in a straight line (see Figure 20).

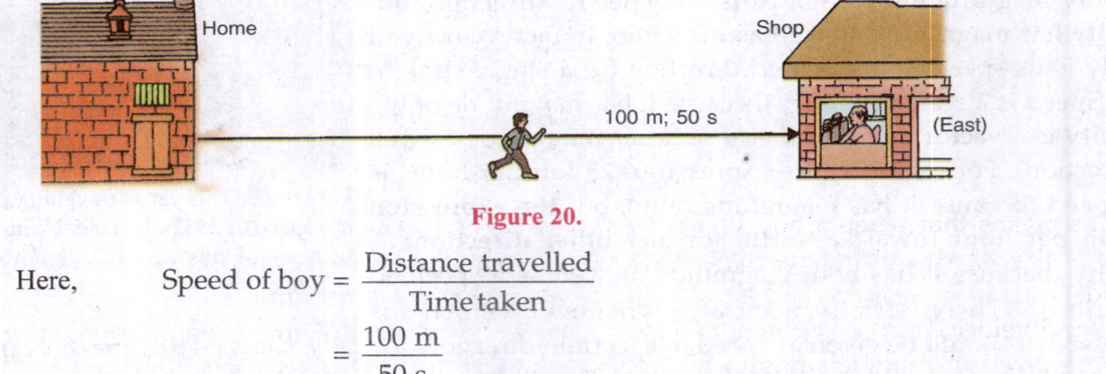

Figure 20.

Here,
$$\text{Speed of boy} = \frac{\text{Distance travelled}}{\text{Time taken}}$$
$$= \frac{100\text{ m}}{50\text{ s}}$$
$$= 2\text{ m/s} \quad \text{... (1)}$$

Since the boy runs in a specified direction (East) in a straight line path, therefore, the displacement here will be equal in magnitude to the distance travelled. The displacement will actually be 100 m towards East. Thus,

$$\text{Velocity of boy} = \frac{\text{Displacement}}{\text{Time taken}}$$
$$= \frac{100\text{ m towards East}}{50\text{ s}}$$
$$= 2\text{ m/s towards East} \quad \text{...(2)}$$

We can see that in this case the magnitude (or size) of speed and velocity of the boy is equal (being 2 m/s).

Please note that **the magnitude of speed and velocity of a moving body is equal only if the body moves in a single straight line** (like the boy in the above case). **If, however, a body does not move in a**

single straight line, then the speed and velocity of the body are not equal. This will become clear from the following example.

Suppose the boy first runs a distance of 100 metres in 50 seconds in going from his home to the shop in the East direction, and then runs a distance of 100 metres again in 50 seconds in the reverse direction from the shop to reach back home from where he started (see Figure 21).

Figure 21.

In this case, the total distance travelled is 100 m + 100 m = 200 m and the total time taken is 50 s + 50 s = 100 s. Thus,

$$\text{Speed of boy} = \frac{\text{Distance travelled}}{\text{Time taken}}$$

$$= \frac{200\text{ m}}{100\text{ s}}$$

$$= 2\text{ m/s} \qquad \text{... (3)}$$

The boy runs 100 m towards East and then 100 m in opposite direction (towards West), and reaches at the starting point, his home. So, the displacement (distance travelled in a given direction) will be 100 m – 100 m = 0 m. The total time taken is 50 s + 50 s = 100 s. In this case :

$$\text{Velocity of boy} = \frac{\text{Displacement}}{\text{Time taken}}$$

$$= \frac{0\text{ m}}{100\text{ s}}$$

$$= 0\text{ m/s} \qquad \text{... (4)}$$

This means that when a boy first runs a distance of 100 metres towards East in 50 seconds and then changes direction and runs the same distance of 100 metres in the reverse direction (towards West) in 50 seconds, then his **average speed is 2m/s** but his **average velocity is 0 m/s**. So, in this case the magnitude of speed and velocity of the boy is not equal. This is an unusual situation. It has happened because the boy has not moved in a single straight line. He has changed (or rather reversed) his direction of motion after reaching the shop.

In most of the cases, the bodies (or objects) move in single straight line (without changing direction). The values of speed and velocity will be the same in these cases. The difference in the values of speed and velocity arises only when a body (or object) does not move in a single straight line (and changes its direction of motion at some point of time). From this discussion we conclude that **though the average speed of a moving body can never be zero, but the average velocity of a moving body can be zero**. Let us solve some problems now.

Sample Problem 1. A car travels a distance of 200 km from Delhi to Ambala towards North in 5 hours. Calculate (*i*) speed, and (*ii*) velocity, of the car for this journey.

Solution. (*i*) $\text{Speed} = \frac{\text{Distance travelled}}{\text{Time taken}}$

$$= \frac{200\text{ km}}{5\text{ h}}$$

$$= 40\text{ km/h}$$

Thus, the speed (or average speed) of the car is 40 km/h.

(*ii*) $$\text{Velocity} = \frac{\text{Displacement}}{\text{Time taken}}$$

$$= \frac{\text{200 km towards North}}{\text{5 h}}$$

$$= \text{40 km/h towards North}$$

So, the velocity (or average velocity) of the car is 40 km/h towards North.

Sample Problem 2. A bus covers a distance of 250 km from Delhi to Jaipur towards West in 5 hours in the morning and returns to Delhi in the evening covering the same distance of 250 km in the same time of 5 hours. Find (*a*) average speed, and (*b*) average velocity, of the bus for the whole journey.

Solution. (*i*) $$\text{Average speed} = \frac{\text{Total distance travelled}}{\text{Total time taken}}$$

$$= \frac{250\text{ km} + 250\text{ km}}{5\text{ h} + 5\text{ h}}$$

$$= \frac{500\text{ km}}{10\text{ h}} = 50\text{ km/h}$$

Thus, the average speed of the bus for the whole journey (both ways) is 50 kilometres per hour.

(*ii*) In this case, the bus travels 250 km from Delhi to Jaipur towards West and then comes back to starting point Delhi in the reverse direction. So, the total displacement (or total distance travelled in a specified direction) will be 250 km – 250 km = 0 km. Now,

$$\text{Average velocity} = \frac{\text{Total displacement}}{\text{Total time taken}}$$

$$= \frac{250\text{ km} - 250\text{ km}}{5\text{ h} + 5\text{ h}}$$

$$= \frac{0\text{ km}}{10\text{ h}}$$

$$= 0\text{ km/h}$$

Thus, the average velocity of the bus for the whole journey (both ways) is 0 kilometres per hour. No direction can be stated in this case of zero velocity.

ACCELERATION

When the velocity of a body is increasing, the body is said to be accelerating. Suppose a car starts off from rest (initial velocity is zero) and its velocity increases at a steady rate so that after 5 seconds its velocity is 10 metres per second. Now, in 5 seconds the velocity has increased by 10 – 0 = 10 metres per second and in 1 second the velocity increases by $\frac{10}{5}$ = 2 metres per second. In other words, the rate at which the velocity increases is 2 metres per second every second. The car is said to have an acceleration of 2 metres per second per second. This gives us the following definition of acceleration : **Acceleration of a body is defined as the rate of change of its velocity with time.** That is,

$$\textbf{Acceleration} = \frac{\textbf{Change in velocity}}{\textbf{Time taken for change}}$$

Now, the change in velocity is the difference between the final velocity and the initial velocity. That is,

Change in velocity = Final velocity – Initial velocity

So, $$\text{Acceleration} = \frac{\text{Final velocity} - \text{Initial velocity}}{\text{Time taken}}$$

Suppose the initial velocity of a body is u and it changes to a final velocity v in time t, then :

$$a = \frac{v-u}{t}$$

where a = acceleration of the body
v = final velocity of the body
u = initial velocity of the body
and t = time taken for the change in velocity

Since acceleration is the change in velocity divided by time, therefore, the unit of acceleration will also be the unit of velocity (metres per second) divided by the unit of time (second). Thus, **the SI unit of acceleration is "metres per second per second" or "metres per second square"** which is written as m/s^2 or $m\,s^{-2}$. The other units of acceleration which are also sometimes used are "centimetres per second square" (cm/s^2 or $cm\,s^{-2}$) and "kilometres per hour square" (km/h^2 or $km\,h^{-2}$). If the motion is in a straight line, acceleration takes place in the direction of velocity, therefore, **acceleration is a vector quantity.** It is clear from the definition of acceleration, that is, $a = \frac{v-u}{t}$ that **when a body is moving with uniform velocity, its acceleration will be zero,** because then the change in velocity $(v - u)$ is zero. Thus : (*i*) when the velocity of a body is uniform, acceleration is zero, and (*ii*) when the velocity of a body is not uniform (it is changing), the motion is accelerated.

(*a*) A car starting off from the traffic lights (or green signal). Speed is *changing*

(*b*) A car speeding up when it leaves the city and speed limit ends. Speed is *changing*

(*c*) A car moving round a bend at constant speed. Here the direction of motion is *changing*

(*d*) A ball being hit by a tennis racket. Both the ball's speed and direction are *changing*

Figure 22. Some examples of objects accelerating.

Uniform Acceleration

When the velocity of a car increases, the car is said to be accelerating. If the velocity increases at a uniform rate, the acceleration is said to be uniform. **A body has a uniform acceleration if it travels in a straight line and its velocity increases by equal amounts in equal intervals of time.** In other words, **a body has a uniform acceleration if its velocity changes at a uniform rate.** Here are some examples of the uniformly accelerated motion :

(*i*) The motion of a freely falling body is an example of uniformly accelerated motion.

(*ii*) The motion of a bicycle going down the slope of a road when the rider is not pedalling and wind resistance is negligible, is also an example of uniformly accelerated motion.

(*iii*) The motion of a ball rolling down an inclined plane is an example of uniformly accelerated motion.

As we will see later on in this chapter, **the velocity-time graph of a body having uniformly accelerated motion is a straight line.**

Non-Uniform Acceleration

A body has a non-uniform acceleration if its velocity increases by unequal amounts in equal intervals of time. In other words, **a body has a non-uniform acceleration if its velocity changes at a non-uniform rate.** The speed (or velocity) of a car running on a crowded city road changes continuously. At one moment the velocity of car increases whereas at another moment it decreases. So, the movement of a car on a crowded city road is an example of non-uniform acceleration. **The velocity-time graph for a body having non-uniform acceleration is a curved line.**

Retardation (or Deceleration or Negative Acceleration)

Acceleration takes place when the velocity of a body changes. The velocity of a body may increase or decrease, accordingly the acceleration is of two types – positive acceleration and negative acceleration. **If the velocity of a body increases, the acceleration is positive, and if the velocity of a body decreases, the acceleration is negative.** Usually, most people use the word acceleration in those cases where the velocity of a body is increasing whereas decrease in the velocity of a body or slowing down is known as retardation, deceleration or negative acceleration. **A body is said to be retarded if its velocity is decreasing.** For example, a train is retarded when it slows down on approaching a Station because then its velocity decreases. **Retardation is measured in the same way as acceleration, that is, retardation is equal to $\frac{\text{change in velocity}}{\text{time taken}}$ and has the same units of "metres per second per second"** (m/s^2 or $m\ s^{-2}$). **Retardation is actually acceleration with the negative sign.** Here is one example. When a car driver travelling at an initial velocity of 10 m/s applies brakes and brings the car to rest in 5 seconds (final velocity becomes zero), then :

$$\text{Acceleration, } a = \frac{\text{Final velocity} - \text{Initial velocity}}{\text{Time taken}}$$

Here, Initial velocity = 10 m/s

Final velocity = 0 m/s (The car stops)

And Time taken = 5 s

So, $a = \frac{(0-10)}{5}$

or $a = -2\ m/s^2$

Thus, the acceleration of the car is, $-2\ m/s^2$. It is negative in sign, but the negative acceleration is known

Figure 23. A rocket accelerates as it lifts off from the ground. It has a positive acceleration. The force needed for the lift off is provided by the rocket engines by burning a fuel.

Figure 24. If the girl in this picture falls a long way without a parachute, her motion is accelerated and she will hit the ground with a speed of about 50 m/s – the speed of a fast racing car !

Figure 25. Due to its special design to make air resistance as large as possible, a parachute decelerates as it falls towards the ground. It has a negative acceleration. By using parachute, this man will land on the ground safely with a speed of only about 8 m/s.

as retardation, so the car has a retardation of + 2 m/s^2. It should be noted that the acceleration of, – 2 m/s^2 and retardation of, + 2 m/s^2 are just the same. **Negative value of acceleration shows that the velocity of the body is decreasing.** When a body is slowed down then the acceleration acting on it is in a direction opposite to that of the motion of the body. Thus, we can have acceleration in one direction and motion in another direction.

Average Velocity

If the velocity of a body is always changing, but changing at a uniform rate (the acceleration is uniform), then the average velocity is given by the "arithmetic mean" of the initial velocity and final velocity for a given period of time, that is :

$$\textbf{Average velocity} = \frac{\textbf{Initial velocity} + \textbf{Final velocity}}{2}$$

or

$$\bar{v} = \frac{u+v}{2}$$

where v bar (written as $\bar{v}$) denotes the average velocity, u is the initial velocity and v is the final velocity. This formula for calculating the average velocity will be helpful in solving the numerical problems, so it should be memorized. We will now solve a problem based on acceleration. Please note that in many problems involving acceleration the term 'speed' is used instead of 'velocity'. This is merely because speed is a more common term in everyday language.

Sample Problem. A driver decreases the speed of a car from 25 m/s to 10 m/s in 5 seconds. Find the acceleration of the car.

Solution. First of all we should note that in this problem the term 'speed' is being used in the same sense as 'velocity'.

Here, Initial velocity of car, $u = 25$ m/s

Final velocity of car, $v = 10$ m/s

And, Time taken, $t = 5$ s

Now, putting these values in the formula for acceleration :

$$a = \frac{v-u}{t}$$

We get :

$$a = \frac{10-25}{5} \text{ m/s}^2$$

$$a = -\frac{15}{5} \text{ m/s}^2$$

$$a = -3 \text{ m/s}^2$$

Thus, the acceleration of car is, – 3 m/s^2 (minus 3 m/s^2). The negative sign of acceleration means that it is retardation. So, we can also say that the car has a retardation of +3 m/s^2.

We will solve many more problems on acceleration after a while. Before we go further and derive the equations of uniformly accelerated motion, **please answer the following questions and problems :**

Very Short Answer Type Questions

1. Is displacement a scalar quantity ?
2. State whether distance is a scalar or a vector quantity.
3. Change the speed of 6 m/s into km/h.
4. What name is given to the speed in a specified direction ?
5. Give two examples of bodies having non-uniform motion.
6. Name the physical quantity obtained by dividing 'Distance travelled' by 'Time taken' to travel that distance.
7. What do the following measure in a car ?
   (*a*) Speedometer (*b*) Odometer

8. Name the physical quantity which gives us an idea of how slow or fast a body is moving.
9. Under what conditions can a body travel a certain distance and yet its resultant displacement be zero ?
10. In addition to speed, what else should we know to predict the position of a moving body ?
11. When is a body said to have uniform velocity ?
12. Under which condition is the magnitude of average velocity equal to average speed ?
13. Which of the two can be zero under certain conditions : average speed of a moving body or average velocity of a moving body ?
14. Give one example of a situation in which a body has a certain average speed but its average velocity is zero.
15. What is the acceleration of a body moving with uniform velocity ?
16. What is the other name of negative acceleration ?
17. Name the physical quantity whose SI unit is :
    (*a*) m/s (*b*) m/s^2
18. What type of motion is exhibited by a freely falling body ?
19. What is the SI unit of retardation ?
20. Fill in the following blanks with suitable words :
    (*a*) Displacement is a .... quantity whereas distance is a .... quantity.
    (*b*) The physical quantity which gives both, the speed and direction of motion of a body is called its............
    (*c*) A motorcycle has a steady .... of 3 m/s^2. This means that every................its................increases by............
    (*d*) Velocity is the rate of change of ....It is measured in ....
    (*e*) Acceleration is the rate of change of.............. It is measured in ....

Short Answer Type Questions

21. What type of motion, uniform or non-uniform, is exhibited by a freely falling body ? Give reason for your answer.
22. State whether speed is a scalar or a vector quantity. Give reason for your choice.
23. Bus *X* travels a distance of 360 km in 5 hours whereas bus *Y* travels a distance of 476 km in 7 hours. Which bus travels faster ?
24. Arrange the following speeds in increasing order (keeping the least speed first) :
    (*i*) An athlete running with a speed of 10 m/s.
    (*ii*) A bicycle moving with a speed of 200 m/min.
    (*iii*) A scooter moving with a speed of 30 km/h.
25. (*a*) Write the formula for acceleration. Give the meaning of each symbol which occurs in it.
    (*b*) A train starting from Railway Station attains a speed of 21 m/s in one minute. Find its acceleration.
26. (*a*) What term is used to denote the change of velocity with time ?
    (*b*) Give one word which means the same as 'moving with a negative acceleration'.
    (*c*) The displacement of a moving object in a given interval of time is zero. Would the distance travelled by the object also be zero ? Give reason for your answer.
27. A snail covers a distance of 100 metres in 50 hours. Calculate the average speed of snail in km/h.

The snail covers a distance of 100 metres in 50 hours.

The tortoise covers the same distance of 100 metres in 15 minutes.

And this sprinter (in red vest) covers a distance of 100 metres in just 9.83 seconds.

28. A tortoise moves a distance of 100 metres in 15 minutes. What is the average speed of tortoise in km/h ?
29. If a sprinter runs a distance of 100 metres in 9.83 seconds, calculate his average speed in km/h.
30. A motorcyclist drives from place A to B with a uniform speed of 30 km h^{-1} and returns from place B to A with a uniform speed of 20 km h^{-1}. Find his average speed.
31. A motorcyclist starts from rest and reaches a speed of 6 m/s after travelling with uniform acceleration for 3 s. What is his acceleration ?
32. An aircraft travelling at 600 km/h accelerates steadily at 10 km/h per second. Taking the speed of sound as 1100 km/h at the aircraft's altitude, how long will it take to reach the 'sound barrier' ?
33. If a bus travelling at 20 m/s is subjected to a steady deceleration of 5 m/s^2, how long will it take to come to rest ?

Long Answer Type Questions

34. (*a*) What is the difference between 'distance travelled' by a body and its 'displacement' ? Explain with the help of a diagram.
(*b*) An ant travels a distance of 8 cm from P to Q and then moves a distance of 6 cm at right angles to PQ. Find its resultant displacement.
35. Define motion. What do you understand by the terms 'uniform motion' and 'non-uniform motion' ? Explain with examples.
36. (*a*) Define speed. What is the SI unit of speed ?
(*b*) What is meant by (*i*) average speed, and (*ii*) uniform speed ?
37. (*a*) Define velocity. What is the SI unit of velocity ?
(*b*) What is the difference between speed and velocity ?
(*c*) Convert a speed of 54 km/h into m/s.
38. (*a*) What is meant by the term 'acceleration' ? State the SI unit of acceleration.
(*b*) Define the term 'uniform acceleration'. Give one example of a uniformly accelerated motion.
39. The distance between Delhi and Agra is 200 km. A train travels the first 100 km at a speed of 50 km/h. How fast must the train travel the next 100 km, so as to average 70 km/h for the whole journey ?
40. A train travels the first 15 km at a uniform speed of 30 km/h; the next 75 km at a uniform speed of 50 km/h; and the last 10 km at a uniform speed of 20 km/h. Calculate the average speed for the entire train journey.
41. A car is moving along a straight road at a steady speed. It travels 150 m in 5 seconds :
(*a*) What is its average speed ?
(*b*) How far does it travel in 1 second ?
(*c*) How far does it travel in 6 seconds ?
(*d*) How long does it take to travel 240 m ?

Multiple Choice Questions (MCQs)

42. A particle is moving in a circular path of radius r. The displacement after half a circle would be :
(*a*) 0 (*b*) πr (*c*) $2r$ (*d*) $2\pi r$
43. The numerical ratio of displacement to distance for a moving object is :
(*a*) always less than 1 (*b*) equal to 1 or more than 1
(*c*) always more than 1 (*d*) equal to 1 or less than 1
44. A boy is sitting on a merry-go-round which is moving with a constant speed of 10 m s^{-1}. This means that the boy is :
(*a*) at rest (*b*) moving with no acceleration
(*c*) in accelerated motion (*d*) moving with uniform velocity
45. In which of the following cases of motion, the distance moved and the magnitude of displacement are equal ?
(*a*) if the car is moving on straight road (*b*) if the car is moving on circular road
(*c*) if the pendulum is moving to and fro (*d*) if a planet is moving around the sun
46. The speed of a moving object is determined to be 0.06 m/s. This speed is equal to :
(*a*) 2.16 km/h (*b*) 1.08 km/h (*c*) 0.216 km/h (*b*) 0.0216 km/h

47. A freely falling object travels 4.9 m in 1st second, 14.7 m in 2nd second, 24.5 m in 3rd second, and so on. This data shows that the motion of a freely falling object is a case of :
(*a*) uniform motion (*b*) uniform acceleration
(*c*) no acceleration (*d*) uniform velocity

48. When a car runs on a circular track with a uniform speed, its velocity is said to be changing. This is because :
(*a*) the car has a uniform acceleration
(*b*) the direction of car varies continuously
(*c*) the car travels unequal distances in equal time intervals
(*d*) the car travels equal distances in unequal time intervals

49. Which of the following statement is correct regarding velocity and speed of a moving body ?
(*a*) velocity of a moving body is always higher than its speed
(*b*) speed of a moving body is always higher than its velocity
(*c*) speed of a moving body is its velocity in a given direction
(*d*) velocity of a moving body is its speed in a given direction

50. Which of the following can sometimes be 'zero' for a moving body ?
(*i*) average velocity (*ii*) distance travelled (*iii*) average speed (*iv*) displacement
(*a*) only (*i*) (*b*) (*i*) and (*ii*) (*c*) (*i*) and (*iv*) (*d*) only (*iv*)

51. When a car driver travelling at a speed of 10 m/s applies brakes and brings the car to rest in 20 s, then retardation will be :
(*a*) + 2 m/s^2 (*b*) – 2 m/s^2 (*c*) – 0.5 m/s^2 (*d*) + 0.5 m/s^2

52. Which of the following could not be a unit of speed ?
(*a*) km/h (*b*) s/m (*c*) m/s (*d*) mm s^{-1}

53. One of the following is not a vector quantity. This one is :
(*a*) displacement (*b*) speed (*c*) acceleration (*d*) velocity

54. Which of the following could not be a unit of acceleration ?
(*a*) km/s^2 (*b*) cm s^{-2} (*c*) km/s (*d*) m/s^2

Questions Based on High Order Thinking Skills (HOTS)

55. A body is moving along a circular path of radius *R*. What will be the distance travelled and displacement of the body when it completes half a revolution ?

56. If on a round trip you travel 6 km and then arrive back home :
(*a*) What distance have you travelled ?
(*b*) What is your final displacement ?

57. A body travels a distance of 3 km towards East, then 4 km towards North and finally 9 km towards East.
(*i*) What is the total distance travelled ?
(*ii*) What is the resultant displacement ?

58. A boy walks from his classroom to the bookshop along a straight corridor towards North. He covers a distance of 20 m in 25 seconds to reach the bookshop. After buying a book, he travels the same distance in the same time to reach back in the classroom. Find (*a*) average speed, and (*b*) average velocity, of the boy.

59. A car travels 100 km at a speed of 60 km/h and returns with a speed of 40 km/h. Calculate the average speed for the whole journey.

60. A ball hits a wall horizontally at 6.0 m s^{-1}. It rebounds horizontally at 4.4 m s^{-1}. The ball is in contact with the wall for 0.040 s. What is the acceleration of the ball ?

ANSWERS

3. 21.6 km/h **6.** Speed **8.** Speed **9.** When the body comes back to its starting point **10.** Direction of speed **12.** When the body moves along a straight line path **13.** Average velocity **15.** Zero (0) **16.** Retardation (or Deceleration) **17.** (*a*) Speed (or Velocity) (*b*) Acceleration **20.** (*a*) vector ; scalar (*b*) velocity (*c*) acceleration ; second ; speed (or velocity) ; 3 m/s (*d*) displacement ; m/s (*e*) velocity ; m/s^2 **23.** Speed of bus X = 72 km/h ; Speed of bus Y = 68 km/h ; So bus X travels faster **24.** 200 m/min < 30 km/h < 10 m/s **25.** (*b*) 0.35 m/s^2 **26.** (*a*) Acceleration (*b*) Retardation (*c*) No. Because distance is a scalar quantity having magnitude only. It has no specified direction **27.** 0.002 km/h **28.** 0.4 km/h **29.** 36.62 km/h **30.** 24 km h^{-1} **31.** 2 m/s^2 **32.** 50 s **33.** 4 s **34.** (*b*) 10 cm **37.** (*c*) 15 m/s **39.** 116.6 km/h **40.** 40 km/h **41.** (*a*) 30 m/s (*b*) 30 m (*c*) 180 m (*d*) 8 s **42.** (*c*) **43.** (*d*) **44.** (*c*) **45.** (*a*) **46.** (*c*) **47.** (*b*) **48.** (*b*) **49.** (*d*) **50.** (*c*) **51.** (*d*) **52.** (*b*) **53.** (*b*) **54.** (*c*) **55.** πR ; $2R$ **56.** (*a*) 6 km (*b*) zero **57.** (*i*) 16 km (*ii*) 12.6 km **58.** Average speed = 0.8 m/s ; Average velocity = 0 m/s **59.** 48 km/h **60.** – 260 m s^{-2}

EQUATIONS OF UNIFORMLY ACCELERATED MOTION

There are three equations for the motion of those bodies which travel with a uniform acceleration. These equations give relationship between initial velocity, final velocity, time taken, acceleration and distance travelled by the bodies. We will study these equations one by one.

1. First Equation of Motion

The first equation of motion is : $v = u + at$. It gives the velocity acquired by a body in time t. We will now derive this first equation of motion.

Consider a body having initial velocity 'u'. Suppose it is subjected to a uniform acceleration 'a' so that after time 't' its final velocity becomes 'v'. Now, from the definition of acceleration we know that :

$$\text{Acceleration} = \frac{\text{Change in velocity}}{\text{Time taken}}$$

or $$\text{Acceleration} = \frac{\text{Final velocity} - \text{Initial velocity}}{\text{Time taken}}$$

So, $$a = \frac{v-u}{t}$$

$$at = v - u$$

and, $$v = u + at$$

where v = final velocity of the body

u = initial velocity of the body

a = acceleration

and t = time taken

The equation $v = u + at$ is known as the first equation of motion and it is used to find out the velocity 'v' acquired by a body in time 't', the body having an initial velocity 'u' and a uniform acceleration 'a'. In fact, this equation has four values in it, if any three values are known, the fourth value can be calculated. By paying due attention to the sign of acceleration, this equation can also be applied to the problems of retardation.

2. Second Equation of Motion

The second equation of motion is : $s = ut + \frac{1}{2}at^2$. It gives the distance travelled by a body in time t. Let us derive this second equation of motion.

Suppose a body has an initial velocity 'u' and a uniform acceleration 'a' for time 't' so that its final velocity becomes 'v'. Let the distance travelled by the body in this time be 's'. The distance travelled by a moving body in time 't' can be found out by considering its average velocity. Since the initial velocity of the body is 'u' and its final velocity is 'v', the average velocity is given by :

$$\text{Average velocity} = \frac{\text{Initial velocity} + \text{Final velocity}}{2}$$

That is, $$\text{Average velocity} = \frac{u+v}{2}$$

Also, Distance travelled = Average velocity × Time

So, $$s = \frac{(u+v)}{2} \times t \quad \text{... (1)}$$

From the first equation of motion we have, $v = u + at$. Putting this value of v in equation (1), we get :

$$s = \frac{(u+u+at) \times t}{2}$$

or $$s = \frac{(2u+at)\times t}{2}$$

or $$s = \frac{2ut+at^2}{2}$$

or $$\mathbf{s = ut + \frac{1}{2}at^2}$$

where s = distance travelled by the body in time t

u = initial velocity of the body

and a = acceleration

This is the second equation of motion and it is used to calculate the distance travelled by a body in time t. This equation should also be memorized because it will be used to solve numerical problems.

3. Third Equation of Motion

The third equation of motion is : $v^2 = u^2 + 2as$. It gives the velocity acquired by a body in travelling a distance s. We will now derive this third equation of motion.

The third equation of motion can be obtained by eliminating t between the first two equations of motion. This is done as follows.

From the second equation of motion we have :

$$s = ut + \frac{1}{2}at^2 \quad \text{... (1)}$$

And from the first equation of motion we have :

$$v = u + at \quad \text{... (2)}$$

This can be rearranged and written as :

$$at = v - u$$

or $$t = \frac{v-u}{a}$$

Putting this value of t in equation (1), we get :

$$s = \frac{u(v-u)}{a} + \frac{1}{2}a\left(\frac{v-u}{a}\right)^2$$

or $$s = \frac{uv-u^2}{a} + \frac{a\left(v^2+u^2-2uv\right)}{2a^2}$$ [because $(v-u)^2 = v^2 + u^2 - 2vu$]

or $$s = \frac{uv-u^2}{a} + \frac{v^2+u^2-2uv}{2a}$$

or $$s = \frac{2uv-2u^2+v^2+u^2-2uv}{2a}$$

or $$2as = v^2 - u^2$$

or $$\mathbf{v^2 = u^2 + 2as}$$

where v = final velocity

u = initial velocity

$a =$ acceleration

and $s =$ distance travelled

This equation gives us the velocity acquired by a body in travelling a distance s.

We will now solve some problems based on motion. **To solve the problems on motion we should remember that :**

(*i*) **if a body starts from rest, its initial velocity, $u = 0$**

(*ii*) **if a body comes to rest (it stops), its final velocity, $v = 0$**

(*iii*) **if a body moves with uniform velocity, its acceleration, $a = 0$**

Sample Problem 1. A scooter acquires a velocity of 36 km per hour in 10 seconds just after the start. Calculate the acceleration of the scooter.

Solution. First of all we should convert the given velocity into proper units, that is, we should convert the velocity of 36 kilometres per hour into metres per second (because the time is given in seconds).

Now, $1 \text{ km} = 1000 \text{ m}$

So, $36 \text{ km} = 36 \times 1000 \text{ m}$

$= 36{,}000 \text{ m}$ ... (1)

Also, $1 \text{ hour} = 60 \text{ minutes}$

$= 60 \times 60 \text{ seconds}$

$= 3600 \text{ s}$ ... (2)

So, $36 \text{ km per hour} = \dfrac{36{,}000 \text{ m}}{3600 \text{ s}}$

$= 10 \text{ m/s}$ ... (3)

Thus, the given velocity of 36 km per hour is equal to 10 metres per second.

Now, Initial velocity, $u = 0$ (Scooter starts from rest)

Final velocity, $v = 10 \text{ m/s}$ (Calculated above)

Acceleration, $a = ?$ (To be calculated)

And, Time, $t = 10 \text{ s}$

By putting these values in the first equation of motion :

$$v = u + at$$

We get :

$$10 = 0 + a \times 10$$

$$10\,a = 10$$

$$a = \frac{10}{10}$$

$$a = 1 \text{ m/s}^2$$

Thus, the acceleration is 1 m/s^2.

Figure 26. We should always wear a helmet while driving a two-wheeler (like a scooter or a motorcycle). It will protect our head from an injury if (God forbid) we meet with a road accident. We should, however, drive a vehicle on the road only when we turn 18 and obtain a driving licence from Transport Department.

Sample Problem 2. A moving train is brought to rest within 20 seconds by applying brakes. Find the initial velocity, if the retardation due to brakes is 2 m s^{-2}.

Solution. In this problem we have been given the value of retardation but we require the value of acceleration. We know that retardation is negative acceleration. So, if the retardation is, $+ 2 \text{ m s}^{-2}$ (as given here), then the acceleration will be, $- 2 \text{ m s}^{-2}$ (the minus sign here indicates the negative acceleration). Let us solve the problem now.

Here, Initial velocity, $u = ?$ (To be calculated)

Final velocity, $v = 0$ (The train stops)

Acceleration, $a = - 2 \text{ m s}^{-2}$

And, Time, $t = 20 \text{ s}$

Now, putting these values in the formula :

$$v = u + at$$

We get :

$$0 = u + (-2) \times 20$$
$$0 = u - 40$$
$$u = 40 \text{ m s}^{-1}$$

Thus, the initial velocity of the train is 40 metres per second.

Figure 27. Indian Railways is the life-line of our Nation. We should not do anything which may hinder the normal operations of our trains in any way. Some people have a very bad habit of hanging on to the doors of compartments of running trains or of travelling on the roofs of compartments. These practices have resulted in many accidents leading to severe injuries to such people and even deaths. Such undesirable practices must be stopped !

Figure 28. Numerous train accidents take place at unmanned railway level crossings in our country. Even on seeing that a train is approaching fast, some people try to cross railway tracks hurriedly (on foot or on vehicles like motorbikes, cars, buses and tractor trolleys) which results in accidents causing loss of life and property. Can't we have some more patience ! Life is God's best gift to us. Let us keep it safe and secure.

Sample Problem 3. A body starts to slide over a horizontal surface with an initial velocity of 0.5 m/s. Due to friction, its velocity decreases at the rate of 0.05 m/s² (acceleration, – 0.05 m/s²). How much time will it take for the body to stop ?

Solution. Here, Initial velocity, $u = 0.5$ m/s

Final velocity, $v = 0$ (The body stops)

Acceleration, $a = -0.05$ m/s²

And, Time, $t = ?$ (To be calculated)

Now, from the first equation of motion, we have :

$$v = u + at$$

So,

$$0 = 0.5 + (-0.05) \times t$$

or

$$0.05\, t = 0.5$$
$$t = \frac{0.5}{0.05}$$
$$t = 10 \text{ s}$$

Thus, the body will take 10 seconds to stop.

Sample Problem 4. A racing car has a uniform acceleration of 4 m/s². What distance will it cover in 10 seconds after the start ?

Solution. Here, Initial velocity, $u = 0$

Time, $t = 10$ s

Acceleration, $a = 4$ m/s²

And, Distance, $s = ?$ (To be calculated)

Now, putting these values in the second equation of motion :

$$s = ut + \frac{1}{2}at^2$$

We get : $$s = 0 \times 10 + \frac{1}{2} \times 4 \times (10)^2$$

$$s = 200 \text{ m}$$

Thus, the distance covered by the car in 10 seconds is 200 metres.

Figure 29. A racing car can attain a speed of more than 60 m/s (or more than 216 km/h).

Figure 30. This is the Thrust SSC Rocket Car which broke the world land-speed record in 1997. It achieved a top speed of 340 m/s (which is 1224 km/h).

Sample Problem 5. A scooter moving at a speed of 10 m/s is stopped by applying brakes which produce a uniform acceleration of, – 0.5 m/s^2. How much distance will be covered by the scooter before it stops ?

Solution. Here, Initial speed, $u = 10$ m/s

Final speed, $v = 0$ (Scooter stops)

Acceleration, $a = -0.5$ m/s^2

And, Distance covered, $s = ?$ (To be calculated)

Now, putting these values in the third equation of motion :

$$v^2 = u^2 + 2as$$

We get : $$(0)^2 = (10)^2 + 2 \times (-0.5) \times s$$

$$0 = 100 - s$$

$$s = 100 \text{ m}$$

Thus, the distance covered is 100 metres.

Sample Problem 6. A car travelling at 20 km/h speeds up to 60 km/h in 6 seconds. What is its acceleration ?

Solution. Here, Initial speed, $u = 20$ km/h

$$= \frac{20 \times 1000 \text{ m}}{60 \times 60 \text{ s}}$$

$$= 5.55 \text{ m/s} \quad \text{... (1)}$$

Final speed, $v = 60$ km/h

$$= \frac{60 \times 1000 \text{ m}}{60 \times 60 \text{ s}}$$

$$= 16.66 \text{ m/s} \quad \text{... (2)}$$

Acceleration, $a = ?$ (To be calculated)

And, Time, $t = 6$ s

We know that : $$v = u + at$$

So, $$16.66 = 5.55 + a \times 6$$

$$6a = 16.66 - 5.55$$

$$6a = 11.11$$

$$a = \frac{11.11}{6}$$

Thus, Acceleration, $a = 1.85$ m/s^2

Sample Problem 7. A bus increases its speed from 20 km/h to 50 km/h in 10 seconds. Its acceleration is :

(*a*) 30 m/s² (*b*) 3 m/s² (*c*) 18 m/s² (*d*) 0.83 m/s²

Choose the correct answer.

Solution. Here, Initial speed, $u = 20$ km/h

$$= \frac{20 \times 1000 \text{ m}}{60 \times 60 \text{ s}}$$

$$= 5.5 \text{ m/s} \quad \ldots (1)$$

Final speed, $v = 50$ km/h

$$= \frac{50 \times 1000 \text{ m}}{60 \times 60 \text{ s}}$$

$$= 13.8 \text{ m/s} \quad \ldots (2)$$

Acceleration, $a = ?$ (To be calculated)

And, Time, $t = 10$ s

Now, $v = u + at$

So, $13.8 = 5.5 + a \times 10$

$$10\,a = 13.8 - 5.5$$

$$10\,a = 8.3$$

$$a = \frac{8.3}{10}$$

$$a = 0.83 \text{ m/s}^2$$

Thus, the acceleration is 0.83 m/s². The correct answer is (*d*)

Figure 31. Travelling in a bus like this is very dangerous. Only God knows whether the people hanging on to this bus precariously will reach their homes or land in hospital ! We should never put our life at risk like this. If we do not get space in one bus, we should wait for another one.

GRAPHICAL REPRESENTATION OF MOTION

We will now discuss the various types of graphs which can be used to calculate 'speed' (or velocity), 'acceleration' and 'distance travelled' by a body. A very important point to remember here is that in the drawing of graphs, the terms 'speed' and 'velocity' are used in the same sense. In most of the graphs which we are going to discuss now, we will be using the term 'speed'. At some of the places, however, the term 'velocity' will also be used. This is because even in the examination papers, they use both the terms 'speed' as well as 'velocity' in the questions based on graphs. We will first study the 'distance-time graphs' and then 'speed-time graphs' (or velocity-time graphs). Please note that in drawing graphs based on motion, 'time' is always taken along the *x*-axis whereas 'distance' or 'speed' (or velocity) is taken along the *y*-axis.

1. DISTANCE-TIME GRAPHS

When a body moves with uniform speed, it will travel equal distances in equal intervals of time. In other words, the distance travelled is directly proportional to time. Thus, for uniform speed, a graph of distance travelled against time will be a straight line as shown by line *OA* in Figure 32. Please note that we can also write the term "uniform velocity" in place of "uniform speed" in the graph. We can now say that **the distance-time graph of a body moving at uniform speed is always a straight line.** In other words, a straight line graph between distance and time tells us that the body is moving with a uniform speed.

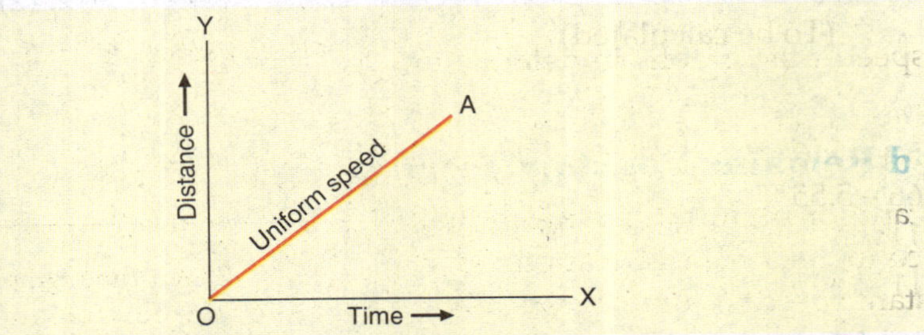

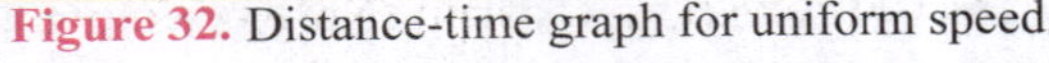

Figure 32. Distance-time graph for uniform speed.

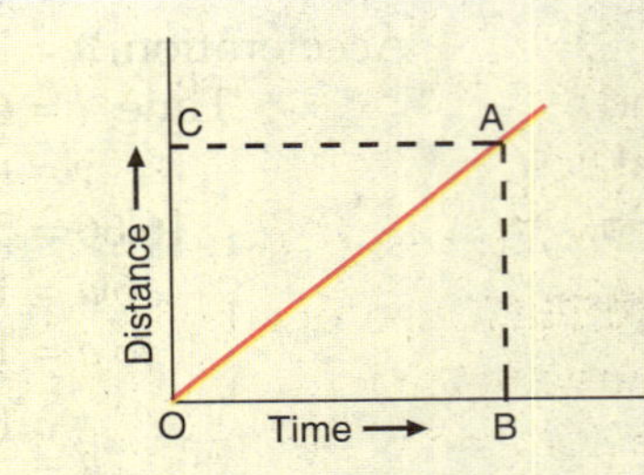

Figure 33. Calculation of speed from distance-time graph.

The slope of a distance-time graph indicates speed of the body. So, **the distance-time graph of a body can be used to calculate the speed of the body.** To find the speed from the distance-time graph of a body, we take any point *A* on the straight line graph (Figure 33), and drop a perpendicular *AB* on the time axis (*x*-axis). It is clear that *AB* represents the distance travelled by the body in the time interval represented by *OB* (Figure 33). We know that :

$$\text{Speed} = \frac{\text{Distance travelled}}{\text{Time taken}}$$

Now, in Figure 33, the distance travelled is *OC* which is in fact equal to *AB*, and the time taken is *OB*. So, putting distance = *AB* and time = *OB* in the above relation, we get :

$$\text{Speed} = \frac{AB}{OB}$$

But $\frac{AB}{OB}$ is known as the slope (or gradient) of the graph line *OA*, therefore, in a distance-time graph for uniform speed, the speed of the body is given by the slope of the graph. In other words, **the slope of a distance-time graph indicates speed.** Thus, we can use a distance-time graph of a body to find the value of speed of the body. All that we have to do is to find out the slope of distance-time graph as shown above and that gives the speed of the body.

We have seen above that if the speed of a body is uniform then its distance-time graph is a straight line (as shown in Figure 32). **If, however, the speed of a body is non-uniform, then the graph between distance travelled and time is a curved line (called a parabola)** as shown in Figure 34.

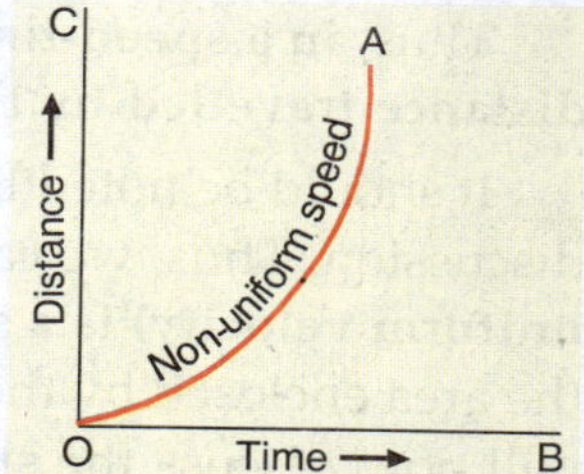

Figure 34. Distance-time graph for non-uniform speed.

We get the following conclusions from the above discussion :

(*i*) If the distance-time graph of a body is a straight line, then its speed is uniform.

(*ii*) If the distance-time graph of a body is a curved line, then its speed is non-uniform.

We know that when a body moves with a non-uniform speed, then its motion is said to be accelerated. So, the curved line *OA* in Figure 34 also represents the distance-time graph of a body moving with accelerated motion.

If a displacement-time graph is drawn, then it will specifically represent 'velocity'. For example, if the displacement-time graph of a moving body is a straight line, then it represents uniform velocity of the body. We will now discuss the speed-time graphs of a moving body. In fact, **the speed-time graphs are also known as velocity-time graphs.** So, whether we write a speed-time graph or a velocity-time graph, it will mean the same thing.

2. SPEED-TIME GRAPHS (OR VELOCITY-TIME GRAPHS)

We can have three types of speed-time graphs for a moving body. These three cases are :

(*i*) When the speed of the body remains constant (and there is no acceleration)

(*ii*) When the speed of the body changes at a uniform rate (there is uniform acceleration)

(*iii*) When the speed of the body changes in a non-uniform way (there is non-uniform acceleration)

We will now discuss these three types of speed-time graphs in detail, one by one.

(*i*) Speed-Time Graph when the Speed Remains Constant

By saying that the speed of a body is constant (or uniform), we mean that the speed does not change with time and hence there is no acceleration. So, a speed-time graph for a body moving with constant speed (or uniform speed) is a straight line parallel to the time axis (as shown by the line *AB* in Figure 35).

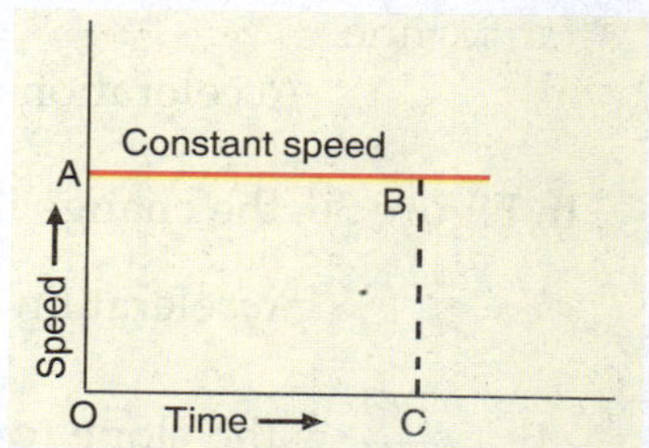

Figure 35. Speed-time graph when the speed remains constant (No acceleration).

In other words, **if the speed-time graph of a body is a straight line parallel to the time axis, then the speed of the body is constant (or uniform).** Since the speed of the body is constant or uniform, there is no acceleration, and hence there is no question of finding the acceleration from such a speed-time graph. We can, however, find the distance travelled by the body in a given time from such a speed-time graph. This is described below.

We know that, $$\text{Speed} = \frac{\text{Distance travelled}}{\text{Time taken}}$$

So, $$\text{Distance travelled} = \text{Speed} \times \text{Time taken} \quad \text{... (1)}$$

Now, to find out the distance travelled by the body at point C (Figure 35), we draw a perpendicular CB at point C which meets the straight-line graph at point B.

Now, Speed at $C = CB$

But $CB = OA$

Thus, Speed at $C = OA$ ... (2)

And, Time at $C = OC$ ... (3)

Now, putting these values of speed and time in relation (1), we get :

Distance travelled $= OA \times OC$ (see Figure 35)

or Distance travelled = Area of rectangle $OABC$

Thus, **in a speed-time graph, the area enclosed by the speed-time curve and the time axis gives us the distance travelled by the body.**

It should be noted that we can also use the term "velocity" in place of "speed" everywhere in the above discussion. Thus, we can say that **the velocity-time graph of an object moving with constant velocity (or uniform velocity) is a straight line parallel to the time axis.** We can also say that in a velocity-time graph, the area enclosed by the velocity-time curve and the time axis gives the distance travelled by the object. We will now discuss the speed-time graph of a body when its speed changes at a uniform rate, that is, when the acceleration of the body is uniform.

(*ii*) Speed-Time Graph when Speed Changes at a Uniform Rate (Uniform Acceleration)

When a body moves with uniform acceleration, its speed changes by equal amounts in equal intervals of time. In other words, the speed becomes directly proportional to time. Thus, **the speed-time graph for a uniformly changing speed (or uniform acceleration) will be a straight line** (as shown by line OP in Figure 36).

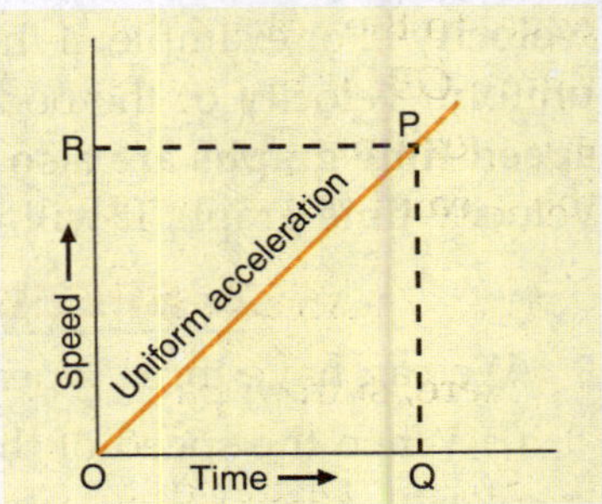

Figure 36. Speed-time graph showing uniform acceleration.

We can find out the value of acceleration from the speed-time graph of a moving body. Now, to calculate the acceleration at a time corresponding to point Q (Figure 36), we draw a perpendicular QP from point Q which touches the straight line graph at point P. We know that :

$$\text{Acceleration} = \frac{\text{Change in speed (or velocity)}}{\text{Time taken}}$$

In Figure 36, the change in speed is represented by PQ whereas time taken is equal to OQ. So,

$$\text{Acceleration} = \frac{PQ}{OQ}$$

But $\frac{PQ}{OQ}$ is the slope (or gradient) of the speed-time graph OP, therefore, we conclude that in a speed-time graph, the acceleration is given by the slope of the graph. In other words, **the slope of a speed-time graph of a moving body gives its acceleration.**

The distance travelled by a moving body in a given time can also be calculated from its speed-time graph. As explained earlier, the distance travelled by the body in the time corresponding to point *Q* (Figure 36) will be equal to the area of the triangle *OPQ*, which is equal to half the area of the rectangle *ORPQ*.

Thus, Distance travelled = Area of triangle *OPQ*

$$= \frac{1}{2} \text{ Area of rectangle } ORPQ$$

$$= \frac{1}{2} \times OR \times OQ \quad \text{(see Figure 36)}$$

Please note that **in a speed-time graph of a body, a straight line sloping upwards** (as in Figure 36) **shows uniform acceleration.** On the other hand, **in a speed-time graph of a body, a straight line sloping downwards** (as in Figure 37) **indicates uniform retardation.**

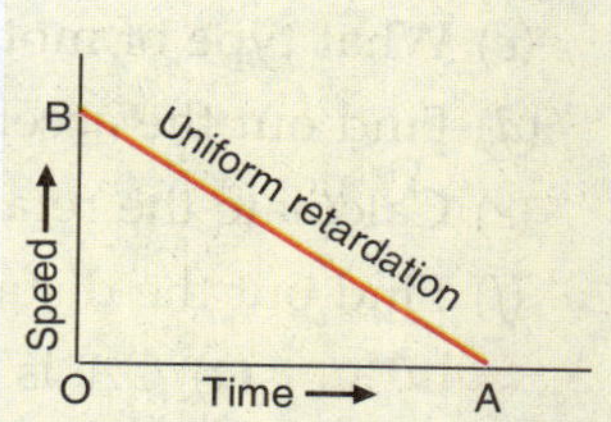

Figure 37. Speed-time graph showing uniform retardation.

It should be noted that we can also use the word "velocity" in place of "speed" everywhere in the above discussion. Thus, we can also say that the velocity-time graph of a body moving with uniform acceleration is a straight line. And that the slope of velocity-time graph of a body indicates its acceleration.

In the speed-time graph shown in Figure 36, we have assumed that the initial speed of the body is zero. It is, however, possible that the body has some initial speed and then it starts accelerating at a uniform rate. So, **we will now discuss the speed-time graph of a body whose initial speed is not zero.**

Speed-Time Graph when the Initial Speed of the Body is Not Zero

Figure 38 shows the speed-time graph of a body having an initial speed equal to *OB* and then accelerating from *B* to *C*. In order to calculate the value of acceleration from such a graph, we will have to subtract the initial speed (*OB*) from the final speed (*AC*), and then divide it by time (*OA*).

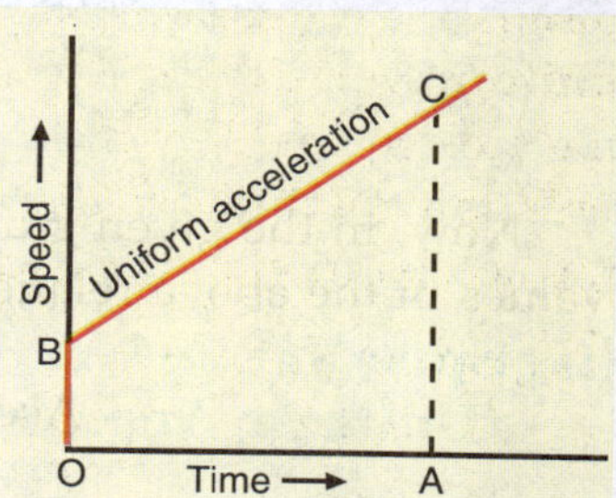

Figure 38. Speed-time graph of a body when its initial speed is not zero.

In such cases also, the distance travelled by the body in a given time is equal to the area between the speed-time graph and the time axis. For example, in this case the distance travelled by the body in time *OA* (Figure 38), will be equal to the area of the figure *OBCA* under the speed-time graph *BC*. Now, the figure *OBCA* has two parallel sides *OB* and *AC* and such a figure is known as a trapezium. Thus, the distance travelled by the body in this case is equal to the area of trapezium *OBCA*. Now,

$$\text{Area of trapezium} = \frac{\text{Sum of two parallel sides} \times \text{Height}}{2}$$

Here, sum of parallel sides is *OB* + *AC* and height is *OA* (see Figure 38).

$$\text{So,} \quad \text{Distance travelled} = \frac{(OB + AC) \times OA}{2}$$

We will now discuss the speed-time graph of a body whose speed does not change at a uniform rate, that is, when the acceleration of the body is non-uniform.

(*iii*) Speed-Time Graph when Speed Changes at a Non-Uniform Rate (Non-Uniform Acceleration)

When the speed of a body changes in an irregular manner, then the speed-time graph of the body is a curved line (as shown by the line *OA* in Figure 39). Even now, the distance travelled by the body is given by the area between the speed-time curve and the time axis.

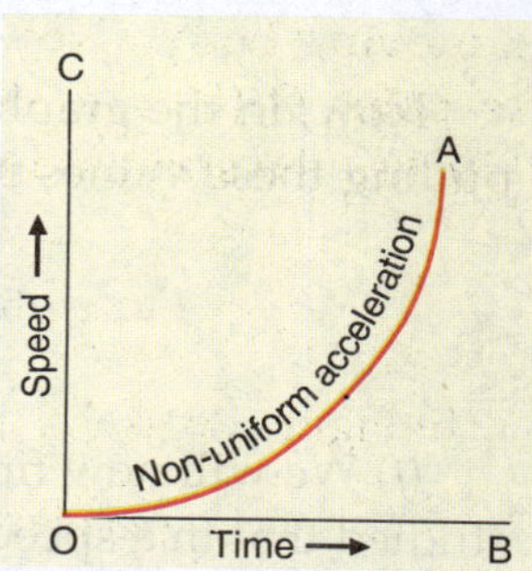

Figure 39. Speed-time graph for non-uniform acceleration.

Once again, please note that we can write the word "velocity" in place of "speed" in the above graph. So, we can also say that the velocity-time graph for non-uniform acceleration is a curved line called parabola. We will now solve some problems based on graphs.

Sample Problem 1. Study the speed-time graph of a body given here and answer the following questions :

(*a*) What type of motion is represented by *OA* ?

(*b*) What type of motion is represented by *AB* ?

(*c*) What type of motion is represented by *BC* ?

(*d*) Find out the acceleration of the body.

(*e*) Calculate the retardation of the body.

(*f*) Find out the distance travelled by the body from *A* to *B*.

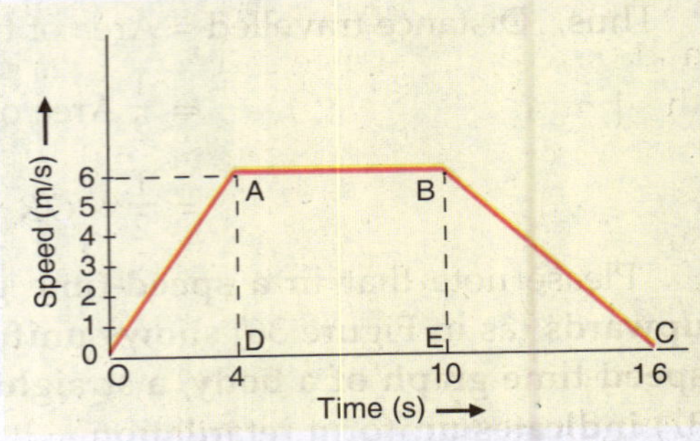

Figure 40. Graph for sample problem 1.

Solution. (*a*) *OA* is a straight line graph between speed and time, and it is sloping upwards from *O* to *A*. Therefore, the graph line *OA* represents uniform acceleration.

(*b*) *AB* is a straight line graph between speed and time, which is parallel to the time axis (*x*-axis). So, *AB* represents uniform speed (or constant speed). There is no acceleration from *A* to *B*.

(*c*) *BC* is a straight line graph between speed and time which is sloping downwards from *B* to *C*. Therefore, *BC* represents uniform retardation (or negative acceleration).

(*d*) Let us find out the acceleration now. We have just seen that the graph line *OA* represents acceleration. So, the slope of speed-time graph *OA* will give us the acceleration of the body. Thus,

$$\text{Acceleration} = \text{Slope of line } OA$$

$$= \frac{AD}{OD}$$

Now, in the given graph (Figure 40), we find that $AD = 6$ m/s and $OD = 4$ seconds. So, putting these values in the above relation, we get :

$$\text{Acceleration} = \frac{6 \text{ m/s}}{4 \text{ s}}$$

$$= 1.5 \text{ m/s}^2 \qquad \text{... (1)}$$

(*e*) Let us calculate the retardation now. We have discussed above that the graph line *BC* represents retardation. So, the slope of speed-time graph *BC* will be equal to the retardation of the body. So,

$$\text{Retardation} = \text{Slope of line } BC$$

$$= \frac{BE}{EC}$$

Now, in the graph given to us (Figure 40), we find that $BE = 6$ m/s and $EC = 16 - 10 = 6$ seconds. So, putting these values in the above relation, we get :

$$\text{Retardation} = \frac{6 \text{ m/s}}{6 \text{ s}}$$

$$= 1 \text{ m/s}^2 \qquad \text{... (2)}$$

(*f*) We will now find out the distance travelled by the body in moving from *A* to *B* (Figure 40). We have studied that in a speed-time graph, the distance travelled by the body is equal to the area enclosed between the speed-time graph and the time-axis. Thus,

Distance travelled from *A* to *B* = Area under the line *AB* and the time axis

= Area of rectangle *DABE*

= $DA \times DE$

Now, from the given graph (Figure 40), we find that $DA = 6$ m/s and $DE = 10 - 4 = 6$ s. Therefore,

Distance travelled from A to $B = 6 \times 6$

$= 36$ m ... (3)

Here is an Exercise for You : Find (*i*) Distance travelled from O to A, (*ii*) Distance travelled from B to C, and (*iii*) Total distance travelled by the body. The answers will be 12 m, 18 m, and 66 m respectively. For this purpose you will require the formula for the area of a triangle. Please note that :

$$\text{Area of a triangle} = \frac{1}{2} \times \text{base} \times \text{height}$$

A yet another point to be noted is that in the graph given in the above sample problem (Figure 40) they could also have written the word "velocity" in place of "speed".

Sample Problem 2. A car is moving on a straight road with uniform acceleration. The following table gives the speed of the car at various instants of time :

Speed (m/s) :	5	10	15	20	25	30
Time (s) :	0	10	20	30	40	50

Draw the speed-time graph by choosing a convenient scale. Determine from it :

(*i*) the acceleration of the car.

(*ii*) the distance travelled by the car in 50 seconds.

Solution. We take a graph paper and plot the above given time values on the x-axis. The corresponding speed values are plotted on the y-axis. The speed-time graph obtained from the given readings is shown in Figure 42. Please note that in this case, when the time is 0, then the speed is not 0. The body has an initial

Figure 41. A car moving on a straight road with uniform acceleration.

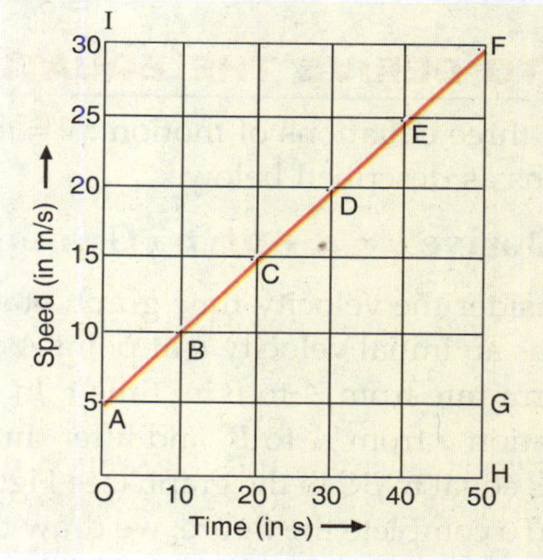

Figure 42. Graph for sample problem 2.

speed of 5 m/s which is represented by point A in Figure 42. We will now answer the questions asked in this sample problem.

(*i*) **Calculation of Acceleration.** We know that :

Acceleration = Slope of speed-time graph

= Slope of line AF (see Figure 42)

$$= \frac{FG}{AG}$$

Now, if we look at the graph shown in Figure 42, we will find that the value of speed at point F is 30 m/s and that at point G is 5 m/s.

Therefore, $FG = 30 - 5$

$= 25$ m/s

Again, at point G, the value of time is 50 seconds whereas that at point A is 0 second.

Thus, $AG = 50 - 0$

$= 50$ s

Now, putting these values of FG and AG in the above relation, we get :

$$\text{Acceleration} = \frac{25 \text{ m/s}}{50 \text{ s}}$$

$$= 0.5 \text{ m/s}^2$$

(*ii*) **Calculation of Distance Travelled.** The distance travelled by the car in 50 seconds is equal to the area under the speed-time curve AF. That is, the distance travelled is equal to the area of the figure $OAFH$ (see Figure 42). But the figure $OAFH$ is a trapezium. So,

$$\text{Distance travelled} = \text{Area of trapezium } OAFH$$

$$= \frac{(\text{Sum of two parallel sides}) \times \text{Height}}{2}$$

In Figure 42, the two parallel sides are OA and HF whereas the height is OH. Therefore,

$$\text{Distance travelled} = \frac{(OA + HF) \times OH}{2}$$

$$= \frac{(5 + 30) \times 50}{2}$$

$$= \frac{35 \times 50}{2}$$

$$= 875 \text{ m}$$

TO DERIVE THE EQUATIONS OF MOTION BY GRAPHICAL METHOD

The three equations of motion : $v = u + at$; $s = ut + \frac{1}{2}at^2$ and $v^2 = u^2 + 2as$ can be derived with the help of graphs as described below.

1. To Derive $v = u + at$ by Graphical Method

Consider the velocity-time graph of a body shown in Figure 43. The body has an initial velocity u at point A and then its velocity changes at a uniform rate from A to B in time t. In other words, there is a uniform acceleration a from A to B, and after time t its final velocity becomes v which is equal to BC in the graph (see Figure 43). The time t is represented by OC. To complete the figure, we draw the perpendicular CB from point C, and draw AD parallel to OC. BE is the perpendicular from point B to OE.

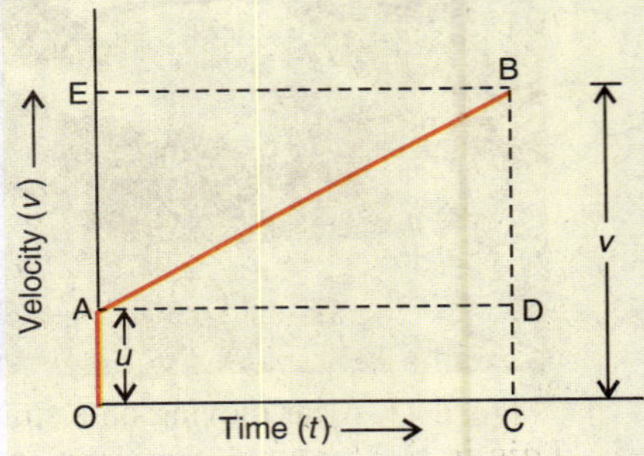

Figure 43. Velocity-time graph to derive the equations of motion.

Now, Initial velocity of the body, $u = OA$ ... (1)

And, Final velocity of the body, $v = BC$ ... (2)

But from the graph $BC = BD + DC$

Therefore, $v = BD + DC$ ... (3)

Again $DC = OA$

So, $v = BD + OA$

Now, From equation (1), $OA = u$

So, $v = BD + u$ ... (4)

We should find out the value of BD now. We know that the slope of a velocity-time graph is equal to acceleration, a.

Thus, Acceleration, a = slope of line AB (see Figure 43)

or
$$a = \frac{BD}{AD}$$

But $AD = OC = t$ (see Figure 43), so putting t in place of AD in the above relation, we get :

$$a = \frac{BD}{t}$$

or
$$BD = at$$

Now, putting this value of BD in equation (4) we get :

$$v = at + u$$

This equation can be rearranged to give :

$$v = u + at$$

And this is the first equation of motion. It has been derived here by the graphical method.

2. To Derive $s = ut + \frac{1}{2}at^2$ by Graphical Method

Suppose the body travels a distance s in time t. In Figure 43, the distance travelled by the body is given by the area of the space between the velocity-time graph AB and the time axis OC, which is equal to the area of the figure $OABC$. Thus :

$$\begin{aligned}\text{Distance travelled} &= \text{Area of figure } OABC \\ &= \text{Area of rectangle } OADC + \text{Area of triangle } ABD\end{aligned}$$

We will now find out the area of the rectangle $OADC$ and the area of the triangle ABD.

(*i*) $$\begin{aligned}\text{Area of rectangle } OADC &= OA \times OC \text{ (see Figure 43)} \\ &= u \times t \\ &= ut \qquad \text{... (5)}\end{aligned}$$

(*ii*) $$\begin{aligned}\text{Area of triangle } ABD &= \frac{1}{2} \times \text{Area of rectangle } AEBD \\ &= \frac{1}{2} \times AD \times BD \\ &= \frac{1}{2} \times t \times at \qquad \text{(because } AD = t \text{ and } BD = at) \\ &= \frac{1}{2}at^2 \qquad \text{... (6)}\end{aligned}$$

So, Distance travelled, s = Area of rectangle $OADC$ + Area of triangle ABD

or
$$s = ut + \frac{1}{2}at^2$$

This is the second equation of motion. It has been derived here by the graphical method.

3. To Derive $v^2 = u^2 + 2as$ by Graphical Method

We have just seen that the distance travelled s by a body in time t is given by the area of the figure $OABC$ which is a trapezium (see Figure 43). In other words,

Distance travelled, s = Area of trapezium $OABC$

$$s = \frac{(\text{Sum of parallel sides}) \times \text{Height}}{2}$$

or
$$s = \frac{(OA + CB) \times OC}{2}$$

Now, $OA + CB = u + v$ and $OC = t$. Putting these values in the above relation, we get :

$$s = \frac{(u+v) \times t}{2} \qquad \text{... (7)}$$

We now want to eliminate t from the above equation. This can be done by obtaining the value of t from the first equation of motion.

Thus, $v = u + at$ (First equation of motion)

And, $at = v - u$

So, $t = \frac{(v-u)}{a}$

Now, putting this value of t in equation (7) above, we get :

$$s = \frac{(u+v)\times(v-u)}{2a}$$

or $2as = v^2 - u^2$ [because $(v + u) \times (v - u) = v^2 - u^2$]

or $v^2 = u^2 + 2as$

This is the third equation of motion. It has been derived by the graphical method.

UNIFORM CIRCULAR MOTION

When a body (or an object) moves in a circle, it is called circular motion. In other words, motion in a circle is circular motion. Before we study the uniform circular motion, we will discuss how a circular path

(*a*) A merry-go-round

(*b*) A CD player

Figure 44. What do merry-go-round and CD player shown in these photographs have in common ? They both use circular motion. The child on a revolving merry-go-round has circular motion, and each and every point on a revolving CD in the CD player has also circular motion.

can be considered to be made up of an indefinite number of tiny sides, and a body moving along such a circular path changes its direction of motion continuously.

Suppose an athlete is running along a square track [see Figure 45(*a*)]. While running along the square track having four sides, the athlete has to change his direction of motion four times (at the four corners of

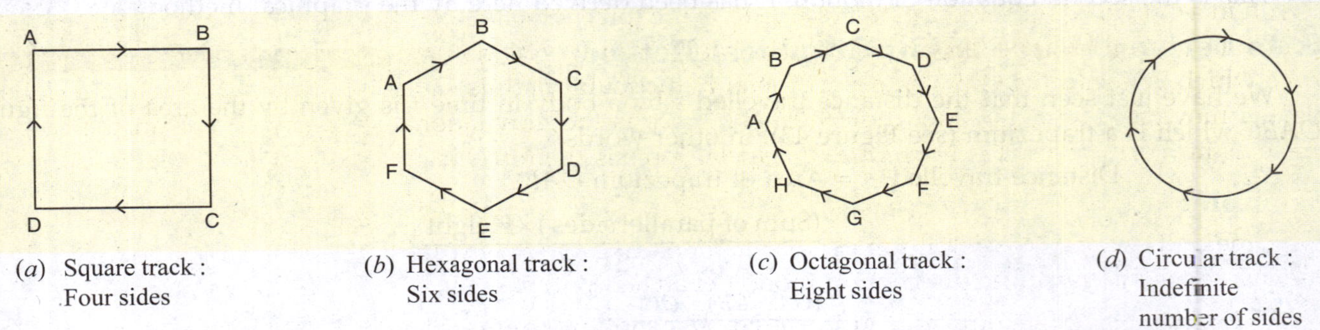

(*a*) Square track : Four sides

(*b*) Hexagonal track : Six sides

(*c*) Octagonal track : Eight sides

(*d*) Circular track : Indefinite number of sides

Figure 45. A circular track (or circular path) can be supposed to be made up of an 'indefinite number' of sides.

the square track : A, B, C and D). Next, suppose the athlete runs along a hexagonal track [see Figure 45(*b*)]. While running along the hexagonal track having six sides, the athlete has to change his direction of motion six times (at the six corners of the hexagonal track : *A, B, C, D, E* and *F*). Again, suppose the athlete now runs along an octagonal track [see Figure 45(*c*)]. While running along the octagonal track having eight sides, the athlete has to change his direction of motion eight times (at the eight corners of the octagonal track : *A, B, C, D, E, F, G* and *H*). Thus, as the number of sides of a track increases, the direction of an athelete running along it changes more and more frequently. Now, if the track has an indefinite number of tiny sides (or point sides), then the shape of track becomes a circle or it becomes a circular track [see Figure 45(*d*)]. And when the athlete runs along a circular track, then his direction of motion changes continuously. In general we can say that : **When a body (or object) moves along a circular path, then its direction of motion (or direction of speed) keeps changing continuously.** So, if an athlete moves with a constant speed along a circular path, then the velocity of the athlete will not be constant because velocity is the speed in a specified direction and here the direction of speed changes continuously. **Since the velocity changes (due to continuous change in direction), therefore, the motion along a circular path is said to be accelerated**. Keeping this point in mind, we will now define uniform circular motion.

When a body moves in a circular path with uniform speed (constant speed), its motion is called uniform circular motion. It is possible for a body to move in a circular path with uniform speed as long as it is travelling equal distances in equal intervals of time. But the velocity of the body moving in a circle with uniform speed is not uniform because the direction of motion is constantly changing. Let us take one example to make this point more clear.

Suppose a stone tied to a thread is rotated in a circular path with uniform speed in clockwise direction as shown in Figure 46. Now, when the stone is at point *A*, then its speed is directed towards east (along the tangent to the circle at *A*). And if the stone is released when it is at *A*, it will fly off in the east direction. When the stone is at point *B*, its speed is directed towards south (along the tangent to the circle at point *B*). And if the stone is released when it is at point *B*, it will fly off in the south direction. This means that when a body moves in a circular path, the direction of speed is not the same at any two points. Since there is a change in the direction of speed of the body, its velocity is not uniform (because velocity is the speed in a specified direction). It is clear that when a body moves in a circle with uniform speed, its velocity changes continuously, so that the motion in a circle is accelerated. In other words, **circular motion is accelerated** even though the speed of the body remains constant. Thus, **the motion in a circle with constant speed is an example of accelerated motion.** *Though the speed may not change, the direction of motion changes continuously.*

Stone
A
East
Thread
B
South

Figure 46. A stone tied to a thread moving with uniform circular motion.

mystudygear

Please note that **a force is needed to produce circular motion.** In other words, a force is needed to make a body move in a circle. Now, when a stone tied to a thread is rotated by a person in a circular path, then the pull of thread is the force which makes the stone move in a circle (This pull is provided by the hand of the person who is holding the thread). **The force which is needed to make an object travel in a circular path is called centripetal force.** In the case of planets moving around the sun, the centripetal force is the gravitational pull of sun, and in the case of satellites moving around the earth, the centripetal force is the force of gravity of earth.

Examples of Uniform Circular Motion

Some of the examples of uniform circular motion are given below. In all these examples, an object does not change its speed but its direction of motion changes continuously.

1. Artificial satellites move in uniform circular motion around the earth. When an artificial satellite goes around the earth in a circular orbit with constant speed, its velocity is not constant because the direction of motion of satellite is changing continuously. Thus, **the motion of a satellite around the earth is accelerated.** It is the force of gravity of earth which keeps the satellite in circular orbit around it.

2. The moon is a natural satellite of the earth. **The moon moves in uniform circular motion around the earth**. So, the motion of moon around the earth is **accelerated**. It is the force of gravity of earth which keeps the moon in circular orbit around it.

3. The earth moves around the sun in uniform circular motion. So, the motion of earth around the sun is **accelerated**. It is the gravitational force of the sun which keeps the earth moving in a circular orbit around it.

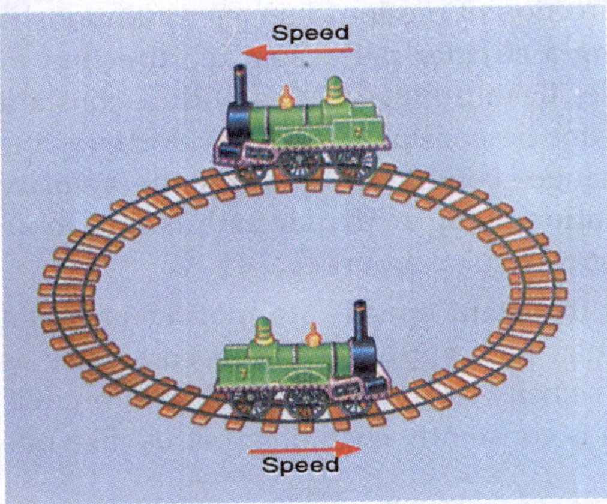

(*a*) This toy train is moving on a circular track. It is in circular motion. Though the speed of train is constant but the direction of motion (or direction of speed) is changing continuously. So, the train is exhibiting accelerated motion

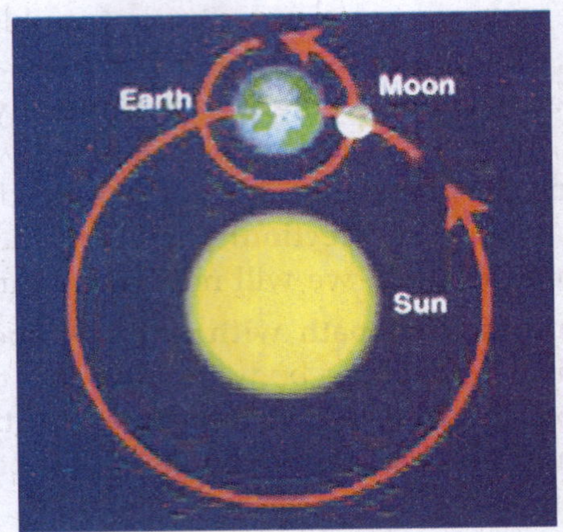

(*b*) The earth is moving around the sun in a circular orbit, and the moon is moving around the earth in another circular orbit. Both the earth and the moon are undergoing circular motion. The direction of motion of the earth and the moon is changing continuously, so their motion is accelerated

(*c*) This athlete (or runner) is running on a circular track with constant speed. Since the direction of her circular motion is changing continuously, it is a case of accelerated motion

Figure 47. Some examples of uniform circular motion.

4. An athlete (or cyclist) moving on a circular track with a constant speed exhibits uniform circular motion. This motion is **accelerated** because of a continuous change in direction of motion.

5. The tip of a seconds' hand of a watch exhibits uniform circular motion on the circular dial of the watch. Please note that though the speed of the tip of seconds' hand is constant but its velocity is not constant (because the direction of motion of tip of seconds' hand changes continuously). Thus, the motion of the tip of seconds' hand of a watch is **accelerated.**

We have already studied uniform linear motion. So, let us see what is the main difference between uniform linear motion and uniform circular motion : In uniform linear motion, the direction of motion is fixed. So, **uniform linear motion is not accelerated.** In uniform circular motion, the direction of motion changes continuously. So, **uniform circular motion is accelerated.** Thus, an important characteristic of circular motion is that the direction of motion in it changes continuously with time, so it is accelerated.

To Calculate the Speed of a Body in Uniform Circular Motion

When a body takes one round of a circular path, then it travels a distance equal to its 'circumference' which is given by $2\pi r$, where r is the radius of the circular path (see Figure 48). The speed of a body (or object) moving along a circular path is given by the formula :

$$v = \frac{2\pi r}{t}$$

where v = speed

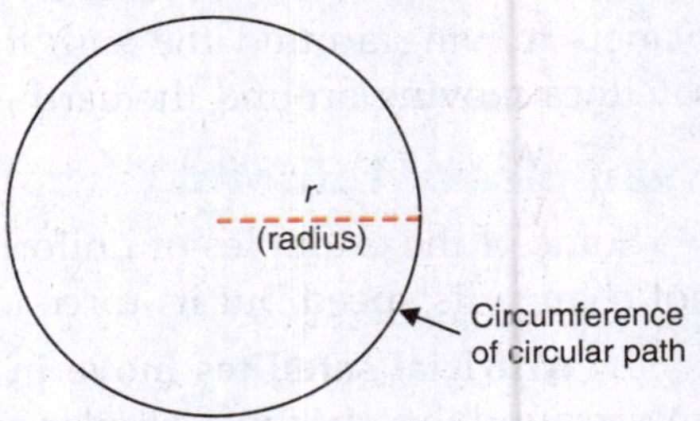

Figure 48. A circular path of radius r. The circumference of this circular path is $2\pi r$.

(pi) $\pi = \frac{22}{7}$ (It is a constant)

r = radius of circular path

and t = time taken for one round of circular path

We will use this formula to solve a numerical problem now.

Sample Problem. A cyclist goes around a circular track once every 2 minutes. If the radius of the circular track is 105 metres, calculate his speed. (Given $\pi = \frac{22}{7}$)

Solution. We know that for a body moving in a circular path :

$$v = \frac{2\pi r}{t}$$

Here, Speed, v = ? (To be calculated)

pi, $\pi = \frac{22}{7}$

Radius of circular track, r = 105 m

And, Time taken for 1 round, t = 2 minutes

= 2 × 60 seconds

= 120 s

Now, putting these values of π, r and t in the above formula, we get :

$$v = \frac{2 \times 22 \times 105}{7 \times 120}$$

$$= 5.5 \text{ m/s}$$

Thus, the speed of cyclist on the circular track is 5.5 metres per second.

We are now in a position to **answer the following questions and problems :**

Very Short Answer Type Questions

1. (*a*) What remains constant in uniform circular motion ?
   (*b*) What changes continuously in uniform circular motion ?
2. State whether the following statement is true or false :
   Earth moves round the sun with uniform velocity.
3. A body goes round the sun with constant speed in a circular orbit. Is the motion uniform or accelerated ?
4. What conclusion can you draw about the velocity of a body from the displacement-time graph shown below :

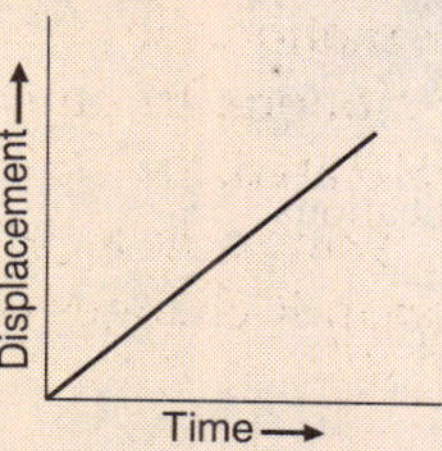

5. Name the quantity which is measured by the area occupied under the velocity-time graph.
6. What does the slope of a speed-time graph indicate ?
7. What does the slope of a distance–time graph indicate ?
8. Give one example of a motion where an object does not change its speed but its direction of motion changes continuously.
9. Name the type of motion in which a body has a constant speed but not constant velocity.
10. What can you say about the motion of a body if its speed-time graph is a straight line parallel to the time axis ?

11. What conclusion can you draw about the speed of a body from the following distance-time graph ?

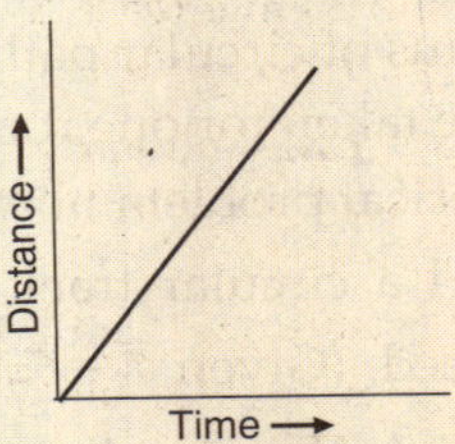

12. What can you say about the motion of a body whose distance-time graph is a straight line parallel to the time axis ?

13. What conclusion can you draw about the acceleration of a body from the speed-time graph shown below ?

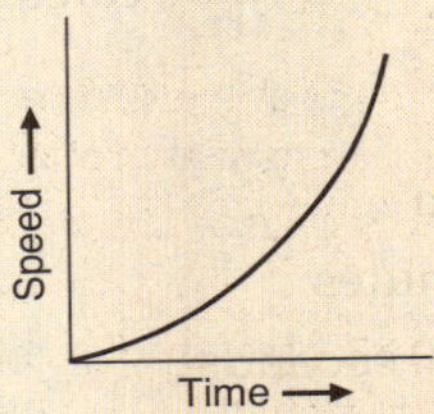

14. A satellite goes round the earth in a circular orbit with constant speed. Is the motion uniform or accelerated ?

This photograph shows a man-made 'communications satellite' going round the earth in a circular orbit (or circular path). We can see the dish antennae, and solar panels (made of solar cells) clearly in this photograph.

This photograph shows a watch. The tip of seconds' hand of this watch moves rapidly on the dial of the watch. The tips of minutes' hand and hours' hand also move on the dial but they move slowly.

15. What type of motion is represented by the tip of the 'seconds' hand' of a watch ? Is it uniform or accelerated ?

16. Fill in the following blanks with suitable words :

(*a*) If a body moves with uniform velocity, its acceleration is ....

(*b*) The slope of a distance-time graph indicates ....of a moving body.

(*c*) The slope of a speed-time graph of a moving body gives its...................

(*d*) In a speed-time graph, the area enclosed by the speed-time curve and the time axis gives the .... by the body.

(*e*) It is possible for something to accelerate but not change its speed if it moves in a ....

Short Answer Type Questions

17. Is the uniform circular motion accelerated ? Give reasons for your answer.
18. Write the formula to calculate the speed of a body moving along a circular path. Give the meaning of each symbol which occurs in it.
19. Explain why, the motion of a body which is moving with constant speed in a circular path is said to be accelerated.
20. What is the difference between uniform linear motion and uniform circular motion ? Explain with examples.
21. State an important characteristic of uniform circular motion. Name the force which brings about uniform circular motion.
22. Find the initial velocity of a car which is stopped in 10 seconds by applying brakes. The retardation due to brakes is 2.5 m/s^2.
23. Describe the motion of a body which is accelerating at a constant rate of 10 m s^{-2}. If the body starts from rest, how much distance will it cover in 2 s ?
24. A motorcycle moving with a speed of 5 m/s is subjected to an acceleration of 0.2 m/s^2. Calculate the speed of the motorcycle after 10 seconds, and the distance travelled in this time.
25. A bus running at a speed of 18 km/h is stopped in 2.5 seconds by applying brakes. Calculate the retardation produced.
26. A train starting from rest moves with a uniform acceleration of 0.2 m/s^2 for 5 minutes. Calculate the speed acquired and the distance travelled in this time.
27. Name the two quantities, the slope of whose graph gives :
    (*a*) speed, and
    (*b*) acceleration
28. A cheetah starts from rest, and accelerates at 2 m/s^2 for 10 seconds. Calculate :
    (*a*) the final velocity
    (*b*) the distance travelled.
29. A train travelling at 20 m s^{-1} accelerates at 0.5 m s^{-2} for 30 s. How far will it travel in this time ?
30. A cyclist is travelling at 15 m s^{-1}. She applies brakes so that she does not collide with a wall 18 m away. What deceleration must she have ?
31. Draw a velocity-time graph to show the following motion :
    A car accelerates uniformly from rest for 5 s ; then it travels at a steady velocity for 5 s.
32. The velocity-time graph for part of a train journey is a horizontal straight line. What does this tell you about (*a*) the train's velocity, and (*b*) about its acceleration ?

Long Answer Type Questions

33. (*a*) Explain the meaning of the following equation of motion :
    $v = u + at$
    where symbols have their usual meanings.
    (*b*) A body starting from rest travels with uniform acceleration. If it travels 100 m in 5 s, what is the value of acceleration ?
34. (*a*) Derive the formula : $v = u + at$, where the symbols have usual meanings.
    (*b*) A bus was moving with a speed of 54 km/h. On applying brakes it stopped in 8 seconds. Calculate the acceleration.
35. (*a*) Derive the formula : $s = ut + \frac{1}{2}at^2$, where the symbols have usual meanings.
    (*b*) A train starting from stationary position and moving with uniform acceleration attains a speed of 36 km per hour in 10 minutes. Find its acceleration.
36. (*a*) Write the three equations of uniformly accelerated motion. Give the meaning of each symbol which occurs in them.
    (*b*) A car acquires a velocity of 72 km per hour in 10 seconds starting from rest. Find (*i*) the acceleration, (*ii*) the average velocity, and (*iii*) the distance travelled in this time.
37. (*a*) What is meant by uniform circular motion ? Give two examples of uniform circular motion.
    (*b*) The tip of seconds' hand of a clock takes 60 seconds to move once on the circular dial of the clock. If the

radius of the dial of the clock be 10.5 cm, calculate the speed of the tip of the seconds' hand of the clock. (Given $\pi = \frac{22}{7}$).

38. Show by means of graphical method that :

$$v = u + at$$

where the symbols have their usual meanings.

39. Show by using the graphical method that :

$$s = ut + \frac{1}{2}at^2$$

where the symbols have their usual meanings.

40. Derive the following equation of motion by the graphical method :

$$v^2 = u^2 + 2as$$

where the symbols have their usual meanings.

Multiple Choice Questions (MCQs)

41. A bus increases its speed from 36 km/h to 72 km/h in 10 seconds. Its acceleration is :
(*a*) 5 m/s^2 (*b*) 2 m/s^2 (*c*) 3.6 m/s^2 (*d*) 1 m/s^2

42. A bus moving along a straight line at 20 m/s undergoes an acceleration of 4 m/s^2. After 2 seconds, its speed will be :
(*a*) 8 m/s (*b*) 12 m/s (*c*) 16 m/s (*d*) 28 m/s

43. The slope of a speed-time graph gives :
(*a*) distance travelled (*b*) velocity (*c*) acceleration (*d*) displacement

44. The area under a speed-time graph represents a physical quantity which has the unit of :
(*a*) m (*b*) m^2 (*c*) m s^{-1} (*d*) m s^{-2}

45. If the displacement of an object is proportional to the square of time, then the object is moving with :
(*a*) uniform velocity (*b*) uniform acceleration
(*c*) increasing acceleration (*d*) decreasing acceleration

46. Four cars A, B, C and D are moving on a levelled, straight road. Their distance-time graphs are shown in the given figure. Which of the following is the correct statement regarding the motion of these cars ?
(*a*) car A is faster than car D. (*b*) car B is the slowest
(*c*) car D is faster than the car C (*d*) car C is the slowest

47. A car of mass 1000 kg is moving with a velocity of 10 m s^{-1}. If the velocity-time graph for this car is a horizontal line parallel to the time axis, then the velocity of car at the end of 25 s will be :
(*a*) 25 m s^{-1} (*b*) 40 m s^{-1} (*c*) 10 m s^{-1} (*d*) 250 m s^{-1}

48. A motorcycle is being driven at a speed of 20 m/s when brakes are applied to bring it to rest in five seconds. The deceleration produced in this case will be :
(*a*) + 4 m/s^2 (*b*) – 4 m/s^2 (*c*) + 0.25 m/s^2 (*d*) – 0.25 m/s^2

49. A sprinter is running along the circumference of a big sports stadium with constant speed. Which of the following do you think is changing in this case ?
(*a*) magnitude of acceleration being produced (*b*) distance covered by the sprinter per second
(*c*) direction in which the sprinter is running (*d*) centripetal force acting on the sprinter

50. In the speed-time graph for a moving object shown here, the part which indicates uniform deceleration of the object is :
(*a*) ST (*b*) QR (*c*) RS (*d*) PQ

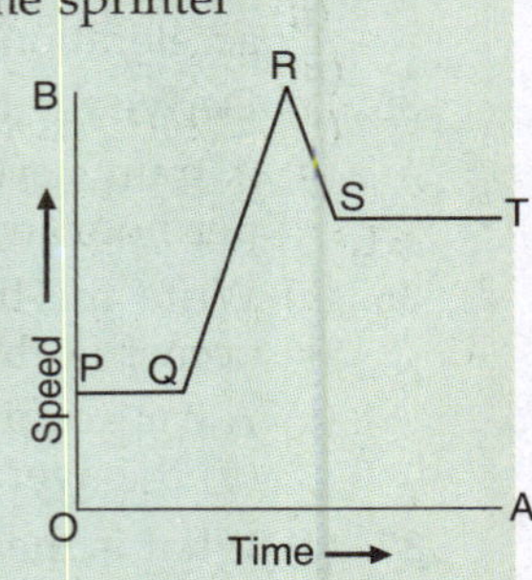

51. A student draws a distance-time graph for a moving scooter and finds that a section of the graph is a horizontal line parallel to the time axis. Which of the following conclusion is correct about this section of the graph ?
(*a*) the scooter has uniform speed in this section
(*b*) the distance travelled by scooter is the maximum in this section
(*c*) the distance travelled by the scooter is the minimum in this section
(*d*) the distance travelled by the scooter is zero in this section

52. Which one of the following is most likely not a case of uniform circular motion ?
(*a*) motion of the earth around the sun
(*b*) motion of a toy train on a circular track
(*c*) motion of a racing car on a circular track
(*d*) motion of hours' hand on the dial of a clock

Questions Based on High Order Thinking Skills (HOTS)

53. The graph given alongside shows the positions of a body at different times. Calculate the speed of the body as it moves from :
(*i*) *A* to *B*,
(*ii*) *B* to *C*, and
(*iii*) *C* to *D*.

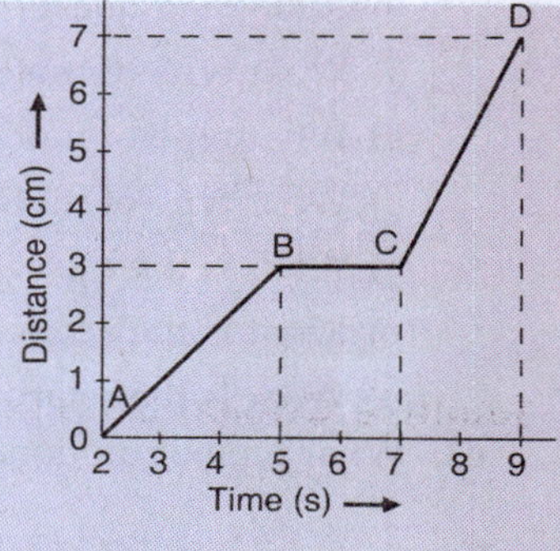

54. What can you say about the motion of a body if :
(*a*) its displacement-time graph is a straight line ?
(*b*) its velocity-time graph is a straight line ?

55. A body with an initial velocity *x* moves with a uniform acceleration *y*. Plot its velocity-time graph.

56. Given alongside is the velocity-time graph for a moving body :
Find : (*i*) Velocity of the body at point *C*.
(*ii*) Acceleration acting on the body between *A* and *B*.
(*iii*) Acceleration acting on the body between *B* and *C*.

57. A body is moving uniformly in a straight line with a velocity of 5 m/s. Find graphically the distance covered by it in 5 seconds.

58. The speed-time graph of an ascending passenger lift is given alongside.
What is the acceleration of the lift :
(*i*) during the first two seconds ?
(*ii*) between second and tenth second ?
(*iii*) during the last two seconds ?

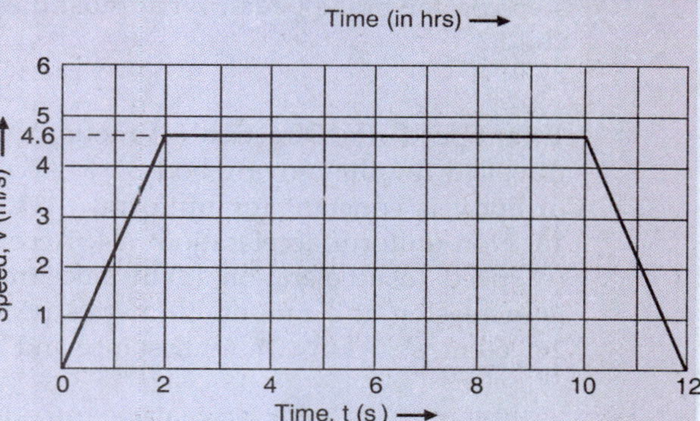

59. A car is moving on a straight road with uniform acceleration. The speed of the car varies with time as follows :

Time (s)	:	0	2	4	6	8	10
Speed (m/s)	:	4	8	12	16	20	24

Draw the speed-time graph by choosing a convenient scale. From this graph :
(*i*) Calculate the acceleration of the car.
(*ii*) Calculate the distance travelled by the car in 10 seconds.

60. The graph given alongside shows how the speed of a car changes with time :
(*i*) What is the initial speed of the car ?
(*ii*) What is the maximum speed attained by the car ?
(*iii*) Which part of the graph shows zero acceleration ?
(*iv*) Which part of the graph shows varying retardation ?
(*v*) Find the distance travelled in first 8 hours.

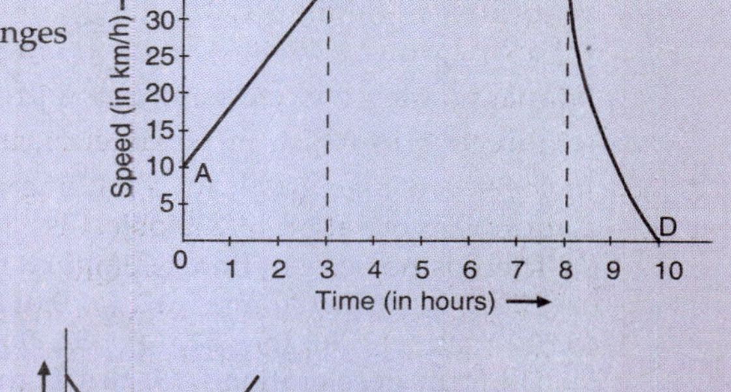

61. Three speed-time graphs are given below :

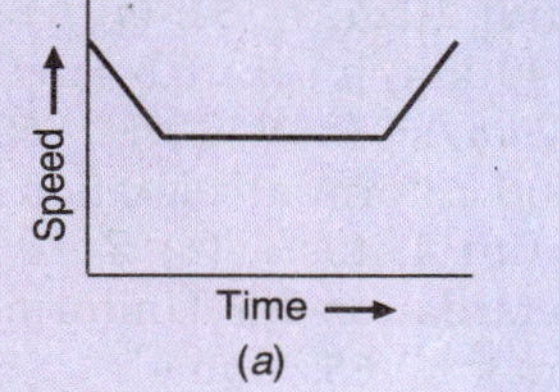

(*a*)

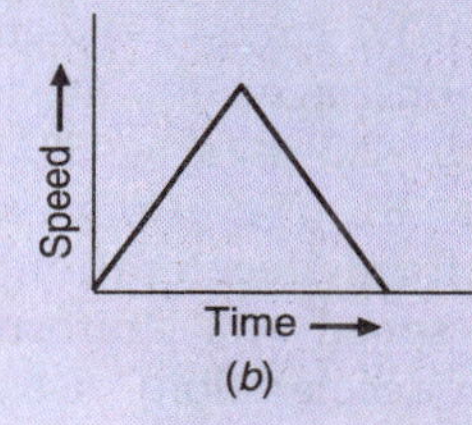

(*b*)

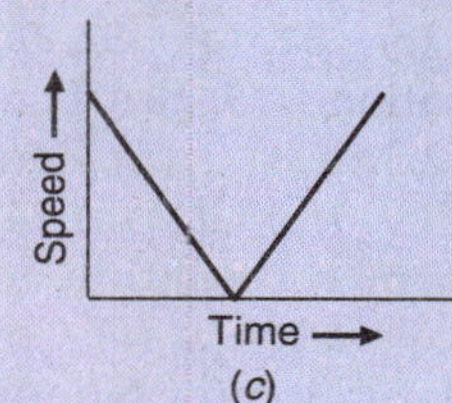

(*c*)

Which graph represents the case of :

(*i*) a cricket ball thrown vertically upwards and returning to the hands of the thrower ?

(*ii*) a trolley decelerating to a constant speed and then accelerating uniformly ?

62. Study the speed-time graph of a car given alongside and answer the following questions :

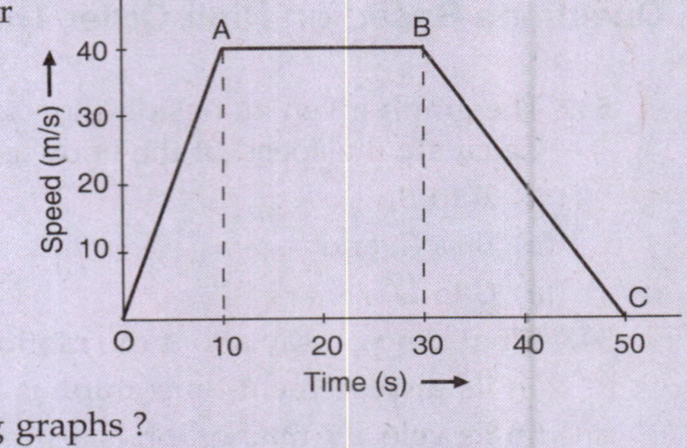

(*i*) What type of motion is represented by *OA* ?

(*ii*) What type of motion is represented by *AB* ?

(*iii*) What type of motion is represented by *BC* ?

(*iv*) What is the acceleration of car from *O* to *A* ?

(*v*) What is the acceleration of car from *A* to *B* ?

(*vi*) What is the retardation of car from *B* to *C* ?

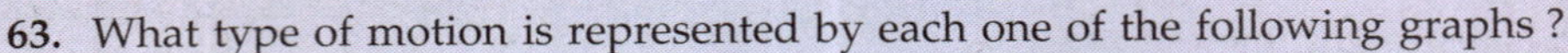

63. What type of motion is represented by each one of the following graphs ?

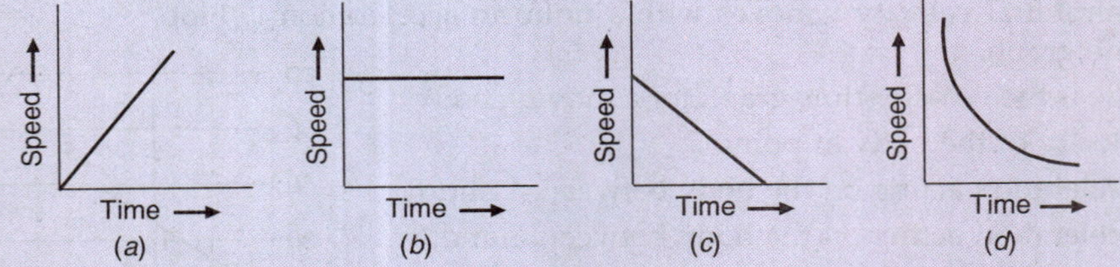

64. A car is travelling along the road at 8 m s^{-1}. It accelerates at 1 m s^{-2} for a distance of 18 m. How fast is it then travelling ?

65. A car is travelling at 20 m/s along a road. A child runs out into the road 50 m ahead and the car driver steps on the brake pedal. What must the car's deceleration be if the car is to stop just before it reaches the child ?

ANSWERS

1. (*a*) Speed (*b*) Direction (of motion) **2.** False **3.** Accelerated **4.** Uniform velocity **5.** Distance travelled (by the moving body) **6.** Acceleration **7.** Speed **9.** Uniform circular motion **10.** The speed of body is constant (or uniform) **11.** Uniform speed **12.** The body is not moving. It is stationary **13.** Non-uniform acceleration **14.** Accelerated **15.** Uniform circular motion ; Accelerated **16.** (*a*) zero (*b*) speed (*c*) acceleration (*d*) distance travelled (*e*) circular path **22.** 25 m/s **23.** The velocity of this body is increasing at a rate of '10 metres per second' every second ; 20 m **24.** 7 m/s ; 60 m **25.** 2 m/s^2 **26.** 60 m/s ; 9 km **27.** (*a*) Distance and Time (*b*) Speed (or Velocity) and Time **28.** (*a*) 20 m/s (*b*) 100 m

29. 825 m **30.** 6.25 m s^{-2} **31.**

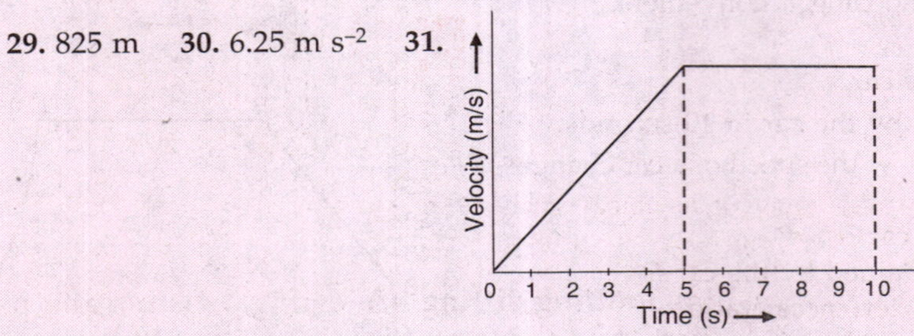

32. (*a*) The train has a uniform velocity (*b*) There is no acceleration **33.** (*b*) 8 m/s^2 **34.** (*b*) – 1.87 m/s^2 **35.** (*b*) 0.016 m/s^2 **36.** (*b*) (*i*) 2 m/s^2 (*ii*) 10 m/s (*iii*) 100 m **37.** (*b*) 0.011 m/s **41.** (*d*) **42.** (*d*) **43.** (*c*) **44.** (*b*) **45.** (*b*) **46.** (*b*) **47.** (*c*) **48.** (*a*) **49.** (*c*) **50.** (*c*) **51.** (*d*) **52.** (*c*) **53.** (*i*) 1 cm/s (*ii*) Zero (*iii*) 2 cm/s **54.** (*a*) Uniform velocity (*b*) Uniform acceleration **55.** See Figure 38 on page 31 **56.** (*i*) 40 km/h (*ii*) 6.6 km/h^2 (*iii*) Zero **57.** 25 m **58.** (*i*) 2.3 m/s^2 (*ii*) Zero (*iii*) –2.3 m/s^2 **59.** (*i*) 2 m/s^2 (*ii*) 140 m **60.** (*i*) 10 km/h (*ii*) 35 km/h (*iii*) BC (*iv*) CD (*v*) 242.5 km **61.** (*i*) *c* (*ii*) *a* **62** (*i*) Uniform acceleration (*ii*) Constant speed (*iii*) Uniform retardation (or Uniform deceleration) (*iv*) 4 m/s^2 (*v*) Zero (*vi*) 2 m/s^2 **63.** (*a*) Uniform acceleration (*b*) Constant speed (*c*) Uniform retardation (or Uniform deceleration) (*d*) Non-uniform retardation (or Non-uniform deceleration) **64.** 10 m s^{-1} **65.** 4 m/s^2

FORCE AND LAWS OF MOTION

When we want to open a door, we have to push the door handle. And when we want to close the door, we have to pull the door handle with our hand. This means that to move a body (or an object), it has either to be pushed or pulled. **A push or pull on a body is called force**. The direction in which a body is pushed or pulled is called the direction of force. We open or close a door by applying force. Now, when we push the door to open it, we apply a force on the door in a direction away from us. And when we pull the door to close it, then we exert a force on the door in a direction towards us.

Figure 1. A push or pull on an object is called force.

Forces are used in our everyday actions like pushing, pulling, lifting, stretching, twisting and pressing. For example, a force is used when we push (kick) a football; a force is used when we pull the drawer of a table ; a force is used when we lift a box from the floor ; a force is used when we stretch a rubber band ; a force is used when we twist a wet cloth to squeeze out water ; and a force is used when we press the brake pedal of a car. The fallen leaves of trees fly away with wind because the force of wind pushes them away. Even the roofs of some huts fly away during a storm because the force of strong winds pushes them away. And when we fly a kite, we can actually feel the force (or push) of the wind on it. We will now describe the effects of force.

(*a*) Weightlifter pulling the weights

(*b*) Weightlifter pushing the weights

Figure 2. This weightlifter first exerts a 'pull' on the weights and then a 'push' on the weights (so as to lift them up). A push or pull on a body is called force. So, this weightlifter is exerting force on the weights.

Effects of Force

A force cannot be seen. A force can be judged only by the effects which it can produce in various bodies (or objects) around us. A force can produce the following effects :

1. A force can ***move*** a stationary body.
2. A force can ***stop*** a moving body.
3. A force can ***change the speed*** of a moving body.
4. A force can ***change the direction*** of a moving body.
5. A force can ***change the shape (and size)*** of a body.

We will now give examples of all these effects produced by a force when it acts on a body (or an object).

If we kick a football kept on the ground with our foot, then the football starts moving (see Figure 3). In this case, the force of our foot moves a stationary football. Similarly, the force of engine can move a stationary car. From these examples we conclude that **a force can make a stationary body move.** It is a common observation that a football moving on the ground stops after some time. In this case, the force of friction of ground stops the moving football. Similarly, the force of brakes can stop a moving car. From these examples we conclude that **a force can make a moving body stop**.

Figure 3. When a player kicks the football, his foot exerts a force on the football. This force causes the football to move.

Suppose we are moving on a bicycle at a certain speed. Now, if someone pushes the moving bicycle from behind, then the speed of bicycle increases and it will move faster. On the other hand, if someone pulls the moving bicycle from behind, then the speed of bicycle decreases and it will move slower. Thus, a push or pull can change the speed of a moving bicycle. But a push or pull is called force. So, we can say that **a force can change the speed of a moving bicycle (or any other moving body)**. If the force is applied in the direction of motion of a body, its speed increases. On the other hand, if the force is applied in the direction opposite to the direction of motion of a body, then its speed decreases. Let us take another example. When a ball is dropped from a height, its speed goes on increasing. **The speed of a falling ball (or any other falling body) increases because the earth applies a pulling force on it which is called the force of gravity.** It is the force of gravity of the earth which pulls a falling ball towards its centre and increases its speed. On the other hand, when a ball is thrown upwards, then its speed goes on decreasing. This is because the earth applies a pulling force of gravity on the ball in the downward direction (opposite to the motion of the ball).

In a tennis match, when a moving tennis ball is hit by a racket, then the direction of tennis ball changes and it goes in a different direction (see Figure 4). In this case, the force exerted by the tennis player's racket changes the direction of a moving tennis ball. Similarly, in a cricket match, when a moving cricket ball is hit by a bat, then the direction of cricket ball changes and it goes in another direction. In this case, the force exerted by the cricket player's bat changes the direction of a moving cricket ball. In the game of carrom, when we take a rebound, then the direction of striker changes. This is because the edge of the carrom board exerts a force on the striker. If we blow air from our mouth on the smoke rising up from a burning incense stick (*agarbatti*), then the direction of motion of smoke changes. In this case, the force exerted by the blowing air changes the direction of moving smoke. From these examples we conclude that **a force can change the direction of motion of a moving body**.

Figure 4. The force from a tennis player's racket can change the direction of motion of the tennis ball.

If we take a light spring and pull it at both the ends with our hands, then the shape and size of the spring changes (see Figure 5). The turns of the spring become farther apart and its length increases. In this case, the force of our hands changes the shape and size of the spring. Here are some more examples in which a force changes the shape (and size) of an object. The shape of dough (kneaded flour) changes on pressing with a rolling pin (*belan*) to make *chapatis*. When we press the dough with a rolling pin, we apply force. So, we can say that the shape of dough changes on applying force. The shape of kneaded wet clay (*geeli mitti*) changes when a potter converts it into pots of different shapes and sizes. This happens because the potter applies force on the kneaded wet clay. The shape of a tooth paste tube (or an ointment tube) changes when we squeeze it because we apply force while squeezing it. Similarly, the shape of a sponge, tomato, balloon, rubber ball or tennis ball changes on pressing. And the shape and size of a rubber band changes on stretching. From all these examples we conclude that **a force can change the shape and size of a body (or object)**.

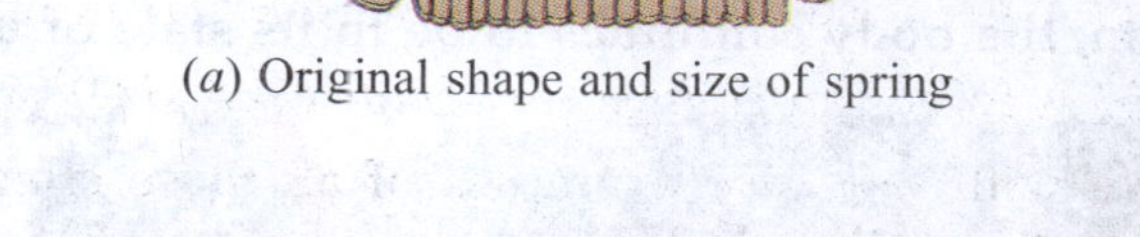

(*a*) Original shape and size of spring

(*b*) Force (of pulling) changes the shape and size of the spring

Figure 5.

We can now define force as follows : **A force is an influence which tends to set a stationary body in motion or stop a moving body ; or which tends to change the speed and direction of a moving body ; or which tends to change the shape (and size) of a body**. We will now discuss the various types of forces.

BALANCED AND UNBALANCED FORCES

Forces are of two types : Balanced forces and Unbalanced forces. We will now discuss balanced and unbalanced forces in detail, one by one. Let us start with balanced forces.

Balanced Forces

If the resultant of all the forces acting on a body is zero, the forces are called balanced forces. A body under the action of balanced forces does not change its position of rest (or of uniform motion) and it appears as if no force is acting on it. This point will become more clear from the following example.

Suppose a heavy box is lying on the ground (Figure 6). Let us push this box with our hands. We find that the box does not move (and remains in its state of rest) though as many as four forces are acting on it. The four forces acting on the box are :

(*i*) Force of our push

(*ii*) Force of friction (which opposes the push and does not allow the box to move)

(*iii*) Force of gravity (which pulls the box downwards)

(*iv*) Force of reaction (exerted by the ground on the box upwards which balances the force of gravity)

Force of reaction
(Exerted by ground)
Force of friction
Heavy box does not move
Force of our push
Force of gravity
(Weight of box)

Figure 6. When balanced forces act on a body (here a heavy box), they do not produce any motion in it.

Now, though the box is at rest, four forces are acting on it. Since the box does not move at all, we conclude that the resultant of all the forces acting on it is zero. The box, therefore, behaves as if no force is acting on it. The forces acting on this stationary box are an example of balanced forces. Please note that the force of our push on the box is balanced by the force of friction, and the force of gravity is balanced by the force of reaction of the ground. Similarly, when we hold a suitcase steady at some height from the ground, the resultant force acting on the suitcase is zero and it does not change its position. Again, in a tug of war, that is, in rope pulling between two teams, if the resultant of forces applied by the two teams is zero, the rope does not move in either direction. The forces exerted by the two teams are balanced. From this discussion we conclude that **if a number of balanced forces act on a stationary body, the body continues to remain in its stationary position.** Similarly, **if a number of balanced forces act on a body in uniform motion, the body continues to be in its state of uniform motion.**

Figure 7. In a tug of war (or rope pulling), when the forces exerted by the two teams on the rope are balanced (equal and opposite), then the rope does not move in either direction.

Figure 8. When a balloon is pressed between hands, then balanced forces (equal and opposite forces) act on balloon due to which the shape of balloon changes.

Though balanced forces cannot produce motion in a stationary body or stop a moving body, they can, however, change the shape of the body. An example of the balanced forces changing the shape of a body is in the squeezing of a rubber ball or balloon. When we press a rubber ball or a balloon between our two hands, the shape of rubber ball or balloon changes from spherical to oblong. In this case we apply two equal and opposite forces (balanced forces) with our hands. Though the ball or balloon does not move, its shape changes. We will now discuss the case of unbalanced forces.

Unbalanced Forces

If the resultant of all the forces acting on a body is not zero, the forces are called unbalanced forces. When unbalanced forces act on a body, they produce a change in its state of rest or of uniform motion. That is, **unbalanced forces can move a stationary body or they can stop a moving body**. In other words, unbalanced forces acting on a body can change its speed or direction of motion. This point will become more clear from the following example.

Suppose a toy car is lying on the ground (see Figure 9). Let us push this car with our hand. We find that the toy car starts moving. Now, in this case also four forces are acting on the toy car. These are :

(*i*) Force of our push
(*ii*) Force of friction
(*iii*) Force of gravity
(*iv*) Force of reaction of ground

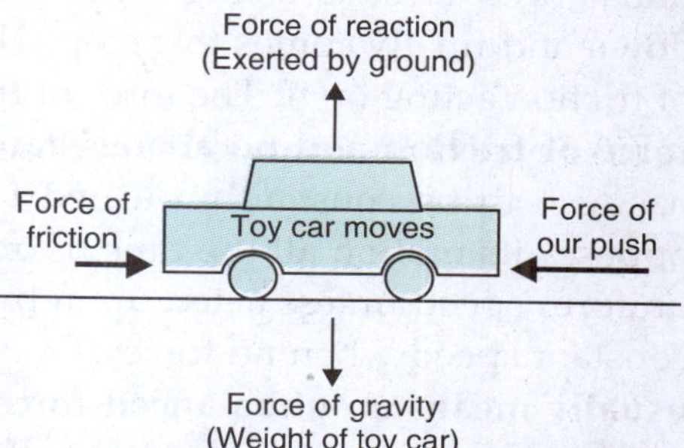

Figure 9. An unbalanced force of our push produces motion in the toy car.

In this case also, the force of gravity on the car acting downwards and the force of reaction of ground acting upwards are equal and opposite, so they balance each other. Now, due to the wheels of the toy car, the opposing 'force of friction' is much less here. The force of our push is, therefore, greater than the force of friction in this case, so they cannot balance each other. Thus, the resultant of all the forces acting on the toy car is not zero. There is a net unbalanced force acting on the toy car which makes the car move from its position of rest. The toy car moves in the direction of greater force (which is the direction of our push). Thus, **to move a stationary object, we have to push it with a force greater than the opposing force of friction.**

Please note that even the heavy box shown in Figure 6 can be moved if pushed with a very strong force (by more than one person). This is because in that case the force of push will become greater than the opposing force of friction. An unbalanced force will then act on the heavy box and make it move.

When we are holding a suitcase above the ground, then the force of gravity acting on the suitcase is balanced by the upward force of our hands. Now, **if we release the suitcase from our hand, then the unbalanced force of gravity acts on it and the suitcase falls to the ground.** In this case the force of gravity

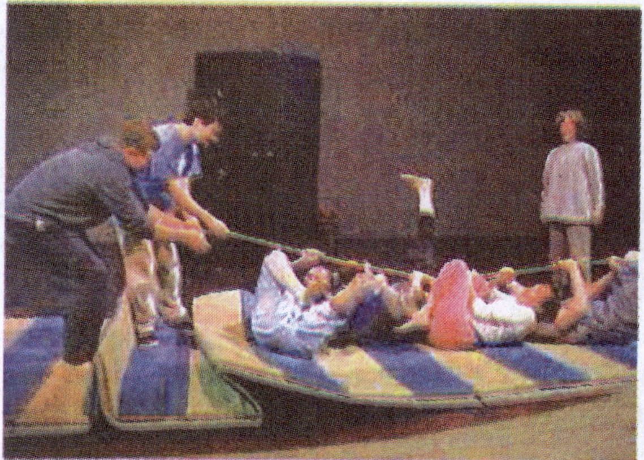

Figure 10. In a tug of war (or rope pulling), if one of the teams suddenly releases the rope, then an unbalanced force acts on the other team due to which it falls backwards.

Figure 11. If there were no unbalanced force of friction and air resistance, then a moving bicycle would go on moving for ever (without stopping).

produces motion in the suitcase. Again, in a tug of war, if one of the teams suddenly releases the rope, an unbalanced force acts on the other team due to which it falls backwards. So, in this case, an unbalanced force results in the motion of the weaker team alongwith the rope they are holding. From the above examples, it is clear that **when an unbalanced force acts on a body, it produces motion in the body**. Another point to be noted is that **an unbalanced force can also stop a moving body**. For example, when a ball is rolling on the ground, an unbalanced force of friction acts on it which brings the ball to a stop after some time.

We have just said that an unbalanced force acting on a body changes its speed or direction of motion. The reverse of this is also true. That is, if the speed or direction of motion of a body changes, then some unbalanced force is acting on it. For example, when we stop pedalling a moving bicycle, then it slows down and finally comes to a stop. The slowing down of the moving bicycle is due to the unbalanced force of friction acting on it. The force of friction opposes the motion of the bicycle. **If there were no unbalanced force of friction and no air resistance, a moving bicycle would go on moving for ever**. Similarly, a cart has also to be constantly pushed to keep it in motion. This is because an unbalanced force of friction opposes its motion all the time. From this discussion we conclude that a body will continue to move with uniform speed unless acted upon by an unbalanced force. It was Galileo who said that objects move with constant speed when no forces act on them. **Please note that when we talk of a force acting on a body, it usually means an unbalanced force**. We will not use the word 'unbalanced' with 'force' again and again for the sake of convenience. We will use only the term 'force' in writing the definitions of Newton's laws of motion. You are, however, free to use the term 'unbalanced force' if you so desire.

NEWTON'S LAWS OF MOTION

Newton has given three laws to describe the motion of bodies. These laws are known as Newton's laws of motion. The Newton's laws of motion give a precise definition of force and establish a relationship between the force applied on a body and the state of motion acquired by it. We will now discuss these laws of motion and consider some of their important applications. Let us start with the first law of motion.

Figure 12. Isaac Newton : The scientist who gave the laws of motion and law of gravitation.

NEWTON'S FIRST LAW OF MOTION

Some of the bodies (or objects) around us are at rest, that is, they are stationary, whereas others are in motion. Newton's first law describes the behaviour of such bodies which are in a state of rest or of uniform motion in a straight line. According to Newton's first law of motion : **A body at rest will remain at rest, and a body in motion will continue in motion in a straight line with a uniform speed, unless it is compelled by an external force to change its state of rest or of uniform motion.** It should be noted that by saying an external force, we mean a force from outside the body. Let us take some examples to make the first law of motion more clear. Suppose a book is lying on the table. It is at rest. The book will not move by itself, that is, it cannot change its position of rest by itself. It can change its state of rest only when compelled by the force of our hands, that is, when we lift the book from the table. Thus, the position of rest of the book has been changed by the external force of our hands. And this observation supports the first part of the first law of motion.

The tendency of a body to remain at rest (stationary) or, if moving, to continue moving in a straight line, is called inertia. Newton's first law recognizes that every body has some inertia. **Inertia is that property of a body due to which it resists a change in its state of rest or of uniform motion.** Greater the inertia of a body, greater will be the force required to bring a change in its state of rest or of uniform motion. In fact, **mass is a measure of the inertia of a body.** If a body has more mass, it has more inertia. That is, **heavier objects have more inertia than lighter objects**. For example, a stone has greater inertia than a football. If we kick a stone, it will not move because of its high inertia but if we kick a football, it will move a long way. Thus, a stone resists a change in its state better than a football does. So, **a stone has more inertia than a football.** Similarly, **a cricket ball has more inertia than a rubber ball of the same size**. A cricket ball has more inertia because it has more mass (it is quite heavy). On the other hand, a rubber ball has less inertia because it has less mass (it is quite light). Thus, **the inertia of a body depends on its mass.** For example, if a body has mass of 1 kilogram and another body has a mass of 20 kilograms, then the body having 20 kilogram mass will have more inertia. It is easier to move a body of mass 1 kilogram by pushing it (because of its small inertia) but it is much more difficult to move a body of mass 20 kilograms by pushing it (because of its very high inertia).

(*a*) A toy car has a small mass, so it has small inertia, and hence can be moved easily by pushing

(*b*) A real car has a large mass, so it has a large inertia, and hence quite difficult to move by pushing

Figure 13. Inertia of a body (or object) depends on its mass.

From the above discussion we conclude that **to overcome the inertia and make a body move from rest, we must apply an external force**. It should be noted that Newton's first law of motion is also some times called Galileo's law of inertia. We can illustrate the Newton's first law of motion or the property of inertia of a body with a simple experiment described below.

We take a glass tumbler and place a thick square card on its mouth as shown in Figure 14(*a*). A coin is then placed above this card in the middle. Let us flick the card hard with our fingers. On flicking, the card moves away but the coin drops into the glass tumbler [see Figure 14(*b*)]. We will now explain how it happens.

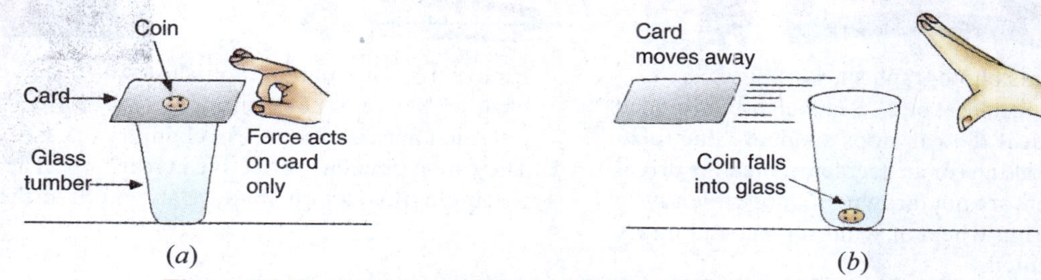

Figure 14. Experiment to illustrate Newton's first law of motion.

Initially, both, the card and the coin, are in the state of rest. Now, when we hit the card with our fingers, a force acts on the card and changes its state of rest to that of motion. Due to this, the card moves away from the mouth of the glass tumbler. The force of our flick, however, does not act on the coin, so the coin continues to be in its state of rest due to its inertia. And when the card (on which the coin had been placed) moves away, the coin falls into the glass tumbler because it prefers to maintain its state of rest due to inertia.

We will now consider the second part of the first law of motion which says that a body in uniform motion will continue to move unless a force compels it to change its state of uniform motion in a straight line. At first sight it would appear to be wrong that a body moving at uniform speed in a straight line will continue to move for ever without coming to rest. Because, if we stop pedalling a bicycle, which is moving at a uniform speed, the bicycle does not go on moving for ever, it comes to rest after some time. The moving bicycle has been compelled to change its state of uniform motion by the external force of air resistance and friction. **If there were no air resistance and no friction to oppose the motion of a bicycle, then according to the first law of motion, a moving bicycle would go on moving for ever. It would not stop by itself.**

We will now describe **some everyday observations which are based on the property of inertia of a body** (due to which it resists a change in its state of rest or of motion). **When a hanging carpet is beaten with a stick, the dust particles start coming out of it.** This is because the force of stick makes the carpet move to-and-fro slightly but the dust particles tend to remain at rest (or stationary) due to their inertia and hence separate from the carpet. **When a tree (having flexible stem) is shaken vigorously, its fruits and leaves fall down.** This is due to the fact that when the tree is shaken, it moves to-and-fro slightly but its fruits and leaves tend to remain at rest (or stationary) due to their inertia and hence detach from the tree and fall down.

We have seen that **when a car or bus starts suddenly, the passengers fall backward.** This is due to the fact that because of their inertia, the passengers tend to remain in their state of rest (or stationary state) even when the car or bus has started moving. **When a running car or bus stops suddenly, the passengers are jerked forward** because due to inertia the passengers tend to remain in their state of motion (which they possessed in a moving car or bus) even though the car or bus has come to rest. The seat belts are

Figure 15. This photograph shows a person sitting in a car wearing a 'seat belt'. Seat belts are provided in cars so that if the car stops suddenly due to an emergency braking (or an accident), then the driver and passengers are not thrown forward violently so as to hit steering wheel or wind screen, and injury can be prevented.

Figure 16. This photograph shows a 'head restrain' at the back of person's neck sitting in a car. Head restrains are provided in cars to reduce neck injury in case of an accident. They are particularly effective in rear-impact accidents (when a vehicle hits from behind). Can you describe how ?

provided in cars so that if a fast running car stops suddenly due to some emergency (or an accident), then the passengers are not thrown forward violently, and injury can be prevented. **When a car or bus turns a corner sharply, we tend to fall sideways** because of our inertia or tendency to continue moving in a straight line. **It is dangerous to jump out of a moving bus** because the jumping man, who is moving with the high speed of the bus, would tend to remain in motion (due to inertia) even on falling to the ground and get hurt due to the resistance offered by ground.

From the above discussion, it is clear that **Newton's first law of motion gives us a definition of force.** It says that **a force is something which changes or tends to change the state of rest or of uniform motion of a body.** In other words, a force is an influence which can produce an acceleration or retardation in a body. **Force is a vector quantity** having magnitude as well as direction.

MOMENTUM

In order to understand Newton's second law of motion, we should first know the meaning of the term 'momentum' of a moving body (or moving object). This is discussed below.

We know that a cricket ball is much more heavy than a tennis ball. Suppose we throw a cricket ball and a tennis ball, both with the same speed or velocity. It will be found that more force is required to stop the cricket ball (which has more mass) and less force is required to stop the tennis ball (which has less mass).

(*a*) A cricket ball hit by a bat

(*b*) A tennis ball hit by a racket

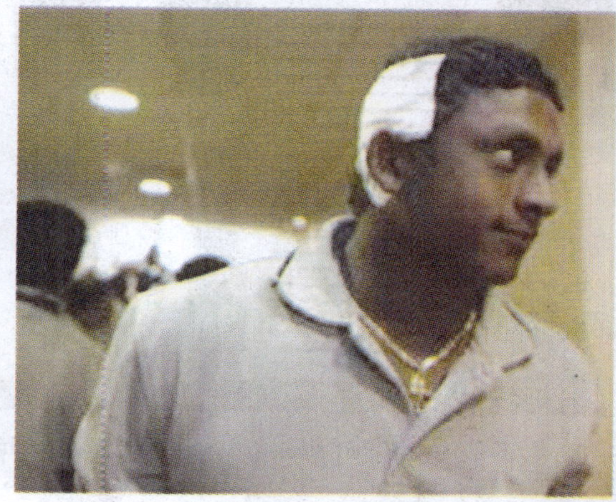

(*c*) A cricketer injured by a fast moving cricket ball

Figure 17. If a cricket ball and a tennis ball, both are moving at the same speed (or same velocity), then more force is required to stop a cricket ball (than a tennis ball). This is because, due to its greater mass, a moving cricket ball has more momentum. Because of its large momentum, a fast moving cricket ball can sometimes cause injuries to a cricketer but a moving tennis ball cannot do so to a tennis player.

We conclude that **the force required to stop a moving body is directly proportional to its mass**. Now, if we throw two cricket balls of the same mass at different speeds or velocities, it will be found that more force is required to stop that cricket ball which is moving with higher velocity and less force is required to stop the cricket ball moving with lower velocity. So, we conclude that **the force required to stop a moving body is also directly proportional to its velocity**. Thus, **the quantity of motion in a body depends on the mass and velocity of the body**. This gives us another term known as "momentum". **The momentum of a body is defined as the product of its mass and velocity.**

Thus, **Momentum = mass × velocity**

or, $p = m \times v$

where p = momentum

m = mass of the body

and v = velocity (or speed) of the body

It is clear that **if a body is at rest, its velocity is zero and hence its momentum is also zero**. Thus, the total momentum of the gun and bullet before firing is zero because their velocity is zero. **Momentum is a vector quantity** and takes place in the direction of velocity. We have just seen that, momentum = mass × velocity. Now, mass is measured in kilograms (kg) and velocity is measured in metres per second (m/s), so **the SI unit of momentum is kilogram metres per second** which is written as **kg.m/s** or **kg.m s^{-1}**.

Every moving body possesses momentum. Since momentum depends on the mass and velocity of a body, so a body will have a large momentum : (*a*) if its mass is large, or (*b*) if its velocity (speed) is large, or (*c*) if both its mass and velocity (speed) are large. We will now discuss some everyday situations which involve large momentum. **A karate player can break a pile of tiles or a slab of ice with a single blow of his hand.** This is because a karate player strikes the pile of tiles or the slab of ice with his hand very, very

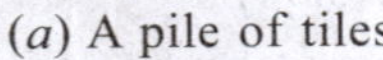

(*a*) A pile of tiles

(*b*) The karate player hits the pile of tiles with a mighty blow of hand

(*c*) All the tiles are broken into pieces

Figure 18. The karate player is able to break so many tiles because he strikes the tiles with his hand very, very fast, producing an extremely large momentum.

fast. In doing so, the large momentum of the fast moving hand is reduced to zero in a very, very short time. This exerts a very large force on the pile of tiles or the ice slab which is sufficient to break them apart.

Though a cricket ball is not very heavy but when it is thrown with a high speed (or high velocity), it acquires a very large momentum and sometimes hurts the batsman. This is why a batsman often ducks to a bouncer. On the other hand, **a car or bus may not be running at a high speed (or high velocity) but because of its high mass, it has a very high momentum which may hurt the person coming in its way**. It is a common observation that **road accidents at high speeds are very much worse than accidents at low speeds**. This is because the momentum of vehicles running at high speeds is very high and causes a lot of damage to the vehicles and injuries to passengers during the collision. Thus, we are afraid of a moving cricket ball or a running vehicle because of the combined effect of their mass and velocity which is called momentum. From this discussion we conclude that the combined effect of mass and velocity of a body is taken into account by a physical quantity called momentum. In fact, **momentum is considered to be a measure of the quantity of motion of a moving body.** We can feel what momentum is if we happen to collide with a person running at top speed ! We will now solve a problem based on momentum.

Sample Problem. What is the momentum of a man of mass 75 kg when he walks with a uniform velocity of 2 m/s ?

Solution. We know that :

$$\text{Momentum} = \text{mass} \times \text{velocity}$$
$$= m \times v$$

Here, Mass, $m = 75$ kg

And, Velocity, $v = 2$ m/s

Putting these values in the above formula, we get :

$$\text{Momentum} = 75 \times 2 \text{ kg.m/s}$$
$$= 150 \text{ kg.m/s}$$

Before we go further and discuss newton's second law of motion, **please answer the following questions :**

Very Short Answer Type Questions

1. What name is given to the product of mass and velocity of a body ?
2. Name the physical quantity which is considered to be a measure of the quantity of motion of a body.
3. What is the SI unit of momentum ?
4. State whether momentum is scalar or vector.
5. What is the total momentum of the bullet and the gun before firing ?
6. Name the physical quantity whose unit is kg.m/s.
7. What will be the momentum of a body of mass *'m'* which is moving with a velocity *'v'* ?
8. What is the usual name of the forces which cannot produce motion in a body but only change its shape ?
9. Name the unbalanced force which slows down a moving bicycle when we stop pedalling it.
10. State whether the following statement is true or false :
    Unbalanced forces acting on a body change its shape.
11. When a ball is dropped from a height, its speed increases gradually. Name the force which causes this change in speed.
12. Name the property of bodies (or objects) to resist a change in their state of rest or of motion.
13. What is the other name of Newton's first law of motion ?
14. The mass of object *A* is 6 kg whereas that of another object *B* is 34 kg. Which of the two objects, *A* or *B*, has more inertia ?
15. Name the scientist who gave the laws of motion.
16. State whether force is a scalar or a vector quantity.
17. With which physical quantity should the speed of a running bull be multiplied so as to obtain its momentum ?
18. Fill in the following blanks with suitable words :
    (*a*) .... is a measure of the inertia of a body.
    (*b*) When a running car stops suddenly, the passengers are jerked ....
    (*c*) When a stationary car starts suddenly, the passengers are jerked ....
    (*d*) Newton's first law of motion is also called Galileo's law of ....
    (*e*) If there were no unbalanced force of .... and no .... resistance, a moving bicycle would go on moving for ever.

Short Answer Type Questions

19. Explain why, it is easier to stop a tennis ball than a cricket ball moving with the same speed.
20. Explain the meaning of the following equation :
    $$p = m \times v$$
    where symbols have their usual meanings.
21. Explain how, a karate player can break a pile of tiles with a single blow of his hand.
22. Calculate the momentum of a toy car of mass 200 g moving with a speed of 5 m/s.
23. What is the change in momentum of a car weighing 1500 kg when its speed increases from 36 km/h to 72 km/h uniformly ?
24. A body of mass 25 kg has a momentum of 125 kg.m/s. Calculate the velocity of the body.
25. Calculate the momentum of the following :
    (*a*) an elephant of mass 2000 kg moving at 5 m/s
    (*b*) a bullet of mass 0.02 kg moving at 400 m/s

An elephant of mass 2000 kg moving at a speed of 5 m/s

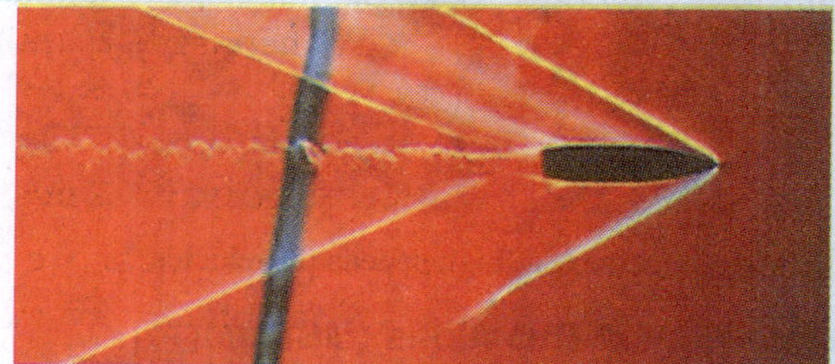

A bullet of mass 0.02 kg moving at a speed of 400 m/s

26. Which of the two, balanced forces or unbalanced forces, can change the shape of an object ? Give an example to illustrate your answer.
27. Describe the term 'inertia' with respect to motion.
28. State Newton's first law of motion. Give two examples to illustrate Newton's first law of motion.
29. On what factor does the inertia of a body depend ? Which has more inertia, a cricket ball or a rubber ball of the same size ?
30. Why do the passengers in a bus tend to fall backward when it starts suddenly ?
31. Explain why, a person travelling in a bus falls forward when the bus stops suddenly.
32. Give reason for the following :
When a hanging carpet is beaten with a stick, the dust particles start coming out of it.
33. When a tree is shaken, its fruits and leaves fall down. Why ?
34. Explain why, it is dangerous to jump out of a moving bus.
35. What is the momentum in kg.m/s of a 10 kg car travelling at (*a*) 5 m/s (*b*) 20 cm/s, and (*c*) 36 km/h ?

Long Answer Type Questions

36. (*a*) Define momentum of a body. On what factors does the momentum of a body depend ?
(*b*) Calculate the change in momentum of a body weighing 5 kg when its velocity decreases from 20 m/s to 0.20 m/s.
37. (*a*) Define the term 'force'.
(*b*) State the various effects of force.
38. Give one example each where :
(*a*) a force moves a stationary body.
(*b*) a force stops a moving body.
(*c*) a force changes the speed of a moving body.
(*d*) a force changes the direction of a moving body.
(*e*) a force changes the shape (and size) of a body.
39. (*a*) What do you understand by the terms "balanced forces" and "unbalanced forces" ? Explain with examples.
(*b*) What type of forces – balanced or unbalanced – act on a rubber ball when we press it between our hands ? What effect is produced in the ball ?
40. (*a*) What happens to the passengers travelling in a bus when the bus takes a sharp turn ? Give reasons for your answer.
(*b*) Why are road accidents at high speeds very much worse than road accidents at low speeds ?

A road accident at high speeds of vehicles

A road accident at low speeds of vehicles

Multiple Choice Questions (MCQs)

41. When a toothpaste tube is squeezed, its shape changes. The force responsible for this is an example of :
(*a*) balanced forces (*b*) centripetal forces (*c*) unbalanced forces (*d*) centrifugal forces

42. The inertia of an object tends to cause an object :
(*a*) to increase its speed (*b*) to decrease its speed
(*c*) to resist a change in its state of motion (*d*) to decelerate due to friction

43. When we talk of a force acting on a body, it usually means :
(*a*) electrical force (*b*) balanced force (*c*) unbalanced force (*d*) nuclear force

44. A passenger in a moving train tosses a coin which falls behind him. This shows that the motion of train is :
(*a*) accelerated (*b*) uniform (*c*) retarded (*d*) along circular track

45. 'When a hanging carpet is beaten with a stick, the dust particles start coming out of it'. This phenomenon can be best explained by making use of :
(*a*) Newton's third law of motion (*b*) Newton's law of gravitation
(*c*) Newton's first law of motion (*d*) Newton's second law of motion

46. A water tanker filled up to two-thirds of its tank with water is running with a uniform speed. When the brakes are suddenly applied, the water in its tank would :
(*a*) move backward (*b*) move forward (*c*) rise upwards (*d*) remain unaffected

47. If we release a magnet held in our hand, it falls to the ground. The force which makes the magnet fall down is an example of :
(*a*) balanced force (*b*) unbalanced force (*c*) magnetic force (*d*) muscular force

48. The inertia of a moving object depends on :
(*a*) momentum of the object (*b*) speed of the object
(*c*) mass of the object (*d*) shape of the object

49. When a rubber balloon held between the hands is pressed, its shape changes. This happens because :
(*a*) balanced forces act on the balloon (*b*) unbalanced forces act on the balloon
(*c*) frictional forces act on the balloon (*d*) gravitational forces act on the balloon

50. Which of the following effect cannot be produced by an unbalanced force acting on a body ?
(*a*) change in speed of the body (*b*) change in shape of the body
(*c*) change in direction of motion of the body (*d*) change in state of rest of the body

Questions Based on High Order Thinking Skills (HOTS)

51. A plastic ball and a clay ball of equal masses, travelling in the same direction with equal speeds, strike against a vertical wall. From which ball does the wall receive a greater amount of momentum ?

52. A moving bicycle comes to rest after sometime if we stop pedalling it. But Newton's first law of motion says that a moving body should continue to move for ever, unless some external force acts on it. How do you explain the bicycle case ?

53. A man throws a ball weighing 500 g vertically upwards with a speed of 10 m/s.
(*i*) What will be its initial momentum ?
(*ii*) What would be its momentum at the highest point of its flight ?

54. A car is moving on a level road. If the driver turns off the engine of the car, the car's speed decreases gradually and ultimately it comes to a stop. A student says that two forces act on the car which bring it to a stop. What could these forces be ? Which of these two forces contributes more to slow down and stop the car ?

55. There are two types of forces X and Y. The forces belonging to type X can produce motion in a stationary object but cannot change the shape of the object. On the other hand, forces belonging to type Y cannot produce motion in a stationary object but can change the shape of the object. What is the general name of the forces such as (*a*) X, and (*b*) Y ?

ANSWERS

1. Momentum **2.** Momentum **4.** Vector **5.** Zero **6.** Momentum **8.** Balanced forces **9.** Force of friction **10.** False **11.** Force of gravity **12.** Inertia **13.** Galileo's law of inertia **14.** B **16.** Vector **17.** Mass (of bull) **18.** (*a*) Mass (*b*) forward (*c*) backward (*d*) inertia (*e*) friction ; air **22.** 1 kg.m/s **23.** 15000 kg.m/s **24.** 5 m/s **25.** (*a*) 10000 kg.m/s (*b*) 8 kg.m/s **35.** (*a*) 50 kg.m/s (*b*) 2 kg.m/s (*c*) 100 kg.m/s **36.** (*b*) 99 kg.m/s decrease **41.** (*a*) **42.** (*c*) **43.** (*c*) **44.** (*a*) **45.** (*c*) **46.** (*b*) **47.** (*b*) **48.** (*c*) **49.** (*a*) **50.** (*b*) **51.** The wall will receive equal momentum from both the balls (because both the balls have equal mass and equal velocity) **53.** (*i*) 5 kg.m/s (*ii*) Zero **54.** Force of friction and Air resistance ; Force of friction **55.** (*a*) Unbalanced forces (*b*) Balanced forces

NEWTON'S SECOND LAW OF MOTION

When two bodies, a heavy one and a light one, are acted upon by the same force for the same time, the light body attains a higher velocity (or higher speed) than the heavy one. But the momentum gained by both the bodies is the same. The link between force and momentum is expressed in Newton's second law of motion.

According to Newton's second law of motion : **The rate of change of momentum of a body is directly proportional to the applied force, and takes place in the direction in which the force acts.** The rate of change of momentum of a body can be obtained by dividing the 'Change in momentum' by 'Time taken' for change. So, Newton's second law of motion can be expressed as :

$$\textbf{Force} \propto \frac{\textbf{Change in momentum}}{\textbf{Time taken}}$$

Consider a body of mass m having an initial velocity u. The initial momentum of this body will be mu. Suppose a force F acts on this body for time t and causes the final velocity to become v. The final momentum of this body will be mv. Now, the change in momentum of this body is $mv - mu$ and the time taken for this change is t. So, according to Newton's second law of motion :

$$F \propto \frac{mv - mu}{t}$$

or

$$F \propto \frac{m(v-u)}{t}$$

But $\frac{v-u}{t}$ represents change in velocity with time which is known as acceleration 'a'. So, by writing 'a' in place of $\frac{v-u}{t}$ in the above relation, we get :

$$F \propto m \times a$$

Thus, the force acting on a body is directly proportional to the product of 'mass' of the body and 'acceleration' produced in the body by the action of the force, and it acts in the direction of acceleration. This is another definition of Newton's second law of motion.

The relation $F \propto m \times a$ can be turned into an equation by putting in a constant k.

Thus, $$F = k \times m \times a \qquad \text{(where } k \text{ is a constant)}$$

The value of constant k in SI units is 1, so the above equation becomes :

$$F = m \times a$$

or **Force = mass × acceleration**

Thus, **Newton's second law of motion gives us a relationship between 'force' and 'acceleration'.** When a force acts on a body, it produces acceleration in the body, the acceleration produced may be positive or negative. **Newton's second law of motion also gives us a method of measuring the force in terms of mass and acceleration.** The force acting on a body can be calculated by using the formula : $F = m \times a$.

We can also write the equation $F = m \times a$ as :

$$a = \frac{F}{m}$$

It is obvious from the above relation that : **The acceleration produced in a body is directly proportional to the force acting on it and inversely proportional to the mass of the body.** Since the acceleration produced is inversely proportional to the mass of a body, therefore, ***if the mass of a body is doubled, its acceleration will be halved. And if the mass is halved then acceleration will get doubled (provided the force remains the same).*** Moreover, since the acceleration produced is inversely proportional to the mass of the body, it means that it will be easier to move light bodies (having less mass) than heavy bodies (having large mass).

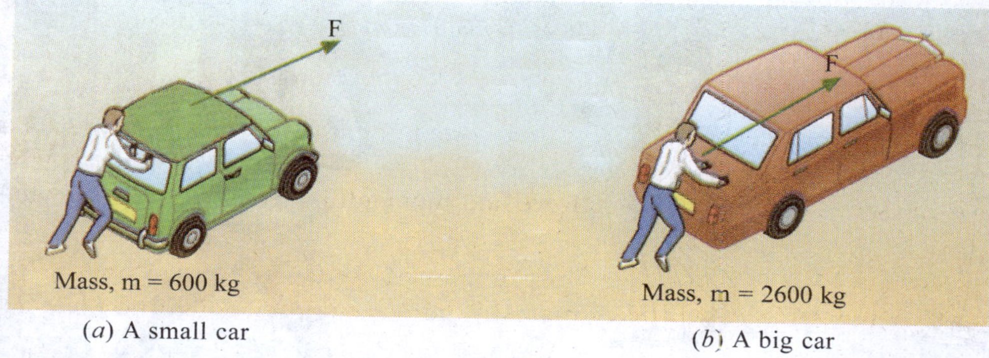

(*a*) A small car (*b*) A big car

Figure 19. Since the acceleration produced is inversely proportional to the mass of car, it is easier to move (or accelerate) a small car (having less mass) than a big car (having large mass) by the force of our push.

The SI unit of force is newton which is denoted by N. **A newton is that force which when acting on a body of mass 1 kg produces an acceleration of 1 m/s² in it.** We have just seen that :

$$F = m \times a$$

Putting $m = 1$ kg and $a = 1$ m/s², F becomes 1 newton.

So, **1 newton = 1 kg × 1 m/s²**

In order to get an idea of 1 newton force, we should hold a weight of 100 grams on our outstretched palm. The force exerted by 100 gram weight on our palm is approximately equal to 1 newton.

The first law of motion discussed earlier is, in fact, a special case of the second law, because when the applied force F is zero, then the acceleration 'a' is also zero and the body remains in its state of rest or of uniform motion. It is obvious that **Newton's second law gives us a relationship between the force applied to a body and the acceleration produced in the body.** The formula $F = m \times a$ should be memorized because it will be used to solve numerical problems.

It should be noted that just as a minus sign for acceleration shows that the acceleration is acting in a direction opposite to the motion of the body, in the same way, **if a minus sign comes with the force, it will indicate that the force is acting in a direction opposite to that in which the body is moving** (just as the force of friction acts in a direction opposite to that of the moving body).

Applications of Newton's Second Law of Motion

Some of the observations of our daily life can be explained on the basis of Newton's second law of motion. In all these cases some technique or arrangement is used to reduce the momentum of a fast moving body more gently (by allowing more time to stop it), so that injury can be prevented or reduced. Here are some examples.

1. Catching a Cricket Ball

A cricket player (or fielder) moves his hands backwards on catching a fast cricket ball. This is done to prevent injury to the hands. We can explain it as follows : A fast moving cricket ball has a large momentum. In stopping (or catching) this cricket ball, its momentum has to be reduced to zero. Now, when a cricket player moves back his hands on catching the fast ball, then the time taken to reduce the momentum of ball to zero is increased (see Figure 20). Due to more time taken to stop the ball, the rate of change of momentum of ball is decreased and hence a small force is exerted on the hands of player. So, the hands of player do not get hurt.

If, however, a cricket player stops a fast moving ball suddenly (keeping his hands stationary), then the large momentum of the ball will be reduced to zero in a very short time. Due to this, the rate of change of momentum of cricket ball will be very large and hence it will exert a large force on player's hands. The player's hands will get hurt.

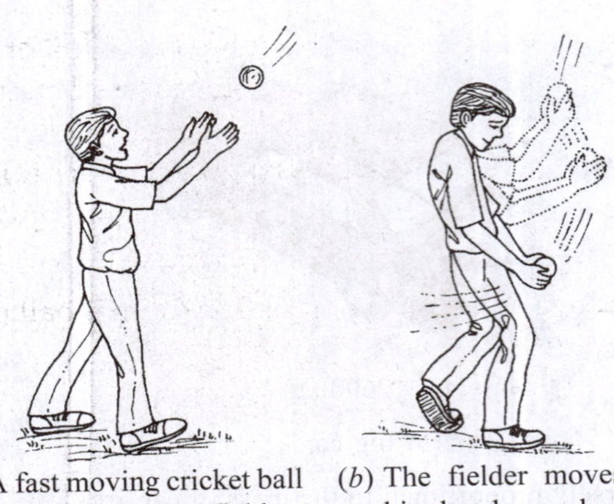

(*a*) A fast moving cricket ball coming towards a fielder

(*b*) The fielder moves back his hands gradually on catching the fast cricket ball to reduce its momentum more gently

Figure 20.

Figure 21. This photograph shows a cricketer (or fielder) drawing back his hands on catching the ball. This action helps reduce the fast moving ball's momentum more gently, exerts less force on the hands, and hence prevents injury to the hands.

2. The Case of a High Jumper

During athletics meet, a high jumping athlete is provided either a cushion or a heap of sand on the ground to fall upon. This is done to prevent injury to the athlete when he falls down after making a high jump. We can explain it as follows : When the high jumper falls on a soft landing site (such as a cushion or a heap of sand), then the jumper takes a longer time to come to a stop. The rate of change of momentum of athlete is less due to which a smaller stopping force acts on the athlete. And the athlete does not get hurt. Thus, **the cushion or sand, being soft, reduces the athlete's momentum more gently.** If, however, a high jumping athlete falls from a height on to hard ground, then his momentum will be reduced to zero in a very short time. The rate of change of momentum will be large due to which a large opposing force will act on the athlete. This can cause serious injuries to the athlete.

Figure 22. A heap of sand (being soft and fluid like) reduces the large momentum of a falling 'high jumping athlete' more gently. Due to this, less opposing force acts on the athlete's body and injuries are prevented.

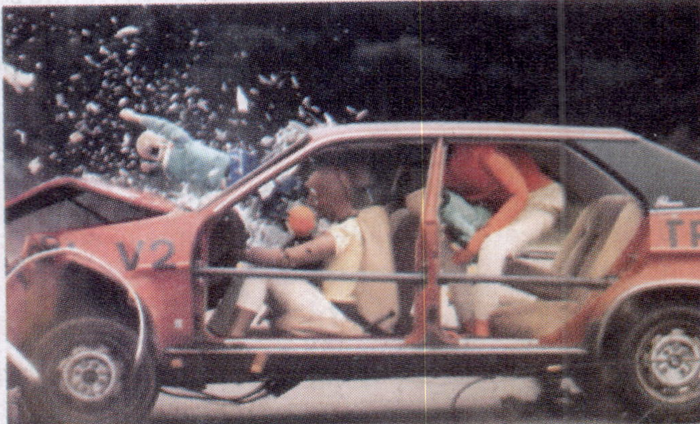

Figure 23. This is what can happen if passengers do not wear seat belts while travelling in a car and the car stops suddenly due to an accident. The large force on the body of passengers produced by rapid decrease in momentum can throw the passengers forward violently causing serious injuries.

3. The Use of Seat Belts in Cars

These days all the cars are provided with seat belts for passengers to prevent injuries in case of an accident. In a car accident, a fast running car stops suddenly. Due to this the car's large momentum is reduced to zero in a very short time. The slightly stretchable seat belts worn by the passengers of the car increase the time taken by the passengers to fall forward. Due to longer time, the rate of change of momentum of passengers is reduced and hence less stopping force acts on them. So, the passengers may either not get injured at all or may get less injuries. It is obvious that seat belts reduce the passengers' momentum more gently and hence prevent injuries.

We will now solve some problems based on Newton's second law of motion.

Sample Problem 1. What force would be needed to produce an acceleration of 4 m/s^2 in a ball of mass 6 kg ?

Solution. The force needed is to be calculated by using the relation :

Force = mass × acceleration

or $F = m \times a$

Here, Force, F = ? (To be calculated)

Mass, m = 6 kg

And, Acceleration, a = 4 m/s^2

Now, putting these values of m and a in the above equation, we get :

$F = 6 \times 4$

or Force, F = 24 N

Thus, the force needed is of 24 newtons.

Sample Problem 2. What is the acceleration produced by a force of 12 newtons exerted on an object of mass 3 kg ?

Solution. Here, Force, F = 12 N

Mass, m = 3 kg

And, Acceleration, a = ? (To be calculated)

We know that : $F = m \times a$

So, $12 = 3 \times a$

$3a = 12$

$a = \frac{12}{3}$ m/s^2

or Acceleration, a = 4 m/s^2

Sample Problem 3. Calculate the force required to impart to a car a velocity of 30 m/s in 10 seconds starting from rest. The mass of the car is 1500 kg.

Solution. Here, Mass, m = 1500 kg

Let us calculate the value of acceleration by using the first equation of motion.

Now, Initial velocity, u = 0 (Car starts from rest)

Final velocity, v = 30 m/s

And, Time taken, t = 10 s

Now, putting these values in the equation :

$v = u + at$

We get, $30 = 0 + a \times 10$

$10a = 30$

$a = \frac{30}{10}$ m/s^2

or Acceleration, a = 3 m/s^2

Now, putting m = 1500 kg and a = 3 m/s^2 in equation :

$F = m \times a$

We get, $F = 1500 \times 3$ N

= 4500 N

Thus, the force required in this case is of 4500 newtons.

Sample Problem 4. The speed-time graph of a car is given alongside. The car weighs 1000 kg.

(*i*) What is the distance travelled by the car in the first two seconds ?

(*ii*) What is the braking force applied at the end of 5 seconds to bring the car to a stop within one second ?

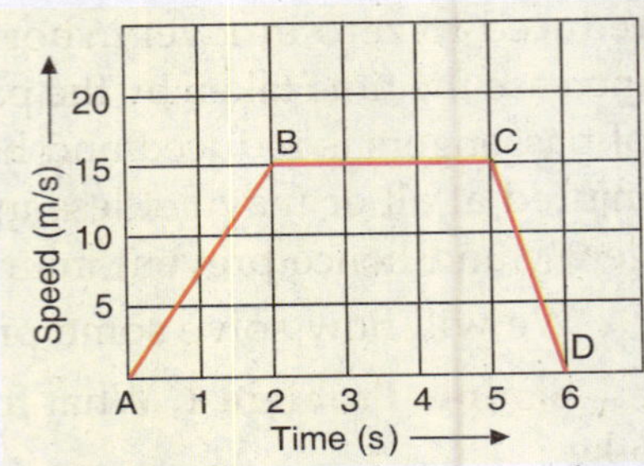

Figure 24. Graph for sample problem 4.

Solution (*i*) We will first calculate the distance travelled in the first two seconds. From the given graph we find that :

$$\text{Distance travelled in first two seconds} = \text{Area under line } AB \text{ and the time axis}$$
$$= \text{Area of triangle } AB2$$
$$= \frac{1}{2} \times \text{Base} \times \text{Height}$$
$$= \frac{1}{2} \times 2 \times 15$$
$$= 15 \text{ m}$$

Thus, the distance travelled by the car in the first two seconds is 15 metres.

(*ii*) The braking force is to be calculated by using the formula :

$$\text{Force} = \text{mass} \times \text{acceleration}$$
or
$$F = m \times a \quad \text{... (1)}$$

Here, the mass of the car is given as 1000 kg but the acceleration in the last one second (from point *C* to point *D*) is to be obtained from the graph shown above. Now, we know that the acceleration is given by the slope of speed-time graph. So,

$$\text{Acceleration in last one second} = \text{Slope of line } CD$$
$$= \frac{\text{Perpendicular}}{\text{Base}}$$
$$= \frac{15}{1}$$
$$= 15 \text{ m/s}^2$$

If we look at the above given graph, we will find that the speed of the car is decreasing from point *C* to point *D*. That is, the acceleration from *C* to *D* is negative and hence it should be written with a minus sign. Thus,

$$\text{Acceleration, } a = -15 \text{ m/s}^2$$

Now, putting $m = 1000$ kg and $a = -15 \text{ m/s}^2$ in formula (1), we get :

$$\text{Force, } F = 1000 \times (-15)$$
$$= -15000 \text{ N}$$

Thus, the force applied by the brakes to stop the car is 15000 newtons. The negative sign of force here shows that the force is being applied in a direction opposite to the motion of the car. That is, it is a retarding force.

Sample Problem 5. A truck starts from rest and rolls down a hill with constant acceleration. It travels a distance of 400 m in 20 s. Find its acceleration. Find the force acting on it if its mass is 7 metric tonnes.

Solution. First of all we will find its acceleration by using the relation :

$$\text{Distance travelled, } s = ut + \frac{1}{2}at^2$$

Figure 25. A truck rolling down the hill with constant acceleration.

Here, Distance travelled, $s = 400$ m
Initial speed, $u = 0$ (It starts from rest)
Time, $t = 20$ s
And, Acceleration, $a = ?$ (To be calculated)

Putting these values in the above formula, we get :

$$400 = 0 \times 20 + \frac{1}{2} \times a \times (20)^2$$

$$400 = 200\,a$$

$$a = \frac{400}{200}$$

Acceleration, $a = 2\ \text{m/s}^2$ ... (1)

We will now calculate the force by using the relation :

$$F = m \times a$$

Here, Mass, $m = 7$ metric tonnes
$= 7 \times 1000$ kg
$= 7000$ kg ... (2)

And, Acceleration, $a = 2\ \text{m/s}^2$ (Calculated above)

So, Force, $F = 7000 \times 2$
$F = 14000$ N

Thus, the force acting on the truck is 14000 newtons.

Sample Problem 6. A force of 5 newtons gives a mass m_1 an acceleration of 8 m/s², and a mass m_2 an acceleration of 24 m/s². What acceleration would it give if both the masses are tied together ?

Solution. (*i*) In the first case :

Force, $F = 5$ N
Mass, $m = m_1$ (To be calculated)
And, Acceleration, $a = 8\ \text{m/s}^2$

Now, $F = m \times a$

So, $5 = m_1 \times 8$

And, $m_1 = \frac{5}{8}$ kg

$m_1 = 0.625$ kg

Thus, the mass m_1 is 0.625 kg.

(*ii*) In the second case :

Force, $F = 5$ N
Mass, $m = m_2$ (To be calculated)
And, Acceleration, $a = 24\ \text{m/s}^2$

Now, $F = m \times a$

So, $5 = m_2 \times 24$

And, $m_2 = \frac{5}{24}$ kg

$m_2 = 0.208$ kg

Thus, the mass m_2 is 0.208 kg.

(*iii*) In the third case :

Force, $F = 5$ N
Total mass, $m = m_1 + m_2$
$= 0.625 + 0.208$
$= 0.833$ kg

And, Acceleration, $a = ?$ (To be calculated)

Now, putting these values in the relation :

$$F = m \times a$$

We get :

$$5 = 0.833 \times a$$

$$a = \frac{5}{0.833}$$

$$a = 6 \text{ m/s}^2$$

Thus, if both the masses are tied together, then the acceleration would be 6 m/s^2.

Sample Problem 7. Which would require a greater force – accelerating a 10 g mass at 5 m/s^2 or a 20 g mass at 2 m/s^2 ?

Solution.

(*i*) In first case : Force, $F = m \times a$

$$= \frac{10}{1000} \text{ kg} \times 5 \text{ m/s}^2$$

$$= 0.05 \text{ N} \quad \text{... (1)}$$

(*ii*) In second case : Force, $F = \frac{20}{1000} \text{ kg} \times 2 \text{ m/s}^2$

$$= 0.04 \text{ N} \quad \text{... (2)}$$

Thus, a greater force of 0.05 N is required for accelerating a 10 g mass.

NEWTON'S THIRD LAW OF MOTION

If a boy wearing roller skates stands facing a wall and pushes the wall with his hands, the boy finds himself moving backwards, away from the wall (see Figure 26). It appears as if the wall also pushes the boy away. Actually, when the boy exerts a force on the wall by pushing it with his hands, then the wall exerts an equal force on the boy in the opposite direction. Since the boy is wearing roller skates, the opposite

(*a*) When the boy exerts a force on the wall, the wall exerts an equal force on the boy in the opposite direction

(*b*) The opposite force exerted by the wall makes the boy on roller skates move backwards

Figure 26.

force exerted by the wall makes him move backwards. In Figure 26(*a*), the boy on roller skates is exerting force on the wall towards left side. The wall exerts an equal force on the boy towards right side. Due to this, the boy moves backwards to the right side [see Figure 26(*b*)]. From this discussion we conclude that **when a boy exerts a force on the wall, the wall exerts an equal and opposite force on the boy.** This is just an illustration of Newton's third law of motion.

When one body influences another body by applying force, we say that the first body is interacting with the second body. In any interaction between two bodies, there are always two forces that come into play. And Newton's third law of motion describes the relationship between the forces that come into play when the two bodies interact with one another.

Figure 27. The man is exerting force on the cow but the cow is exerting an equal force back on the man. This situation illustrates Newton's third law of motion.

According to Newton's third law of motion : **Whenever one body exerts a force on another body, the second body exerts an equal and opposite force on the first body.** The force exerted by the first body on the second body is known as "*action*" and the force exerted by the second body on the first body is known as "*reaction*". It should be noted that "*action*" and "*reaction*" are just forces. We can now write another definition of Newton's third law of motion : **To every action there is an equal and opposite reaction.** Action (force) and reaction (force) act on two different bodies, but they act simultaneously. We will now describe a simple experiment to prove the Newton's third law of motion, that is, to prove that action (force) and reaction (force) are always equal and opposite.

We take two similar spring balances *A* and *B* and join them hook to hook as shown in Figure 28. The other end of spring balance *B* is attached to a hook *H* fixed in a wall. Let us pull the free end of the spring balance *A* to the right side by our hand. We find that both the spring balances show the same reading. For example, in Figure 28, both the spring balances show the same force of 4 N. This can be explained as follows.

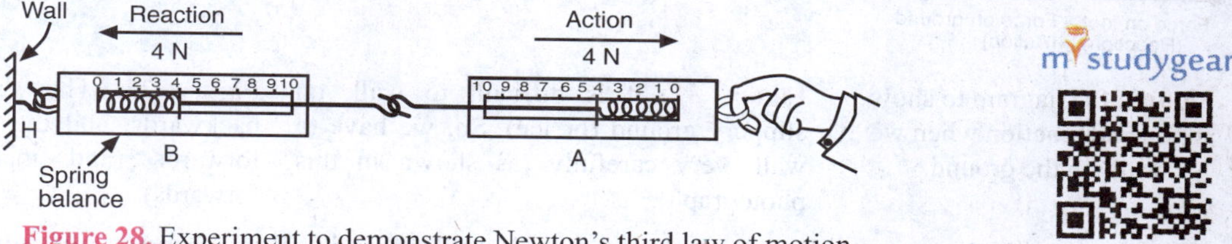

Figure 28. Experiment to demonstrate Newton's third law of motion.

When we pull the balance *A*, it exerts a force of 4 N on the balance *B*. The balance *B* pulls the balance *A* with an equal force of 4 N, but in the opposite direction. In other words, when balance *A* exerts a force of action on balance *B*, then balance *B* exerts an equal and opposite force of reaction on balance *A*. Since both the spring balances show the same reading (of 4 N), we conclude that the action and reaction forces are equal in magnitude. In Figure 28 we find that the action force is acting towards east and the reaction force is acting towards west. Thus, action and reaction forces act in opposite directions.

Action and Reaction Act on Two Different Bodies

Suppose a box is resting on the ground (Figure 29). The box is exerting a downward force of its weight on the ground. The downward weight of the box is balanced by an equal, upward force supplied by the ground. Now, the force exerted by the weight of the box is "action" and it acts on the ground whereas the force exerted by the ground on the box is "reaction" and it acts on the box. Since the box is in equilibrium under the action of two forces, it neither goes up nor goes down, the "action" of the box must be equal and opposite to the "reaction" of the ground. It is obvious that the "action" of the box acts on the ground and "reaction" of the ground acts on the box. Thus, action and reaction act on two different bodies.

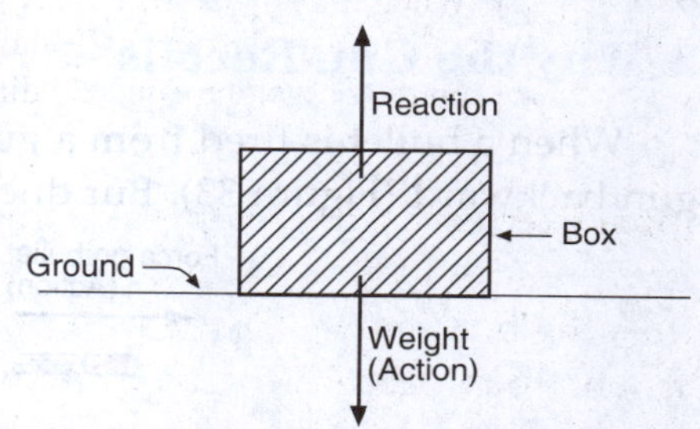

Figure 29. The box exerts "action" on the ground and the ground exerts an equal and opposite "reaction" on the box.

Some Examples to Illustrate Newton's Third Law of Motion

We will now give some examples from our everyday life which will illustrate Newton's third law of motion.

1. How do We Walk

When we walk on the ground, then our foot pushes the ground backward and, in return, the ground pushes our foot forward (Figure 30). The forward reaction exerted by the ground on our foot makes us walk forward. If, however, the ground is slippery or if there is all ice, it becomes very difficult to walk. This is due to the fact that on the slippery ground or ice, the friction is much less, and we cannot exert a backward action force on slippery ground or ice which would produce a forward reaction force on us.

Figure 30. Diagram to show action and reaction when we walk on the ground.

Figure 31. It is difficult to walk on slippery ground (or ice). So, we have to walk very carefully (as shown in this photograph).

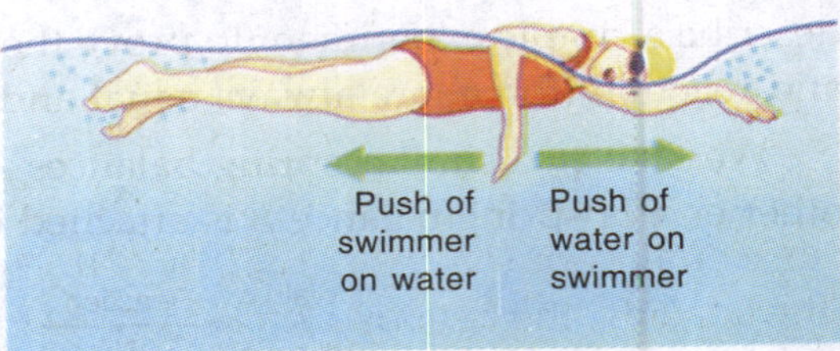

Figure 32. The swimmer pushes the water backwards, and the water pushes the swimmer forwards (and makes the swimmer move forwards).

Let us discuss the case of a swimmer now. A swimmer pushes the water backwards (or applies force on the water backwards) with his hands and feet to move in the forward direction in water. It is the equal and opposite reaction to this force which pushes the swimmer forward.

Please note that **though action and reaction forces are equal in magnitude but they do not produce equal acceleration in the two bodies on which they act**. This is because the two bodies on which action and reaction forces act usually have different masses. So, **the acceleration produced will be more in the body having less mass whereas the acceleration produced will be less in the body having more mass.** This point will become more clear from the following example of the recoil of a gun on firing. 'Recoil' of gun means 'sudden backward movement' or 'jerk' of gun when a bullet is fired from it.

2. Why the Gun Recoils

When a bullet is fired from a gun, the force sending the bullet forward is equal to the force sending the gun backward (Figure 33). But due to high mass of the gun, it moves only a little distance backward and gives a backward jerk or kick to the shoulder of the gunman. The gun is said to have recoiled.

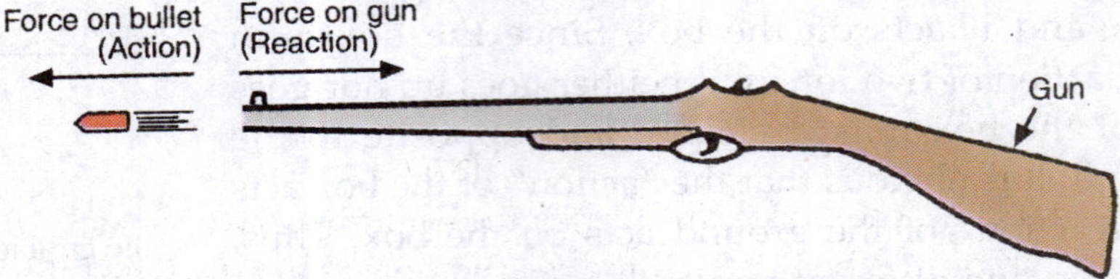

Figure 33. Diagram to show action and reaction when a bullet is fired from the gun.

3. The Flying of Jet Aeroplanes and Rockets

Jet aeroplanes utilise the principle of action and reaction. In the modern jet aircraft, the hot gases obtained by the rapid burning of fuel rush out of a jet (a nozzle) at the rear end (back end) of the aircraft at a great speed. The equal and opposite reaction of the backward going gases pushes the aircraft forward at a great speed.

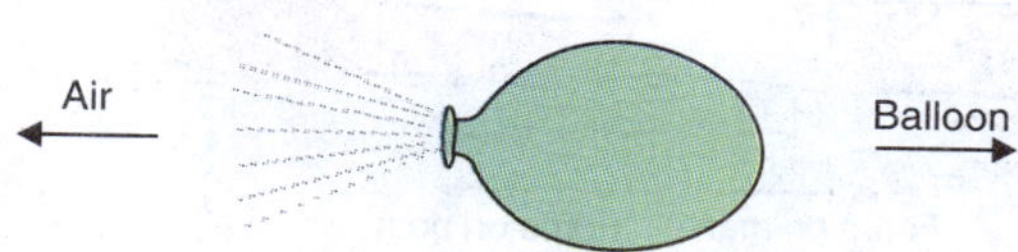

Figure 34. A deflating balloon demonstrates the principle of working of a jet engine.

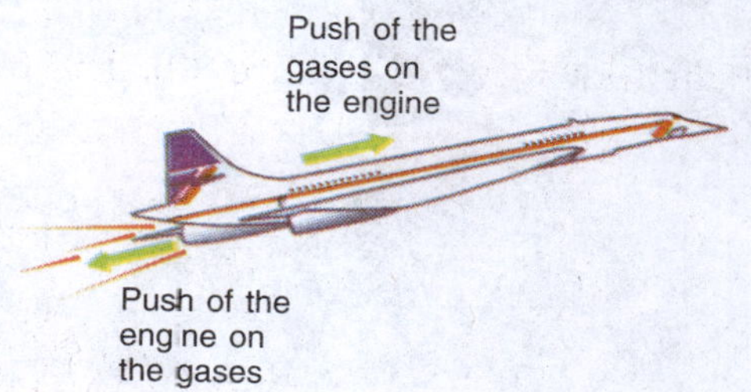

Figure 35. The jet aeroplane's engines exert a backward force on the exhaust gases (produced by the burning of fuel) ; the backward rushing exhaust gases exert a forward force on the engines (which makes the aeroplane move forward).

We can demonstrate the principle of working of a jet engine by using a balloon filled with compressed air as follows : If a balloon filled with compressed air and its mouth untied is released with its mouth on the left side, the balloon moves very fast towards the right side (see Figure 34). This means that the balloon flies off in the opposite direction to that of the escaping air. Here the compressed air present in balloon rushes to the left side with a high speed. The equal and opposite reaction of the left going air pushes the balloon to the right side.

Please note that if the inflated balloon is released with its mouth in the downward direction, then it will move upwards (like a rocket) (see Figure 36). In this case, the air rushes out of balloon in the downward direction. The equal and opposite reaction of downward going air pushes the balloon upwards. We will now discuss the case of rockets. **The rockets also work on the principle of action and reaction.** In a rocket, the hot gases produced by the rapid burning of fuel rush out of a jet at the bottom of the rocket at a very high speed (Figure 37). The equal and opposite reaction force of the downward going gases pushes the rocket upward with a great speed. Please note that a rocket can propel itself even in vacuum (or outer space) because it does not require air for obtaining uplift or for burning its fuel. This is not so in the case of a jet aircraft. A jet aircraft cannot fly in outer space (where there is no air) because it needs air to provide an uplift and also to burn its fuel.

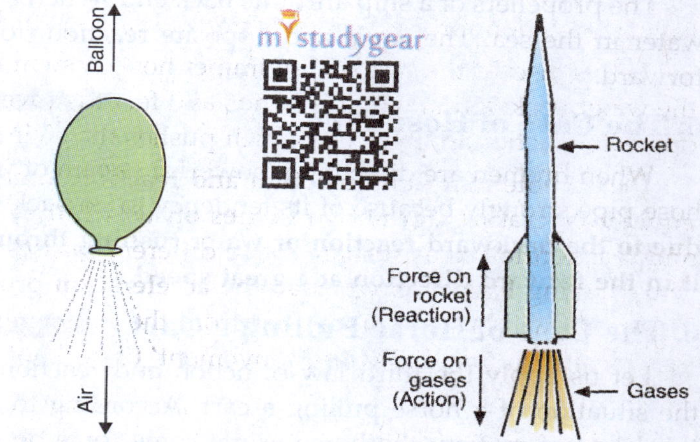

Figure 36. A deflating balloon also demonstrates the principle of working of a rocket.

Figure 37. Diagram to show "action" and "reaction" in the case of a rocket.

4. The Case of a Boat and the Ship

During the rowing of a boat, the boatman pushes the water backwards with the oars. The water exerts an equal and opposite push on the boat which makes the boat move forward. In fact, harder the boatman pushes back the water with oars, greater is the reaction force exerted by water and faster the boat moves forward.

Figure 38. The woman pushes the water backwards with the oars. The backward going water exerts an equal and opposite push on the boat (which makes the boat move forward).

Figure 39. Diagram to show "action" and "reaction" when a man steps out of a boat.

It is a common experience that **when a man jumps out of a boat to the bank of the river (or lake), the boat moves backwards, away from him.** This is due to the fact that to step out of the boat, the man presses the boat with his foot in the backward direction (Figure 39). The push of the man on the boat is the action (force). The boat exerts an equal force on the man in the forward direction which enables him to move forward. This force exerted by the boat on the man is reaction (force). Since the boat is floating on water and not fixed, it moves backward due to the action force exerted by man.

Another point to be noted is that **when a boatman wants to take the boat away from the bank of the river, he sits in the boat and pushes the river bank with his oar.** When the boatman exerts a force of action on the bank (with his oar), the bank exerts an equal and opposite force of reaction on the boat. So, the boat moves away from the bank.

The propellers of a ship are at its back end. When these propellers work, they exert a backward force on water in the sea. The equal and opposite reaction (force) exerted by water on the ship, moves the ship forward.

5. The Case of Hose Pipe

When firemen are directing a powerful stream of water on fire from a hose pipe, they have to hold the hose pipe strongly because of its tendency to go backward. **The backward movement of the hose pipe is due to the backward reaction of water rushing through it in the forward direction at a great speed.**

6. The Case of Horse Pulling a Cart

Let us apply the third law of action and reaction to the situation of a horse pulling a cart. According to the third law of motion, the horse exerts some force on the cart, and the cart exerts an equal and opposite force on the horse. So, at first glance it seems that the forces being equal and opposite cancel out and hence the cart would not move. But it should be noted that it is only the force on the cart which determines whether the cart will move or not, and that the force exerted by the cart on the horse affects the horse alone. Thus, if the horse is able to apply enough force to overcome the frictional forces present, the cart will move. So, **to make the cart move, the horse bends**

Figure 40. To make the cart move, the horse bends forward and presses the ground with its feet. When the forward reaction to the backward push of the horse is greater than the opposing frictional forces of the wheels, the cart moves.

forward and pushes the ground with its feet. When the forward reaction to the backward push of the horse is greater than the opposing frictional forces of the wheels, the cart moves.

In all the above examples, the two interacting bodies are in direct contact with each other. It is not always necessary that two bodies can exert force on one another only when they are in contact. **In some cases the two bodies can also exert force on each other even when they are not in contact with each other.** That is, the interaction can also take place even when the two bodies are not in contact. **In all such cases the forces of action and reaction are equal and opposite**. For example, a magnet can interact with a piece of iron and exert a force on it even when they are separated by a distance. The magnet exerts a force on iron piece, and the iron piece exerts an equal and opposite force on the magnet. The interaction between an electrically charged comb and a piece of paper also takes place from a distance. The electrically charged comb and the piece of paper exert equal and opposite forces on each other. The interaction between a falling stone and the earth also takes place though they are not in contact with each other and two forces come into play. While the earth pulls the stone downwards by the force of gravity, the stone also pulls the earth towards itself with an equal force. It should be clear by now that we cannot think of a single isolated force – for every force there is an equal and opposite force. In other words, **the forces always occur in pairs**, and Newton's third law of motion concerns these pairs of forces.

CONSERVATION OF MOMENTUM

In the second law of motion we have studied that the moving bodies possess momentum which is equal to the product of mass and velocity. That is,

$$\text{Momentum} = \text{mass} \times \text{velocity}$$

We will now take one example to understand the meaning of the term 'conservation of momentum'.

Suppose a speeding truck (fast moving truck) hits a stationary car due to which the car also starts moving. Now, in this collision, the velocity of truck decreases but the velocity of car increases. Due to this the momentum of the truck decreases, and the momentum of car increases. It has been found that the increase in the momentum of car is equal to the decrease in the momentum of truck, so that there is no loss of momentum in the collision. The momentum lost by the truck has been gained by the car. This is an illustration of the law of conservation of momentum.

According to the law of conservation of momentum : **When two (or more) bodies act upon one another, their total momentum remains constant (or conserved) provided no external forces are acting.** The law of conservation of momentum means that whenever one body gains momentum, then some other body must lose an equal amount of momentum. This law can also be stated as : **Momentum is never created or destroyed.** The law of conservation of momentum is also known as the principle of conservation of momentum. The principle of conservation of momentum is in accord with Newton's third law of motion which says that action and reaction (forces) are equal and opposite. We will now take an example to prove the law of conservation of momentum.

Suppose two bodies, a truck and a car, are moving in the same direction (towards east) but with different speeds or velocities [see Figure 41(*a*)]. Let the mass of the truck be m_1 and its velocity be u_1 so that its initial momentum is m_1u_1. Let the mass of the car be m_2 and its velocity be u_2 so that the initial momentum of the car is m_2u_2. Thus, the total momentum of the truck and the car before collision is $m_1u_1 + m_2u_2$.

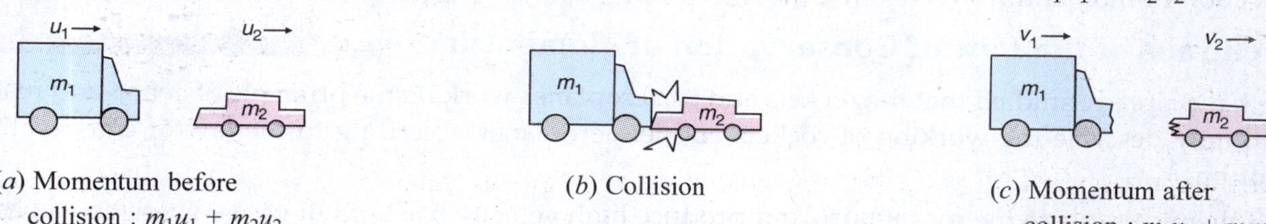

(*a*) Momentum before collision : $m_1u_1 + m_2u_2$

(*b*) Collision

(*c*) Momentum after collision : $m_1v_1 + m_2v_2$

Figure 41. Conservation of momentum : $m_1u_1 + m_2u_2 = m_1v_1 + m_2v_2$

Suppose the truck and the car collide for a short time t [see Figure 41(b)]. Due to collision, the velocities of the truck and the car will change. Let the velocity of the truck after the collision be v_1, and the velocity of the car after the collision be v_2 [see Figure 41(c)]. So the momentum of the truck after the collision will be m_1v_1, and the momentum of the car after the collision will be m_2v_2. In this way, the total momentum of the truck and the car after the collision will be $m_1v_1 + m_2v_2$.

Suppose that during collision, the truck exerts a force F_1 on the car and, in turn, the car exerts a force F_2 on the truck. We will now find out the values of the forces F_1 and F_2. This can be done as follows :

(i) When the force F_1 of the truck acts on the car for a time t, then the velocity of car changes from u_2 to v_2. So,

$$\text{Acceleration of car, } a_2 = \frac{(v_2 - u_2)}{t}$$

But, force = mass × acceleration, so the force F_1 exerted by the truck on the car is given by :

$$F_1 = m_2 \times \frac{(v_2 - u_2)}{t} \quad \text{... (1)}$$

(ii) When the force F_2 of the car reacts on the truck for a time t, then the velocity of the truck changes from u_1 to v_1 . So,

$$\text{Acceleration of truck, } a_1 = \frac{(v_1 - u_1)}{t}$$

But, force = mass × acceleration, so the force F_2 exerted by car on the truck is given by :

$$F_2 = m_1 \times \frac{(v_1 - u_1)}{t} \quad \text{... (2)}$$

Now, the force F_1 exerted by the truck is the 'action' and the force F_2 exerted by the car is the 'reaction'. But according to the third law of motion, the action and reaction are equal and opposite. That is,

$$F_1 = -F_2$$

Now, putting the values of F_1 and F_2 from equations (1) and (2), we get :

$$\frac{m_2\,(v_2 - u_2)}{t} = -\frac{m_1(v_1 - u_1)}{t}$$

Cancelling t from both sides, we get :

$$m_2\,(v_2 - u_2) = -m_1\,(v_1 - u_1)$$

or $$m_2v_2 - m_2u_2 = -m_1v_1 + m_1u_1$$

or $$m_2v_2 + m_1v_1 = m_2u_2 + m_1u_1$$

or $$m_1u_1 + m_2u_2 = m_1v_1 + m_2v_2$$

Now, $m_1u_1 + m_2u_2$ represents total momentum of the truck and car before collision whereas $m_1v_1 + m_2v_2$ represents the total momentum of the truck and car after collision. This means that :

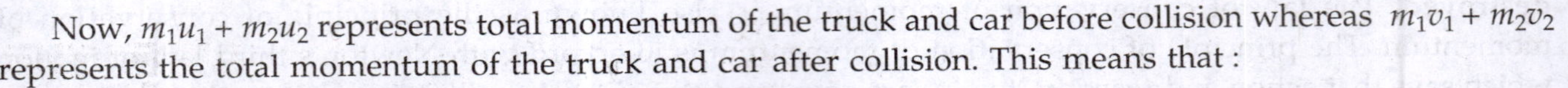

Total momentum before collision = **Total momentum after collision**

It is obvious that the total momentum of the two bodies before and after the collision is the same. This means that the momentum of the two bodies remains constant (or conserved). And this result proves the law of conservation of momentum. We will now describe some of the important applications of the law of conservation of momentum.

Applications of the Law of Conservation of Momentum

We have already studied that the rockets and jet aeroplanes work on the principle of action and reaction. We will now describe the working of rockets and jet aeroplanes according to the law of conservation of momentum.

The chemicals inside the rocket burn and produce high velocity blast of hot gases. These gases pass out through the tail nozzle of the rocket in the downward direction with tremendous speed or velocity, and the rocket moves up to balance the momentum of the gases. Although the mass of gases emitted is comparatively small, but they have a very high velocity and hence a very large momentum. An equal momentum is imparted to the rocket in the opposite direction, so that, inspite of its large mass, the rocket goes up with a high velocity.

Figure 42. A rocket works on the principle of conservation of momentum.

Figure 43. A jet aeroplane also works on the principle of conservation of momentum.

In jet aeroplanes, a large volume of gases produced by the combustion of fuel is allowed to escape through a jet in the backward direction. Due to the very high speed or velocity, the backward rushing gases have a large momentum. They impart an equal and opposite momentum to the jet aeroplane due to which the jet aeroplane moves forward with a great speed. Thus, **we can also say that the rockets and jet aeroplanes work on the principle of conservation of momentum.**

We will now describe how the momentum is conserved when a bullet is fired from a gun. Initially, before a bullet is fired from a gun, both, the bullet and the gun, are at rest. So, before a bullet is fired, the initial momentum of the bullet and the gun is zero (because their velocities are zero).

Now, when a bullet is fired from a gun, then the bullet has the momentum given by : *mass of bullet × velocity of bullet*. The bullet imparts an equal and opposite momentum to the gun due to which the gun jerks backwards. The gun is said to recoil. The backward velocity of the gun is called recoil velocity. The momentum acquired by the gun is : *mass of gun × recoil velocity of gun*. Now, according to the law of conservation of momentum :

$$\text{Momentum of bullet} = \text{Momentum of gun}$$

or

$$\textit{Mass of bullet} \times \textit{Velocity of bullet} = \textit{Mass of gun} \times \textit{Recoil velocity of gun}$$

We should remember this relation because it will be used to solve the numerical problems. Let us solve some problems now.

Sample Problem 1. A bullet of mass 10 g is fired from a gun of mass 6 kg with a velocity of 300 m/s. Calculate the recoil velocity of the gun.

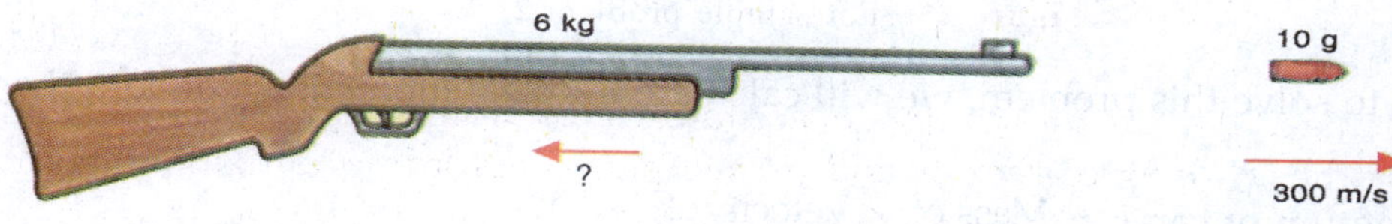

Figure 44. For sample problem 1.

Solution. Here, Mass of bullet = 10 g

$= \frac{10}{1000}$ kg

= 0.01 kg

Velocity of bullet = 300 m/s

Mass of gun = 6 kg

And, Recoil velocity of gun = ? (To be calculated)

Now, putting these values in the relation :

Mass of bullet × Velocity of bullet = Mass of gun × Recoil velocity of gun

We get : 0.01 × 300 = 6 × Recoil velocity of gun

So, Recoil velocity of gun $= \frac{0.01 \times 300}{6}$

= 0.5 m/s

Note. The above problem can also be solved by calculating the momentum of bullet and the gun separately as follows :

Momentum of bullet = Mass of bullet × Velocity of bullet

= 0.01 × 300

= 3 kg.m/s

Now, suppose the recoil velocity of gun is v m/s.

So, Momentum of gun = Mass of gun × Recoil velocity of gun

= 6 × v kg.m/s

According to the law of conservation of momentum :

Momentum of bullet = Momentum of gun

So, $3 = 6 \times v$

And, $v = \frac{3}{6}$ m/s

Recoil velocity of gun, v = 0.5 m/s

Sample Problem 2. The car *A* of mass 1500 kg, travelling at 25 m/s collides with another car *B* of mass 1000 kg travelling at 15 m/s in the same direction. After collision the velocity of car *A* becomes 20 m/s. Calculate the velocity of car *B* after the collision.

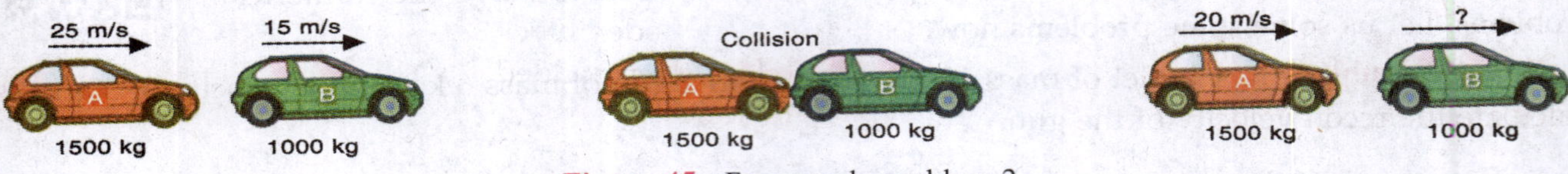

Figure 45. For sample problem 2.

Solution. In order to solve this problem, we will calculate the total momentum of both the cars, before and after the collision.

(*a*) Momentum of car *A* (before collision) = Mass of car *A* × Velocity of car *A*

= 1500 × 25

$= 37500$ kg.m/s

Momentum of car B (before collision) $=$ Mass of car B $\times$ Velocity of car B

$= 1000 \times 15$

$= 15000$ kg.m/s

Total momentum of car A and car B (before collision) $= 37500 + 15000$

$= 52500$ kg.m/s ...(1)

(*b*) After collision, the velocity of car A of mass 1500 kg becomes 20 m/s.

So, Momentum of car A (after collision) $= 1500 \times 20$

$= 30000$ kg.m/s

After collision, suppose the velocity of car B of mass 1000 kg becomes v m/s.

So, Momentum of car B (after collision) $= 1000 \times v$

$= 1000\, v$ kg.m/s

Total momentum of car A and car B (after collision) $= 30000 + 1000\, v$ ...(2)

Now, according to the law of conservation of momentum :

Total momentum before collision $=$ Total momentum after collision

That is,

$$52500 = 30000 + 1000\, v$$

$$1000\, v = 52500 - 30000$$

$$1000\, v = 22500$$

$$v = \frac{22500}{1000}$$

$$v = 22.5 \text{ m/s}$$

Thus, the velocity of car B after the collision will be 22.5 m/s.

Sample Problem 3. A bullet of mass 10 g moving with a velocity of 400 m/s gets embedded in a freely suspended wooden block of mass 900 g. What is the velocity acquired by the block ?

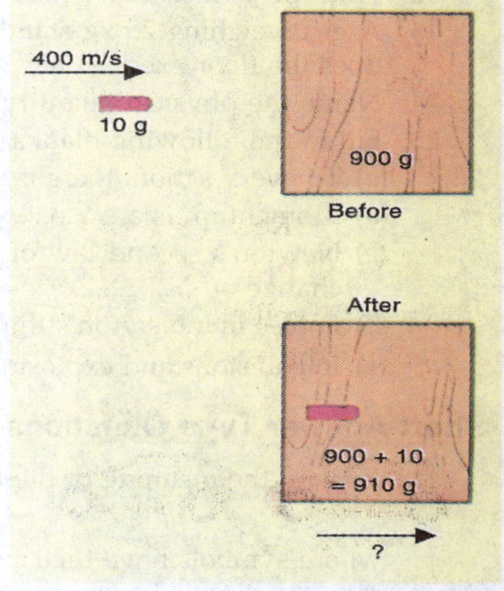

Figure 46. For sample problem 3.

Solution. Here, Mass of the bullet, $m_1 = 10$ g

$= \frac{10}{1000}$ kg

$= 0.01$ kg

And, Velocity of the bullet, $v_1 = 400$ m/s

So, Momentum of the bullet $= m_1 \times v_1$

$= 0.01 \times 400$ kg.m/s ... (1)

Now, this bullet of mass 10 g gets embedded into a wooden block of mass 900 g. So, the mass of wooden block alongwith the embedded bullet will become 900 + 10 = 910 g. Thus,

Mass of wooden block + Bullet, $m_2 = 900 + 10$

$= 910$ g

$= \frac{910}{1000}$ kg

$= 0.91$ kg

And, Velocity of wooden block + bullet, v_2 = ? (To be calculated)

So, Momentum of wooden block + bullet $= m_2 \times v_2$

$= 0.91 \times v_2$ kg.m/s ... (2)

Now, according to the law of conservation of momentum, the two momenta as given by equations (1) and (2) should be equal.

So, $m_1 \times v_1 = m_2 \times v_2$

or $0.01 \times 400 = 0.91 \times v_2$

And, $v_2 = \frac{0.01 \times 400}{0.91}$

$= 4.4$ m/s

Thus, the velocity acquired by the wooden block (having the bullet embedded in it) is 4.4 metres per second.

We are now in a position to **answer the following questions :**

Very Short Answer Type Questions

1. Which physical quantity corresponds to the rate of change of momentum ?
2. State the relation between the momentum of a body and the force acting on it.
3. What is the unit of force ?
4. Define one newton force.
5. What is the relationship between force and acceleration ?
6. If the mass of a body and the force acting on it are both doubled, what happens to the acceleration ?
7. Name the physical quantity whose unit is 'newton'.
8. Which physical principle is involved in the working of a jet aeroplane ?
9. Name the principle on which a rocket works.
10. Is the following statement true or false :
    A rocket can propel itself in a vacuum.
11. What is the force which produces an acceleration of 1 m/s² in a body of mass 1 kg ?
12. Find the acceleration produced by a force of 5 N acting on a mass of 10 kg.
13. A girl weighing 25 kg stands on the floor. She exerts a downward force of 250 N on the floor. What force does the floor exert on her ?
14. Name the physical quantity which makes it easier to accelerate a small car than a large car.
15. Fill in the following blanks with suitable words :
    (*a*) To every action, there is an .... and .... reaction
    (*b*) Momentum is a ....quantity. Its unit is ....
    (*c*) Newton's second law of motion can be written as Force = mass × .... or Force = ... of change of ....
    (*d*) Forces in a Newton's third law pair have equal .... but act in opposite...............
    (*e*) In collisions and explosions, the total .... remains constant, provided that no external................acts.

Short Answer Type Questions

16. Explain the meaning of the following equation :
    $F = m \times a$
    where symbols have their usual meanings.
17. To take the boat away from the bank of a river, the boatman pushes the bank with an oar. Why ?
18. Why does a gunman get a jerk on firing a bullet ?
19. If action is always equal to reaction, explain why a cart pulled by a horse can be moved.

A gunman gets a jerk on firing a bullet.

20. Explain how a rocket works.
21. Do action and reaction act on the same body or different bodies ? How are they related in magnitude and direction ? Are they simultaneous or not ?
22. If a man jumps out from a boat, the boat moves backwards. Why ?
23. Why is it difficult to walk on a slippery road ?
24. Explain why, a runner presses the ground with his feet before he starts his run.
25. A 60 g bullet fired from a 5 kg gun leaves with a speed of 500 m/s. Find the speed (velocity) with which the gun recoils (jerks backwards).
26. A 10 g bullet travelling at 200 m/s strikes and remains embedded in a 2 kg target which is originally at rest but free to move. At what speed does the target move off ?
27. A body of mass 2 kg is at rest. What should be the magnitude of force which will make the body move with a speed of 30 m/s at the end of 1 s ?
28. A body of mass 5 kg is moving with a velocity of 10 m/s. A force is applied to it so that in 25 seconds, it attains a velocity of 35 m/s. Calculate the value of the force applied.
29. A car of mass 2400 kg moving with a velocity of 20 m s^{-1} is stopped in 10 seconds on applying brakes. Calculate the retardation and the retarding force.
30. For how long should a force of 100 N act on a body of 20 kg so that it acquires a velocity of 100 m/s ?
31. How long will it take a force of 10 N to stop a mass of 2.5 kg which is moving at 20 m/s ?
32. The velocity of a body of mass 10 kg increases from 4 m/s to 8 m/s when a force acts on it for 2 s.
    (*a*) What is the momentum before the force acts ?
    (*b*) What is the momentum after the force acts ?
    (*c*) What is the gain in momentum per second ?
    (*d*) What is the value of the force ?
33. A gun of mass 3 kg fires a bullet of mass 30 g. The bullet takes 0.003 s to move through the barrel of the gun and acquires a velocity of 100 m/s. Calculate :
    (*i*) the velocity with which the gun recoils.
    (*ii*) the force exerted on gunman due to recoil of the gun
34. Draw a diagram to show how a rocket engine provides a force to move the rocket upwards. Label the diagram appropriately.
35. Name the laws involved in the following situations :
    (*a*) the sum of products of masses and velocities of two moving bodies before and after their collision remains the same.
    (*b*) a body of mass 5 kg can be accelerated more easily by a force than another body of mass 50 kg under similar conditions
    (*c*) when person A standing on roller skates pushes another person B (also standing on roller skates) and makes him move to the right side, then the person A himself gets moved to the left side by an equal distance.
    (*d*) if there were no friction and no air resistance, then a moving bicycle would go on moving for ever.

Long Answer Type Questions

36. (*a*) State and explain Newton's second law of motion.
    (*b*) A 1000 kg vehicle moving with a speed of 20 m/s is brought to rest in a distance of 50 metres :
    (*i*) Find the acceleration.
    (*ii*) Calculate the unbalanced force acting on the vehicle.
37. (*a*) Explain why, a cricket player moves his hands backwards while catching a fast cricket ball.
    (*b*) A 150 g ball, travelling at 30 m/s, strikes the palm of a player's hand and is stopped in 0.05 second. Find the force exerted by the ball on the hand.
38. (*a*) State Newton's third law of motion and give two examples to illustrate the law.
    (*b*) Explain why, when a fireman directs a powerful stream of water on a fire from a hose pipe, the hose pipe tends to go backward.

A fireman directing a powerful stream of water on a fire from a hose pipe.

39. (*a*) State the law of conservation of momentum.

(*b*) Discuss the conservation of momentum in each of the following cases :

(*i*) a rocket taking off from ground.

(*ii*) flying of a jet aeroplane.

40. (*a*) If a balloon filled with air and its mouth untied, is released with its mouth in the downward direction, it moves upwards. Why ?

(*b*) An unloaded truck weighing 2000 kg has a maximum acceleration of 0.5 m/s^2. What is the maximum acceleration when it is carrying a load of 2000 kg ?

Multiple Choice Questions (MCQs)

41. The rockets work on the principle of conservation of :

(*a*) mass (*b*) energy (*c*) momentum (*d*) velocity

42. An object of mass 2 kg is sliding with a constant velocity of 4 m/s on a frictionless horizontal table. The force required to keep this object moving with the same velocity is :

(*a*) 32 N (*b*) 0 N (*c*) 2 N (*d*) 8 N

43. The physical quantity which makes it easier to accelerate a small car than a large car is measured in the unit of :

(*a*) m/s (*b*) kg (*c*) kg.m/s (*d*) kg.m/s^2

44. According to the third law of motion, action and reaction :

(*a*) always act on the same body but in opposite directions

(*b*) always act on different bodies in opposite directions

(*c*) have same magnitudes and directions

(*d*) act on either body at normal to each other

45. The unit of measuring momentum of a moving body is :

(*a*) m s^{-1} (*b*) kg.m s^{-1} (*c*) kg.m s^{-2} (*d*) Nm^2 kg^{-2}

46. A boy of mass 50 kg standing on ground exerts a force of 500 N on the ground. The force exerted by the ground on the boy will be :

(*a*) 50 N (*b*) 25000 N (*c*) 10 N (*d*) 500 N

47. A Honda City car, a Maruti Alto car, a Tata Nano car and a Mahindra Scorpio car, all are running at the same speed of 50 m/s under identical conditions. If all these cars are hit from behind with the same force and they continue to move forward, the maximum acceleration will be produced in :

(*a*) Honda City (*b*) Maruti Alto (*c*) Tata Nano (*d*) Mahindra Scorpio

1150 kg

720 kg

600 kg

2510 kg

48. The acceleration produced by a force of 5 N acting on a mass of 20 kg in m/s^2 is :

(*a*) 4 (*b*) 100 (*c*) 0.25 (*d*) 2.5

49. Which of the following situations involves the Newton's second law of motion ?

(*a*) a force can stop a lighter vehicle as well as a heavier vehicle which are moving

(*b*) a force can accelerate a lighter vehicle more easily than a heavier vehicle which are moving

(*c*) a force exerted by a lighter vehicle on collision with a heavier vehicle results in both the vehicles coming to a standstill

(*d*) a force exerted by the escaping air from a balloon in the downward direction makes the balloon to go upwards

50. A fielder pulls his hands backwards after catching the cricket ball. This enables the fielder to :

(*a*) exert larger force on the ball (*b*) reduce the force exerted by the ball

(*c*) increase the rate of change of momentum (*d*) keep the ball in hands firmly

Questions Based on High Order Thinking Skills (HOTS)

51. Why are car seat-belts designed to stretch somewhat in a collision ?
52. The troops (soldiers) equipped to be dropped by parachutes from an aircraft are called paratroopers. Why do paratroopers roll on landing ?
53. Why would an aircraft be unable to fly on the moon ?
54. Explain why it is possible for a small animal to fall from a considerable height without any injury being caused when it reaches the ground.
55. A boy of mass 50 kg running at 5 m/s jumps on to a 20 kg trolley travelling in the same direction at 1.5 m/s. What is their common velocity ?
56. A girl of mass 50 kg jumps out of a rowing boat of mass 300 kg on to the bank, with a horizontal velocity of 3 m/s. With what velocity does the boat begin to move backwards ?

Paratroopers being dropped from an aircraft.

57. A truck of mass 500 kg moving at 4 m/s collides with another truck of mass 1500 kg moving in the same direction at 2 m/s. What is their common velocity just after the collision if they move off together ?
58. A ball *X* of mass 1 kg travelling at 2 m/s has a head-on collision with an identical ball *Y* at rest. *X* stops and *Y* moves off. Calculate the velocity of *Y* after the collision.
59. A heavy car A of mass 2000 kg travelling at 10 m/s has a head-on collision with a sports car B of mass 500 kg. If both cars stop dead on colliding, what was the velocity of car B ?
60. A man wearing a bullet-proof vest stands still on roller skates. The total mass is 80 kg. A bullet of mass 20 grams is fired at 400 m/s. It is stopped by the vest and falls to the ground. What is then the velocity of the man ?

ANSWERS

1. Force **6.** Acceleration remains the same **7.** Force **8.** Principle of conservation of momentum **10.** True **11.** 1 newton (1 N) **12.** 0.5 m/s^2 **13.** 250 N **14.** Mass (of the car) **15.** (*a*) equal ; opposite (*b*) vector ; kg.m/s (*c*) acceleration ; rate ; momentum (*d*) magnitude ; directions (*e*) momentum ; force **25.** 6 m/s **26.** 0.99 m/s **27.** 60 N **28.** 5 N **29.** – 2 m/s^2 ; – 4800 N **30.** 20 s **31.** 5 s **32.** (*a*) 40 kg.m/s (*b*) 80 kg.m/s (*c*) 20 kg.m/s^2 (*d*) 20 N **33.** (*i*) 1 m/s (*ii*) 1000 N **35.** (*a*) Law of conservation of momentum (*b*) Newton's second law of motion (*c*) Newton's third law of motion (*d*) Newton's first law of motion **36.** (*b*) (*i*) – 4 m/s^2 (*ii*) – 4000 N **37.** (*b*) 90 N **40.** (*b*) 0.25 m/s^2 **41.** (*c*) **42.** (*b*) **43.** (*b*) **44.** (*b*) **45.** (*b*) **46.** (*d*) **47.** (*c*) **48.** (*c*) **49.** (*b*) **50.** (*b*) **51.** So that by stretching somewhat the seat-belts allow the large momentum of a passenger to reduce gently, the passenger is prevented from being thrown forward violently, and injury is prevented (or reduced) during a collision **53.** An aircraft needs air because (*i*) air moving under the wings of aircraft is strong enough to hold it up, and (*ii*) air burns the fuel in aircraft engines. Since there is no air on moon, an aircraft cannot fly on the moon. **54.** This is because a small animal has small mass, so the momentum produced is less. When the small animal falls to the ground with less momentum, less opposing force of ground (less force of reaction) acts on the small animal and hence no injury is caused **55.** 4 m/s **56.** 0.5 m/s **57.** 2.5 m/s **58.** 2 m/s **59.** 40 m/s **60.** 0.1 m/s

GRAVITATION

In the previous chapter we have studied that a force is necessary to make a body move. That is, **a force is necessary to produce motion in a body**. Now, if we drop a piece of stone from some height, the stone falls down towards the earth. Since the stone starts moving downwards (it is in motion), therefore, a force must be acting on it. This force is due to the attraction between the earth and the stone and it is called the gravitational force of earth (or gravity of earth). Thus, **a stone dropped from a height falls towards the earth because the earth exerts a force of attraction (called gravity) on the stone and pulls it down.**

It is said that once the great English scientist Isaac Newton was sitting in his garden under an apple tree when an apple from the tree fell on him. Newton said that an apple falls down from the tree towards

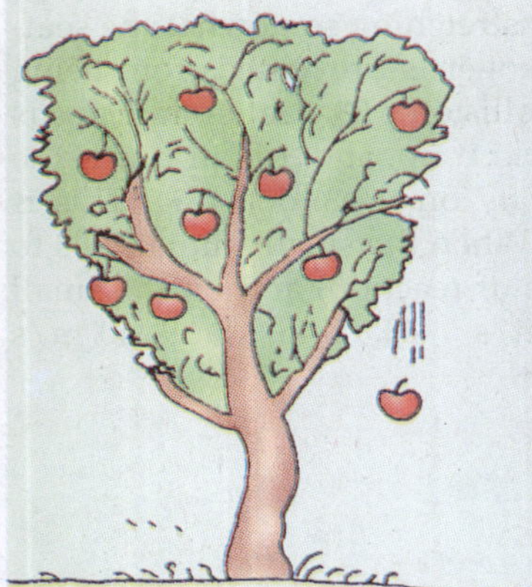

Figure 1. Newton said that an apple falls down from a tree because the earth exerts a force of attraction on it. This force of attraction is called gravitational force of earth or gravity (of earth).

Figure 2. Rain falls down from the sky to the earth due to the gravitational force of earth or gravity (of earth).

Figure 3. The gravitational force of earth or gravity (of earth) also causes water to flow down the rivers.

the earth because the earth exerts a 'force of attraction' on the apple in the downward direction. This force of attraction exerted by the earth is called its gravity. Similarly, a leaf falls down from a tree due to gravity of earth. In fact, **the earth attracts (or pulls) all the objects towards its centre. The force with which the earth pulls the objects towards it is called the gravitational force of earth or gravity (of earth)**. It is due to the gravitational force of earth that all the objects fall towards the earth when released from a height.

The gravitational force of earth (or gravity of earth) is responsible for holding the atmosphere above the earth; for the rain falling to the earth ; and for the flow of water in the rivers. It is also the gravitational force of earth (or gravity of earth) which keeps us firmly on the ground (and we do not float here and there). Similarly, a ball thrown upwards also falls back to the earth due to the gravitational force of the earth. Since the gravitational force of earth (or gravity of earth) pulls the objects in the downward direction, therefore, a force has to be applied by us to raise an object to a height above the surface of earth (to overcome the gravitational force of earth).

Every Object in the Universe Attracts Every Other Object

When we drop an object, it falls towards the earth. This means that the earth attracts the various objects towards its centre. Newton said that it is not only the earth which attracts the other objects, in fact, every object attracts every other object. So, **according to Newton, every object in this universe attracts every other object with a certain force. The force with which two objects attract each other is called gravitational force (or gravity)**. The gravitational force between two objects acts even if the two objects are not connected by any means.

If the masses of the objects (or bodies) are small, then the gravitational force between them is very small (which cannot be detected easily). For example, 'two stones' lying on the ground attract each other but since their masses are small, the gravitational force of attraction between them is small and hence we do not see one stone moving towards the other stone. **If, however, one of the objects (or bodies) is very big (having a very large mass), then the gravitational force becomes very large (and its effect can be seen easily)**. For example, a stone (lying at a height) and the earth attract each other, and since the earth has a very large mass, the gravitational force of attraction between them is very large due to which when the stone is dropped, it moves down towards the earth. Please note that **the 'gravitational force' or 'gravity' is always a force of attraction between two objects (or two bodies).** We will now study the universal law of gravitation.

UNIVERSAL LAW OF GRAVITATION

The universal law of gravitation was given by Newton. So, it is also known as Newton's law of gravitation. According to universal law of gravitation : **Every body in the universe attracts every other body with a force which is directly proportional to the product of their masses and inversely proportional to the square of the distance between them.** The direction of force is along the line joining the centres of the two bodies.

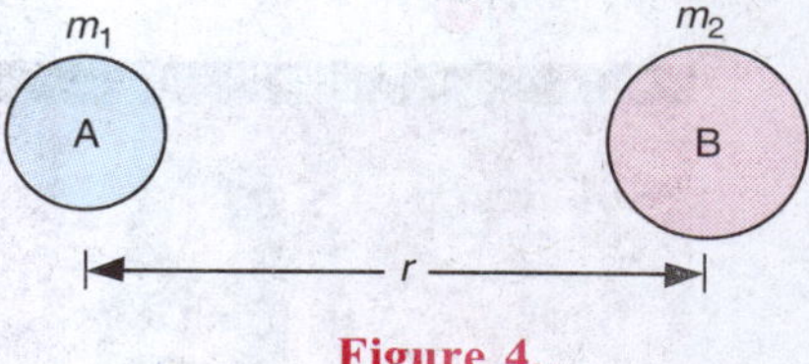

Figure 4.

Suppose two bodies A and B of masses m_1 and m_2 are lying at a distance r from each other (see Figure 4). Let the force of attraction between these two bodies be F. Now, according to the universal law of gravitation :

(*i*) **the force between two bodies is directly proportional to the product of their masses.** That is,

$$F \propto m_1 \times m_2 \quad \text{... (1)}$$

(*ii*) **the force between two bodies is inversely proportional to the square of the distance between them.** That is,

$$F \propto \frac{1}{r^2} \quad \text{... (2)}$$

Combining (1) and (2), we get :

$$F \propto \frac{m_1 \times m_2}{r^2}$$

Gravitational force, $$F = G \times \frac{m_1 \times m_2}{r^2}$$

where G is a constant known as "universal gravitational constant". The value of gravitational constant G does not depend on the medium between the two bodies. It also does not depend on the masses of the bodies or the distance between them.

The above formula gives the gravitational force of attraction F between two bodies of masses m_1 and m_2 which are at a distance r from one another. This formula is applicable anywhere in this universe, and it is a mathematical expression of universal law of gravitation. Since the gravitational force between two bodies is inversely proportional to the square of the distance between them, therefore, **if we double the distance between two bodies, the gravitational force becomes one-fourth** and **if we halve the distance between two bodies, then the gravitational force becomes four times.**

Newton's law of gravitation is called universal law of gravitation because it is applicable to all the bodies having mass : whether the bodies are big or small ; whether the bodies are terrestrial (which are on earth) or celestial (which are in outer space) such as the stars, planets and satellites.

Units of Gravitational Constant, G

According to universal law of gravitation, the gravitational force F between two bodies of masses m_1 and m_2 placed at a distance r apart is given by :

$$F = G \times \frac{m_1 \times m_2}{r^2}$$

This can be rearranged to get an expression for the gravitational constant G as follows :

$$G = F \times \frac{r^2}{m_1 \times m_2}$$

Now, the unit of force F is newton (N), the unit of distance r is metre (m), and the unit of masses m_1 and m_2 is kilogram (kg). So, the SI unit of gravitational constant G becomes :

$$\frac{\text{newton(metre)}^2}{\text{(kilogram)}^2} \quad \text{or} \quad \frac{\text{Nm}^2}{\text{kg}^2} \quad \text{or} \quad \text{Nm}^2/\text{kg}^2 \quad \text{or} \quad \text{Nm}^2\ \text{kg}^{-2}$$

Value of Gravitational Constant, G

If the masses m_1 and m_2 of the two bodies are 1 kg each and the distance r between them is 1 m, then putting $m_1 = 1$ kg; $m_2 = 1$ kg and $r = 1$ m in the above formula, we get :

$$F = G \quad (\text{when } m_1 = m_2 = 1 \text{ kg and } r = 1 \text{ m})$$

Figure 5. The value of universal gravitational constant G is 6.67×10^{-11} Nm^2/kg^2.

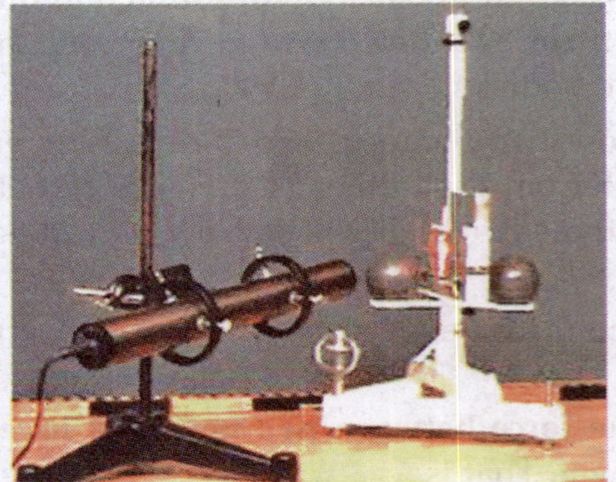

Figure 6. This photograph shows the experimental set-up of Cavendish method for determining the value of universal gravitational constant G.

Thus, **the gravitational constant G is numerically equal to the force of gravitation which exists between two bodies of unit masses kept at a unit distance from each other. The value of universal gravitational constant G has been found to be 6.67×10^{-11} Nm²/kg².** The extremely small value of gravitational constant (G) tells us that the force of gravitation between any two ordinary objects will be very, very weak.

The value of gravitational constant G has been determined by performing careful experiments with two gold balls. Two heavy gold balls were suspended near each other by strong but delicate threads. The force between the two gold balls was then measured. Knowing the force, the masses of the gold balls, and the distance between them, the value of G was calculated by using Newton's gravitation formula. The experiment with gold balls gave the value of gravitational constant G as 6.67×10^{-11} Nm^2/kg^2. Please note that though the exact value of gravitational constant G is 6.67×10^{-11} Nm^2/kg^2 but many times it is taken as 6.7×10^{-11} Nm^2/kg^2 in the numerical problems just for the sake of convenience in calculations.

The formula : $F = G \times \frac{m_1 \times m_2}{r^2}$ can be used to calculate the gravitational force anywhere in this universe. In all the cases, the value of G is 6.67×10^{-11} Nm^2/kg^2 and m_1 and m_2 are the masses of the two bodies and r is the distance between the centres of the two bodies. **The force of gravitation is a vector quantity** and it acts along the line joining the centres of mass of the two bodies.

Gravitational Force Between Objects of Small Size and Big Size

Suppose two balls of 1 kg each are placed with their centres 1 m apart, then they attract each other with a force given by,

$$F = G \times \frac{m_1 \times m_2}{r^2}$$

Putting $G = 6.67 \times 10^{-11}$ Nm^2/kg^2; $m_1 = 1$ kg; $m_2 = 1$ kg and $r = 1$ m

We get : $$F = \frac{6.67 \times 10^{-11} \times 1 \times 1}{(1)^2} \text{ newtons}$$

or $$F = 6.67 \times 10^{-11} \text{ newtons}$$

It is obvious that the gravitational force of attraction between two balls of 1 kg each and 1 m apart is 6.67×10^{-11} newtons and this is a very small force.

Though the various objects on this earth attract one another constantly, they do not cause any motion because the gravitational force of attraction between them is very small. If, however, at least one of the bodies is large (like the sun or the earth), then the gravitational force becomes very large. For example, the earth has a very large mass and this force is quite large between the earth and other objects. Hence, objects when thrown up, fall back to the earth. This point will become more clear from the following example in which we are calculating the gravitational force between a ball having 1 kilogram mass and the earth.

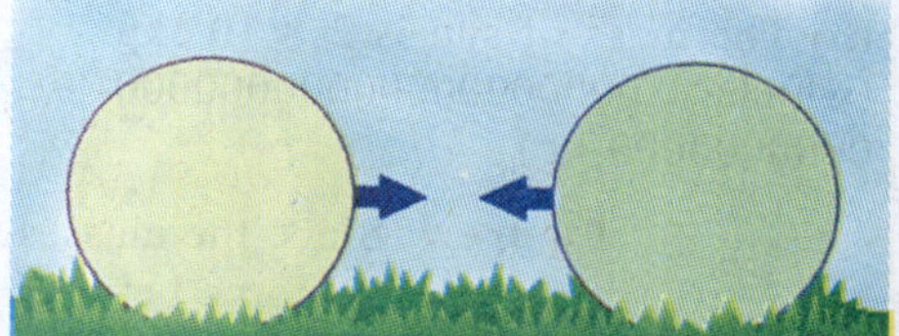

Figure 7. Though these balls attract each other but they do not show any motion because, due to their small masses, the gravitational force of attraction between them is very, very small.

Sample Problem 1. Calculate the force of gravitation due to earth on a ball of 1 kg mass lying on the ground. (Mass of earth = 6×10^{24} kg; Radius of earth = 6.4×10^3 km; and $G = 6.7 \times 10^{-11}$ Nm^2/kg^2)

Solution. The force of gravitation is calculated by using the formula :

$$F = G \times \frac{m_1 \times m_2}{r^2}$$

Here, Gravitational constant, $G = 6.7 \times 10^{-11}$ Nm^2/kg^2

Mass of earth, $m_1 = 6 \times 10^{24}$ kg

Mass of ball, $m_2 = 1$ kg

And, Distance between centre, r = Radius of earth of earth and ball

$$= 6.4 \times 10^3 \text{ km}$$
$$= 6.4 \times 10^3 \times 1000 \text{ m}$$
$$= 6.4 \times 10^6 \text{ m}$$

Now, putting these values in the above formula, we get :

$$F = \frac{6.7 \times 10^{-11} \times 6 \times 10^{24} \times 1}{(6.4 \times 10^6)^2}$$

or $$F = 9.8 \text{ newtons}$$

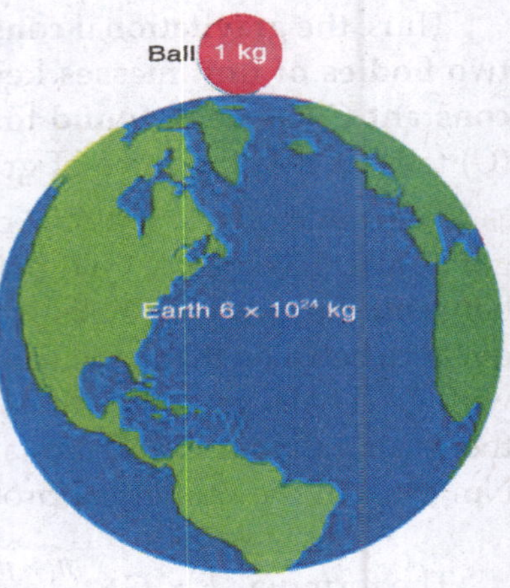

Figure 8. For sample problem 1.

Thus, the earth exerts a gravitational force of 9.8 newtons on a ball of mass 1 kilogram. This is a comparatively large force. It is due to this large gravitational force exerted by earth that when the 1 kg ball is dropped from a height, it falls to the earth.

It is clear from the above discussion that we can ignore the gravitational force between two balls of 1 kilogram each because it is very small. But we cannot ignore the gravitational force between a 1 kilogram ball and the earth because it is quite large (due to the large mass of earth). And **when both the objects (or bodies) are very big, having very large masses, then the gravitational force of attraction between them becomes extremely large**. For example, the sun, the earth and the moon have

(*a*) The mass of sun is 2×10^{30} kg (which is 2000000000000000000000000000000 kg)

(*b*) The mass of earth is 6×10^{24} kg (which is 6000000000000000000000000 kg)

(*c*) The mass of moon is 7.4×10^{22} kg (which is 74000000000000000000000 kg)

Figure 9. Since the masses of the sun, the earth, and the moon are extremely large, therefore, the gravitational force between the sun and the earth, and the earth and the moon is extremely large.

extremely large masses, therefore, the gravitational force of attraction between the sun and the earth (or other planets), or between the earth and the moon, is extremely large. This point will become more clear from the following example in which we are calculating the gravitational force between the earth and the moon.

Sample Problem 2. The mass of the earth is 6×10^{24} kg and that of the moon is 7.4×10^{22} kg. If the distance between the earth and the moon be 3.84×10^5 km, calculate the force exerted by the earth on the moon. ($G = 6.7 \times 10^{-11}$ Nm^2 kg^{-2})

Solution. The force exerted by one body on another body is given by the Newton's formula :

$$F = G \times \frac{m_1 \times m_2}{r^2}$$

Here, Gravitational constant, $G = 6.7 \times 10^{-11}$ Nm^2 kg^{-2}

Mass of the earth, $m_1 = 6 \times 10^{24}$ kg

Mass of the moon, $m_2 = 7.4 \times 10^{22}$ kg

And, Distance between the earth and moon, $r = 3.84 \times 10^5$ km

$= 3.84 \times 10^5 \times 1000$ m

$= 3.84 \times 10^8$ m

Putting these values in the above formula, we get :

$$F = \frac{6.7 \times 10^{-11} \times 6 \times 10^{24} \times 7.4 \times 10^{22}}{(3.84 \times 10^8)^2}$$

$$F = 2.01 \times 10^{20} \text{ newtons}$$

Thus, the gravitational force exerted by the earth on the moon is 2.01×10^{20} newtons. And this is an extremely large force. It is this extremely large gravitational force exerted by the earth on the moon which makes the moon revolve around the earth.

Gravitational Force Holds the Solar System Together

In the solar system, planets move in almost circular orbits around the sun ; and satellites move in circular orbits around the planets. A force (called centripetal force) is needed to make an object move in a circular orbit (or circular path). In the case of planets moving around the sun, the centripetal force is provided

Figure 10. This picture shows the solar system. The sun is at the centre of solar system and the 8 planets are revolving around it. The planets move in orbits around the sun due to the gravitational force of attraction of the sun.

by the gravitational force of the sun. And in the case of satellites moving around the planets, the centripetal force is provided by the gravitational force of the planets. We will now discuss the case of 'the sun and the earth' and that of 'the earth and the moon'.

Since the masses of the sun (which is a star) and the earth (which is a planet) are very, very large, they exert very large force on one another. **It is the gravitational force between the sun and the earth which keeps the earth in uniform circular motion around the sun.** Similarly, the gravitational force between the earth and the moon makes the moon revolve at uniform speed around the earth. Thus, the gravitational

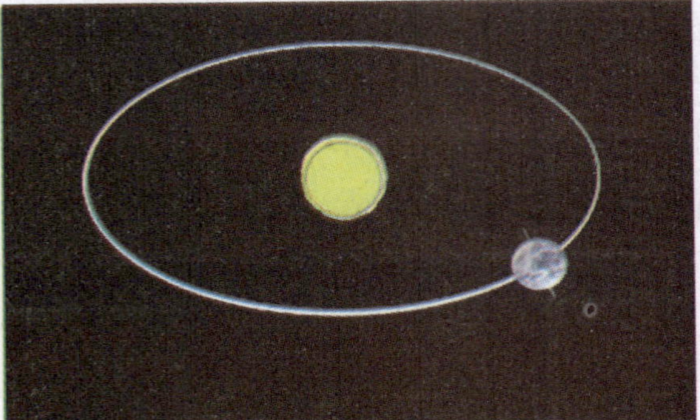

Figure 11. The earth moves around the sun due to the gravitational force exerted by the sun.

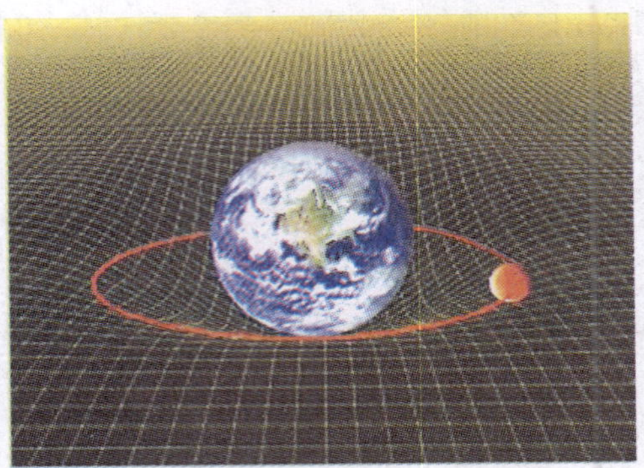

Figure 12. The moon moves around the earth due to the gravitational force exerted by the earth.

force is responsible for the existence of our solar system. **The tides in the sea formed by the rising and falling of water level in the sea, are due to the gravitational force of attraction which the moon and the sun exert on the water surface in the sea.** Thus, Newton used his theory of gravitation to give the first satisfactory explanation of many natural phenomena such as : motion of planets around the sun ; motion of moon around the earth ; and formation of tides in the sea (or ocean). He also explained Kepler's laws of

(*a*) Low tide : The water level in the sea falls

(*b*) High tide : The water level in the sea rises

Figure 13. The photograph on the left side shows low tide. If we stand at this place for a few hours, we will see the high tide (as shown in the photograph on the right side). The tides are caused mainly by the gravitational force of the moon (and to a smaller extent of the sun) acting on the surface of sea.

planetary motion. Here are some more applications of Newton's law of gravitation or universal law of gravitation. The universal law of gravitation is used to determine the masses of the sun, the earth and the moon accurately. It also helps in discovering new stars and planets.

KEPLER'S LAWS OF PLANETARY MOTION

Johannes Kepler was a 16th century astronomer who established three laws which govern the motion of planets (around the sun). These are known as Kepler's laws of planetary motion. The same laws also describe the motion of satellites (like the moon) around the planets (like the earth). The Kepler's laws of planetary motion are given on the next page.

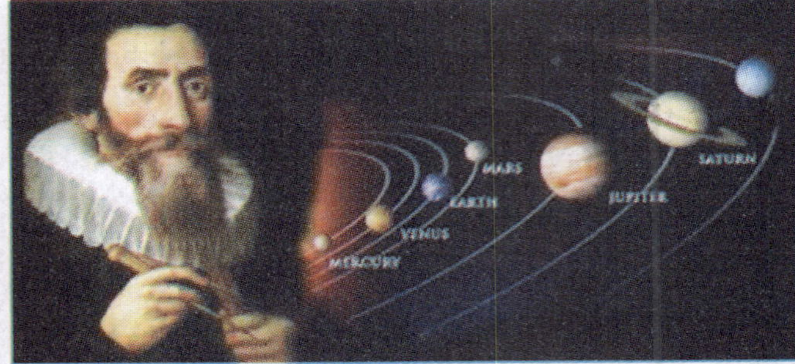

Figure 14. Johannes Kepler : The scientist who gave three laws to describe the motion of planets around the sun.

1. Kepler's first law states that : **The planets move in elliptical orbits around the sun, with the sun at one of the two foci of the elliptical orbit**. This law means that the orbit (or path) of a planet around the sun is an ellipse (oval-shaped) and not an exact circle. An elliptical path has two foci, and the sun is at one of the two foci of the elliptical path (*foci* is the plural of *focus*). This is shown in Figure 15. In Figure 15, a planet P is moving around the sun S in an elliptical orbit. The elliptical orbit has two foci F_1 and F_2. The sun is situated at the focus F_1 (see Figure 15).

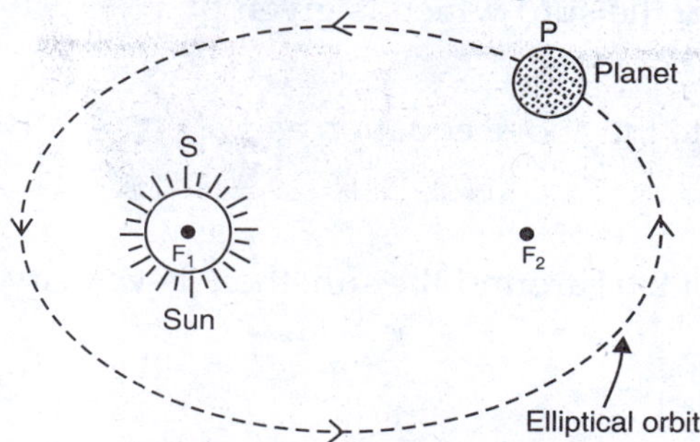

Figure 15. Diagram for Kepler's first law of planetary motion.

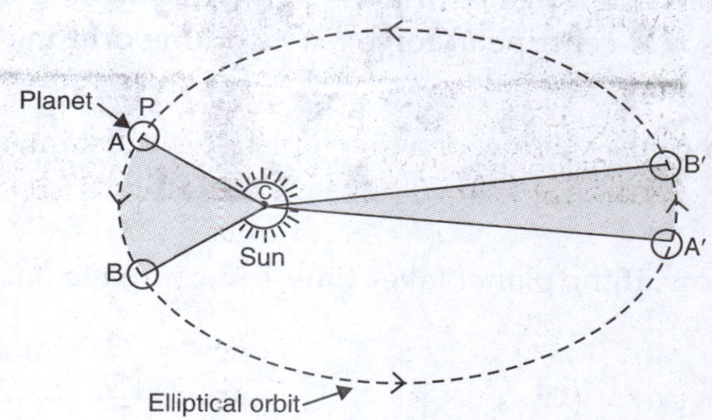

Figure 16. Diagram for Kepler's second law of planetary motion.

2. Kepler's second law states that : **Each planet revolves around the sun in such a way that the line joining the planet to the sun sweeps over equal areas in equal intervals of time**. We know that a planet moves around the sun in an elliptical orbit with sun at one of its focus. Now, since the line joining the planet and the sun sweeps over equal areas in equal intervals of time, it means that **a planet moves faster when it is closer to the sun, and moves slowly when it is farther from the sun.** This point will become more clear from Figure 16.

In Figure 16, a planet P is moving in an elliptical orbit around the sun. When the planet is nearer to the sun at position A, it travels faster and sweeps over an area ABC in time t. On the other hand, when the same planet is farther from the sun at position A', then it moves slowly but sweeps over an equal area $A'B'C$ in the same time t. Thus, the Kepler's second law tells us that **a planet does not move with constant speed around the sun. The speed is greater when the planet is nearer the sun, and less when the planet is farther away from the sun**. A planet could move around the sun with constant speed only if its orbit were a true circle (and not an ellipse).

3. Kepler's third law states that : **The cube of the mean distance of a planet from the sun is directly proportional to the square of time it takes to move around the sun**. This law can be expressed as :

$$r^3 \propto T^2$$

or
$$r^3 = \text{constant} \times T^2$$

or
$$\frac{r^3}{T^2} = \text{constant}$$

where r = mean distance of planet from the sun

and T = time period of the planet (around the sun)

Though Kepler gave the laws of planetary motion but he could not give a theory to explain the motion of planets. It was Newton who showed that **the cause of the motion of planets is the gravitational force which the sun exerts on them**. In fact, Newton used the Kepler's third law of planetary motion to develop the law of universal gravitation. This is discussed below.

How Did Newton Guess the Inverse-Square Rule

The statement made by Newton in his universal law of gravitation that 'the force between two bodies is inversely proportional to the square of distance between them' is called the inverse-square rule. That is, the inverse-square rule is :

$$F \propto \frac{1}{r^2}$$

Newton got the idea of the inverse-square rule for gravitational force between two bodies by applying Kepler's third law to the orbit of a planet around the sun. An important assumption made for this purpose is that the orbit of a planet around the sun is 'circular'. Newton derived the inverse-square rule for gravitational force as follows.

Consider a planet of mass m moving with a velocity (or speed) v around the sun in a circular orbit of radius r. A centripetal force F acts on the orbiting planet (due to the sun) which is given by :

$$F = \frac{mv^2}{r}$$

Since the mass m of a given planet is constant, so we can write the above equation as :

$$F \propto \frac{v^2}{r} \quad ...(1)$$

Now, if the planet takes time T to complete one revolution (of $2\pi r$) around the sun, then its velocity v is given by :

$$v = \frac{2\pi r}{T}$$

Here the factor 2π is a constant, so we can write this equation as :

$$v \propto \frac{r}{T}$$

Now, taking square on both sides, we get :

$$v^2 \propto \frac{r^2}{T^2}$$

If we multiply as well as divide the right side of this relation by r, we get :

$$v^2 \propto \frac{r^3}{T^2} \times \frac{1}{r}$$

Now, by Kepler's third law of planetary motion, the factor $\frac{r^3}{T^2}$ is constant. So, the above relation becomes :

$$v^2 \propto \frac{1}{r} \quad ...(2)$$

By putting $\frac{1}{r}$ in place of v^2 in relation (1), we get :

$$F \propto \frac{1}{r \times r}$$

or

$$F \propto \frac{1}{r^2}$$

Thus, the gravitational force between the sun and a planet is inversely proportional to the square of distance between them. It was this conclusion obtained by using Kepler's third law of planetary motion which helped Newton to formulate universal law of gravitation.

NEWTON'S THIRD LAW OF MOTION AND GRAVITATION

Newton's third law of motion says that : *If an object exerts a force on another object, then the second object exerts an equal and opposite force on the first object.* **The Newton's third law of motion also holds good for the force of gravitation. This means that when earth exerts a force of attraction on an object, then the object also exerts an equal force on the earth, in the opposite direction.** Thus, even a falling object attracts the earth towards itself. When an object, say a stone, is dropped from a height, it gets accelerated and falls towards the earth and we say that the stone comes down due to the gravitational force of attraction exerted by the earth. Now, **if the stone also exerts an equal and opposite force on the earth, then why don't we see the earth rising up towards the stone ?** We will try to answer this question now.

From Newton's second law of motion, we know that :

$$\text{Force} = \text{Mass} \times \text{Acceleration}$$

$$\text{So,} \quad \text{Acceleration} = \frac{\text{Force}}{\text{Mass}}$$

$$\text{or} \quad a = \frac{F}{m}$$

It is clear from this formula that the acceleration produced in a body is inversely proportional to the mass of the body. Now, **the mass of a stone is very small, due to which the gravitational force produces a large acceleration in it.** Due to large acceleration of stone, we can see the stone falling towards the earth. The mass of earth is, however, very, very large. **Due to the very large mass of the earth, the same gravitational force produces very, very small acceleration in the earth.** Actually, the acceleration produced in the earth is so small that it cannot be observed. And hence we do not see the earth rising up towards the stone.

It can be shown by calculations that the gravitational force between the earth and a 1 kilogram stone produces an acceleration of 9.8 m/s^2 in the stone. **Since the acceleration produced in the stone is quite large, we can see the stone falling towards the earth.** Now, the same gravitational force produces an acceleration of 1.63×10^{-24} m/s^2 in the earth. **Since the acceleration produced in the earth is extremely small, we cannot see the motion of the earth towards the falling stone.**

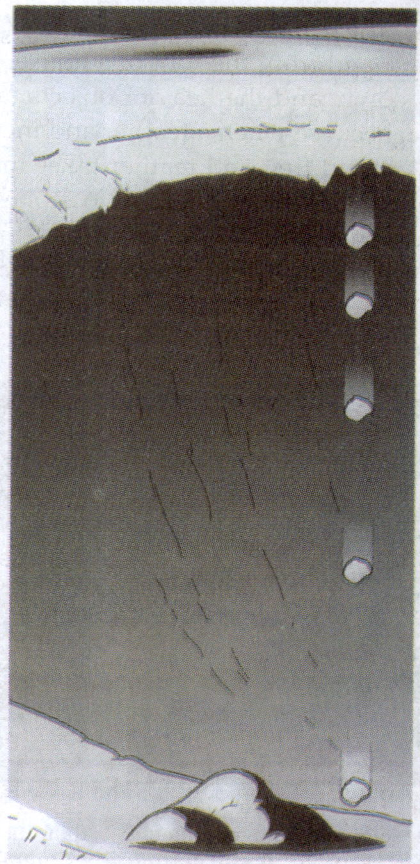

Figure 17. When the earth attracts a stone downwards with a certain force, the stone attracts the earth upwards with an equal force. We can see the stone falling down because due to its small mass, the acceleration produced in it is large. On the other hand, because of the extremely large mass of earth, the same force produces a very, very small (or negligible) acceleration in the earth due to which we do not see the earth moving up towards the falling stone.

FREE FALL

The falling of a body (or object) from a height towards the earth under the gravitational force of earth (with no other forces acting on it) is called free fall. And such a body is called 'freely falling body' (or 'freely falling object'). So, whenever a body (or object) falls towards the earth on its own, we say that it is under free fall or that it is a freely falling body (or freely falling object). Let us discuss this in a little more detail.

Figure 18. This bungee-jumper is falling down only under the gravitational force of the earth. He is said to be in free fall (or falling freely towards the earth).

Figure 19. This is the leaning tower of Pisa (in Italy) where Galileo experimented with falling objects. When two stones of different masses were dropped from the top of leaning tower of Pisa, they hit the ground at the same time showing that the acceleration of a freely falling object does not depend on the mass of the object.

Our earth attracts all the bodies (or objects) which are near its surface so that when a body (say, a stone) is dropped from the roof of a house, it falls down to the earth. Earlier it was thought that the lighter objects fall slowly and the heavier objects fall more rapidly when dropped from the same height and at the same time, because when a feather and metal coin are dropped simultaneously from a roof, the metal coin reaches the ground first and feather takes more time to reach the ground. This was later on found to be wrong by Galileo. Galileo dropped two stones of different masses from the top of the leaning tower of Pisa, and found that they hit the ground at the same time. From this Galileo concluded that **the acceleration of an object falling freely towards the earth does not depend on the mass of the object.** During free fall, the heavier objects as well as the lighter objects accelerate at the same rate. It was suggested by Galileo that the slow speed of feather, while falling, is due to the fact that its surface area is very large as compared to its

Figure 20. Galileo Galilei : The scientist who conducted experiments on freely falling objects.

Figure 21. Robert Boyle : The scientist who showed that in the absence of air resistance (that is, in vacuum) even a feather and a coin fell at the same rate.

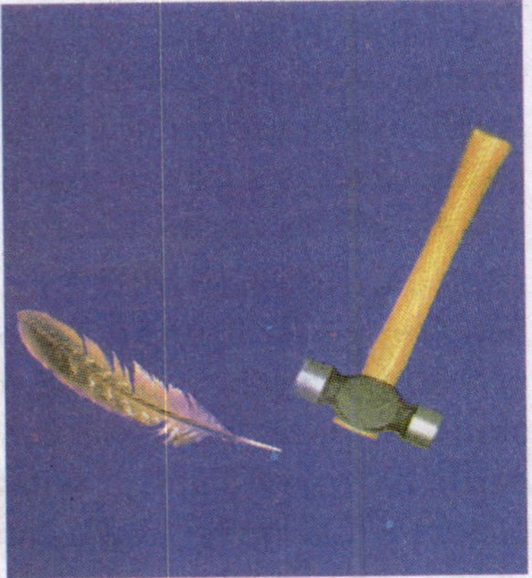

Figure 22. Recreating the feather and coin experiment by using feather and hammer. The air was pumped out from the glass tube. A feather and a hammer were then released. In the absence of air resistance, both fell down at the same rate.

mass, so the feather experiences much more resistance from air and its speed is slowed down. The metal coin, being small and heavy, does not get so much resistance from air and falls to the ground at a faster rate. If there were no air, the feather and the coin would fall at the same rate. This has been shown to be so by means of experiments done in vacuum by Robert Boyle. The feather and the coin, both, were put in a tall glass jar and the air from the jar was removed by using a vacuum pump. When this jar was inverted, both, feather and the coin fell to the bottom of the jar at the same time showing that in the absence of air resistance, that is, in vacuum, all the objects fall at the same rate. In other words, **the acceleration produced in the freely falling bodies is the same for all the bodies and it does not depend on the mass of the falling body.**

Acceleration due to Gravity (g)

When an object is dropped from some height, its velocity increases at a constant rate. In other words, **when an object is dropped from some height, a uniform acceleration is produced in it by the gravitational pull of the earth** and this acceleration does not depend on the mass of the falling object. **The uniform acceleration produced in a freely falling body due to the gravitational force of the earth is known as acceleration due to gravity** and it is denoted by the letter g. The value of g does not depend on the mass of the body. The value of g changes slightly from place to place but for most of the purposes it is taken as 9.8 m/s^2. Thus, **the acceleration due to gravity, $g = 9.8\ m/s^2$.** In other words, when an object falls to the ground under the action of earth's gravity, its velocity increases at the constant rate of 9.8 metres per second for every second of time it is falling. **When a body is dropped freely, it falls with an acceleration of 9.8 m/s² and when a body is thrown vertically upwards, it undergoes a retardation of 9.8 m/s².** So, the velocity of a body thrown vertically upwards will decrease at the rate of 9.8 m/s². The velocity decreases until it reaches zero. The body then falls back to the earth like any other body dropped from that height.

Before we go further and derive a formula to calculate the acceleration due to gravity of earth, please remember that when a body (or object) is 'on the surface of earth' or 'near the surface of earth' then the distance of the body from the centre of earth is taken as equal to radius of earth (R). So, in this case the distance r in the formula for gravitational force becomes 'radius of earth' R.

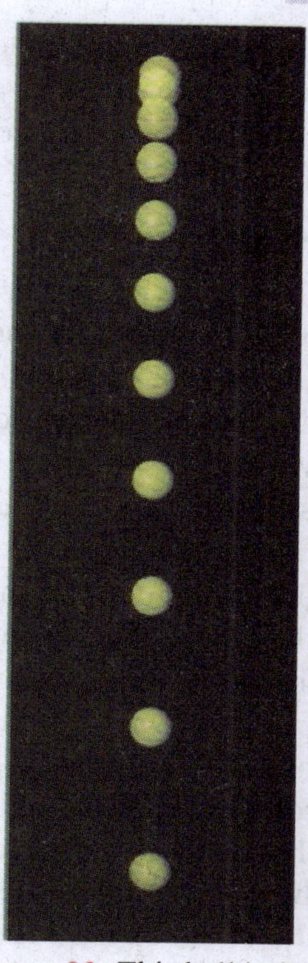

Figure 23. This ball is falling to the ground under the action of earth's gravity. Its velocity is increasing at a constant rate of 9.8 m/s for every second of time it is falling

Calculation of the Acceleration Due to Gravity (*g*)

If we drop a body (say, a stone) of mass m from a distance R from the centre of the earth of mass M, then the force exerted by the earth on the body is given by universal law of gravitation as :

$$F = G \times \frac{M \times m}{R^2} \quad (G = \text{Gravitational constant}) \ \ldots (1)$$

This force exerted by the earth produces acceleration in the stone due to which the stone moves downwards. We also know that :

$$\text{Force} = \text{Mass} \times \text{Acceleration}$$

or

$$F = m \times a$$

So, Acceleration of stone, $a = \dfrac{F}{m}$ ... (2)

Putting the value of force F from equation (1) in the above relation, we get :

$$\text{Acceleration,} \quad a = \frac{G \times M \times m}{R^2 \times m}$$

or

$$a = G \times \frac{M}{R^2}$$

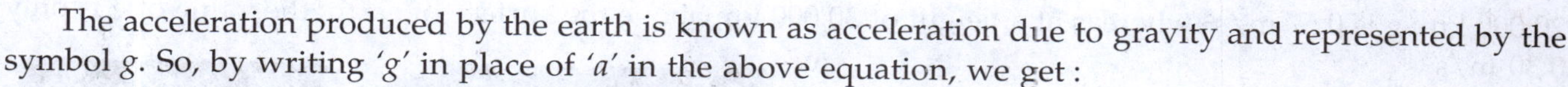

The acceleration produced by the earth is known as acceleration due to gravity and represented by the symbol g. So, by writing 'g' in place of 'a' in the above equation, we get :

$$\text{Acceleration due to gravity,} \quad g = G \times \frac{M}{R^2}$$

where G = gravitational constant

M = mass of the earth

and R = radius of the earth

This is the formula for calculating the acceleration due to gravity on or near the surface of the earth. To calculate the value of g, we should put the values of G, M and R in the above formula.

Now, Gravitational constant, $G = 6.7 \times 10^{-11}\ \text{Nm}^2/\text{kg}^2$

Mass of the earth, $M = 6 \times 10^{24}$ kg

And, Radius of the earth, $R = 6.4 \times 10^6$ m

Putting these values of G, M and R in the above formula, we get :

$$g = \frac{6.7 \times 10^{-11} \times 6 \times 10^{24}}{(6.4 \times 10^6)^2}$$

or

$$g = 9.8\ \text{m/s}^2$$

Thus, the value of acceleration due to gravity is 9.8 m/s^2. But sometimes, to make the calculations easy, the value of g is taken as a round figure of 10 m/s^2. This is done just for the sake of convenience. Please note that this acceleration due to gravity acts in the direction of the line joining the body to the centre of the earth.

Variation of Acceleration Due to Gravity (g)

The value of acceleration due to gravity of earth (g) depends on the values of gravitational constant (G), mass of the earth (M), and radius of the earth (R). As gravitational constant (G) and mass of earth (M) are always constant , the value of acceleration due to gravity (g) is constant as long as the radius of earth R remains constant. Hence the value of g is constant at a given place on the surface of the earth. Please note that **the value of acceleration due to gravity, g, is not constant at all the places on the surface of the earth.** This is due to the fact that the earth is not a perfect sphere, so the value of its radius R is not the same at all the places on its surface. In other words, due to the flattening of the earth at the poles, all the places on its surface are not at the same distance from its centre and so the value of g varies with latitude. **Since the radius of the earth at the poles is minimum, the value of g is maximum at the poles.** Again, **the radius of earth is maximum at the equator, so the value of g is minimum at the equator** (because radius occurs in the denominator of the formula for g).

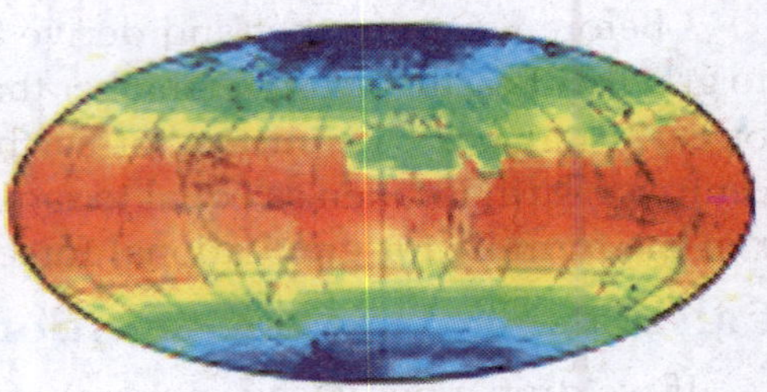

Figure 24. The earth is not a perfect sphere. Due to the flattening of earth at the poles, the radius of earth is the minimum at the poles and hence the value of g is the maximum at the poles. On the other hand, the radius of the earth is the maximum at the equator and hence the value of g is the minimum at the equator of earth.

We have just seen that :

$$g = G \times \frac{M}{R^2}$$

We find that the value of g is inversely proportional to the square of distance from the centre of the earth. Now, **as we go up from the surface of the earth, the distance from the centre of the earth increases, and hence the value of g decreases** (because R increases in this case). The value of acceleration due to gravity, g, at an altitude of 200 km above the surface of the earth is 9.23 m/s^2; at an altitude of 1000 km, g is 7.34 m/s^2; at 5,000 km above earth g is 3.08 m/s^2; at 10,000 km g is 1.49 m/s^2; at 20,000 km, g is 0.57 m/s^2 whereas at a height of 30,000 km above the surface of earth, the value of g is only 0.30 m/s^2.

The above formula suggests that the value of g should increase on going down inside the earth because then the value of R decreases. This, however, is not true. Actually this formula for g is not applicable at any point inside the surface of earth. At the moment, it will be sufficient for us to know that **the value of g also decreases as we go down inside the earth**, and it becomes zero at the centre of the earth. Please note that **the value of acceleration due to gravity, g, is maximum on the surface of the earth, it decreases on going above the surface of earth or on going inside the surface of the earth.**

Figure 25. The value of acceleration due to gravity (g) is the maximum on the surface of the earth. The value of g decreases on going above the surface of earth as well as on going below the surface of earth (or inside the earth).

Acceleration Due to Gravity (g) Does Not Depend on the Mass of a Body

Let us write down the formula for the acceleration due to gravity, g, once again :

$$g = G \times \frac{M}{R^2}$$

where G = gravitational constant
M = mass of earth
and R = radius of earth

We find that this formula for the acceleration due to gravity involves only the mass of earth. It does not involve the mass of the body on which the force of gravity of earth acts. **Since the acceleration due to gravity does not depend on the mass of the body, all the bodies (whether heavy or light) fall with the same acceleration towards the surface of the earth.** Thus, a big stone will fall with the same acceleration as a small stone because the acceleration due to gravity of earth (which acts on them during their free fall) does not depend on their mass. Both the stones are acted upon by the same acceleration of 9.8 m/s^2. In other words, **if a big stone and a small stone are dropped from the roof of a house simultaneously, they will reach the ground at the same time.** Let us solve some problems now.

Sample Problem 1. Calculate the value of acceleration due to gravity on the surface of the moon. (Given : Mass of the moon = 7.4×10^{22} kg; Radius of moon = 1740 km; $G = 6.7 \times 10^{-11}$ Nm^2/kg^2)

Solution. The formula for calculating the acceleration due to gravity is :

$$g = G \times \frac{M}{R^2}$$

Here, Gravitational constant, $G = 6.7 \times 10^{-11}$ Nm^2/kg^2
Mass of the moon, $M = 7.4 \times 10^{22}$ kg
And, Radius of the moon, R = 1740 km
= 1740×1000 m
= 1.74×10^6 m

Now, putting these values of G, M and R in the above formula, we get :

$$g = \frac{6.7 \times 10^{-11} \times 7.4 \times 10^{22}}{(1.74 \times 10^6)^2}$$

or $$g = 1.63 \text{ m/s}^2$$

Thus, the acceleration due to gravity, g, on the surface of the moon is 1.63 m/s^2.

Figure 26. The value of acceleration due to gravity (g) on the moon is only about one-sixth $\left(\frac{1}{6}\right)$ of the value of g on the earth. This is because both, the mass and radius of moon are smaller than that of the earth.

Figure 27. This photograph shows an astronaut on the surface of moon. Since the value of g on the moon is only about one-sixth of the value of g on earth, the weight of this astronaut on the moon will also be only about one-sixth of his weight on the earth (though his mass on the moon and the earth will be the same).

Please note that **the value of g on the moon is about one-sixth $\left(\frac{1}{6}\right)$ of the value of g on the earth** (the value of acceleration due to gravity on the earth being 9.8 m/s^2).

Sample Problem 2. The earth's gravitational force causes an acceleration of 5 m/s^2 in a 1 kg mass somewhere in space. How much will the acceleration of a 3 kg mass be at the same place ?

Solution. The acceleration produced by the gravitational force of earth does not depend on the mass of the object. So, the acceleration produced in the 3 kg mass will be the same as that produced in 1 kg mass. That is, the acceleration produced will be 5 m/s^2.

EQUATIONS OF MOTION FOR FREELY FALLING BODIES

Since the freely falling bodies fall with uniformly accelerated motion, the three equations of motion derived earlier for bodies under uniform acceleration can be applied to the motion of freely falling bodies. For freely falling bodies, the acceleration due to gravity is 'g', so we replace the acceleration 'a' of the equations by 'g' and since the vertical distance of the freely falling bodies is known as height 'h', we replace the distance 's' in our equations by the height 'h'. This gives us the following modified equations for the motion of freely falling bodies :

	General equations of motion		Equations of motion for freely falling bodies
(i)	$v = u + at$	changes to	$v = u + gt$
(ii)	$s = ut + \frac{1}{2}at^2$	changes to	$h = ut + \frac{1}{2}gt^2$
(iii)	$v^2 = u^2 + 2as$	changes to	$v^2 = u^2 + 2gh$

We will use these modified equations to solve numerical problems. Before we do that, we should remember the following important points for the motion of freely falling bodies :

(a) **When a body is falling vertically downwards, its velocity is increasing, so the acceleration due to gravity, g, is taken as positive.**
That is, Acceleration due to gravity = + 9.8 m/s^2 for a freely falling body

(b) **When a body is thrown vertically upwards, its velocity is decreasing, so the acceleration due to gravity, g, is taken as negative.**
That is, Acceleration due to gravity = – 9.8 m/s^2 for a body thrown upwards

(c) **When a body is dropped freely from a height, its initial velocity 'u' is zero.**

(d) **When a body is thrown vertically upwards, its final velocity 'v' becomes zero.**

(e) **The time taken by a body to rise to the highest point is equal to the time it takes to fall from the same height.**

We will now solve some problems based on the motion of freely falling bodies.

Figure 28. The height of a bridge over a river can be estimated by dropping a stone from the bridge and noting the time it takes to touch the water surface in the river.

Sample Problem 1. To estimate the height of a bridge over a river, a stone is dropped freely in the river from the bridge. The stone takes 2 seconds to touch the water surface in the river. Calculate the height of the bridge from the water level (g = 9.8 m/s^2).

Solution. The stone is being dropped freely from rest, so the initial velocity of the stone, $u = 0$. Again, the velocity of stone is increasing as it comes down, so the acceleration due to gravity, g, is to be taken as positive.

Now, Initial velocity of stone, $u = 0$

Time taken, $t = 2$ s

Acceleration due to gravity, $g = 9.8 \text{ m/s}^2$ (Stone comes down)

And, Height of the bridge, $h = ?$ (To be calculated)

We know that for a freely falling body :

$$\text{Height, } h = ut + \frac{1}{2}gt^2$$

Putting the above values in this formula, we get :

$$h = 0 \times 2 + \frac{1}{2} \times 9.8 \times (2)^2$$

or $$h = \frac{1}{2} \times 9.8 \times 4$$

or $$h = 19.6 \text{ m}$$

Thus, the height of bridge above the water level is 19.6 metres.

Sample Problem 2. When a ball is thrown vertically upwards, it goes through a distance of 19.6 m. Find the initial velocity of the ball and the time taken by it to rise to the highest point. (Acceleration due to gravity, $g = 9.8 \text{ m/s}^2$)

Figure 29. A ball thrown vertically upwards.

Solution. Here, the ball is going up against the attraction of earth, so its velocity is decreasing continuously. In other words, we can say that the ball is being retarded. Thus, the acceleration in the ball is negative which means that the value of g is to be used here with the negative sign.

Here, Initial velocity of ball, $u = ?$ (To be calculated)

Final velocity of ball, $v = 0$ (It stops)

Acceleration due to gravity, $g = -9.8 \text{ m/s}^2$ (Ball goes up)

And, Height, $h = 19.6$ m

Now, putting all these values in the formula :

$$v^2 = u^2 + 2gh$$

we get : $$(0)^2 = u^2 + 2 \times (-9.8) \times 19.6$$

$$0 = u^2 - 19.6 \times 19.6$$

$$u^2 = (19.6)^2$$

So, $$u = 19.6 \text{ m/s}$$

Thus, the initial velocity of the ball is 19.6 m/s which means that the ball has been thrown upwards with a velocity of 19.6 m/s.

Let us now calculate the time taken by the ball to reach the highest point. Now, we know the initial velocity, the final velocity and the acceleration due to gravity, so the time taken can be calculated by using the equation :

$$v = u + gt$$

Here, Final velocity, $v = 0$ (The ball stops)

Initial velocity, $u = 19.6$ m/s (Calculated above)

Acceleration due to gravity, $g = -9.8 \text{ m/s}^2$ (Ball goes up)

And, Time, $t = ?$ (To be calculated)

So, putting these values in the above equation, we get :

$$0 = 19.6 + (-9.8) \times t$$
$$0 = 19.6 - 9.8\,t$$
$$9.8\,t = 19.6$$
$$t = \frac{19.6}{9.8}$$
$$t = 2 \text{ s}$$

Thus, the ball takes 2 seconds to reach the highest point of its upward journey. Please note that the ball will take an equal time, that is, 2 seconds to fall back to the ground. In other words, the ball will take a total of 2 + 2 = 4 seconds to reach back to the thrower.

Sample Problem 3. A cricket ball is dropped from a height of 20 metres.

(*a*) Calculate the speed of the ball when it hits the ground.

(*b*) Calculate the time it takes to fall through this height. ($g = 10 \text{ m/s}^2$)

Solution. (*a*) Here, Initial speed, $u = 0$

Final speed, $v = ?$ (To be calculated)

Acceleration due to gravity, $g = 10 \text{ m/s}^2$ (Ball comes down)

And, Height, $h = 20$ m

Now, we know that for a freely falling body :

$$v^2 = u^2 + 2gh$$

So,

$$v^2 = (0)^2 + 2 \times 10 \times 20$$
$$v^2 = 400$$
$$v = \sqrt{400}$$

or

$$v = 20 \text{ m/s}$$

Thus, the speed of cricket ball when it hits the ground will be 20 metres per second.

(*b*) Now, Initial speed, $u = 0$

Final speed, $v = 20$ m/s (Calculated above)

Acceleration due to gravity, $g = 10 \text{ m/s}^2$

And, Time, $t = ?$ (To be calculated)

Putting these values in the formula :

$$v = u + gt,$$

we get :

$$20 = 0 + 10 \times t$$
$$10\,t = 20$$
$$t = \frac{20}{10}$$
$$t = 2 \text{ s}$$

Thus, the ball takes 2 seconds to fall through a height of 20 metres.

Sample Problem 4. A ball is thrown up with a speed of 15 m/s. How high will it go before it begins to fall ? ($g = 9.8 \text{ m/s}^2$)

Solution. Please note that here the ball is going up against the gravity, so the value of g is to be taken as negative.

Here, Initial speed of ball, $u = 15$ m/s

Final speed of ball, $v = 0$ (The ball stops)

Acceleration due to gravity, $g = -9.8 \text{ m/s}^2$ (Retardation)

And, Height, $h = ?$ (To be calculated)

Now, putting all these values in the formula,

$$v^2 = u^2 + 2gh,$$

we get :

$$(0)^2 = (15)^2 + 2 \times (-9.8) \times h$$
$$0 = 225 - 19.6\,h$$
$$19.6\,h = 225$$

or

$$h = \frac{225}{19.6}$$
$$h = 11.4 \text{ m}$$

Thus, the ball will go to a maximum height of 11.4 metres before it begins to fall.

MASS

The mass of a body is the quantity of matter (or material) contained in it. Mass is a **scalar quantity** which has only magnitude but no direction. The mass of a body (or object) is commonly measured by an equal arm balance (see Figure 30). **The SI unit of mass is kilogram** which is written in short form as **kg.** A body contains the same quantity of matter wherever it be—whether on earth, moon or even in outer space. So, the mass of an object is the same everywhere. For example, if the mass of an object is 5 kilograms on the earth, then it will have the same mass of 5 kilograms even when it is taken to any other planet, or moon, or in outer space. Thus, **the mass of a body (or object) is constant and does not change from place to place**. Mass of a body is usually denoted by the small *'m'*. Mass of a body is a measure of inertia of the body and it is also known as inertial mass. **The mass of a body cannot be zero.**

Figure 30. A common beam balance.

Figure 31. This is a chemical balance. It is used for the accurate measurement of mass in a science laboratory.

WEIGHT

The earth attracts every body (or object) towards its centre with a certain force which depends on the mass of the body and the acceleration due to gravity at that place. **The weight of a body is the force with which it is attracted towards the centre of the earth.** In other words, the force of earth's gravity acting on a body is known as its weight.

We know that, Force = mass × acceleration

The acceleration produced by the force of attraction of the earth is known as acceleration due to gravity and written as *'g'*. Thus, the downward force acting on a body of mass *'m'* is given by :

Force = mass × acceleration due to gravity

or Force = $m \times g$

But, by definition, the force of attraction of earth on a body is known as weight W of the body, so by writing weight W in place of force in the above equation, we get :

Weight, $W = m \times g$

where m = mass of the body

and g = acceleration due to gravity

Weight is measured in the same units as force. We know that the SI unit of force is newton (N). So, **the SI unit of weight is also newton** which is denoted by the letter **N**. Let us calculate the weight of 1 kilogram mass. We know that :

$$\text{Weight, } W = m \times g$$
$$= 1 \text{ kg} \times 9.8 \text{ m/s}^2$$
$$= 9.8 \times 1 \text{ kg} \times 1 \text{ m/s}^2$$

Now, by definition 1 kg × 1 m/s^2 is equal to 1 newton, so :

Weight, W = 9.8 newtons (or 9.8 N)

Thus, **the weight of 1 kilogram mass is 9.8 newtons**. This means that the force acting on a mass of 1 kilogram at the surface of the earth is 9.8 newtons.

We have just seen that : $W = m \times g$. Now, at a given place, the value of g is constant, therefore, at a given place $W \propto m$, that is, at a given place, the weight of a body is directly proportional to its mass. It is due to this reason that at a given place, we can use the weight of a body as a measure of mass of the body.

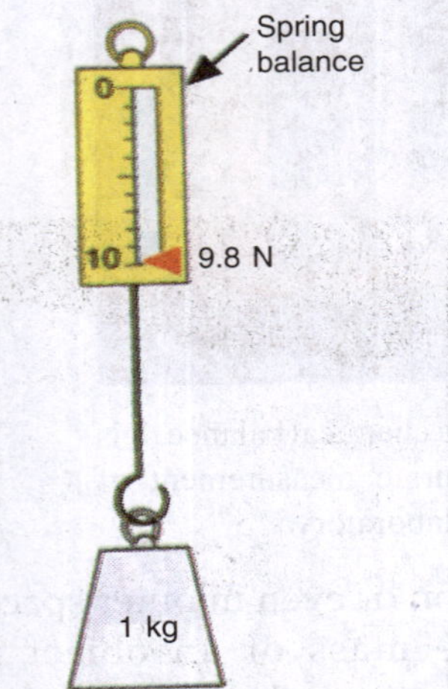

Figure 32. The weight of 1 kilogram mass is 9.8 newtons.

Figure 33. The weight of an apple of mass 100 grams is 1 newton.

Figure 34. An astronaut in 'weightless' orbit near his spacecraft. In this interplanetary space, the force of gravity is zero, so the astronaut has no weight. He is weightless. Under these conditions of weightlessness, the astronaut has to use small jets of gas to manoeuvre his moves.

Weight is a vector quantity having magnitude as well as direction. The weight of a body acts in vertically downward direction. The weight of a body is usually denoted by W. The weight of a body is given by $W = m \times g$, and since the value of g (the acceleration due to gravity) changes from place to place, therefore, **the weight of a body also changes from place to place**. Thus, **the weight of a body is not constant.** In the interplanetary space, where $g = 0$, the weight of a body becomes zero and we feel true weightlessness. Thus, **the weight of a body can be zero.**

We know that the value of acceleration due to gravity, g, decreases as we go down inside the earth and becomes zero at the centre of the earth. So, **whatever be the weight of a body on the surface of the earth, its weight becomes zero when it is taken to the centre of the earth** (because the value of g is zero at the centre of the earth). The weight of an object is measured with a spring balance (see Figures 35 and 36). The spring balance gives us the weight of the object because the extension of the spring depends on the force with which it is pulled downwards by the earth. Thus, **it is the gravitational force acting on an object which operates a spring balance, and not its mass.**

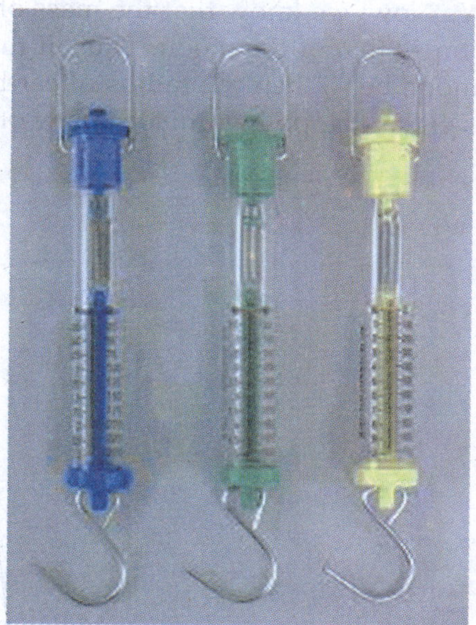

Figure 35. These are spring balances. They are used to measure weight of objects.

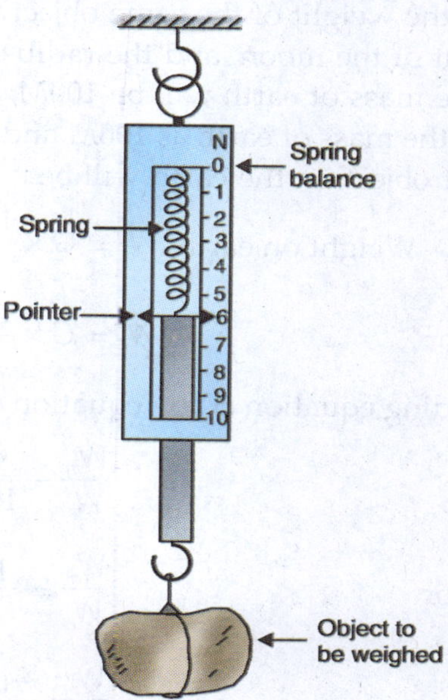

Figure 36. The spring balance reading here shows that the weight of object suspended from its hook is 6 newtons (or 6 N).

Weight of an Object on the Moon

Just as the weight of an object on the earth is the force with which the earth attracts the object, in the same way, the weight of an object on the moon is the force with which the moon attracts that object. The gravitational force of the moon is about one-sixth that of the earth, therefore, **the weight of an object on the moon will be about one-sixth of what it is on the earth.** Thus, a spring balance which shows the weight of a body to be 6 N on earth will show a weight of only 1 N when taken to the moon. The weight of an object on the moon is less than that on the earth because the mass and radius of moon are less than that of earth (due to which it exerts a lesser force of gravity).

Figure 37. This is a moon-buggy on the surface of moon. The mass of a moon-buggy is the same on the earth and on the moon. The weight of moon-buggy on the moon is, however, only about one-sixth $\left(\frac{1}{6}\right)$ of its weight on the earth. This is because the value of g on the moon is about one-sixth of the value of g on the earth.

To Show That the Weight of an Object on the Moon is $\frac{1}{6}$th of Its Weight on the Earth

Suppose we have an object of mass m. Let its weight on the moon be W_m. Again suppose that the mass of the moon is M and its radius is R. Now, according to universal law of gravitation, the weight (force) of the object on the moon will be :

$$\text{Weight on moon, } W_m = G \times \frac{M \times m}{R^2} \quad \text{... (1)}$$

This weight is actually the force with which the moon attracts the object.

Suppose the weight of the same object on the earth be W_e. Now, we know that the mass of the earth is 100 times that of the moon, and the radius of the earth is 4 times that of the moon. Thus, if mass of moon is M, then the mass of earth will be $100M$; and if radius of moon be R, then the radius of earth will be $4R$. Now, taking the mass of earth as $100M$ and radius of earth as $4R$, and applying universal law of gravitation, the weight of object on the earth will be :

$$\text{Weight on earth, } W_e = G \times \frac{100\,M \times m}{(4R)^2}$$

or

$$W_e = G \times \frac{100\,M \times m}{16R^2} \quad \text{... (2)}$$

Now, dividing equation (1) by equation (2), we get :

$$\frac{W_m}{W_e} = \frac{G \times M \times m \times 16R^2}{R^2 \times G \times 100M \times m}$$

or

$$\frac{W_m}{W_e} = \frac{16}{100}$$

or

$$\frac{W_m}{W_e} = \frac{1}{6}$$

or

$$\frac{\text{Weight on moon}}{\text{Weight on earth}} = \frac{1}{6}$$

or

$$\text{Weight on moon} = \frac{1}{6}\text{ Weight on earth}$$

Please note that the mass of the object is the same on the moon and the earth, but its weight on the moon is only one-sixth $\left(\frac{1}{6}\right)$ of the weight on the earth. We will now solve some problems based on mass and weight. Please note that if the value of acceleration due to gravity of earth, g, is not given in the numerical problems, then we should take its value to be 9.8 m/s^2.

Sample Problem 1. Mass of a body is 5 kg. What is its weight ?

Solution. The weight of a body is calculated by using the formula :

Weight, $W = m \times g$

Here, Mass of the body, m = 5 kg

And, Acceleration due to gravity, g = 9.8 m/s^2

So, Weight, $W = 5 \times 9.8$

$= 49$ N

Thus, the weight of the body is 49 newtons.

Sample Problem 2. What is the mass of an object whose weight is 49 newtons ?

Solution. Here, Weight, W = 49 N

Mass, m = ? (To be calculated)

And, Acceleration due to gravity, g = 9.8 m/s^2

Now, putting these values in the formula,

$$W = m \times g$$

we get :

$$49 = m \times 9.8$$

$$m = \frac{49}{9.8}$$

$$m = 5 \text{ kg}$$

Thus, the mass of the object is 5 kilograms.

Sample Problem 3. A man weighs 600 N on the earth. What is his mass ? (take $g = 10 \text{ m s}^{-2}$). If he were taken to the moon, his weight would be 100 N. What is his mass on the moon ? What is the acceleration due to gravity on the moon ?

Solution. First of all we will find out the mass of man on the earth. This can be done by using the formula :

$$W = m \times g$$

Here, Weight of man on earth, $W = 600$ N

Mass of man on earth, $m = ?$ (To be calculated)

And, Acceleration due to gravity, $g = 10 \text{ m s}^{-2}$ (on earth)

Now, putting these values in the above formula, we get :

$$600 = m \times 10$$

So,

$$m = \frac{600}{10}$$

$$m = 60 \text{ kg}$$

Thus, the mass of man on the earth is 60 kilograms. Now, the mass of a body remains the same everywhere in the universe. So, the mass of this man on the moon will also be 60 kilograms.

We will now calculate the value of acceleration due to gravity on the moon by using the same formula :

$$W = m \times g$$

Now, Weight of man on the moon, $W = 100$ N

Mass of the man on moon, $m = 60$ kg (Calculated above)

And, Acceleration due to gravity, $g = ?$ (To be calculated) (on the moon)

By putting these values in the above formula, we get :

$$100 = 60 \times g$$

So,

$$g = \frac{100}{60}$$

$$g = 1.66 \text{ m s}^{-2}$$

Thus, the acceleration due gravity on the surface of the moon is 1.66 m s^{-2}.

Sample Problem 4. How much would a 70 kg man weigh on the moon ? What would be his mass on the earth and on the moon ? (Acceleration due to gravity on moon = 1.63 m/s^2)

Solution. We will first calculate the weight of the man on the moon.

Here, Mass of the man on moon, $m = 70$ kg

Acceleration due to gravity, $g = 1.63 \text{ m/s}^2$ (on the moon)

We know that :

$$W = m \times g$$

So,

$$W = 70 \times 1.63$$

$$W = 114.1 \text{ N}$$

Thus, the man would weigh 114.1 newtons on the moon. Please note that the mass of a body is constant everywhere in the universe. So, the mass of this man would be the same on the earth as well as on the moon, that is, the mass will be 70 kg on the earth as well as on the moon.

Before we end this discussion on mass and weight, we would like to give the main differences between mass and weight in tabular form.

Differences Between Mass and Weight

Mass	*Weight*
1. The mass of an object is the quantity of matter contained in it.	**1.** The weight of an object is the force with which it is attracted towards the centre of the earth.
2. The SI unit of mass is kilogram (kg).	**2.** The SI unit of weight is newton (N).
3. The mass of an object is constant.	**3.** The weight of an object is not constant. It changes with the change in acceleration due to gravity (g).
4. The mass of an object can never be zero.	**4.** The weight of an object can be zero. For example, in the interplanetary space, where $g = 0$, the weight of an object becomes zero.

Before we go further and discuss thrust and pressure, **please answer the following questions and problems :**

Very Short Answer Type Questions

1. What is the value of gravitational constant G (*i*) on the earth, and (*ii*) on the moon ?

2. Which force is responsible for the moon revolving round the earth ?

3. Does the acceleration produced in a freely falling body depend on the mass of the body ?

4. Name the scientist who gave the three laws of planetary motion.

5. Name the scientist who explained the motion of planets on the basis of gravitational force between the sun and planets.

6. State the Kepler's law which is represented by the relation $r^3 \propto T^2$.

7. Which of the Kepler's laws of planetary motion led Newton to establish the inverse-square rule for gravitational force between two bodies ?

8. Name the property of earth which is responsible for extremely small acceleration being produced in it as a result of attraction by other small objects.

9. What is the acceleration produced in a freely falling body of mass 10 kg ? (Neglect air resistance)

10. When an object is dropped from a height, it accelerates and falls down. Name the force which accelerates the object.

11. Give the formula for the gravitational force F between two bodies of masses M and m kept at a distance d from each other.

12. What force is responsible for the earth revolving round the sun ?

13. What name has been given to the force with which two objects lying apart attract each other ?

14. What type of force is involved in the formation of tides in the sea ?

15. Which force is responsible for holding the solar system together ?

16. What is the weight of a 1 kilogram mass on the earth ? ($g = 9.8\ m/s^2$).

17. On what factor/factors does the weight of a body depend ?

18. As the altitude of a body increases, do the weight and mass both vary ?

19. If the same body is taken to places having different gravitational field strength, then what will vary : its weight or mass ?

20. If the mass of an object be 10 kg, what is its weight ? ($g = 9.8\ m/s^2$).

21. The weight of a body is 50 N. What is its mass ? ($g = 9.8\ m/s^2$).

22. A body has a weight of 10 kg on the surface of earth. What will be its weight when taken to the centre of the earth ?

23. Write down the weight of a 50 kg mass on the earth. ($g = 9.8\ m/s^2$).

24. If the weight of a body on the earth is 6 N, what will it be on the moon ?

25. State whether the following statements are true or false :

(*a*) A falling stone also attracts the earth.

(*b*) The force of gravitation between two objects depends on the nature of medium between them.

(c) The value of G on the moon is about one-sixth $\left(\frac{1}{6}\right)$ of the value of G on the earth.

(d) The acceleration due to gravity acting on a freely falling body is directly proportional to the mass of the body.

(e) The weight of an object on the earth is about one-sixth of its weight on the moon.

26. Fill in the following blanks with suitable words :

(a) The acceleration due to gravity on the moon is about .... of that on the earth.

(b) In order that the force of gravitation between two bodies may become noticeable and cause motion, one of the bodies must have an extremely large ....

(c) The weight of an object on the earth is about .... of its weight on the moon.

(d) The weight of an object on the moon is about .... of its weight on the earth.

(e) The value of g on the earth is about .... of that on the moon.

(f) If the weight of a body is 6 N on the moon, it will be about...............on the earth.

Short Answer Type Questions

27. Explain what is meant by the equation :

$$g = G \times \frac{M}{R^2}$$

where the symbols have their usual meanings.

28. (a) What do you mean by the term 'free fall' ?

(b) During a free fall, will heavier objects accelerate more than lighter ones ?

29. Can we apply Newton's third law to the gravitational force ? Explain your answer.

30. Give reason for the following :

The force of gravitation between two cricket balls is extremely small but that between a cricket ball and the earth is extremely large.

31. Describe how the gravitational force between two objects depends on the distance between them.

32. What happens to the gravitational force between two objects when the distance between them is :

(i) doubled ?

(ii) halved ?

33. State two applications of universal law of gravitation.

34. Explain why, if a stone held in our hand is released, it falls towards the earth.

35. Calculate the force of gravitation between two objects of masses 50 kg and 120 kg respectively kept at a distance of 10 m from one another. (Gravitational constant, $G = 6.7 \times 10^{-11}$ Nm^2 kg^{-2})

36. What is the force of gravity on a body of mass 150 kg lying on the surface of the earth ? (Mass of earth = 6×10^{24} kg; Radius of earth = 6.4×10^6 m; $G = 6.7 \times 10^{-11}$ Nm^2/kg^2)

37. The mass of sun is 2×10^{30} kg and the mass of earth is 6×10^{24} kg. If the average distance between the sun and the earth be 1.5×10^8 km, calculate the force of gravitation between them.

38. A piece of stone is thrown vertically upwards. It reaches the maximum height in 3 seconds. If the acceleration of the stone be 9.8 m/s^2 directed towards the ground, calculate the initial velocity of the stone with which it is thrown upwards.

39. A stone falls from a building and reaches the ground 2.5 seconds later. How high is the building ? (g = 9.8 m/s^2)

40. A stone is dropped from a height of 20 m.

(i) How long will it take to reach the ground ?

(ii) What will be its speed when it hits the ground ? (g = 10 m/s^2)

41. A stone is thrown vertically upwards with a speed of 20 m/s. How high will it go before it begins to fall ? (g = 9.8 m/s^2)

42. When a cricket ball is thrown vertically upwards, it reaches a maximum height of 5 metres.

(a) What was the initial speed of the ball ?

(b) How much time is taken by the ball to reach the highest point ? (g =10 m s^{-2})

43. Write the differences between mass and weight of an object.

44. Can a body have mass but no weight ? Give reasons for your answer.

45. A force of 20 N acts upon a body whose weight is 9.8 N. What is the mass of the body and how much is its acceleration ? (g = 9.8 m s^{-2}).
46. A stone resting on the ground has a gravitational force of 20 N acting on it. What is the weight of the stone ? What is its mass ? (g = 10 m/s^2).
47. An object has mass of 20 kg on earth. What will be its (*i*) mass, and (*ii*) weight, on the moon ? (g on moon = 1.6 m/s^2).
48. Which is more fundamental, the mass of a body or its weight ? Why ?
49. How much is the weight of an object on the moon as compared to its weight on the earth ? Give reason for your answer.

It is quite difficult to lift heavy weights on the earth but it becomes very easy to lift the same heavy weights on the moon. Why ?

Long Answer Type Questions

50. (*a*) Define mass of a body. What is the SI unit of mass ?
    (*b*) Define weight of a body. What is the SI unit of weight ?
    (*c*) What is the relation between mass and weight of a body ?
51. (*a*) State the universal law of gravitation. Name the scientist who gave this law.
    (*b*) Define gravitational constant. What are the units of gravitational constant ?
52. (*a*) What do you understand by the term 'acceleration due to gravity of earth' ?
    (*b*) What is the usual value of the acceleration due to gravity of earth ?
    (*c*) State the SI unit of acceleration due to gravity.
53. (*a*) Is the acceleration due to gravity of earth 'g' a constant ? Discuss.
    (*b*) Calculate the acceleration due to gravity on the surface of a satellite having a mass of 7.4×10^{22} kg and a radius of 1.74×10^6 m ($G = 6.7 \times 10^{-11}$ Nm^2/kg^2). Which satellite do you think it could be ?
54. State and explain Kepler's laws of planetary motion. Draw diagrams to illustrate these laws.
55. The mass of a planet is 6×10^{24} kg and its diameter is 12.8×10^3 km. If the value of gravitational constant be 6.7×10^{-11} Nm^2/kg^2, calculate the value of acceleration due to gravity on the surface of the planet. What planet could this be ?

Multiple Choice Questions (MCQs)

56. An object is thrown vertically upwards with a velocity u, the greatest height h to which it will rise before falling back is given by :
    (*a*) u/g (*b*) $u^2/2g$ (*c*) u^2/g (*d*) $u/2g$
57. The mass of moon is about 0.012 times that of earth and its diameter is about 0.25 times that of earth. The value of G on the moon will be :
    (*a*) less than that on the earth (*b*) more than that on the earth
    (*c*) same as that on the earth (*d*) about one-sixth of that on the earth
58. The value of g on the surface of the moon :
    (*a*) is the same as on the earth (*b*) is less than that on the earth
    (*c*) is more than that on the earth (*d*) keeps changing day by day
59. The atmosphere consisting of a large number of gases is held to the earth by :
    (*a*) winds (*b*) clouds (*c*) earth's magnetic field (*d*) gravity
60. The force of attraction between two unit point masses separated by a unit distance is called :
    (*a*) gravitational potential (*b*) acceleration due to gravity
    (*c*) gravitational field strength (*d*) universal gravitational constant

61. The weight of an object at the centre of the earth of radius R is :
(*a*) zero
(*b*) R times the weight at the surface of the earth
(*c*) infinite
(*d*) $1/R^2$ times the weight at the surface of the earth

62. Two objects of different masses falling freely near the surface of moon would :
(*a*) have same velocities at any instant
(*b*) have different accelerations
(*c*) experience forces of same magnitude
(*d*) undergo a change in their inertia

63. The value of acceleration due to gravity of earth :
(*a*) is the same on equator and poles
(*b*) is the least on poles
(*c*) is the least on equator
(*d*) increases from pole to equator

64. The law of gravitation gives the gravitational force between :
(*a*) the earth and a point mass only
(*b*) the earth and the sun only
(*c*) any two bodies having some mass
(*d*) any two charged bodies only

65. The value of quantity G in the formula for gravitational force :
(*a*) depends on mass of the earth only
(*b*) depends on the radius of earth only
(*c*) depends on both mass and radius of earth
(*d*) depends neither on mass nor on radius of earth

66. Two particles are placed at some distance from each other. If, keeping the distance between them unchanged, the mass of each of the two particles is doubled, the value of gravitational force between them will become :
(*a*) 1/4 times (*b*) 1/2 times (*c*) 4 times (*d*) 2 times

67. In the relation $F = G \times M \times m/d^2$, the quantity G :
(*a*) depends on the value of g at the place of observation
(*b*) is used only when the earth is one of the two masses
(*c*) is the greatest on the surface of the earth
(*d*) is of the same value irrespective of the place of observation

68. The gravitational force of attraction between two objects is x. Keeping the masses of the objects unchanged, if the distance between the objects is halved, then the magnitude of gravitational force between them will become :
(*a*) $x/4$ (*b*) $x/2$ (*c*) $2x$ (*d*) $4x$

69. An apple of mass 100 g falls from a tree because of gravitational attraction between the earth and the apple. If the magnitude of force exerted by the earth on the apple be F_1 and the magnitude of force exerted by the apple on the earth be F_2, then :
(*a*) F_1 is very much greater than F_2
(*b*) F_2 is very much greater than F_1
(*c*) F_1 is only a little greater than F_2
(*d*) F_1 and F_2 are exactly equal

70. According to one of the Kepler's laws of planetary motion :
(*a*) $r^2 \propto T^3$ (*b*) $r \propto T^2$ (*c*) $r^3 \propto T^2$ (*d*) $r^3 \propto \frac{1}{T^2}$

Questions Based on High Order Thinking Skills (HOTS)

71. If the distance between two masses is increased by a factor of 5, by what factor would the mass of one of them have to be altered to maintain the same gravitational force ? Would this be an increase or decrease in the mass ?

72. Universal law of gravitation states that every object exerts a gravitational force of attraction on every other object. If this is true, why don't we notice such forces ? Why don't the two objects in a room move towards each other due to this force ?

73. Suppose a planet exists whose mass and radius both are half those of the earth. Calculate the acceleration due to gravity on the surface of this planet.

The universal law of gravitation states that every object exerts a gravitational force of attraction on every other object. If this is true, then why don't we see the various objects in a room moving towards one another ?

74. A coin and a piece of paper are dropped simultaneously from the same height. Which of the two will touch the ground first ? What will happen if the coin and the piece of paper are dropped in vacuum ? Give reasons for your answer.

75. A stone and the earth attract each other with an equal and opposite force. Why then we see only the stone falling towards the earth but not the earth rising towards the stone ?

76. What is the actual shape of the orbit of a planet around the sun ? What assumption was made by Newton regarding the shape of an orbit of a planet around the sun for deriving his inverse square rule from Kepler's third law of planetary motion ?

77. The values of g at six distances A, B, C, D, E and F from the surface of the earth are found to be 3.08 m/s^2, 9.23 m/s^2, 0.57 m/s^2, 7.34 m/s^2, 0.30 m/s^2 and 1.49 m/s^2, respectively.

(*a*) Arrange these values of g according to the increasing distances from the surface of the earth (keeping the value of g nearest to the surface of the earth first)

(*b*) If the value of distance F be 10000 km from the surface of the earth, state whether this distance is deep inside the earth or high up in the sky. Give reason for your answer.

ANSWERS

1. (*i*) 6.67×10^{-11} Nm^2/kg^2 (*ii*) 6.67×10^{-11} Nm^2/kg^2 **2.** Gravitational force **3.** No **8.** Extremely large mass of earth **9.** 9.8 m/s^2 **10.** Gravitational force (of earth) **11.** $F = G \times \frac{M \times m}{d^2}$ **12.** Gravitational force **13.** Gravitational force **14.** Gravitational force (exerted mainly by the moon and to some extent by the sun) **15.** Gravitational force (of the sun) **16.** 9.8 N **18.** Weight varies ; Mass does not vary **19.** Weight **20.** 19.6 N **21.** 5.102 kg **24.** About 1 N **25.** (*a*) True (*b*) False (*c*) False (*d*) False (*e*) False **26.** (*a*) one-sixth (*b*) mass (*c*) six times (*d*) one-sixth (*e*) six times (*f*) 36 N **28.** (*b*) No **32.** (*i*) Becomes one-fourth (*ii*) Becomes four times **35.** 4.02×10^{-9} N **36.** 1472 N **37.** 3.57×10^{22} N **38.** 29.4 m/s **39.** 30.6 m **40.** (*i*) 2s (*ii*) 20 m/s **41.** 20.4 m **42.** (*a*) 10 m/s (*b*) 1 s **44.** Yes **45.** 1 kg ; 20 m/s^2 **46.** 20 N ; 2 kg **47.** (*i*) 20 kg (*ii*) 32 N **48.** Mass **49.** About one-sixth $\left(\frac{1}{6}\right)$ **53.** (*a*) No (*b*) 1.63 m/s^2 ; Moon **55.** 9.8 m/s^2 ; Earth **56.** (*b*) **57.** (*c*) **58.** (*b*) **59.** (*d*) **60.** (*d*) **61.** (*a*) **62.** (*a*) **63.** (*c*) **64.** (*c*) **65.** (*d*) **66.** (*c*) **67.** (*d*) **68.** (*d*) **69.** (*d*) **70.** (*c*) **71.** 25 times ; Increase **72.** In order to be able to notice the gravitational force of attraction between any two objects, at least one of the objects on the earth should have an extremely large mass. Since no object on the earth has an extremely large mass, we cannot notice such forces ; The two objects in a room do not move towards each other because due to their small masses, the gravitational force of attraction between them is very, very weak **73.** 19.6 m/s^2 , **76.** Elliptical ; That the orbit of a planet around the sun is 'circular' **77.** (*a*) 9.23 m/s^2 , 7.34 m/s^2 , 3.08 m/s^2, 1.49 m/s^2, 0.57 m/s^2, 0.30 m/s^2 (*b*) This distance F of 10000 km is high up in the sky ; The distance of 10000 km cannot be deep inside the earth because the radius of earth is only about 6400 km and the value of g at the centre of earth becomes 0 (zero).

THRUST AND PRESSURE

If we push hard on a piece of wood with our thumb, the thumb does not go into the wood [see Figure 38(*a*)]. But if we push a drawing pin into the wood with the same force of our thumb, the drawing pin goes into the wood [see Figure 38(*b*)]. These observations can be explained as follows :

Our thumb does not go into the wood because the force of thumb is falling on a large area of the wood due to which the 'force per unit area' (or pressure) on the wood is small. The drawing pin goes into the wood because due to the sharp tip of the drawing pin, the force of thumb is falling on a very small area of the wood due to which the 'force per unit area' (or pressure) on the wood becomes very large. It is clear from this example that *pressure is the force acting on a unit area of the object (here wood)*. The force of thumb produces small pressure when it acts on a large area of wood but the same force of thumb produces much greater pressure when it acts on a very small area of wood through the tip of drawing pin. Thus, **the effect**

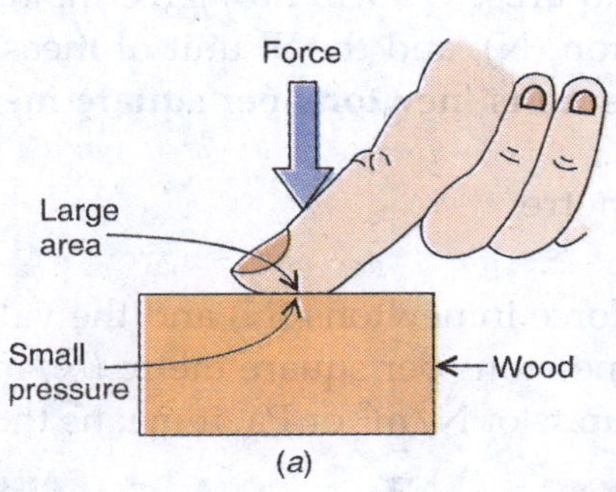

(a)

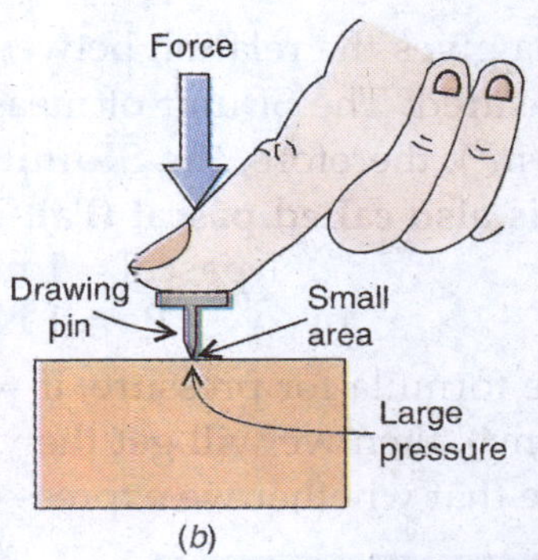

(b)

Figure 38.

of a force depends on the area of the object on which it acts.

Please note that **the weight of a body is also a force. And it always acts in the downward direction.** We will now discuss the pressure exerted by a brick on the ground in two different positions—in the lying position and in the standing position.

In Figure 39, two similar bricks (having the same weight) are placed in two different positions on the ground. The brick in Figure 39(*a*) is in the lying position whereas the brick in Figure 39(*b*) is in the standing position. The two bricks exert the same force on the ground because they have the same weight. But the two bricks exert different pressures on the ground because their areas in contact with the ground are different.

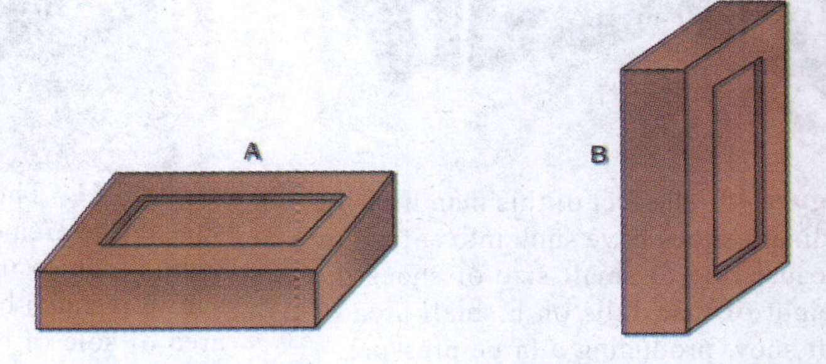

(*a*) A lying brick exerts less pressure on ground (*b*) A standing brick exerts greater pressure on ground

Figure 39.

(*i*) The brick *A* is in the lying position so its area in contact with the ground is large [see Figure 39(*a*)]. So, in this case the force of the weight of brick falls on a larger area of the ground and 'the force per unit area' (or pressure) on the ground is small (or less). Thus, the brick *A* in the lying position exerts smaller pressure on the ground.

(*ii*) The brick *B* is in the standing position so its area in contact with the ground is small [see Figure 39(*b*)]. In this case the force of the weight of brick falls on a smaller area of the ground, and 'the force per unit area' (or pressure) on the ground becomes large. Thus, the brick *B* in the standing position exerts a greater pressure on the ground.

From the above discussion we conclude that the pressure depends on two factors :

1. Force applied, and
2. Area over which force acts.

The same force can produce different pressures depending on the area over which it acts. For example, **when a force acts over a large area of an object, it produces a small pressure.** But **if the same force acts over a small area of the object, it produces a large pressure.**

We can now define pressure as follows : **Pressure is the force acting perpendicularly on a unit area of the object.** To obtain the value of pressure, we should divide the force acting on an object by the area of the object on which it acts. So, the formula for calculating pressure is :

$$\textbf{Pressure} = \frac{\textbf{Force}}{\textbf{Area}}$$

This formula gives the relation between pressure, force and area. We will now give the units in which pressure is measured. The SI unit of measuring force is newton (N), and the SI unit of measuring area is 'square metre' (m^2), therefore, **the SI unit of measuring pressure is 'newtons per square metre' (N/m^2 or $N\ m^{-2}$) which is also called pascal (Pa).** Thus,

$$1 \text{ pascal} = 1 \text{ newton per square metre}$$

or $$1 \text{ Pa} = 1 \text{ N/m}^2$$

In the above formula for pressure, if we put the value of force in newtons (N) and the value of area in square metres (m^2), then we will get the value of pressure in newtons per square metre (N/m^2) or pascals (Pa). Please note that whether we express the pressure in the units of N/m^2 or Pa, it means the same thing.

Figure 40. The feet of this man wearing ordinary shoes have sunk into soft snow because due to small size of shoes the weight of man falls on a small area of soft snow producing a large pressure.

Figure 41. These are snow shoes. The area of snow shoes (which comes in contact with snow) is much bigger than the area of sole of ordinary shoes worn by us in everyday life.

Figure 42. This man wearing snow shoes can walk easily on soft snow (without sinking into it). This is because due to large area of snow shoes, the weight of man is spread over a large area of soft snow producing small pressure.

We will now solve some numerical problems based on pressure.

Sample Problem 1. A force of 100 N is applied to an object of area 2 m^2. Calculate the pressure.

Solution. Here, Force = 100 N

And, Area = 2 m^2

Now, putting these values in the formula :

$$\text{Pressure} = \frac{\text{Force}}{\text{Area}}$$

we get :

$$\text{Pressure} = \frac{100 \text{ N}}{2 \text{ m}^2}$$

$$= 50 \text{ N/m}^2 \quad (\text{or } 50 \text{ Pa})$$

Thus, the pressure is 50 newtons per square metre or 50 pascals.

Sample Problem 2. A woman is wearing sharp-heeled shoes or pencil-heeled shoes (called stilettos). If the mass of this woman is 50 kg and the area of one heel is 1 cm^2, calculate the pressure exerted on the ground when the woman stands on just one heel. ($g = 10 \text{ m/s}^2$).

Figure 43. A woman wearing sharp-heeled shoes (called stilettos).

Solution. In this case the force will be the weight of woman which is given by $m \times g$ (where m is the mass of woman and g is the acceleration due to gravity). So,

$$\text{Force} = m \times g$$

$$(\text{Weight of woman}) = 50 \times 10 \text{ N}$$

$= 500 \text{ N}$

And $\quad$ Area $= 1 \text{ cm}^2$

$= \frac{1}{10000} \text{ m}^2$

Now, $\quad$ Pressure $= \frac{\text{Force}}{\text{Area}}$

$= \frac{500 \times 10000}{1}$

$= 5000{,}000 \text{ N/m}^2$ (or 5000,000 Pa)

Thus, the pressure exerted by a 50 kg woman wearing sharp-heeled shoes and standing on only one heel of area 1 cm^2 is 5000,000 Nm^2 (which is a very, very large pressure).

Sample Problem 3. A rectangular wooden block has mass of 4 kg. The length, breadth and height of this wooden block are 50 cm, 25 cm and 10 cm, respectively. Find the pressure on the table top :

(*a*) when the wooden block is kept with its surface measuring 50 cm × 25 cm on the table.

(*b*) when the wooden block is kept with its surface measuring 25 cm × 10 cm on the table.

(Assume : Acceleration due to gravity, $g = 10 \text{ m/s}^2$)

Solution. Here, $\quad$ Mass of wooden block, $m = 4$ kg

Acceleration due to gravity, $g = 10 \text{ m/s}^2$

So, $\quad$ Weight of wooden block, $W = m \times g$

$= 4 \times 10$

$= 40 \text{ N}$

Since weight is a force, so we can say that the force exerted by the wooden block on the table top is 40 N. We will now calculate the pressure in the two cases.

(*a*) *In the first case* : $\quad$ Force = 40 N $\quad$ (Calculated above)

And, $\quad$ Area $= 50 \text{ cm} \times 25 \text{ cm}$

$= \frac{50}{100} \text{ m} \times \frac{25}{100} \text{ m}$

$= 0.5 \text{ m} \times 0.25 \text{ m}$

$= 0.125 \text{ m}^2$

Now, $\quad$ Pressure $= \frac{\text{Force}}{\text{Area}}$

$= \frac{40}{0.125}$

$= 320 \text{ N m}^{-2}$ (or 320 Pa)

Figure 44.

Thus, the pressure exerted by the wooden block on table top when kept on its face measuring 50 cm × 25 cm is 320 N m^{-2} or 320 pascals (see Figure 44).

(*b*) *In the second case* : $\quad$ Force = 40 N $\quad$ (Same as above)

And, $\quad$ Area $= 25 \text{ cm} \times 10 \text{ cm}$

$= \frac{25}{100} \text{ m} \times \frac{10}{100} \text{ m}$

$= 0.25 \text{ m} \times 0.1 \text{ m}$

$= 0.025 \text{ m}^2$

Now, $\quad$ Pressure $= \frac{\text{Force}}{\text{Area}}$

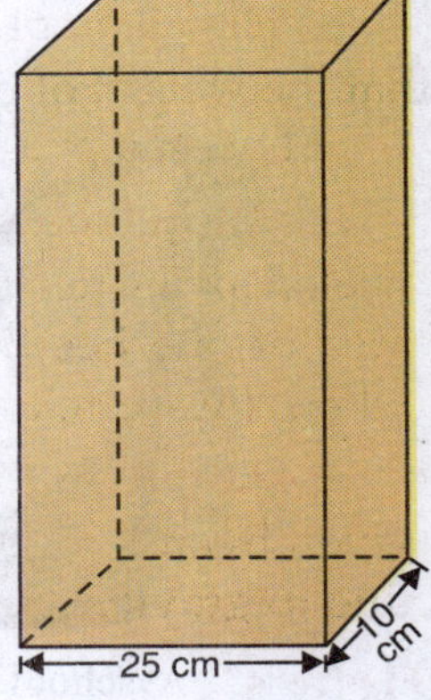

Figure 45.

$$= \frac{40}{0.025}$$

$$= 1600 \text{ N m}^{-2} \quad \text{(or 1600 Pa)}$$

Thus, the pressure exerted by the wooden block on table top when kept on its face measuring 25 cm × 10 cm is 1600 N m^{-2} or 1600 pascals (see Figure 45).

Please note that the **SI unit of pressure is pascal** whose symbol is **Pa.** Actually, pascal is a very small unit of pressure, so many times a bigger unit of pressure called 'kilopascal' (kPa) is used.

We have just defined pressure in terms of force. Pressure can also be defined in terms of 'thrust'. **The force acting on a body perpendicular to its surface is called thrust.** Actually, thrust is the total force acting on the surface of a body. So, we can also define pressure as follows : **Thrust per unit area is called pressure.** That is :

$$\textbf{Pressure} = \frac{\textbf{Thrust}}{\textbf{Area}}$$

The unit of thrust is the same as that of force. That is, **the SI unit of thrust is newton (N).** Actually, for most of the purposes, the terms 'force' and 'thrust' are used in the same sense. So, we will be using the term 'force' in all our discussions. The students are, however, free to use the term 'thrust.'

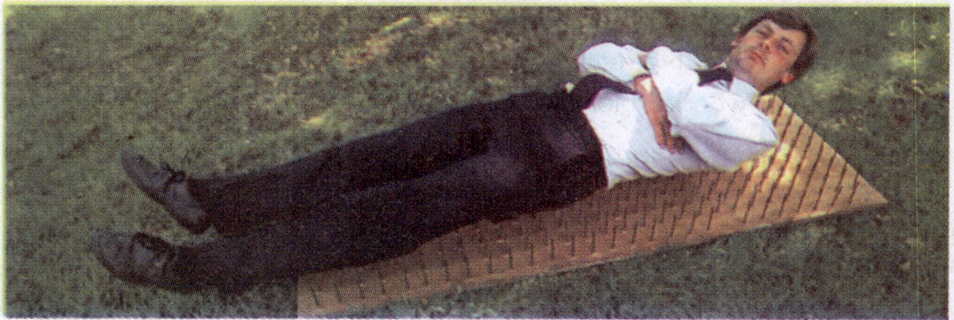

Figure 46. Explain why, a person can lie on a bed of nails if there is a very large number of nails (Please don't try it yourself. It may prove to be dangerous).

Explanation of Some Everyday Observations on the Basis of Pressure

We have just studied that 'pressure is the force per unit area'. This definition of pressure can be used to explain many observations of our daily life. An important point to be kept in mind in this regard is that **the same force produces less pressure if it acts on a large area but it can produce high pressure if it acts on a small area.**

1. Why School Bags have Wide Straps. A school bag has wide strap made of thick cloth (canvas) so that the weight of bag may fall over a large area of the shoulder of the child producing less pressure on the

Figure 47. A school bag has a wide strap so that the weight of books may spread over a large area of child's shoulder producing less pressure (and hence less pain).

Figure 48. A sharp knife cuts things better because due to very thin edge of its blade, the force of hands falls on a very small area of object being cut, producing high pressure.

shoulder. And due to less pressure, it is more comfortable to carry the heavy school bag. On the other hand, if the school bag has a strap made of thin string, then the weight of school bag will fall over a small area of the shoulder. This will produce a large pressure on the shoulder of the child and it will become very painful to carry the heavy school bag.

2. Why a Sharp Knife Cuts Better than a Blunt Knife. A sharp knife has a very thin edge to its blade. A sharp knife cuts objects (like vegetables) better because due to its very thin edge, the force of our hand falls over a very small area of the object producing a large pressure. And this large pressure cuts the object easily. On the other hand, a blunt knife has a thicker edge. A blunt knife does not cut an object easily because due to its thicker edge, the force of our hand falls over a larger area of the object and produces lesser pressure. This lesser pressure cuts the object with difficulty.

3. Why the Tip of a Needle is Sharp. The tip of a sewing needle is sharp so that due to its sharp tip, the needle may put the force on a very small area of the cloth, producing a large pressure sufficient to pierce the cloth being stitched. A nail has a pointed tip, so that when it is hammered, the force of hammer falls on a very small area of wood (or wall) creating a large pressure which pushes the nail into wood (or wall).

4. Why the Pressure on Ground is More when a Man is Walking than when He is Standing. When a man is walking, then at one time only his one foot is on the ground. Due to this, the force of weight of man falls on a smaller area of the ground and produces more pressure on the ground. On the other hand, when the man is standing, then both his feet are on the ground. Due to this the force of weight of the man falls on a larger area of the ground and produces lesser pressure on the ground.

5. Why the Depression is Much More when a Man Stands on the Cushion than when He Lies Down on it. When a man stands on a cushion then only his two feet (having small area) are in contact with the cushion. Due to this the weight of man falls on a small area of the cushion producing a large pressure. This large pressure causes a big depression in the cushion. On the other hand, when the same man is lying on the cushion, then his whole body (having large area) is in contact with the cushion. In this case the weight of man falls on a much larger area of the cushion producing much smaller pressure. And this smaller pressure produces a very little depression in the cushion.

The tractors have broad tyres so that there is less pressure on the ground and the tyres do not sink into comparatively soft ground in the fields. A wide steel belt is provided over the wheels of army tanks so that they exert less pressure on the ground and do not sink into it. Wooden sleepers (or concrete sleepers) are kept below the railway line so that there is less pressure of the train on the ground and railway line may not sink into the ground. The snow shoes have large, flat soles so that there is less pressure on the soft snow and stop the wearer from sinking into it.

Figure 49. The wide tyres of this tractor spread the weight of tractor and its trolley over a large area of ground producing lesser pressure on ground so that it can travel over soft or muddy ground without sinking in it.

Figure 50. Concrete sleepers (or wooden sleepers) are kept below the iron rails of railway track so that the weight of passing train is spread over a large area of ground and the track may not sink into the ground.

It is easier to walk on soft sand if we have flat shoes rather than shoes with sharp heels (or pencil heels). This is because a flat shoe has a greater area in contact with the soft sand due to which there is less pressure on the soft sand. Due to this the flat shoes do not sink much in soft sand and it is easy to walk on it. On the other hand, a sharp heel has a small area in contact with the soft sand and so exerts a greater pressure on the soft sand. Due to this greater pressure, the sharp heels tend to sink deep into soft sand making it difficult for the wearer to walk on soft sand.

From the above discussion we conclude that in some everyday situations, the effect of force has to be increased whereas in other situations, the effect of force has to be decreased. For example, **the effect of force is increased in tools like knives, axes, nails and pins, etc., by decreasing the area on which the force acts (so that the pressure is more).** On the other hand, **the effect of force is decreased in laying the foundations of buildings and dams by increasing the area on which the force acts (so that the pressure is less).** For example, the foundations of buildings and dams are laid on a larger area of ground so that the weight of the building or dam (to be constructed) produces less pressure on ground (and the building or dam may not sink into the ground).

PRESSURE IN FLUIDS

Water is a liquid. When we pour some water on a table, it 'flows'. Air is a gas (or rather a mixture of gases). Air flows from one place to another. **Those substances which can flow easily are called fluids. All the liquids and gases are fluids.** Water and air are the two most common fluids. We have already studied that solids exert pressure on a surface due to their weight. Fluids also have weight. So, fluids (liquids and gases) also exert pressure on the container in which they are enclosed. **A fluid (liquid or gas) exerts pressure in all directions – even upwards !** We will now discuss buoyancy which is a property exhibited by fluids.

Figure 51. Water is a fluid (because it can flow). In fact, all the liquids and gases are fluids. Fluids exert pressure in all directions—even upwards !

BUOYANCY

When an object is placed in a liquid, the liquid exerts an 'upward force' on it. For example, when a piece of cork is held below the surface of water by applying the force of our thumb and then released, the cork immediately rises to the surface (see Figure 52). It appears as if some upward force is exerted by water on the cork which pushes it to the surface.

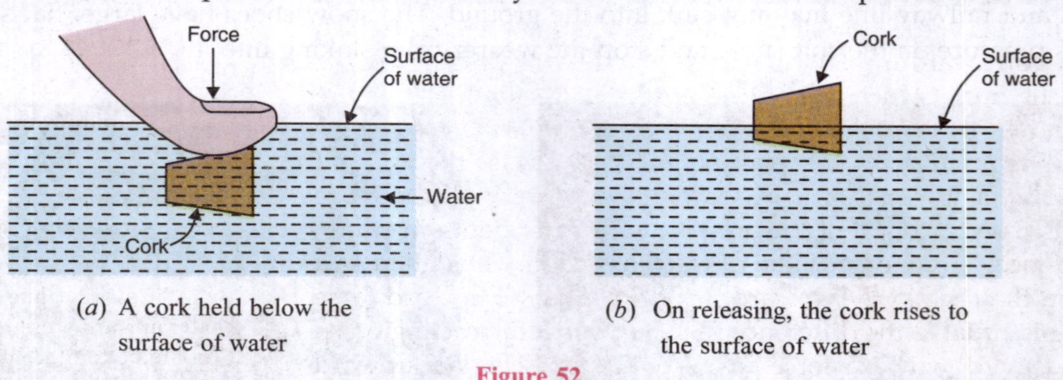

(*a*) A cork held below the surface of water

(*b*) On releasing, the cork rises to the surface of water

Figure 52.

If we lift a stone lying at the bottom of a pond, it appears to be light as long as it is being lifted inside water. But as soon as the stone is lifted out of water into air, the same stone feels to be much heavier. This means that some upward force acts on the stone when it is immersed in water and makes it feel lighter. Let us take another example. While taking bath, we find that as long as the mug filled with water remains immersed in the bucket full of water, it appears to be light and hence easy to lift. But as soon as the mug filled with water is lifted out of the bucket of water, it feels much heavier. This observation also shows that as long as the mug filled with water is inside the water surface, some upward force acts on it which reduces its effective weight and makes it appear lighter. In general, ***whenever an object (or body) is immersed in water (or any other liquid), it appears to lose some weight and feels lighter.***

From all the above examples, we conclude that **the objects appear to be less heavy when submerged in water than they are in air.** The objects appear to be less heavy in water because the water exerts an upward force on them. It is not only water which exerts an upward force on the objects immersed in it. In fact, **every liquid exerts an upward force on the objects immersed in it.** The tendency of a liquid to exert an upward force on an object placed in it, is called **buoyancy.** Even the gases exhibit the property of buoyancy. We will now discuss the buoyant force.

Buoyant Force

When an object is immersed in a liquid, it experiences an upward force. This upward force is called buoyant force. Thus, **the upward force acting on an object immersed in a liquid is called buoyant force.** It is due to the upward 'buoyant force' exerted by a liquid that the weight of an object appears to be less in the liquid than its actual weight in air. **The upward force exerted by a liquid is also known as 'upthrust'.** In other words, **the buoyant force is also known as upthrust.** It is due to the upward force ('buoyant force' or 'upthrust') exerted by water that we are able to swim in water and ships float in water. If there were no upward force of water, we would not be able to swim, and the ships would also sink. **It is the buoyant force which makes the heavy objects seem lighter in water.** We will now discuss the cause of buoyant force.

Figure 53. This sea diver is lifting an object lying under water in the sea. He finds that it is very easy to lift the object lying under water at the bottom of sea. This is because sea-water exerts an upward force (buoyant force or upthrust) on the object submerged in water and makes it feel much lighter (than that on ground).

Cause of Buoyant Force

In order to understand why liquids exert an upward buoyant force, let us consider a mug filled with water immersed in a bucket containing water as shown in Figure 54. Water exerts force on the sides of the mug as well as on its top and bottom (shown by arrows). The sideways forces exerted by water on the mug, being equal and opposite, cancel out. Now, there is a force of water acting on the top of the mug (which acts in the downward direction), and a force of water acting on the bottom of the mug (which acts in the upward direction) (see Figure 54). It is known that ***the pressure exerted by a liquid increases with depth and acts in all directions (even upwards).*** Now, as the top *A* of the mug is at a lower depth in water, it experiences less force downwards. The bottom *B* of the mug is at a greater depth in water, so it experiences more force in the upward direction. Thus, there is a net force on the mug in the upward direction. The net upward force on the mug is equal to the difference in the upward force acting on its bottom and the downward force acting on its top. This net upward force acting on the mug is the buoyant force (which reduces the effective weight of mug and makes it feel lighter inside the water). From this discussion we conclude that : **As we lower an object into a liquid, the greater upward pressure of liquid underneath it provides an upward force called the buoyant force (or upthrust).**

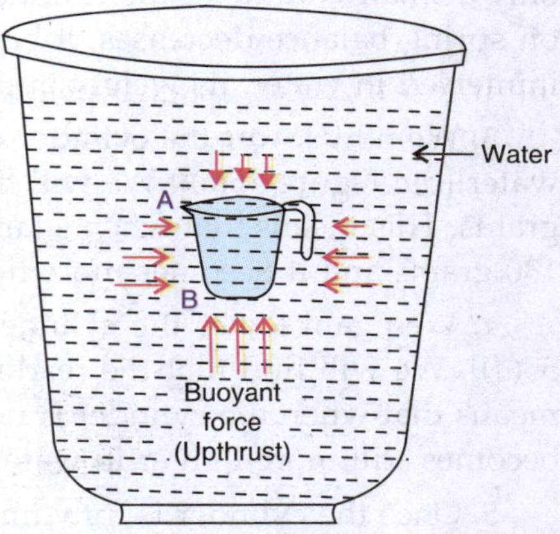

Figure 54. Cause of buoyant force is the greater upward pressure exerted by water on the bottom of mug because it is at a greater depth inside the water.

We will now describe an experiment to study the magnitude of buoyant force acting on a body when the body is gradually dipped in a liquid like water.

Experiment to Study the Magnitude of Buoyant Force

The experiment to study the magnitude of buoyant force can be performed as follows :

1. We take a small metal cylinder *C* and suspend it from the hook of a spring balance *B* as shown in Figure 55(*a*). The reading of spring balance will give the weight of metal cylinder in air. We can see from Figure 55(*a*) that the weight of metal cylinder in air is 150 grams. This is the real weight of the metal cylinder (because it has been taken in air).

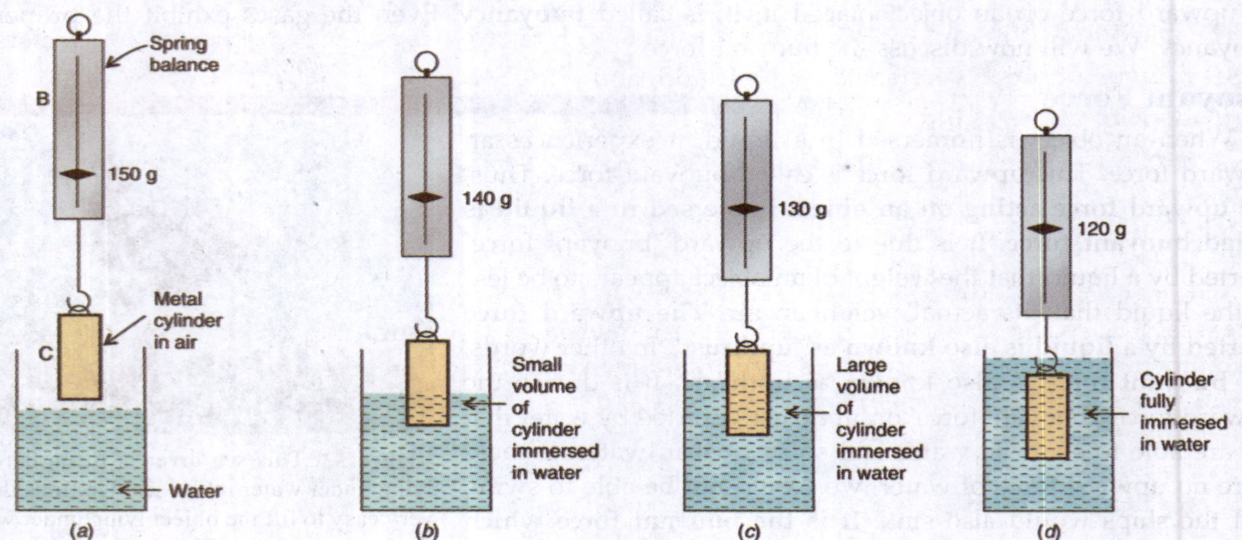

Figure 55. Experiment to study the magnitude of buoyant force.

2. Let us lower the cylinder attached to the spring balance in a container of water in such a way that only a small volume of the cylinder is immersed in water [see Figure 55(*b*)]. We will find that the reading on spring balance decreases, it becomes 140 grams. This means that when a small part of the cylinder is immersed in water, its weight appears to decrease from 150 grams to 140 grams, and it becomes lighter.

3. We now lower the cylinder further down in water so that a large volume of cylinder is immersed in water [see Figure 55(*c*)]. We will find that the reading on spring balance decreases further, it becomes 130 grams. This means that when a large volume of cylinder is dipped in water, its weight decreases further to 130 grams and it becomes more lighter in water.

4. We again lower the cylinder further so that the cylinder gets fully immersed in water [see Figure 55(*d*)]. We will find that the reading on spring balance decreases still further, it becomes 120 grams. This means that when the cylinder is fully immersed in water, its weight decreases further to 120 grams, and it becomes still more lighter in water.

5. Once the cylinder is fully immersed in water, then the maximum loss in the weight of cylinder takes place. Any further lowering of cylinder in water does not reduce the weight of cylinder. In the above experiment, the maximum loss in weight of cylinder on fully immersing in water is 150 – 120 = 30 grams. Now, even if we lower the fully immersed cylinder more and more in water, there will be no further loss in its weight.

From the above discussion we conclude that as more and more volume of an object is immersed in a liquid, the apparent weight of the object goes on decreasing and it seems to become more and more lighter. But once the object is completely immersed under the liquid, then further lowering it in liquid does not make it any more lighter. This means that **the maximum loss in weight of an object takes place when it is fully immersed in a liquid.**

We know that an object immersed in a liquid appears to lose weight and become lighter due to the upward buoyant force of the liquid. This means that **as more and more volume of the object is immersed in a liquid, the upward buoyant force acting on it increases.** But once the object is completely immersed in a liquid, then lowering it further in the liquid does not increase the buoyant force. This means that **the maximum upward 'buoyant force' acts on an object when it is completely immersed in the liquid.** We will now discuss the factors which affect the buoyant force.

Factors Affecting Buoyant Force

The magnitude of buoyant force acting on an object immersed in a liquid depends on two factors :

(*i*) **volume of object immersed in the liquid,** and

(*ii*) **density of the liquid.**

Let us discuss these two factors in somewhat detail, one by one.

1. The buoyant force exerted by a liquid depends on the volume of the solid object immersed in the liquid

As the volume of solid object immersed inside the liquid increases, the upward 'buoyant force' also increases. And when the object is completely immersed in the liquid, the buoyant force becomes the maximum and remains constant. Please note that **the magnitude of buoyant force acting on a solid object does not depend on the nature of the solid object.** It depends only on its volume. For example, if two balls made of different metals having different weights but equal volumes are fully immersed in a liquid, they will experience an equal upward 'buoyant force' (and undergo an equal loss in weight). This is because both the balls displace equal weight of the liquid due to their equal volumes.

2. The buoyant force exerted by a liquid depends on the density of the liquid in which the object is immersed

The liquid having higher density exerts more upward buoyant force on an object than another liquid having lower density. Thus, **as the density of liquid increases, the buoyant force exerted by it also increases.** For example, sea-water has higher density than fresh water, therefore, sea-water will exert more buoyant force on an object immersed in it than the fresh water. **It is easier to swim in sea-water because sea-water**

(*a*) Groundnut oil has lower density than water. So, groundnut oil will exert less buoyant force on an object immersed in it (than water)

(*b*) The density of water is more than groundnut oil but less than that of glycerine. So, water will exert more buoyant force than groundnut oil but less than that exerted by glycerine, on an object immersed in it

(*c*) The density of glycerine is higher than that of water. So, glycerine will exert more buoyant force on an object immersed in it (than water)

Figure 56. The buoyant force (or upward force) exerted by a liquid on an object immersed in it depends on the density of the liquid. As the density of liquid increases, the buoyant force exerted by it also increases.

exerts a greater buoyant force on the swimmer (due to its higher density). The fresh-water in a swimming pool, however, exerts a comparatively smaller buoyant force on the swimmer (due to its lower density than sea-water). Mercury is a liquid having very high density. So, mercury will exert a very great buoyant force on an object immersed in it. **Even a very heavy material like an iron block floats in mercury because mercury exerts a very high buoyant force on iron block due to its very high density.**

Before we go further and study Archimedes' principle, we should know the meaning of the term *'displaced liquid'*. This is discussed below. Suppose we have a bucket filled with water upto the brim. Now, if we immerse an object into this bucket full of water, then the object will occupy some of the volume in the bucket which was earlier occupied by water. Due to this the object will 'push out' some of the water from the bucket. This *'pushed out water'* is the *'displaced water'*. So, we can now say that when an object is immersed in a bucket filled with water, it displaces some of the water which overflows from the bucket. And **when an object is completely immersed in water, then the volume of water displaced will be equal to the volume of the object itself.**

Please note that water can flow out from a bucket on immersing an object in it only when the bucket is filled to the brim. If, however, we immerse an object in a bucket of water which is not filled to the brim, then the object will displace water due to which the level of water will rise in the bucket but no water will flow out. **The Archimedes' principle which we will study now gives a relationship between the buoyant force exerted by a liquid on an object and the weight of liquid displaced by it.** Please note that the mass of water (or any other liquid) is expressed in kilograms (or grams) but the weight of water is a force and hence it should be expressed in the unit of force called 'newton' (N). **The weight of 1 kilogram mass of water is about 10 newtons (or 10 N).**

ARCHIMEDES' PRINCIPLE

When a solid object is immersed (or dipped) in a liquid, an upward 'buoyant force' acts on the object. The magnitude of this buoyant force is given by Archimedes' principle. According to Archimedes' principle : **When an object is wholly (or partially) immersed in a liquid, it experiences a buoyant force (or upthrust) which is equal to the weight of liquid displaced by the object.** In other words :

Buoyant force (or Upthrust) acting on an object = Weight of liquid displaced by that object

For example, if a stone, on being immersed in water, displaces '10 newtons' weight of water, then according to Archimedes' principle, the buoyant force acting on this stone will be equal to '10 newtons'. Thus, **the magnitude of buoyant force acting on an object immersed in a liquid is equal to the weight of liquid displaced by the immersed object.**

Figure 57. Archimedes : The scientist who said that when an object is wholly (or partially) submerged in a liquid, it experiences an upward force which is equal to the weight of liquid displaced by the object.

Please note that **even gases (like air) exert an upward force (or buoyant force) on the objects placed in them** but in most cases it is so small that we usually ignore it. In fact, Archimedes' principle is applicable to objects in liquids as well as gases. Now, liquids and gases are known by the common name of 'fluids'. So, sometimes the word 'liquid' in the definition of Archimedes' principle is replaced by 'fluid' to make it more general. Thus, Archimedes' principle can also be stated as : *When an object is wholly (or partially) immersed in a fluid, it experiences a buoyant force (or upthrust) which is equal to the weight of fluid displaced by the object.* **It is the buoyant force (or upthrust) due to displaced air which makes a balloon rise in air.** We will now solve a numerical problem based on Archimedes' principle.

Figure 58. It is the buoyant force (or upthrust) due to displaced air which makes this hot-air balloon rise up in the air.

Sample Problem. When an aluminium object is immersed in water, it displaces 5 kg of water. How much is the buoyant force acting on the aluminium object in newtons ? (g = 10 m/s²).

Solution. According to Archimedes' principle, the buoyant force acting on this aluminium object will be equal to the weight of water displaced by this aluminium object. So, all that we have to do is to find the weight of water displaced in 'newtons'. That will give us the buoyant force. We know that :

$$\text{Weight, } W = m \times g$$

Here, Mass of water, m = 5 kg

And, Acceleration due to gravity, $g = 10 \text{ m/s}^2$

Now, putting these values of m and g in the above formula, we get :

$$\text{Weight of water, } W = 5 \times 10 \text{ N}$$
$$= 50 \text{ N}$$

Now, since the weight of water displaced by the aluminium object is 50 newtons, therefore, the buoyant force acting on the aluminium object (due to water) will also be 50 newtons.

Applications of Archimedes' Principle

Archimedes' principle has many applications (or uses). The important applications of Archimedes' principle are given below :

1. Archimedes' principle is used in determining the relative density of a substance.
2. The hydrometers used for determining the density of liquids are based on Archimedes' principle.
3. The lactometers used for determining the purity of milk are based on Archimedes' principle.
4. Archimedes' principle is used in designing ships and submarines.

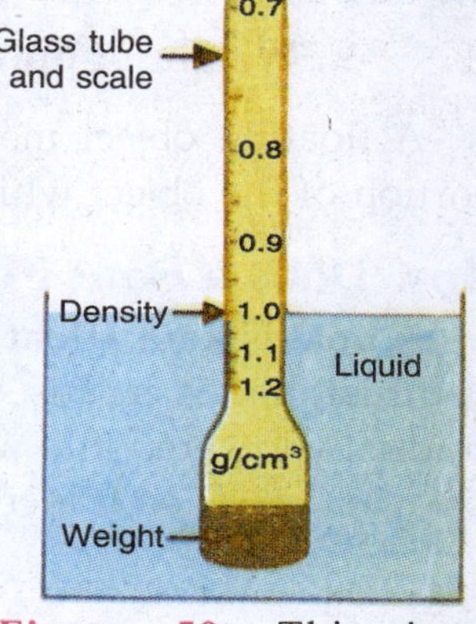

Figure 59. This is a hydrometer. It is used to measure density of liquids. Hydrometer works on Archimedes' principle.

We will describe all these applications of Archimedes' principle in detail in higher classes. At the moment, we will explain why some objects float whereas others sink in a liquid.

WHY OBJECTS FLOAT OR SINK IN A LIQUID

When a piece of wood is placed in water, it floats but when a piece of iron is put in the same water, it sinks to the bottom. We will now discuss why some objects float and others sink in the same liquid. **When an object is put in a liquid, then two forces act on it :**

(i) **Weight of the object acting downwards (which tends to pull down the object),** and

(ii) **Buoyant force (or upthrust) acting upwards (which tends to push up the object).**

Now, whether an object will float or sink in a liquid will depend on the relative magnitudes of these two forces (weight and buoyant force) acting on the object in opposite directions. Three cases arise :

(*a*) If the buoyant force (or upthrust) exerted by the liquid is less than the weight of the object, the object will sink in the liquid.

(*b*) If the buoyant force (or upthrust) exerted by the liquid is equal to the weight of the object, then the object will float in the liquid.

(*c*) If the buoyant force (or upthrust) exerted by the liquid is more than the weight of the object, the object will rise in the liquid and then float.

From the above discussion we conclude that **an object will float in a liquid if the upward buoyant force it receives from the liquid is great enough to overcome the downward force of its weight.** We will now discuss the principle of flotation of objects (or bodies).

The Principle of Flotation

When the weight of an object acting downwards is equal to the upward buoyant force exerted by the liquid, the buoyant force will balance the weight of object due to which the object will float in the liquid. So, for an object to float in a liquid, *the weight of object should be equal to buoyant force acting on it* (see Figure 60). But by Archimedes' principle, *the buoyant force acting on an object is equal to the weight of liquid displaced by it*. So, we can say that *the condition for an object to float in a liquid is that the weight of object should be equal to the weight of liquid displaced by it*. This condition gives us the principle of flotation which can be stated as follows.

Block of wood floats
Weight of block of wood
Water
Buoyant force exerted by water

Figure 60. This block of wood floats in water because its downward acting 'weight' is balanced by the upward acting 'buoyant force' exerted by water.

According to the principle of flotation : **An object will float in a liquid if the weight of object is equal to the weight of liquid displaced by it.** That is, for flotation :

Weight of object = Weight of liquid displaced by it

A floating object may be partly or totally submerged in the liquid. The liquid is displaced by that portion of the object which is submerged under liquid.

How Does a Boat Float in Water

A boat is kept afloat by an upward force from the water. This upward force is called buoyant force (or upthrust) and it is caused by the pressure of water 'pushing up' on the bottom of the boat. When a boat is gradually lowered into water (in a river or sea), it displaces more and more water due to which the upward 'buoyant force' on it increases. The boat stops sinking down into water when the buoyant force acting on it

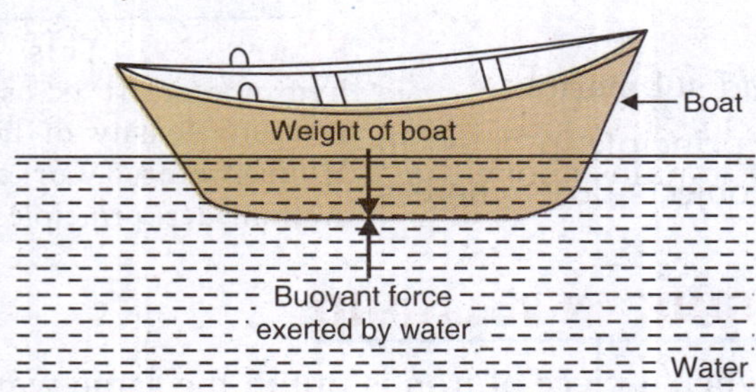

Figure 61. A floating boat displaces water equal to its own weight. This displaced water exerts buoyant force to balance the weight of boat and keep it afloat.

Figure 62. This boat is overloaded with people. Let us hope that this boat will reach the other side of the river safely. Many people in our country meet their watery graves when they travel in boats like this.

is just enough to support the weight of boat (see Figure 61). Now, Archimedes' principle says that the buoyant force is equal to the weight of liquid displaced by the boat. So, **when a boat is floating, the weight of water displaced by the submerged part of the boat is equal to the weight of the boat.**

As more and more people get into the boat, the boat becomes lower and lower in water. When the boat becomes lower in water, it displaces more water. Due to greater weight of water displaced, the buoyant force on the boat increases. And this greater buoyant force enables the extra weight of the people in the boat to be supported. If, however, the water level reaches the upper edge of boat, no further increase in buoyant force is possible because the boat cannot displace any more water. If any more people get into the boat in this condition, the boat will sink.

The Density of Floating Objects

We have just learnt that for an object to float in a liquid, the weight of liquid displaced by it should be equal to its own weight. This can happen if the object has a lower density (or lower average density) than the liquid. If, however, the object has a higher density than the liquid, then the weight of liquid displaced will be less than the weight of the object and the object will not float, it will sink.

We can tell whether an object will float (or sink) in a liquid by comparing its density (or average density) with that of the liquid.

1. An object will float in a liquid if its density (or average density) is less than that of the liquid (see Figure 63). This point will become more clear from the following examples :

(*i*) The density of cork is less than that of water, so cork floats in water.

(*ii*) The density of wood is less than that of water, therefore, wood floats in water.

(*iii*) The density of ice is less than that of water, so ice floats in water.

(*iv*) The density of glass is less than that of mercury, so a piece of glass floats in mercury.

(*v*) The density of iron is less than that of mercury, therefore, a nail of iron floats in mercury.

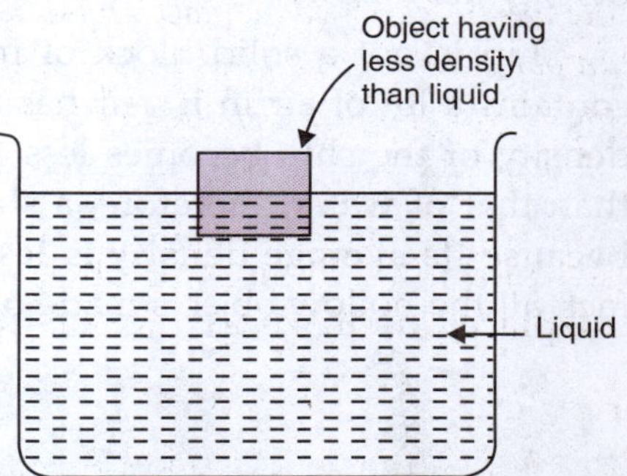

Figure 63. If the density of an object is less than that of liquid, it floats in the liquid.

Please note that if the density of an object is less than that of the liquid, then the object floats in the liquid in such a way that a portion of the object is inside the liquid (or submerged in the liquid) and the remaining portion is above the surface of liquid (as shown in Figure 63).

2. An object will also float in a liquid if its density is equal to that of the liquid (see Figure 64). For example, tar has the same density as water, so tar just floats in water. Please note that when the density of an object is equal to that of the liquid, then the object floats in the liquid in such a way that all of it remains submerged in water (as shown in Figure 64). No part of it remains above the surface of water.

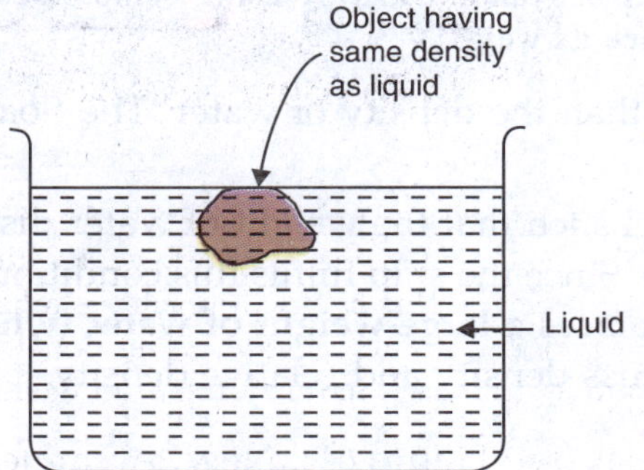

Figure 64. If the density of an object is equal to that of the liquid, it just floats in the liquid.

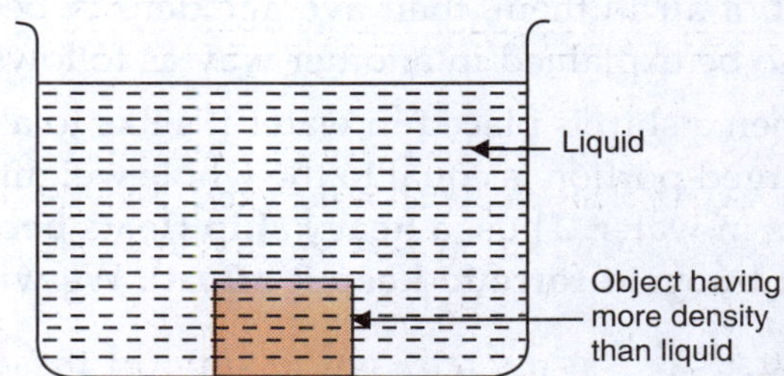

Figure 65. If the density of an object is more than that of the liquid, it sinks in the liquid.

3. An object will sink in a liquid if its density is more than that of the liquid (see Figure 65). This point will become more clear from the following examples :

(*i*) Iron (or steel) has more density than water, so a nail of iron (or steel) will sink in water. This is why when a nail of iron (or steel) is placed on the surface of water in a trough, it immediately sinks to the bottom.

(*ii*) Glass has more density than water, so a piece of glass will sink in water.

(*iii*) Aluminium as well as gold have higher densities than water, therefore, a solid piece of aluminium or of gold will sink in water.

(*iv*) Mercury is a liquid metal having higher density than water, so mercury also sinks in water.

Why Ships Float

When we put a piece of iron in water, it sinks immediately because iron is denser than water. Why should then ships made from iron and steel float in water ? This can be explained on the basis of 'average density' as follows.

Ship is not a solid block of iron and steel. A ship is a hollow object made of iron and steel which contains a lot of air in it. Air has a very low density. Due to the presence of a lot of air in it, the average density of the ship becomes less than the density of water. And since the average density of ship is less than that of water, therefore, a ship floats in water. Thus, **a ship made of iron and steel floats in water because its average density is less than that of water (due to the presence of a lot of air space in it).** In fact, all the hollow objects made of dense materials (like metals) float in water because due to the presence

Figure 66. A ship floating in water. When the ship is inside the sea, it sinks in the sea water to a certain level such that the weight of sea water displaced by its submerged part is equal to the whole weight of the ship.

Figure 67. A submarine sinks in the sea by taking water into its buoyancy tanks (so as to increase its weight). Submarine can again come to the surface of sea by blowing water out of its buoyancy tanks by using compressed air (so as to reduce its weight).

of a lot of air in them, their average density becomes less than the density of water. The floating of ships can also be explained in another way as follows.

When a ship is placed in water it sinks to a certain level such that the weight of water displaced by its submerged portion is equal to the whole weight of the ship. Since the ship fulfils this condition of flotation, it floats in water. Thus, **a heavy ship floats because it displaces a large weight of water (which provides a great buoyant force to keep it afloat).** We will now discuss density and relative density.

DENSITY

Some substances appear to be heavy whereas others are light. For example, iron is heavier than aluminium and water is heavier than alcohol. In physics we describe the lightness or heaviness of different substances by using the word density. **The density of a substance is defined as mass of the substance per unit volume.** That is :

$$\text{Density} = \frac{\text{Mass of the substance}}{\text{Volume of the substance}}$$

The formula for density of a substance can also be written as :

$$\textbf{Density} = \frac{\textbf{Mass}}{\textbf{Volume}}$$

The SI unit of mass is kilogram (kg) and the SI unit of volume is cubic metre (m^3), so the **SI unit of density is 'kilograms per cubic metre'** (which is written in short form as **kg/m^3** or **$kg\ m^{-3}$**). The values of densities of some of the common substances in SI units are given below :

Densities of Some Common Substances in SI Units

Substance	*Density*	*Density can also be written as*
1. Cork	240 kg/m^3	0.24×10^3 kg/m^3
2. Wood	800 kg/m^3	0.8×10^3 kg/m^3
3. Ice	920 kg/m^3	0.92×10^3 kg/m^3
4. Water	**1000 kg/m^3**	**1.0×10^3 kg/m^3**
5. Glycerine	1260 kg/m^3	1.26×10^3 kg/m^3
6. Glass	2500 kg/m^3	2.5×10^3 kg/m^3
7. Aluminium	2700 kg/m^3	2.7×10^3 kg/m^3
8. Iron	7800 kg/m^3	7.8×10^3 kg/m^3
9. Mercury	13600 kg/m^3	13.6×10^3 kg/m^3
10. Gold	19300 kg/m^3	19.3×10^3 kg/m^3

From the above table we can see that the density of water is 1000 kg/m^3. **By saying that the density of water is 1000 kilograms per cubic metre we mean that the mass of 1 cubic metre volume of water is 1000 kilograms.** Please note that the density of water of 1000 kg/m^3 can also be expressed as 1.0×10^3 kg/m^3 (by using the powers of 10).

Figure 68. The mass of 1 cubic metre volume (1 m^3) of a substance is known as its density.

The SI unit of density (kilograms per cubic metre) is a very big unit of density because it involves the mass of 1 cubic metre volume of the substance. So, **many times a smaller unit of density called 'grams per cubic centimetre' is also used.** It is written as **g/cm^3 or $g\ cm^{-3}$**. When the mass of a substance is taken in 'grams' (g) and its volume is taken in 'cubic centimetres' (cm^3), then its density will come in the unit of 'grams per cubic centimetre' (g/cm^3 or $g\ cm^{-3}$). Grams per cubic centimetre is the common unit of density. The densities of some of the substances in common units are given below :

Substance	*Density*	*Substance*	*Density*
1. Cork	0.24 g/cm^3	6. Glass	2.5 g/cm^3
2. Wood	0.8 g/cm^3	7. Aluminium	2.7 g/cm^3
3. Ice	0.92 g/cm^3	8. Iron	7.8 g/cm^3
4. Water	**1.0 g/cm^3**	9. Mercury	13.6 g/cm^3
5. Glycerine	1.26 g/cm^3	10. Gold	19.3 g/cm^3

The density of a substance, under specified conditions, is always the same. So, **the density of a substance is one of its characteristic properties.** The density of a given substance can help us to determine its purity. We will study this in higher classes. Please note that **if the density of a substance is more than the density of water, then the substance will be heavier than water and hence sink in water.** On the other hand, **if**

the density of a substance is less than the density of water, then the substance will be lighter than water and hence float in water. We will now solve some numerical problems based on density.

Sample Problem 1. The mass of 2 m^3 of steel is 15600 kg. Calculate the density of steel in SI units.

Solution. We know that : $\text{Density} = \frac{\text{Mass}}{\text{Volume}}$

$$= \frac{15600 \text{ kg}}{2 \text{ m}^3}$$

$$= 7800 \text{ kg/m}^3$$

Thus, the density of steel in SI units is 7800 kg/m^3.

Figure 69. Aluminium is a light metal having comparatively low density. Aircraft is made from aluminium alloys to give it a low density (to keep it light), and high strength.

Figure 70. The separation of two (or more) immiscible liquids by a separating funnel is based on the difference in their densities. In this photograph, a student is separating a mixture of water and oil by using a separating funnel. Water is denser than oil so it sinks to the bottom of separating funnel. When the tap is opened, the water can be run off first.

Sample Problem 2. An object of mass 50 g has a volume of 20 cm^3. Calculate the density of the object. If the density of water be 1 g/cm^3, state whether the object will float or sink in water.

Solution. We know that :

$$\text{Density} = \frac{\text{Mass of the object}}{\text{Volume of the object}}$$

Here, Mass of the object = 50 g

And, Volume of the object = 20 cm^3

Now, putting these values of mass and volume of the object in the above formula, we get :

$$\text{Density of object} = \frac{50 \text{ g}}{20 \text{ cm}^3}$$

$$= 2.5 \text{ g/cm}^3$$

Thus, the density of object is 2.5 g/cm^3.

Since the density of object (2.5 g/cm^3) is greater than the density of water (1 g/cm^3), therefore, the object will sink in water.

RELATIVE DENSITY

The relative density of a substance is the ratio of its density to that of water. That is :

$$\text{Relative density of a substance} = \frac{\text{Density of the substance}}{\text{Density of water}}$$

We know that, Density $= \frac{\text{Mass}}{\text{Volume}}$, so by writing $\frac{\text{Mass}}{\text{Volume}}$ in place of the density in the above relation, we get:

$$\text{Relative density of a substance} = \frac{\text{Mass of the substance}}{\text{Volume of the substance}} \times \frac{\text{Volume of water}}{\text{Mass of water}}$$

Now, if we take 'equal volumes of the substance and of water', then the two volume factors of the above relation cancel out, and we are left with :

$$\text{Relative density of a substance} = \frac{\text{Mass of the substance}}{\text{Mass of an equal volume of water}}$$

This relation gives us the following definition of relative density. **The relative density of a substance is the ratio of the mass of any volume of the substance to the mass of an equal volume of water.** In other words, the relative density of a substance is the mass of the substance relative to the mass of an equal volume of water. **As the relative density is a ratio of two similar quantities (masses), it has no units.** Thus, relative density is a pure number. The relative density values of some of the common substances are given below :

Relative Densities of Some Common Substances

Substance	*Relative density*	*Substance*	*Relative density*
1. Cork	0.24	6. Glass	2.5
2. Wood	0.8	7. Aluminium	2.7
3. Ice	0.92	8. Iron	7.8
4. Water	**1**	9. Mercury	13.6
5. Glycerine	1.26	10. Gold	19.3

The relative density of a substance expresses the heaviness (or density) of the substance in comparison to water. For example, the relative density of iron is 7.8. Now, **by saying that the relative density of iron is 7.8 we mean that iron is 7.8 times as heavy as an equal volume of water.** Thus, the relative density of a substance is a number which tells us how many times the substance is heavier than an equal volume of water. The relative density of water is 1. Now, if the relative density of a substance is more than 1, then it will be heavier than water and hence it will sink in water. On the other hand, if the relative density of a substance is less than 1, then it will be lighter than water and hence float in water.

Relative density is very important in the accurate determination of density. Actually, the relative density of a substance is found accurately by using Archimedes' principle. And this relative density is then used to calculate the density of the substance. We will now solve some numerical problems based on relative density.

Sample Problem 1. The relative density of silver is 10.8. If the density of water be 1.0×10^3 kg m^{-3}, calculate the density of silver in SI units.

Solution. We know that :

$$\text{Relative Density of a substance} = \frac{\text{Density of the substance}}{\text{Density of water}}$$

Here, Relative density of silver = 10.8

Density of silver = ? (To be calculated)

And, Density of water = 1.0×10^3 kg m^{-3}

Now, putting these values of relative density of silver and density of water in the above formula, we get :

$$10.8 = \frac{\text{Density of silver}}{1.0 \times 10^3}$$

So, Density of silver = $10.8 \times 1.0 \times 10^3$ kg m^{-3}

$= 10.8 \times 10^3$ kg m^{-3}

Thus, the density of silver in SI units is 10.8×10^3 kg m^{-3}. This can also be written as 10800 kg m^{-3}.

It is obvious from the above calculations that **the density of a substance can be obtained by multiplying its 'relative density' by the 'density of water'.** Please note that sometimes the density of water is not given in the numerical problems. So, we should remember the density of water ourselves.

Sample Problem 2. The volume of a solid of mass 500 g is 350 cm^3

(*a*) What will be the density of this solid ?

(*b*) What will be the mass of water displaced by this solid ?

(*c*) What will be the relative density of the solid ?

(*d*) Will it float or sink in water ?

Solution. (*a*) Density of solid $= \frac{\text{Mass of solid}}{\text{Volume of solid}}$

$$= \frac{500 \text{ g}}{350 \text{ cm}^3}$$

$$= 1.42 \text{ g/cm}^3$$

Thus, the density of the given solid is 1.42 g/cm^3.

(*b*) The solid will displace water equal to its own volume. Since the volume of solid is 350 cm^3 so it will displace 350 cm^3 of water. Now, volume of water displaced is 350 cm^3 and the density of water in common units is 1 g/cm^3. Putting these values for water in the formula :

$$\text{Density of water} = \frac{\text{Mass of water}}{\text{Volume of water}}$$

we get, $1 \text{ g/cm}^3 = \frac{\text{Mass of water}}{350 \text{ cm}^3}$

So, Mass of water = $1 \text{ g/cm}^3 \times 350 \text{ cm}^3$

$= 350$ g

Thus, the mass of water displaced is 350 grams.

(*c*) $$\text{Relative density of solid} = \frac{\text{Density of solid}}{\text{Density of water}}$$

$$= \frac{1.42 \text{ g/cm}^3}{1 \text{ g/cm}^3}$$

$$= 1.42$$

Thus, the relative density of the solid is 1.42.

(*d*) Since the relative density of this solid (1.42) is greater than the relative density of water (which is 1), therefore, this solid is heavier than water and hence it will sink in water.

(*a*) Wood floats in water because the density of wood is less than that of water

(*b*) Ice floats in water because the density of ice is less than that of water

(*c*) Iron floats in mercury because the density of iron is less than that of mercury

Figure 71. An object floats in a liquid if its density is less than that of the liquid.

We are now in a position to **answer the following questions and problems :**

Very Short Answer Type Questions

1. Write the common unit of density.
2. What is the density of water in SI units ?
3. What is the value of relative density of water ?
4. Name the quantity whose one of the units is pascal (Pa).
5. State the units in which pressure is measured.
6. State whether the following statements are true or false :
   (*a*) The buoyant force depends on the nature of object immersed in the liquid.
   (*b*) Archimedes' principle can also be applied to gases.
7. In which direction does the buoyant force on an object due to a liquid act ?
8. What is the other name of buoyant force ?
9. Name the force which makes heavy objects appear light when immersed in a liquid.
10. What is upthrust ?
11. Name the principle which gives the magnitude of buoyant force acting on an object immersed in a liquid.
12. The relative density of mercury is 13.6. What does this statement mean ?
13. What name is given to 'thrust per unit area' ?
14. What is the scientific name of the 'upward force' acting on an object immersed in a liquid ?
15. What is meant by the term 'buoyancy' ?
16. What causes buoyant force (or upthrust) on a boat ?
17. Why does ice float in water ?
18. What force acting on an area of 0.5 m^2 will produce a pressure of 500 Pa ?
19. An object of weight 200 N is floating in a liquid. What is the magnitude of buoyant force acting on it ?
20. Name the scientist who gave the magnitude of buoyant force acting on a solid object immersed in a liquid.
21. The density of gold is 19 g/cm^3. Find the volume of 95 g of gold.
22. What is the mass of 5 m^3 of cement of density 3000 kg/m^3 ?
23. What is the density of a substance of mass 100 g and volume 10 cm^3 ?
24. Why does a block of wood held under water rise to the surface when released ?
25. The density of a body is 800 kg/m^3. Will it sink or float when dipped in a bucket of water ? (Density of water = 1000 kg/m^3).
26. Fill in the following blanks with suitable words :
   (*a*) Force acting on a unit area is called..................
   (*b*) It is the................ force which makes objects appear lighter in water.
   (*c*) A heavy ship floats in water because its...................density is less than that of water.

(d) In fluids (liquids and gases), pressure acts in....................directions, and pressure.................as the depth increases.

(e) In order to sink in a fluid, the density of an object must be .... than the .... of the fluid.

(f) Snow shoes work by spreading out a person's .... over a much bigger ....

(g) If the area of a snow shoe is five times........................ than the area of an ordinary shoe, then the pressure of a snow shoe on the snow is five times...............

Short Answer Type Questions

27. (a) What is the difference between the density and relative density of a substance ?
    (b) If the relative density of a substance is 7.1, what will be its density in SI units ?
28. Define thrust. What is its unit ?
29. A mug full of water appears light as long as it is under water in the bucket than when it is outside water. Why ?
30. What happens to the buoyant force as more and more volume of a solid object is immersed in a liquid ? When does the buoyant force become maximum ?
31. Why do we feel light on our feet when standing in a swimming pool with water up to our armpits ?
32. Explain why, big boulders can be moved easily by flood.
33. An iron nail sinks in water but it floats in mercury. Why ?
34. Explain why, a piece of glass sinks in water but it floats in mercury.
35. Steel sinks in water but a steel boat floats. Why ?
36. Explain why, school bags are provided with wide straps to carry them.
37. Why does a sharp knife cut objects more effectively than a blunt knife ?
38. Explain why, wooden (or concrete) sleepers are kept below the railway line.
39. Explain why, a wide steel belt is provided over the wheels of an army tank.

A wide steel belt is provided over the wheels of an army tank.

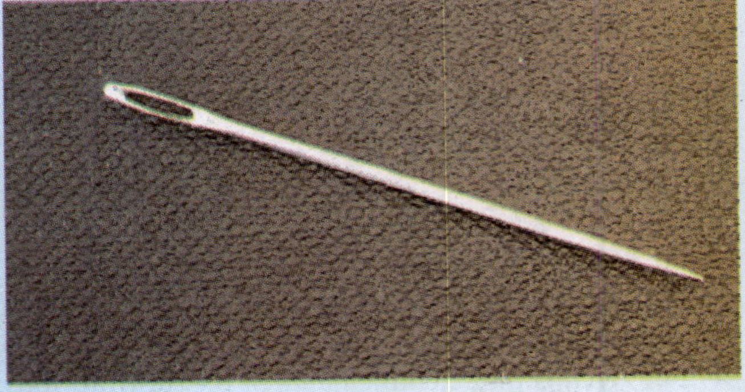

The tip of a sewing needle is sharp.

40. Explain why, the tip of a sewing needle is sharp.
41. When is the pressure on the ground more—when a man is walking or when a man is standing ? Explain.
42. Explain why, snow shoes stop you from sinking into soft snow.
43. Explain why, when a person stands on a cushion, the depression is much more than when he lies down on it.
44. Use your ideas about pressure to explain why it is easier to walk on soft sand if you have flat shoes rather than shoes with sharp heels.
45. Explain why, a nail has a pointed tip.

A nail has a pointed tip

The density of iron or steel is much higher than that of water, so an object made of iron or steel (like this car) sinks in water.

46. Explain why, buildings and dams have wide foundations.
47. Why does a ship made of iron and steel float in water whereas a small piece of iron sinks in it ?
48. Why do camels have large flat feet ?

A camel.

A large flat foot of camel.

49. Name these forces :
   (*a*) the upward push of water on a submerged object
   (*b*) the force which wears away two surfaces as they move over one another
   (*c*) the force which pulled the apple off Isaac Newton's tree.
   (*d*) the force which stops you falling through the floor.
50. A pressure of 10 Pa acts on an area of 3.0 m^2. What is the force acting on the area ? What force will be exerted by the application of same pressure if the area is made one-third ?
51. A girl is wearing a pair of flat shoes. She weighs 550 N. The area of contact of one shoe with the ground is 160 cm^2. What pressure will be exerted by the girl on the ground :
   (*a*) if she stands on two feet ?
   (*b*) if she stands on one foot ?
52. Calculate the density of an object of volume 3 m^3 and mass 9 kg. State whether this object will float or sink in water. Give reason for your answer.
53. An object weighs 500 grams in air. This object is then fully immersed in water. State whether it will weigh less in water or more in water. Give reason for your answer.
54. (*a*) Write down an equation that defines density.
   (*b*) 5 kg of material A occupy 20 cm^3 whereas 20 kg of material B occupy 90 cm^3. Which has the greater density : A or B ? Support your answer with calculations.

Long Answer Type Questions

55. (*a*) Define buoyant force. Name two factors on which buoyant force depends.
   (*b*) What is the cause of buoyant force ?
   (*c*) When a boat is partially immersed in water, it displaces 600 kg of water. How much is the buoyant force acting on the boat in newtons ? ($g = 10 \text{ m s}^{-2}$)
56. (*a*) State the principle of flotation.
   (*b*) A floating boat displaces water weighing 6000 newtons.
      (*i*) What is the buoyant force on the boat ?
      (*ii*) What is the weight of the boat ?
57. (*a*) Define density. What is the SI unit of density ?
   (*b*) Define relative density. What is the SI unit of relative density ?
   (*c*) The density of turpentine is 840 kg/m^3. What will be its relative density ? (Density of water = 1000 kg/m^3)
58. (*a*) Define pressure.
   (*b*) What is the relation between pressure, force and area ?
   (*c*) Calculate the pressure when a force of 200 N is exerted on an area of :
      (*i*) 10 m^2
      (*ii*) 5 m^2

59. (*a*) What are fluids ? Name two common fluids.
(*b*) State Archimedes' principle.
(*c*) When does an object float or sink when placed on the surface of a liquid ?

60. (*a*) How does a boat float in water ?
(*b*) A piece of steel has a volume of 12 cm^3, and a mass of 96 g. What is its density :
(*i*) in g/cm^3 ?
(*ii*) in kg/m^3 ?

61. An elephant weighing 40,000 N stands on one foot of area 1000 cm^2 whereas a girl weighing 400 N is standing on one 'stiletto' heel of area 1 cm^2.

An elephant standing on one foot.

A girl standing on one 'stiletto' heel.

(*a*) Which of the two, elephant or girl, exerts a larger force on the ground and by how much ?
(*b*) What pressure is exerted on the ground by the elephant standing on one foot ?
(*c*) What pressure is exerted on the ground by the girl standing on one heel ?
(*d*) Which of the two exerts larger pressure on the ground : elephant or girl ?
(*e*) What is the ratio of pressure exerted by the girl to the pressure exerted by the elephant ?

Multiple Choice Questions (MCQs)

62. An object weighs 10 N in air. When immersed fully in a liquid, it weighs only 8 N. The weight of liquid displaced by the object will be :
(*a*) 2 N (*b*) 8 N (*c*) 10 N (*d*) 12 N

63. A rectangular wooden block has length, breadth and height of 50 cm, 25 cm and 10 cm, respectively. This wooden block is kept on ground in three different ways, turn by turn. Which of the following is the correct statement about the pressure exerted by this block on the ground ?
(*a*) the maximum pressure is exerted when the length and breadth form the base
(*b*) the maximum pressure is exerted when length and height form the base
(*c*) the maximum pressure is exerted when breadth and height form the base
(*d*) the minimum pressure is exerted when length and height form the base

64. An object is put in three liquids having different densities, one by one. The object floats with $\frac{1}{9}, \frac{2}{11}$ and $\frac{3}{7}$ parts of its volume outside the surface of liquids of densities d_1, d_2 and d_3 respectively. Which of the following is the correct order of the densities of the three liquids ?
(*a*) $d_1 > d_2 > d_3$ (*b*) $d_2 > d_3 > d_1$
(*c*) $d_1 < d_2 < d_3$ (*d*) $d_3 > d_2 > d_1$

65. A metal in which even iron can float is :
(*a*) sodium (*b*) magnesium (*c*) mercury (*d*) manganese

66. Four balls, A, B, C and D displace 10 mL, 24 mL, 15 mL and 12 mL of a liquid respectively, when immersed completely. The ball which will undergo the maximum apparent loss in weight will be :
(*a*) A (*b*) B (*c*) C (*d*) D

67. The relative densities of four liquids P, Q, R and S are 1.26, 1.0, 0.84 and 13.6 respectively. An object is floated in all these liquids, one by one. In which liquid the object will float with its maximum volume submerged under the liquid ?
(*a*) P (*b*) Q (*c*) R (*d*) S

68. A solid of density 900 kg/m^3 floats in oil as shown in the given diagram. The oil floats on water of density 1000 kg/m^3 as shown. The density of oil in kg/m^3 could be :

(*a*) 850 (*b*) 900

(*c*) 950 (*b*) 1050

69. The density of water is 1000 kg/m^3 and the density of copper is 8900 kg/m^3. Which of the following statements is incorrect ?

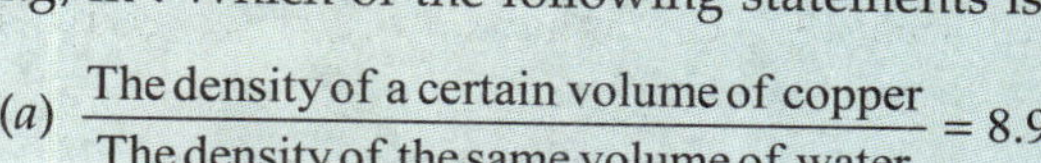

(*a*) $\dfrac{\text{The density of a certain volume of copper}}{\text{The density of the same volume of water}} = 8.9$

(*b*) $\dfrac{\text{The volume of a certain mass of copper}}{\text{The volume of the same mass of water}} = 8.9$

(*c*) $\dfrac{\text{The weight of a certain volume of copper}}{\text{The weight of the same volume of water}} = 8.9$

(*d*) $\dfrac{\text{The mass of a certain volume of copper}}{\text{The mass of the same volume of water}} = 8.9$

70. The diagrams represent four measuring cylinders containing liquids. The mass and volume of the liquid in each cylinder are stated. Which two measuring cylinders could contain an identical liquid ?

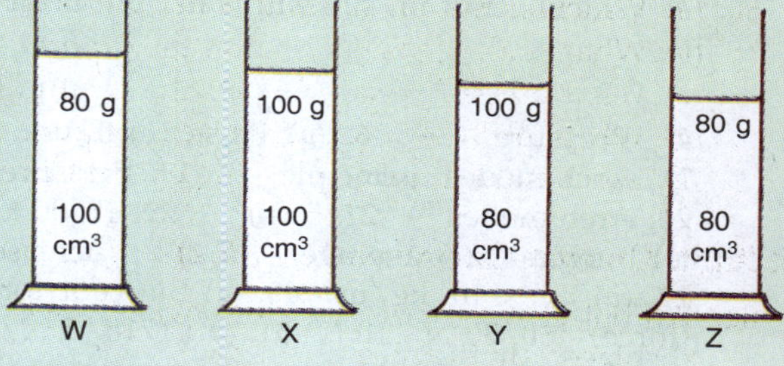

(*a*) W and X
(*b*) W and Y
(*c*) X and Y
(*d*) X and Z

71. Consider the following information in respect of four objects A, B, C and D :

Object	*Density (kg/m^3)*	*Volume (m^3)*	*Mass (kg)*
A		2	4000
B	8000	4	
C	2000		1000
D		4	2000

Which object would float on water ?

(*a*) A (*b*) B (*c*) C (*d*) D

Questions Based on High Order Thinking Skills (HOTS)

72. If two equal weights of unequal volumes are balanced in air, what will happen when they are completely dipped in water ? Why ?

73. Two different bodies are completely immersed in water and undergo the same loss in weight. Is it necessary that their weights in air should also be the same ? Explain.

74. A body floats in kerosene of density 0.8×10^3 kg/m^3 up to a certain mark. If the same body is placed in water of density 1.0×10^3 kg/m^3, will it sink more or less ? Give reason for your answer.

75. Giving reasons state the reading on a spring balance when it is attached to a floating block of wood which weighs 50 g in air.

76. If a fresh egg is put into a beaker filled with water, it sinks. On dissolving a lot of salt in the water, the egg begins to rise and then floats. Why ?

77. A beaker full of water is suspended from a spring balance. Will the reading of the balance change :
(*a*) if a cork is placed in water ?
(*b*) if a piece of heavy metal is placed in it ?
Give reasons for your answer.

78. When a golf ball is lowered into a measuring cylinder containing water, the water level rises by 30 cm^3 when the ball is completely submerged. If the mass of ball in air is 33 g, find its density.

79. A boy gets into a floating boat.
(*a*) What happens to the boat ?
(*b*) What happens to the weight of water displaced ?
(*c*) What happens to the buoyant force on the boat ?

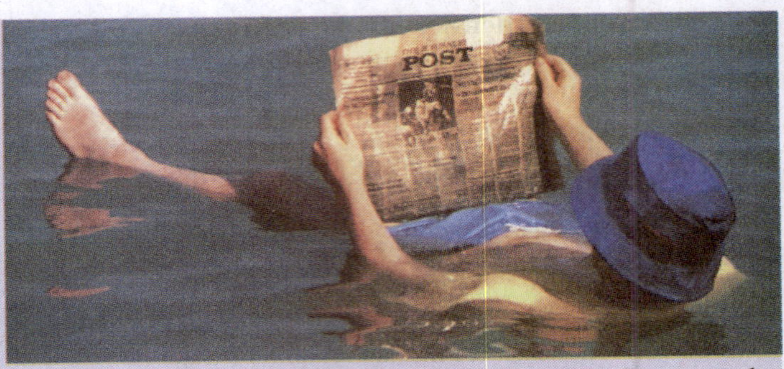

The Dead Sea lies between Israel and Jordan. It is the most salty sea in the world. The salty water of Dead Sea has such a high density and exerts such a high upward force (buoyant force or upthrust) that a person can float in it sitting up and even read a newspaper in this position (as shown in the above photograph). It is called Dead Sea because due to its very high salt content, no living things (plants and animals) can exist in it.

80. A $\frac{1}{2}$ kg sheet of tin sinks in water but if the same sheet is converted into a box or boat, it floats. Why ?

ANSWERS

4. Pressure **6.** (*a*) False (*b*) True **7.** Upward direction 8. Upthrust **9.** Buoyant force **11.** Archimedes' principle **13.** Pressure **14.** Buoyant force (or Upthrust) **18.** 250 N **19.** 200 N **20.** Archimedes **21.** 5 cm^3 **22.** 15000 kg **23.** 10 g/cm^3 **25.** Float in water **26.** (*a*) pressure (*b*) buoyant (*c*) average (*d*) all ; increases (*e*) more ; density (*f*) weight ; area (*g*) bigger ; smaller **27.** (*b*) 7.1×10^3 kg/m^3 **49.** (*a*) Buoyant force (*b*) Force of friction (*c*) Gravitational force (*d*) Reaction (force) **50.** 30 N ; 10 N **51.** (*a*) 17187.5 N/m^2 (*b*) 34375 N/m^2 **52.** 3 kg/m^3; Float in water ; Because the density of object is less than the density of water **53.** It will weigh less in water ; Because an upward force (buoyant force) equal to the weight of water displaced acts on the object when immersed in water which reduces its apparent weight **54.** (*b*) A **55.** (*c*) 6000 N **56.** (*b*) (*i*) 6000 N (*ii*) 6000 N **57.** (*c*) 0.84 **58.** (*c*) (*i*) 20 Pa (*ii*) 40 Pa **60.** (*b*) (*i*) 8 g/cm^3 (*ii*) 8000 kg/m^3 **61.** (*a*) Elephant has a larger weight of 40000 N, therefore, elephant exerts a larger force on the ground ; Elephant exerts a larger force on the ground by 40000 N – 400 N = 39600 N (*b*) 400,000 N/m^2 (*c*) 4000,000 N/m^2 (*d*) Girl (*e*) 4000,000 : 400,000 = 10 : 1 ; The pressure exerted by girl is 10 times greater than that exerted by the elephant **62.** (*a*) **63.** (*c*) **64.** (*c*) **65.** (*c*) **66.** (*b*) **67.** (*c*) **68.** (*c*) **69.** (*b*) **70.** (*d*) **71.** (*d*) **72.** The two equal weights of unequal volumes will get unbalanced when they are completely immersed in water ; This is because due to their unequal volumes, they will displace unequal volumes of water and hence suffer unequal loss in weight when completely dipped in water **73.** No, it is not necessary that their weights in air should also be the same ; This is because the two bodies have undergone the same loss in weight on completely immersing in water due to their equal volumes and not because of their equal weights, so they may have different weights in air **74.** The body will sink less in water ; This is because the density of water (1×10^3 kg/m^3) is more than the density of kerosene (0.8×10^3 kg/m^3) due to which water will exert a greater 'upward' buoyant force on the body **75.** The reading on spring balance will be 0 (zero) ; This is because the weight of floating block of wood is fully supported by the liquid in which it is floating and hence it does not exert any force on the spring balance **76.** When a lot of salt is dissolved in water, then the density of salt solution becomes much more than pure water. Due to its much higher density, the salt solution exerts a greater 'upward' buoyant force on the egg making it rise and then float **77.** (*a*) The reading of spring balance will not change if a cork is placed in water because cork, being lighter than water, floats in water (*b*) The reading of spring balance will change if a piece of heavy metal is placed in water because heavy metal, being denser than water, sinks in water **78.** 1.1 g/cm^3 **79.** (*a*) The boat sinks a little more in water, that is, the boat floats lower in water (*b*) The weight of water displaced (by the submerged part of boat) increases (*c*) The buoyant force acting on the boat increases **80.** The sheet of tin sinks in water because the density of tin is higher than that of water ; When the same sheet of tin is converted into a box (or boat) then due to the trapping of lot of 'light' air in the box (or boat) the average density of box (or boat) made of tin sheet becomes lower than that of water and hence it floats in water.

WORK AND ENERGY

We have already studied force and motion in the previous chapters of this book. We will now study that **whenever a force makes a body move, then work is said to be done. For doing work, energy is required**. When the work is done by human beings or animals (like horses), then the energy for doing work is supplied by the food which they eat. And when the work is done by machines, then energy is supplied by fuels (such as petrol and diesel, etc.) or by electricity. **When work is done, an equal amount of energy is used up**. In this chapter we will study work, energy and power. Let us discuss the work first.

WORK

In ordinary language the word "work" means almost any physical or mental activity but in physics it has only one meaning : **Work is done when a force produces motion.** For example, when an engine moves a train along a railway line, it is said to be doing work; a horse pulling the cart is also doing work; and a man climbing the stairs of a house is also doing work in moving himself against the force of gravity.

Figure 1. When an engine applies force on a train, the train moves. So, work is said to be done by the engine.

Figure 2. When a horse applies force on the cart, the cart moves. So, work is said to be done by the horse.

The work done by a force on a body depends on two factors :

(*i*) Magnitude of the force, and

(*ii*) Distance through which the body moves (in the direction of force).

We can now define work as follows : **Work done in moving a body is equal to the product of force exerted on the body and the distance moved by the body in the direction of force.** That is,

Work = Force × Distance moved in the direction of force

But usually we write :

Work = Force × Distance

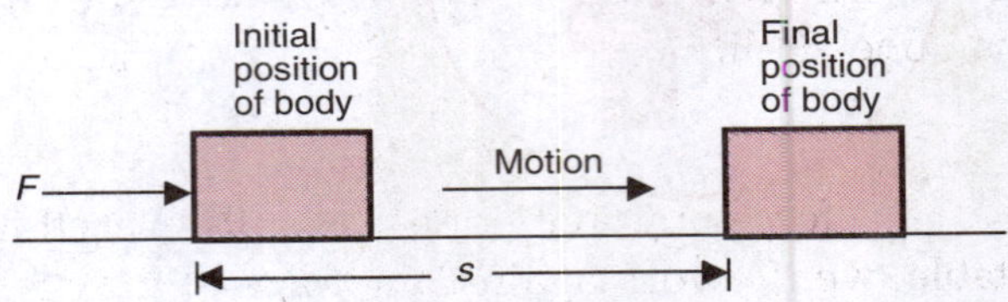

Figure 3. When a force F moves a body by distance s in its own direction, then work done, $W = F \times s$.

If a force F acts on a body and moves it a distance s in its own direction, then :

Work done = Force × Distance

or $W = F \times s$

This formula will be used to solve numerical problems on work. It should be noted that **when a body is moved on the ground by applying force, then the work is done against friction** (which opposes the motion of the body).

Please note that though most of the books use the term 'distance' in the definition of work but a few books also use the term 'displacement' in the definition of work. So, we can also write the definition of work as follows : *Work done in moving a body is equal to the product of force and the displacement of the body in the direction of force.* That is,

Work = Force × Displacement in the direction of force

or Work = Force × Displacement

or $W = F \times s$

Thus, in the discussion on work, whether we use the term 'distance' or 'displacement', it will mean the same thing. We will now discuss the unit of work.

Unit of Work

Work is the product of force and distance. Now, unit of force is newton (N) and that of distance is metre (m), so **the unit of work is newton metre** which is written as **Nm.** This unit of work is called joule which can be defined as follows : **When a force of 1 newton moves a body through a distance of 1 metre in its own direction, then the work done is known as 1 joule.** That is,

1 joule = 1 newton × 1 metre

or 1 J = 1 Nm

Thus, **the SI unit of work is joule** which is denoted by the letter J. **Work is a scalar quantity.** It should be noted that **the condition for a force to do work is that it should produce motion in an object**. That is, it should make the object move through some distance. If, however, the distance moved is zero, then the work done "on the object" is always zero. For example, **a man may get completely exhausted in trying to push a stationary wall, but since there is no displacement (the wall does not move), the work done by the man on the wall is**

Figure 4. When a force is applied to the wall (by pushing it), the wall does not move. So, no work is done on the wall.

zero (see Figure 4). However, the work done on the body of the man himself is not zero. This is because when the man pushes the wall, his muscles are stretched and blood is displaced to the strained muscles more rapidly. These changes consume energy and the man feels tired. Here is another example. **A man standing still at a bus stop with heavy suitcases in his hands may get tired soon but he does no work in this situation**. This is because the suitcases held by the man do not move at all. From the above discussion it is clear that it is not necessary that whenever a force is applied to an object, then work is done. Work is done only when a force is able to move the object. If the object does not move on applying force, no work is done at all.

Work Done Against Gravity

The force of gravity of earth pulls everything towards the surface of earth. So, if we lift a book from a table, we do work against the force of gravity. Please note that when a body is lifted vertically upwards, then the force required to lift the body is equal to its weight. So, **whenever work is done against gravity, the amount of work done is equal to the product of weight of the body and the vertical distance through which the body is lifted.**

Suppose a body of mass m is lifted vertically upwards through a distance h. In this case, the force required to lift the body will be equal to weight of the body, $m \times g$ (where m is mass and g is acceleration due to gravity). Now,

Work done in lifting a body = Weight of body × Vertical distance

or $W = m \times g \times h$

where W = work done

m = mass of the body

g = acceleration due to gravity

and h = height through which the body is lifted

We will use this formula to calculate the work done in all those cases where the object is being lifted upwards, against the force of gravity.

Figure 5 shows a man of mass m climbing the stairs having a vertical height h. In this case the work done by the man in lifting his body upwards against the force of gravity of earth is $m \times g \times h$ (where g is the acceleration due to gravity). We will now solve some numerical problems based on work.

Mass, m · Height h · Weight ($m \times g$)

Figure 5. A man climbing the stairs is doing work against gravity.

Sample Problem 1. How much work is done by a force of 10 N in moving an object through a distance of 1 m in the direction of the force ?

Solution. The work done is calculated by using the formula :

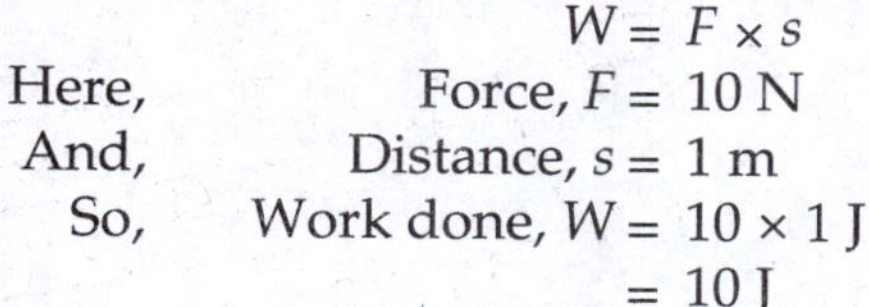

$$W = F \times s$$

Here, Force, F = 10 N

And, Distance, s = 1 m

So, Work done, $W = 10 \times 1$ J

$= 10$ J

Thus, the work done is 10 joules.

Sample Problem 2. Calculate the work done in lifting 200 kg of water through a vertical height of 6 metres (Assume $g = 10$ m/s^2).

Solution. In this case work is being done against gravity in lifting water. Now, the formula for calculating the work done against gravity is :

$$W = m \times g \times h$$

Here, Mass of water, m = 200 kg

Acceleration due to gravity, $g = 10 \text{ m/s}^2$

And, Height, $h = 6$ m

Now, putting these values in the above formula, we get :

$$W = 200 \times 10 \times 6$$

$$W = 12000 \text{ J}$$

Thus, the work done is 12000 joules.

Figure 6. In lifting the books from floor, this man is doing work against gravity,

Figure 7. In lifting the weights, this weightlifter is doing work against gravity.

Figure 8. The electric motor of this 'lift' (or 'elevator') in a building is doing work in moving up the load of people standing in it, against gravity.

Sample Problem 3. A car weighing 1000 kg and travelling at 30 m/s stops at a distance of 50 m decelerating uniformly. What is the force exerted on it by the brakes ? What is the work done by the brakes ?

Solution. In order to calculate the force, we have to find out the acceleration (or rather retardation) first.

Now, Initial speed, $u = 30$ m/s

Final speed, $v = 0$ (The car stops)

Acceleration, $a = ?$ (To be calculated)

And, Distance, $s = 50$ m

Now, we know that :

$$v^2 = u^2 + 2as$$

So,

$$(0)^2 = (30)^2 + 2 \times a \times 50$$

$$100\,a = -900$$

$$a = -\frac{900}{100}$$

Thus, Acceleration, $a = -9 \text{ m/s}^2$

The force exerted by the brakes can now be calculated by using the formula :

$$F = m \times a$$

Here, Mass, $m = 1000$ kg (Given)

And, Acceleration, $a = -9 \text{ m/s}^2$ (Calculated above)

So, Force, $F = 1000 \times (-9)$

$$F = -9000 \text{ N}$$

Thus, the force exerted by the brakes on the car is of 9000 newtons. The negative sign shows that it is a retarding force.

The work done by the brakes can be calculated by using the relation :

$$W = F \times s$$

Here, Force, $F = 9000$ N

Distance, $s = 50$ m

So, Work done, $W = 9000 \times 50$ J

$= 450000$ J

$= 4.5 \times 10^5$ J

Thus, the work done by the brakes is 4.5×10^5 joules.

WORK DONE BY A FORCE ACTING OBLIQUELY

So far we have considered only that case of work in which the body moves in the direction of the applied force. This, however, is not always so. **In many cases, the movement of the body is at an angle to the direction of the applied force.** For example, when a child pulls a toy car with a string attached to it, the car moves horizontally on the ground, but the force applied by the child is along the string held in his hand making some angle with the ground. This is shown in Figure 9, in which the toy car moves along the horizontal ground surface *OX* but the force is being applied along the string *OA*, the direction of force making an angle θ with the direction of motion.

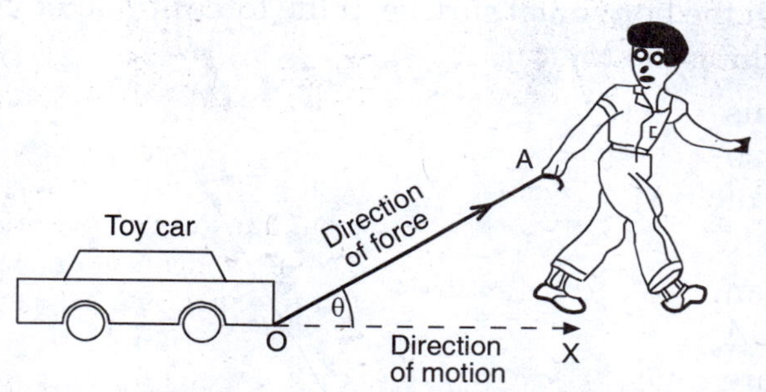

Figure 9. When a child pulls a toy car, the toy car moves on the horizontal ground *OX* but the force applied is along the string *OA*, at an angle θ to the direction of motion.

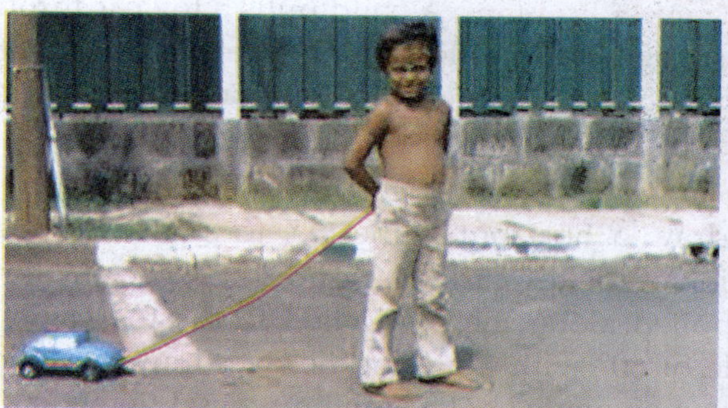

Figure 10. This photograph shows a child pulling a toy car. Look at the string (or thread) tied to the toy car and held in child's hand. This string is at an angle to the horizontal surface of ground. The child applies the pulling force to the toy car along this string.

Please note that **in such cases we cannot use the formula $W = F \times s$ to calculate the work done because the distance moved, *s*, is not exactly in the direction of force applied.** In this case, the whole of force *F* is not being used in pulling the toy car, only its horizontal component along the ground is the effective force pulling the toy car. We will now derive a formula for the work done when the body moves at an angle theta, θ, to the direction of force.

Formula for Work Done When a Body Moves at an Angle to the Direction of Force

Suppose a body lying at point *O* is being pulled by a man (see Figure 11). Now, though the body is moving on the horizontal floor and reaches point *X* after covering a distance *s*, but the force *F* is being applied in the direction of the string *OA*, making an angle θ with the direction of motion of the body. Please note that in this case all the force *F* is not utilised in pulling the body, only the horizontal component of force *F* is the effective force which is pulling the body along the ground. Thus, **the work done in pulling**

the body will be equal to the product of horizontal component of the force and distance moved by body. In this case the horizontal component of force F is $F \cos \theta$ and the distance moved is s. Thus, work done :

$$W = F \cos \theta \times s$$

where F = force applied

θ = angle between the direction of force and direction of motion

and s = distance moved

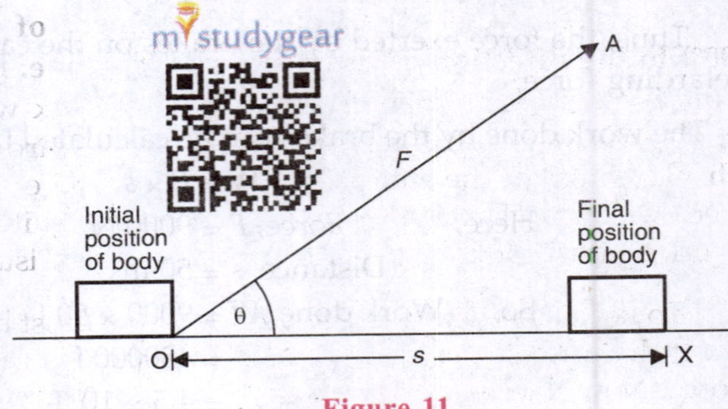

Figure 11.

All the problems on work done by a force acting obliquely can be solved by using the formula : $F \cos \theta \times s$. The most important point to remember while applying this formula is that **θ is the angle between the direction of motion of body and the direction of force applied.** The calculation of work done when a body moves at an angle to the direction of applied force will become clear from the following example.

Sample Problem. A child pulls a toy car through a distance of 10 metres on a smooth, horizontal floor. The string held in child's hand makes an angle of 60° with the horizontal surface. If the force applied by the child be 5 N, calculate the work done by the child in pulling the toy car.

Solution. We will first draw the diagram for this problem. The toy car is moving along horizontal floor, so we draw a horizontal line OX to show the direction of motion of the toy car (see Figure 12). Now, the force of 5 N is applied along the string tied to the toy car making an angle of 60° with the floor. So, we draw another line OA making an angle of 60° with horizontal floor OX. In Figure 12, OX represents the direction of motion and OA represents the direction of force, the angle between them being 60°. Now, we know that the formula for work done when a body moves at an angle to the direction of force is :

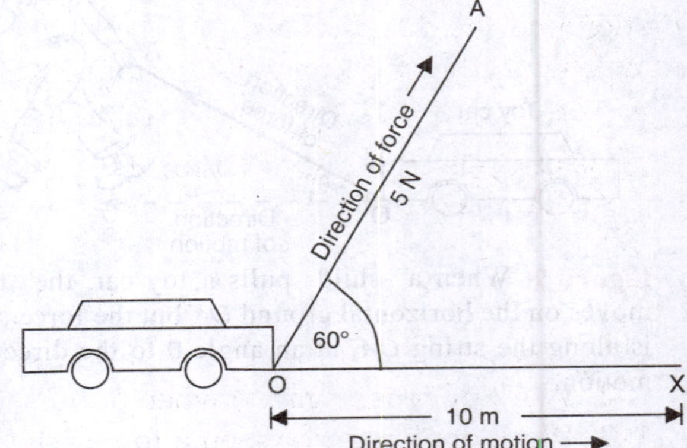

Figure 12. Diagram for sample problem.

$$W = F \cos \theta \times s$$

Here, Force, $F = 5$ N

Angle, $\theta = 60°$

And, Distance, $s = 10$ m

So, putting these values in the above formula, we get :

$$\text{Work done, } W = 5 \times \cos 60° \times 10$$

Now, if we look up the table of natural cosines, we will find that $\cos 60° = 0.5$. So, putting this value of $\cos 60°$ in the above relation, we get :

$$W = 5 \times 0.5 \times 10$$
$$= 25 \text{ J}$$

Thus, the work done is 25 joules.

Work Done When the Force Acts at Right Angles to the Direction of Motion

If the force acts at right angles to the direction of motion of a body, then the angle θ between the direction of motion and direction of force is 90°. Now, $\cos 90° = 0$, so the component of force, $F \cos 90°$, acting in the direction of displacement becomes zero and hence the work done also becomes zero. That is,

$$\text{Work done, } W = F \cos 90° \times s$$
$$= F \times 0 \times s \quad \text{(Because } \cos 90° = 0\text{)}$$
$$\text{Work done, } W = 0$$

This means that **when the displacement of the body is perpendicular (at 90°) to the direction of force, no work is done.** For example, if a man carries a suitcase strictly horizontally, he does no work with respect to gravity because the force of gravity acts vertically downwards and the angle between the displacement of the suitcase and the direction of force becomes 90°, and cos 90° becomes zero (Though the man carrying the suitcase horizontally may be doing work against the forces like friction and air resistance).

Figure 13. A man carrying suitcases strictly horizontally does no work in respect to gravity.

mystudygear

To keep a body moving in a circle, there must be a force acting on it directed towards the centre. This force is called centripetal force. Now, **the work done on a body moving in a circular path is also zero.** This is because when a body moves in a circular path, then the centripetal force acts along the radius of the circle, and it is at right angles to the motion of the body. Thus, **the work done in the case of earth moving round the sun is zero,** and **the work done in the case of a satellite moving round the earth is also zero.** From this discussion it is clear that it is possible that a force is acting on a body but still the work done is zero.

Work Done When the Force Acts Opposite to the Direction of Motion

If the force acts opposite to the direction of motion of a body, then the angle θ between the direction of motion and the direction of force is 180°. In this case, the component of force *F* acting in the direction of motion of the body becomes, $-F$ (minus *F*). So, the work done by the force is :

$$W = -F \times s$$

It is obvious that the work done by the force in this case is negative. This means that when a force acts opposite to the direction in which the body moves, then the work done by the force is negative.

Positive, Negative and Zero Work

The work done by a force can be positive, negative or zero.

1. Work done is positive when a force acts in the direction of motion of the body.
2. Work done is negative when a force acts opposite to the direction of motion of the body.
3. Work done is zero when a force acts at right angles to the direction of motion of the body.

Positive work done by a force increases the speed of a body : negative work done by a force decreases the speed of a body ; whereas zero work done by a force has no effect on the speed of a body. We will now give examples of positive work, negative work and zero work.

If we kick a football lying on the ground, then the football starts moving. The force of our kick has moved the football. Here we have applied the force in the direction of motion of football (see Figure 14). So, the work done on the football in this case is positive (and it increases the speed of football).

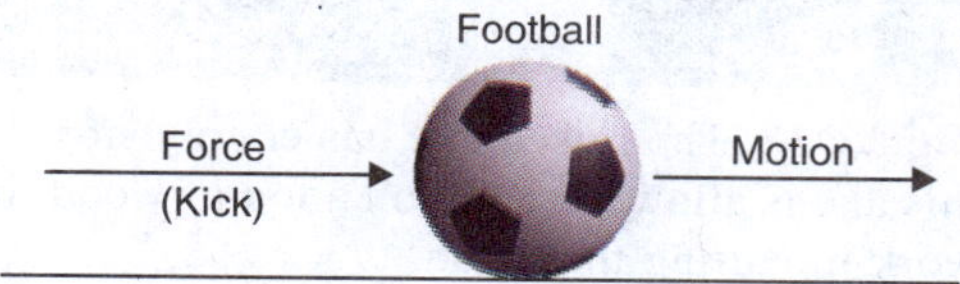

Figure 14. The force (of kick) acts in the direction of motion of football, so the work done is positive here.

Figure 15. The force (of friction) acts opposite to the direction of motion of football, so the work cone is negative in this case.

A football moving on the ground slows down gradually and ultimately stops. This is because a force due to friction (of ground) acts on the football. The force of friction acts in a direction opposite to the direction of motion of football (see Figure 15). So, in this case the work done by the force of friction on the football is negative (and it decreases the speed of football).

The satellites (like the moon) move around the earth in a circular path. In this case the gravitational force of earth acts on the satellite at right angles to the direction of motion of satellite (see Figure 16). So,

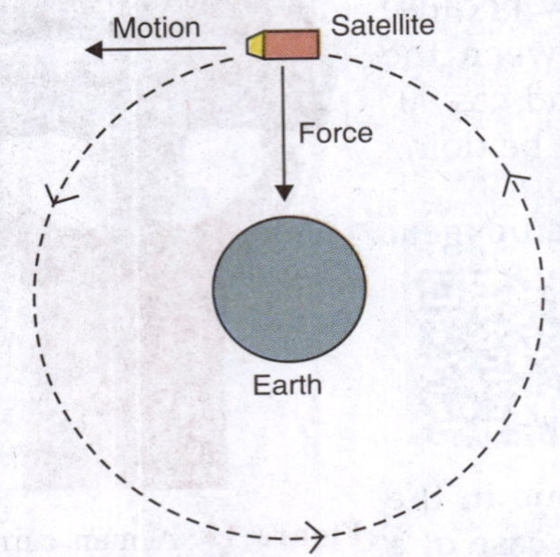

Figure 16. The force of gravity of earth acts on the satellite at right angles to the direction of motion of satellite, so the work done by the force of gravity of earth is zero.

Figure 17. This picture shows a communications satellite moving in circular orbit around the earth.

the work done by the earth on the satellite moving around it in circular path is zero. Similarly, the work done by the sun on planets (like the earth) moving around it in circular orbits is zero.

When a boy throws a ball vertically upwards, then the force applied by the boy on the ball does positive work (because the force acts in the direction of motion of ball). But the gravitational force of earth acting on the upward going ball does negative work (because it acts opposite to the direction of motion of ball).

ENERGY

If a person can do a lot of work we say that he has a lot of energy or he is very energetic. In physics also, anything which is able to do work is said to possess energy. Thus, **energy is the ability to do work.** Let us take one example to understand it more clearly. To cut a log of wood into small pieces, we have to raise the axe vertically above the log of wood and some work has to be done in raising the axe. If the axe is now allowed to fall on wood, it can do work in cutting the wood. Thus, the work done in raising the axe has been stored up in it, giving it the ability for doing work. Now, when the axe is resting on the log of wood, it can no longer do any work. To give it the ability to do work again, work has to be done in raising it above the log of wood once again. We say that the raised axe has the energy or ability for doing work. **The amount of energy possessed by a body is equal to the amount of work it can do when its energy is released.** It should be noted that whenever work is done, energy is consumed.

Figure 18. The raised axe has energy stored in it. If this axe is allowed to fall on a log of wood, it can do work in cutting the wood.

A body having energy can do work as follows : A body which possesses energy can exert a force on another object. During this process, some of the energy of the body is transferred to the object. By gaining energy, the object moves. And when the object moves, work is said to be done. **Energy is a scalar quantity**. It has only magnitude but no direction.

Unit of Energy

The units of work and energy are the same. So, **the SI unit of energy is joule** (which is denoted by the letter J). Whenever work is done, an equal amount of energy is consumed. Keeping this is mind, we can define 1 joule energy as follows : **The energy required to do 1 joule of work is called 1 joule energy**. Joule is a small unit of energy, so sometimes a bigger unit of energy called 'kilojoule' is also used. The symbol of kilojoule is kJ. Now,

1 kilojoule = 1000 joules

or 1 kJ = 1000 J

The unit of energy called 'joule' is named after a British physicist James Prescott Joule.

Figure 19. James Prescott Joule : The scientist after whom the unit of energy called 'joule' is named.

Different Forms of Energy

Energy exists in many forms. The main forms of energy are :

1. Kinetic energy
2. Potential energy
3. Chemical energy
4. Heat energy
5. Light energy
6. Sound energy
7. Electrical energy
8. Nuclear energy

In this class we will discuss only kinetic energy and potential energy in detail. The 'kinetic energy' and 'potential energy' taken together is known as 'mechanical energy'.

Figure 20. Mechanical energy refers to the total potential energy and kinetic energy possessed by a moving object. This combination of horse (and jockey) have a lot of mechanical energy which is enabling them to jump the fence.

KINETIC ENERGY

A moving cricket ball can do work in pushing back the stumps (see Figure 21) ; moving water can do work in turning a turbine for generating electricity; and moving wind can do work in turning the blades of wind-mill. Thus, a moving body is capable of doing work and hence possesses energy. **The energy of a body due to its motion is called kinetic energy.**

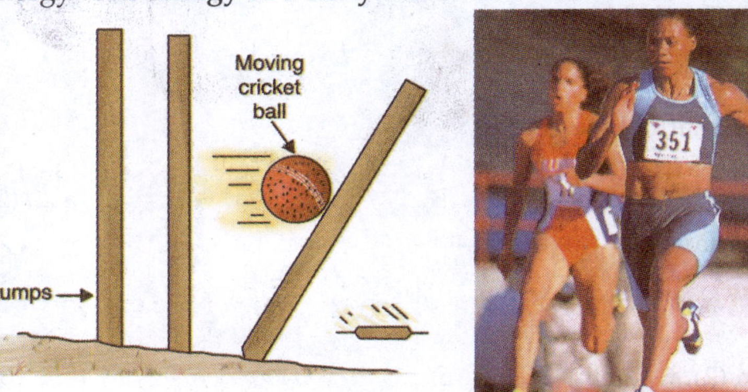

Figure 21. A moving cricket ball possesses kinetic energy.

Figure 22. These runners possess kinetic energy.

Figure 23. This running motorcycle possesses kinetic energy.

A moving hammer drives a nail into wood because of its kinetic energy and a moving bullet can penetrate even a steel plate due to its kinetic energy which it has on account of its high speed. In fact, every object around us which is moving possesses kinetic energy. In other words, every object around us which has speed, possesses kinetic energy. For example, a runner has kinetic energy ; a running motorcycle has kinetic energy ; a running car (or bus) has kinetic energy; a falling stone has kinetic energy ; and an arrow flying through the air has also kinetic energy. When a moving body is brought to rest (stopped) by an opposing force, the kinetic energy is lost, being used up to do work in overcoming the resistance of opposing force. We will now derive a formula for calculating the kinetic energy of a moving body.

Formula for Kinetic Energy

The kinetic energy of a moving body is measured by the amount of work it can do before coming to rest. Suppose a body, such as a ball, of mass m and moving with a velocity v is at position A (see Figure 24). Let it enter into a medium M, such as air, which opposes the motion of the body with a constant force F. As a result of the opposing force, the body will be constantly retarded, that is, its velocity decreases gradually and it will come to rest (or stop) at position B after travelling a distance s. So, the final velocity V of the body becomes zero.

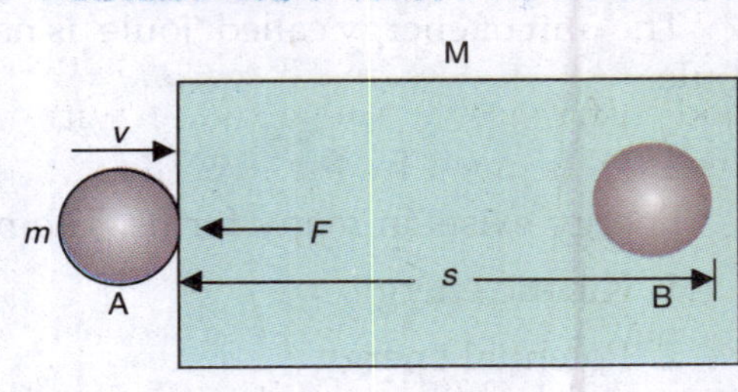

Figure 24.

(*i*) In going through the distance s against the opposing force F, the body has done some work. This work is given by :

$$\text{Work} = \text{Force} \times \text{Distance}$$

or $$W = F \times s$$

At position B the body is at rest, that is, it has no motion and hence no kinetic energy. This means that all the kinetic energy of the body has been used up in doing the work W. So, the kinetic energy must be equal to this work W. Thus,

$$\text{Kinetic energy} = W$$

or $$\text{Kinetic energy} = F \times s \qquad \text{... (1)}$$

(*ii*) If a body has an initial velocity 'v', final velocity 'V', acceleration 'a' and travels a distance 's', then according to the third equation of motion :

$$V^2 = v^2 + 2as$$

(Please note that we have written $V^2 = v^2 + 2as$ instead of the usual $v^2 = u^2 + 2as$. But it should not make any difference)

In the above example, we have :

Initial velocity of the body = v (Supposed)

Final velocity of the body, V = 0 (The body stops)

Acceleration = $-a$ (Retardation)

and Distance travelled = s

Now, putting these values in the above equation, we get :

$$(0)^2 = v^2 - 2as$$

or $$v^2 = 2as \qquad \text{... (2)}$$

From Newton's second law of motion, we have :

$$F = m \times a$$

or $$a = \frac{F}{m}$$

Putting this value of acceleration 'a' in equation (2), we get :

$$v^2 = \frac{2 \times F \times s}{m}$$

or $$F \times s = \frac{1}{2} mv^2 \qquad \text{... (3)}$$

But from equation (1), $F \times s$ = Kinetic energy. So, comparing equations (1) and (3), we get :

$$\text{Kinetic energy} = \frac{1}{2}mv^2$$

where m = mass of the body

and v = velocity of the body (or speed of the body)

Thus, a body of mass m and moving with a velocity v has the capacity of doing work equal to $\frac{1}{2}mv^2$ before it stops.

Some Important Conclusions

We have just seen that the kinetic energy of a body of mass m and moving with a velocity (or speed) v is given by the formula :

$$\text{Kinetic energy} = \frac{1}{2}mv^2$$

From this formula, it is clear that :

(*i*) the kinetic energy of a body is directly proportional to the mass of the body, and

(*ii*) the kinetic energy of a body is directly proportional to the square of velocity of the body (or square of the speed of the body).

Figure 25. The kinetic energy of this running elephant depends on the mass of elephant and its speed (of running). Actually, the kinetic energy is directly proportional to (*i*) mass of elephant, and (*ii*) square of speed (or velocity) of elephant. This elephant of mass 2000 kg and running at a speed of 5 m/s will have a kinetic energy of 25,000 joules. Calculate the kinetic energy yourself by using the formula $\frac{1}{2}mv^2$.

Since the kinetic energy of a body is directly proportional to its mass, therefore, **if the mass of a body is doubled, its kinetic energy also gets doubled** and **if the mass of a body is halved, its kinetic energy also gets halved** (provided its velocity remains the same). Again, since the kinetic energy of a body is directly proportional to the square of its velocity, therefore, **if the velocity of a body is doubled, its kinetic energy becomes four times,** and **if the velocity of a body is halved, then its kinetic energy becomes one-fourth.** It is obvious that doubling the velocity has a greater effect on the kinetic energy of a body than doubling its mass.

Since the kinetic energy of a body depends on its mass and velocity, therefore, heavy bodies moving with high velocities have more kinetic energy (they can do more work), than slow moving bodies of small mass. This is the reason why a blacksmith uses a heavier hammer than the one used by a goldsmith. It has been found that a driver increases the speed (velocity) of his car on approaching a hilly road. Let us see why this is done. When a car is moving on a flat road, it has to do work to overcome the friction of the road and air resistance but no work is done against the force of gravity. On the other hand, when the car is going up the hill, then in addition to friction and air resistance,

Figure 26. This car is going up the hill, so in addition to friction and air resistance, it has also to do work against gravity. A driver increases the speed of car on approaching a hilly road to give more kinetic energy to the car so that it may go up the hill against the force of gravity.

it has to do work against the force of gravity. Thus, **a driver increases the speed of his car on approaching a hilly road to give more kinetic energy to the car so that it may go up against gravity.** Please note that in the above discussion on kinetic energy we have mostly used the term "velocity". The term "speed" can also be used in place of "velocity" everywhere in the above description of kinetic energy. Another point to be noted is that 'Kinetic Energy' is also denoted by the symbol K.E. A yet another symbol for kinetic energy is E_k (where E stands for Energy and k for kinetic). We will now solve some numerical problems based on kinetic energy.

Sample Problem 1. Calculate the kinetic energy of a body of mass 2 kg moving with a velocity of 0.1 metre per second.

Solution. The formula for calculating kinetic energy is :

$$\text{Kinetic energy} = \frac{1}{2} mv^2$$

Here, Mass, $m = 2$ kg

And, Velocity, $v = 0.1$ m/s

So, putting these values in the above formula, we get :

$$\text{Kinetic energy} = \frac{1}{2} \times 2 \times (0.1)^2$$

$$= \frac{1}{2} \times 2 \times 0.1 \times 0.1$$

$$= 0.01 \text{ J}$$

Thus, the kinetic energy of the body is 0.01 joule.

Figure 27. Kinetic energy of a moving body depends on the square of its velocity (or speed).

Sample Problem 2. Two bodies of equal masses move with uniform velocities v and $3v$ respectively. Find the ratio of their kinetic energies.

Solution. In this problem, the masses of the two bodies are equal, so let the mass of each body be m. We will now write down the expressions for the kinetic energies of both the bodies separately.

(*i*) Mass of first body = m

Velocity of first body = v

So, K.E. of first body $= \frac{1}{2} mv^2$ ... (1)

(*ii*) Mass of second body = m

Velocity of second body = $3v$

So, K.E. of second body $= \frac{1}{2} m (3v)^2$

$$= \frac{1}{2} m \times 9v^2$$

$$= \frac{9}{2} mv^2 \quad \text{... (2)}$$

Now, to find out the ratio of kinetic energies of the two bodies, we should divide equation (1) by equation (2), so that :

$$\frac{\text{K.E. of first body}}{\text{K.E. of second body}} = \frac{\frac{1}{2}mv^2}{\frac{9}{2}mv^2}$$

or

$$\frac{\text{K.E. of first body}}{\text{K.E. of second body}} = \frac{1}{9} \quad \text{... (3)}$$

Thus, the ratio of the kinetic energies is 1 : 9.

We can also write down the equation (3) as follows :

K.E. of second body = 9 × K.E. of first body

That is, the kinetic energy of second body is 9 times the kinetic energy of the first body. It is clear from this example that **when the velocity (or speed) of a body is "tripled" (from v to $3v$), then its kinetic energy becomes "nine times".**

Sample Problem 3. How much work should be done on a bicycle of mass 20 kg to increase its speed from 2 m s^{-1} to 5 m s^{-1} ? (Ignore air resistance and friction).

Solution. We know that whenever work is done, an equal amount of energy is used up. So, the work done in this case will be equal to the change in kinetic energy of bicycle when its speed changes from 2 m s^{-1} to 5 m s^{-1}.

Figure 28. For sample problem 3.

(*a*) *In the first case* :

Mass of bicycle, $m = 20$ kg

And, Speed of bicycle, $v = 2$ m s^{-1}

So, Kinetic energy, $E_k = \frac{1}{2}mv^2$

$= \frac{1}{2} \times 20 \times (2)^2$

$= 10 \times 4$

$= 40$ J

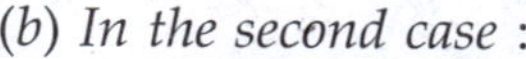

(*b*) *In the second case* :

Mass of bicycle, $m = 20$ kg

And, Speed of bicycle, $v = 5$ m s^{-1}

So, Kinetic energy, $E_k = \frac{1}{2}mv^2$

$= \frac{1}{2} \times 20 \times (5)^2$

$= 10 \times 25$

$= 250$ J

Now, Work done = Change in kinetic energy

$= 250 - 40$

$= 210$ J

Thus, the work done is 210 joules.

POTENTIAL ENERGY

Suppose a brick is lying on the ground. It has no energy so it cannot do any work. Let us lift this brick to the roof of a house (see Figure 29). Now, some work has been done in lifting this brick against the force of gravity. This work gets stored up in the brick in the form of potential energy. Thus, the energy of a brick

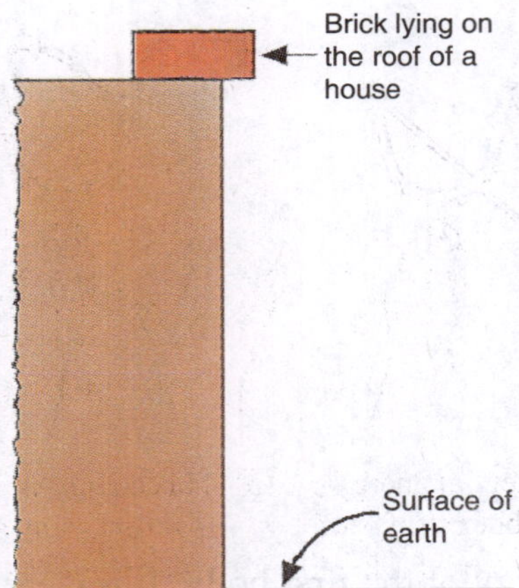

Figure 29. A brick lying on the roof of a house has potential energy in it due to its higher position above the surface of earth. This is actually gravitational potential energy.

Figure 30. This car has been raised into the air for repairs by a hydraulic jack. This raised car has potential energy in it. Since this car is stationary (not moving), therefore, it has no kinetic energy.

lying on the roof of a house is due to its higher position with respect to the ground. And if this brick falls from the roof-top, it can do some (undesirable) work in breaking the window-panes or somebody's head ! The energy of brick lying on the roof-top is known as gravitational potential energy because it has been acquired by doing work against gravity.

Another type of potential energy is elastic potential energy, which is due to a change in the shape of the body. The change in shape of a body can be brought about by compressing, stretching, bending or twisting. Some work has to be done to change the shape of a body (temporarily). This work gets stored in the deformed body in the form of elastic potential energy. When this deformed body is released, it comes back to its original shape and size and the potential energy is given out in some other form. For example, a wound-up circular spring possesses elastic potential energy which drives a wound-up toy (such as a toy car) . Figure 31(*a*) shows the normal shape of the circular spring used in winding toys. When we wind-up the spring of a toy-car by using a winding key, then some work is done by us due to which the spring gets coiled more tightly [see Figure 31(*b*)]. The work done in winding the spring gets stored up in the tightly coiled-up spring (or wound-up spring) in the form of elastic potential energy. When the wound-up spring is slowly released, its potential energy is gradually converted into kinetic energy which turns the wheels of the toy car and makes it run. Thus, a wound-up spring can do work in returning to its original shape during unwinding. The potential energy of a wound-up spring is not due to its position above the ground, it is due to the change in its shape. Let us take another example.

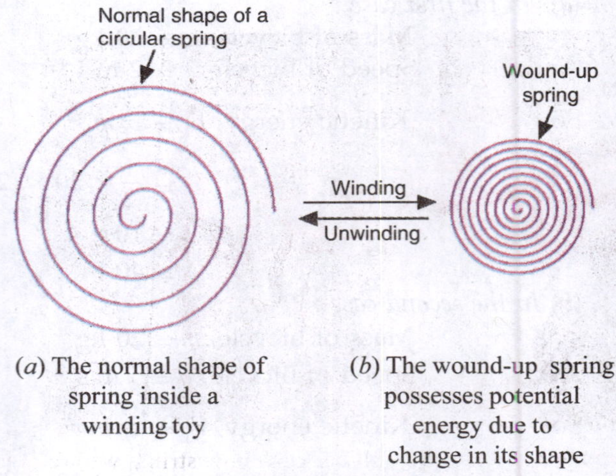

(*a*) The normal shape of spring inside a winding toy

(*b*) The wound-up spring possesses potential energy due to change in its shape

Figure 31. An example of elastic potential energy.

When we do work in stretching the rubber strings of a catapult (*gulel*), then the work done by us gets stored in the stretched rubber strings in the form of elastic potential energy [see Figure 32(*a*)]. The stretched strings of a catapult possess potential energy due to a change in their shape (because they become long and thin). This energy of the stretched strings of the catapult can be used to throw away a piece of stone with a high speed [see Figure 32(*b*)]. We can now say that: **The energy of a body due to its position or change in shape is known as potential energy.** Actually, **the energy of a body due to its position above the ground is called gravitational potential energy and the energy of a body due to a change in its shape and size is called elastic potential energy.** Elastic potential energy is associated with the state of 'compression' or 'extension' of an object. For example, the energy possessed by a 'compressed spring' or an 'extended spring' (stretched spring) is the elastic potential energy. **The gravitational potential energy as well as elastic potential energy are commonly known as just potential energy.**

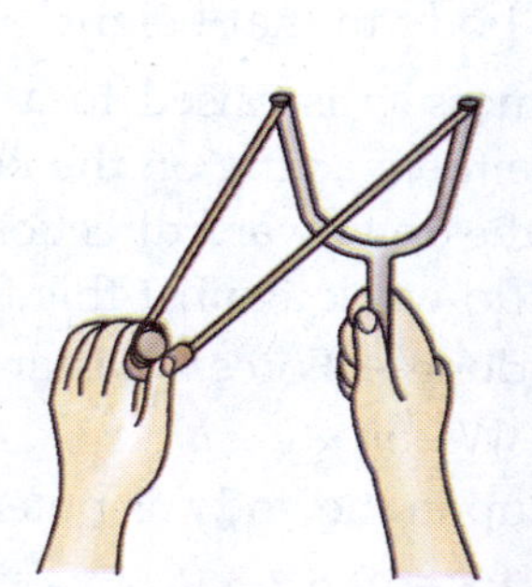

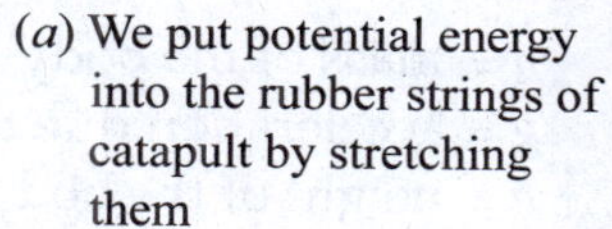

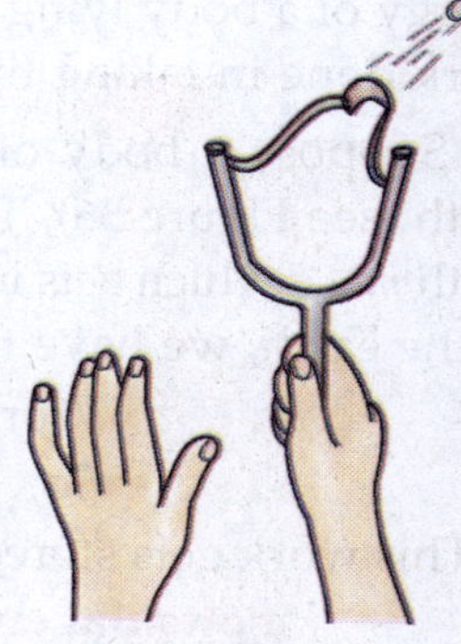

(*a*) We put potential energy into the rubber strings of catapult by stretching them

(*b*) This energy is used to throw away a piece of stone

Figure 32. Another example of elastic potential energy.

The water in a tank on the roof of a building possesses potential energy due to its position (height) above the ground. A stretched rubber band and compressed gas in a cylinder also possess potential energy but this is due to their change in shape or configuration. A ceiling fan which has been switched off, water in the reservoir of a dam, a spring expanded beyond its normal shape, a rubber band lying on the table, and a stretched rubber band lying on the ground, all possess potential energy. A bent bow has also potential energy stored in it. The potential energy stored in the bent bow (due to change in its shape) is used in the form of kinetic energy in throwing off an arrow. It is obvious that **a body may possess energy even when it is not in motion.** And this energy is called potential energy.

Figure 33. When we pull back the bow string, we are storing potential energy in it. So, a bent bow possesses potential energy.

Figure 34. A bird sitting at a height has only potential energy.

Figure 35. A bird flying in the sky has potential energy as well as kinetic energy.

A body can have both potential energy as well as kinetic energy at the same time. **The sum of the potential and kinetic energies of a body is called its mechanical energy.** A flying bird, a flying aeroplane, and a man climbing a hill, all have kinetic energy as well as potential energy. A stationary stone lying at the top of a hill has only potential energy. When this stone starts rolling downwards, it has both kinetic and potential energy. And when the stone reaches the bottom of the hill, it has only kinetic energy. We will now derive a formula for calculating the gravitational potential energy of a body.

Formula for Potential Energy

The potential energy of a body is due to its higher position above the earth and it is equal to the work done on the body, against gravity, in moving the body to that position. So, to find out the potential energy of a body lying at a certain height, all that we have to do is to find out the work done in taking the body to that height.

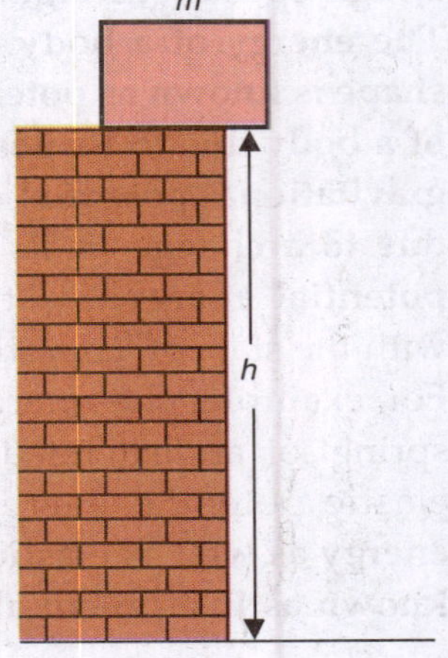

Figure 36.

Suppose a body of mass m is raised to a height h above the surface of the earth (see Figure 36). The force acting on the body is the gravitational pull of the earth $m \times g$ which acts in the downward direction. To lift the body above the surface of the earth, we have to do work against this force of gravity. Now,

Work done = Force × Distance

So, $W = m \times g \times h$

This work gets stored up in the body as potential energy. Thus,

Potential energy = $m \times g \times h$

where m = mass of the body

g = acceleration due to gravity

and h = height of the body above a reference point, say the surface of earth

We will now solve some problems based on potential energy. Please note that 'Potential Energy' is usually denoted by the letters P.E. Another symbol for potential energy is E_p (where E stands for Energy and p for potential).

Sample Problem 1. If acceleration due to gravity is 10 m/s², what will be the potential energy of a body of mass 1 kg kept at a height of 5 m ?

Solution. The potential energy of a body is calculated by using the formula :

Potential energy = $m \times g \times h$

In this case, Mass, m = 1 kg

Acceleration due to gravity, g = 10 m/s²

And, Height, h = 5 m

So, putting these values in the above formula, we get :

Potential energy = $1 \times 10 \times 5$

= 50 J

Thus, the potential energy of the body is 50 joules.

Sample Problem 2. A bag of wheat weighs 200 kg. To what height should it be raised so that its potential energy may be 9800 joules ? (g = 9.8 m s^{-2})

Solution. Here, Potential energy, P.E. = 9800 J

Mass, m = 200 kg

Acceleration due to gravity, g = 9.8 m s^{-2}

And, Height, h = ? (To be calculated)

Now, putting these values in the formula :

P.E. = $m \times g \times h$

We get : $9800 = 200 \times 9.8 \times h$

So, $$h = \frac{9800}{200 \times 9.8}$$

h = 5 m

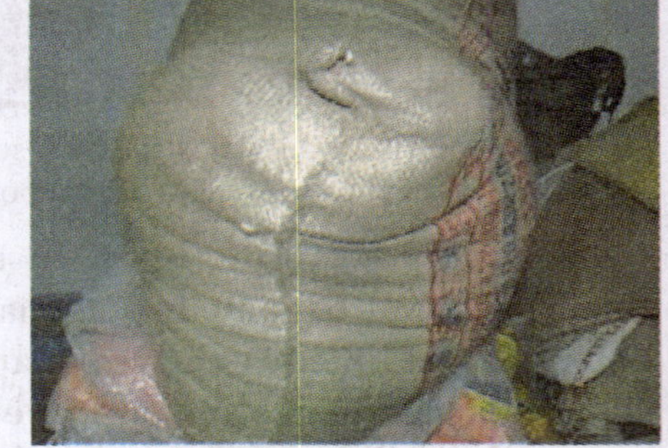
Figure 37. For sample problem 2.

Thus, the bag of wheat should be raised to a height of 5 metres.

Before we go further and discuss power, **please answer the following questions and problems :**

Very Short Answer Type Questions

1. How much work is done when a body of mass *m* is raised to a height *h* above the ground ?
2. State the SI unit of work.
3. Is work a scalar or a vector quantity ?
4. Define 1 joule of work.
5. What is the condition for a force to do work on a body ?
6. Is energy a vector quantity ?
7. What are the units of (*a*) work, and (*b*) energy ?
8. What is the work done against gravity when a body is moved horizontally along a frictionless surface ?
9. By how much will the kinetic energy of a body increase if its speed is doubled ?
10. Write an expression for the kinetic energy of a body of mass *m* moving with a velocity *v*.
11. If the speed of a body is halved, what will be the change in its kinetic energy ?
12. On what factors does the kinetic energy of a body depend ?
13. Which would have a greater effect on the kinetic energy of an object : doubling the mass or doubling the velocity ?
14. How fast should a man of 50 kg run so that his kinetic energy be 625 J ?
15. State whether the following objects possess kinetic energy, potential energy, or both :
    (*a*) A man climbing a hill
    (*b*) A flying aeroplane
    (*c*) A bird running on the ground
    (*d*) A ceiling fan in the off position
    (*e*) A stretched spring lying on the ground.
16. Two bodies *A* and *B* of equal masses are kept at heights of *h* and 2*h* respectively. What will be the ratio of their potential energies ?
17. What is the kinetic energy of a body of mass 1 kg moving with a speed of 2 m/s ?
18. Is potential energy a vector or a scalar quantity ?
19. A load of 100 kg is pulled up by 5 m. Calculate the work done. ($g = 9.8 \text{ m/s}^2$)
20. State whether the following statement is true or false :
    The potential energy of a body of mass 1 kg kept at a height of 1 m is 1 J.
21. What happens to the potential energy of a body when its height is doubled ?
22. What kind of energy is possessed by the following ?
    (*a*) A stone kept on roof-top.
    (*b*) A running car.
    (*c*) Water stored in the reservoir of a dam.
    (*d*) A compressed spring.
    (*e*) A stretched rubber band.
23. Fill in the following blanks with suitable words :
    (*a*) Work is measured as a product of .... and ....
    (*b*) The work done on a body moving in a circular path is ....
    (*c*) 1 joule is the work done when a force of one .... moves an object through a distance of one........... in the direction of ....
    (*d*) The ability of a body to do work is called .... The ability of a body to do work because of its motion is called................
    (*e*) The sum of the potential and kinetic energies of a body is called .... energy.

Short Answer Type Questions

24. What are the quantities on which the amount of work done depends ? How are they related to work ?
25. Is it possible that a force is acting on a body but still the work done is zero ? Explain giving one example.

26. A boy throws a rubber ball vertically upwards. What type of work, positive or negative, is done :
    (*a*) by the force applied by the boy ?
    (*b*) by the gravitational force of earth ?
27. Write the formula for work done on a body when the body moves at an angle to the direction of force. Give the meaning of each symbol used.
28. How does the kinetic energy of a moving body depend on its (*i*) speed, and (*ii*) mass ?
29. Give one example each in which a force does (*a*) positive work (*b*) negative work, and (*c*) zero work.
30. A ball of mass 200 g falls from a height of 5 metres. What is its kinetic energy when it just reaches the ground ? ($g = 9.8\ m/s^2$).
31. Find the momentum of a body of mass 100 g having a kinetic energy of 20 J.
32. Two objects having equal masses are moving with uniform velocities of 2 m/s and 6 m/s respectively. Calculate the ratio of their kinetic energies.
33. A body of 2 kg falls from rest. What will be its kinetic energy during the fall at the end of 2 s ? (Assume $g = 10\ m/s^2$)
34. On a level road, a scooterist applies brakes to slow down from a speed of 10 m/s to 5 m/s. If the mass of the scooterist and the scooter be 150 kg, calculate the work done by the brakes. (Neglect air resistance and friction)
35. A man drops a 10 kg rock from the top of a 5 m ladder. What is its speed just before it hits the ground ? What is its kinetic energy when it reaches the ground ? ($g = 10\ m/s^2$)
36. Calculate the work done by the brakes of a car of mass 1000 kg when its speed is reduced from 20 m/s to 10 m/s ?
37. A body of mass 100 kg is lifted up by 10 m. Find :
    (*i*) the amount of work done.
    (*ii*) potential energy of the body at that height (value of $g = 10\ m/s^2$).
38. A boy weighing 50 kg climbs up a vertical height of 100 m. Calculate the amount of work done by him. How much potential energy does he gain ? ($g = 9.8\ m/s^2$).
39. When is the work done by a force on a body : (*a*) positive, (*b*) negative, and (*c*) zero ?
40. To what height should a box of mass 150 kg be lifted, so that its potential energy may become 7350 joules ? ($g = 9.8\ m/s^2$).
41. A body of mass 2 kg is thrown vertically upwards with an initial velocity of 20 m/s. What will be its potential energy at the end of 2 s ? (Assume $g = 10\ m/s^2$).
42. How much work is done when a force of 1 N moves a body through a distance of 1 m in its own direction ?
43. A car is being driven by a force of 2.5×10^{10} N. Travelling at a constant speed of 5 m/s, it takes 2 minutes to reach a certain place. Calculate the work done.
44. Explain by an example that a body may possess energy even when it is not in motion.
45. (*a*) On what factors does the gravitational potential energy of a body depend ?
    (*b*) Give one example each of a body possessing : (*i*) kinetic energy, and (*ii*) potential energy.
46. Give two examples where a body possesses both, kinetic energy as well as potential energy.
47. How much is the mass of a man if he has to do 2500 joules of work in climbing a tree 5 m tall ? ($g = 10\ m\ s^{-2}$)
48. If the work done by a force in moving an object through a distance of 20 cm is 24.2 J, what is the magnitude of the force ?
49. A boy weighing 40 kg makes a high jump of 1.5 m.
    (*i*) What is his kinetic energy at the highest point ?
    (*ii*) What is his potential energy at the highest point ? ($g = 10\ m/s^2$).
50. What type of energy is possessed :
    (*a*) by the stretched rubber strings of a catapult ?
    (*b*) by the piece of stone which is thrown away on releasing the stretched rubber strings of catapult ?

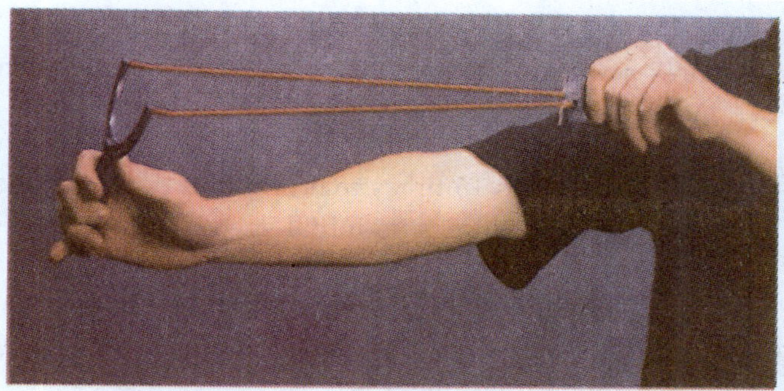

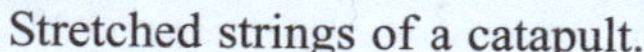

Stretched strings of a catapult.

A weightlifter in action

51. A weightlifter is lifting weights of mass 200 kg up to a height of 2 metres. If $g = 9.8 \text{ m s}^{-2}$, calculate :

(*a*) potential energy acquired by the weights.

(*b*) work done by the weightlifter.

Long Answer Type Questions

52. (*a*) Define the term 'work'. Write the formula for the work done on a body when a force acts on the body in the direction of its displacement. Give the meaning of each symbol which occurs in the formula.

(*b*) A person of mass 50 kg climbs a tower of height 72 metres. Calculate the work done. ($g = 9.8 \text{ m s}^{-2}$)

53. (*a*) When do we say that work is done ? Write the formula for the work done by a body in moving up against gravity. Give the meaning of each symbol which occurs in it.

(*b*) How much work is done when a force of 2 N moves a body through a distance of 10 cm in the direction of force ?

54. (*a*) What happens to the work done when the displacement of a body is at right angles to the direction of force acting on it ? Explain your answer.

(*b*) A force of 50 N acts on a body and moves it a distance of 4 m on a horizontal surface. Calculate the work done if the direction of force is at an angle of 60° to the horizontal surface.

55. (*a*) Define the term 'energy' of a body. What is the SI unit of energy.

(*b*) What are the various forms of energy ?

(*c*) Two bodies having equal masses are moving with uniform speeds of v and $2v$ respectively. Find the ratio of their kinetic energies.

56. (*a*) What do you understand by the kinetic energy of a body ?

(*b*) A body is thrown vertically upwards. Its velocity goes on decreasing. What happens to its kinetic energy as its velocity becomes zero ?

(*c*) A horse and a dog are running with the same speed. If the weight of the horse is ten times that of the dog, what is the ratio of their kinetic energies ?

57. (*a*) Explain by an example what is meant by potential energy. Write down the expression for gravitational potential energy of a body of mass m placed at a height h above the surface of the earth.

(*b*) What is the difference between potential energy and kinetic energy ?

(*c*) A ball of mass 0.5 kg slows down from a speed of 5 m/s to that of 3 m/s. Calculate the change in kinetic energy of the ball. State your answer giving proper units.

58. (*a*) What is the difference between gravitational potential energy and elastic potential energy ? Give one example of a body having gravitational potential energy and another having elastic potential energy.

(*b*) If 784 J of work was done in lifting a 20 kg mass, calculate the height through which it was lifted. ($g = 9.8 \text{ m/s}^2$)

Multiple Choice Questions (MCQs)

59. A car is accelerated on a levelled road and acquires a velocity 4 times of its initial velocity. During this process, the potential energy of the car :
(*a*) does not change
(*b*) becomes twice that of initial potential energy
(*c*) becomes 4 times that of initial potential energy
(*d*) becomes 16 times that of initial potential energy

60. A car is accelerated on a levelled road and attains a speed of 4 times its initial speed. In this process, the kinetic energy of the car :
(*a*) does not change
(*b*) becomes 4 times that of initial kinetic energy
(*c*) becomes 8 times that of initial kinetic energy
(*d*) becomes 16 times that of initial kinetic energy

61. In case of negative work, the angle between the force and displacement is :
(*a*) 0° (*b*) 45° (*c*) 90° (*d*) 180°

62. An iron sphere of mass 10 kg has the same diameter as an aluminium sphere of mass 3.5 kg. Both the spheres are dropped simultaneously from a tower. When they are 10 m above the ground, they have the same :
(*a*) acceleration (*b*) momentum (*c*) potential energy (*d*) kinetic energy

63. A girl is carrying a school bag of 3 kg mass on her back and moves 200 m on a levelled road. If the value of *g* be 10 m/s^2, the work done by the girl against the gravitational force will be :
(*a*) 6000 J (*b*) 0.6 J (*c*) 0 J (*d*) 6 J

64. The work done on an object does not depend on the :
(*a*) displacement
(*b*) angle between force and displacement
(*c*) force applied
(*d*) initial velocity of the object

65. Water stored in a dam possesses :
(*a*) no energy (*b*) electrical energy (*c*) kinetic energy (*d*) potential energy

66. The momentum of a bullet of mass 20 g fired from a gun is 10 kg.m/s. The kinetic energy of this bullet in kJ will be :
(*a*) 5 (*b*) 1.5 (*c*) 2.5 (*d*) 25

67. Each of the following statement describes a force acting. Which force is causing work to be done ?
(*a*) the weight of a book at rest on a table
(*b*) the pull of a moving railway engine on its coaches
(*c*) the tension in an elastic band wrapped around a parcel
(*d*) the push of a person's feet when standing on the floor

68. A girl weighing 400 N climbs a vertical ladder. If the value of *g* be 10 m s^{-2}, the work done by her after climbing 2 m will be :
(*a*) 200 J (*b*) 800 J (*c*) 8000 J (*d*) 2000 J

69. Which of the following does not possess the ability to do work not because of motion ?
(*a*) a sparrow flying in the sky
(*b*) a sparrow moving slowly on the ground
(*c*) a sparrow in the nest on a tree
(*d*) a squirrel going up a tree

70. A stone is thrown upwards as shown in the diagram. When it reaches P, which of the following has the greatest value for the stone ?
(*a*) its acceleration
(*b*) its kinetic energy
(*c*) its potential energy
(*d*) its weight

P
stone

Questions Based on High Order Thinking Skills (HOTS)

71. A boy tries to push a truck parked on the roadside. The truck does not move at all. Another boy pushes a bicycle. The bicycle moves through a certain distance. In which case was the work done more : on the truck or on the bicycle ? Give a reason to support your answer.

72. The work done by a force acting obliquely is given by the formula : $W = F \cos \theta \times s$. What will happen to the work done if angle θ between the direction of force and motion of the body is increased gradually ? Will it increase, decrease or remain constant ?

73. What should be the angle between the direction of force and the direction of motion of a body so that the work done is zero ?

74. In which of the following case the work done by a force will be maximum : when the angle between the direction of force and direction of motion is 0° or 90° ?

75. How much work is done by the gravitational force of earth acting on a satellite moving around it in a circular path ? Give reason for your answer.

76. A man is instructed to carry a package from the base camp at *B* to summit *A* of a hill at a height of 1200 metres. The man weighs 800 N and the package weighs 200 N. If $g = 10$ m/s^2,
(*i*) how much work does man do against gravity ?
(*ii*) what is the potential energy of the package at *A* if it is assumed to be zero at *B* ?

77. When a ball is thrown vertically upwards, its velocity goes on decreasing. What happens to its potential energy as its velocity becomes zero ?

78. A man X goes to the top of a building by a vertical spiral staircase. Another man Y of the same mass goes to the top of the same building by a slanting ladder. Which of the two does more work against gravity and why ?

79. When a ball is thrown inside a moving bus, does its kinetic energy depend on the speed of the bus ? Explain.

80. A bullet of mass 15 g has a speed of 400 m/s. What is its kinetic energy ? If the bullet strikes a thick target and is brought to rest in 2 cm, calculate the average net force acting on the bullet. What happens to the kinetic energy originally in the bullet ?

ANSWERS

1. $m \times g \times h$ **5.** The force should produce motion in the body **8.** Zero **9.** Becomes four times **11.** Becomes one-fourth **13.** Doubling the velocity **14.** 5 m/s **15.** (*a*) Both kinetic energy and potential energy (*b*) Both kinetic energy and potential energy (*c*) Only kinetic energy (*d*) Only potential energy (*e*) Only potential energy (rather elastic potential energy) **16.** 1 : 2 **17.** 2 J **19.** 4900 J **20.** False **21.** Potential energy gets doubled **22.** (*a*) Potential energy (*b*) Kinetic energy (*c*) Potential energy (*d*) Potential energy (*e*) Potential energy **23.** (*a*) force ; distance (*b*) zero (*c*) newton ; metre ; force (*d*) energy ; kinetic energy (*e*) mechanical **26.** (*a*) Positive (*b*) Negative **30.** 9.8 J **31.** 2 kg.m/s **32.** 1 : 9 **33.** 400 J **34.** 5625 J **35.** 10 m/s ; 500 J **36.** 150 kJ **37.** (*i*) 10,000 J (*ii*) 10,000 J **38.** 4.9×10^4 J ; 4.9×10^4 J **40.** 5 m **41.** 400 J **42.** 1 J **43.** 1.5×10^{13} J **47.** 50 kg **48.** 121 N **49.** (*i*) Zero (*ii*) 600 J **50.** (*a*) Potential energy (*b*) Both potential energy and Kinetic energy **51.** (*a*) 3920 J (*b*) 3920 J **52.** (*b*) 35280 J **53.** (*b*) 0.2 J **54.** (*b*) 100 J **55.** (*c*) 1 : 4 **56.** (*b*) Kinetic energy becomes zero (*c*) 10 : 1 **57.** (*c*) 4 J **58.** (*b*) 4 m **59.** (*a*) **60.** (*d*) **61.** (*d*) **62.** (*a*) **63.** (*c*) **64.** (*d*) **65.** (*d*) **66.** (*c*) **67.** (*b*) **68.** (*b*) **69.** (*c*) **70.** (*c*) **71.** More work is done on the bicycle. This is because the bicycle moves through a certain distance on applying force (push) ; No work is done on the truck because it does not move at all on applying force (push) **72.** Decrease **73.** 90° **74.** When the angle between the direction of force and direction of motion is 0° **75.** Zero ; Because the gravitational force acts along the radius of circular path, at right angles (90°) to the motion of satellite **76.** (*i*) 12×10^5 J (*ii*) 2.4×10^5 J **77.** Potential energy becomes the maximum **78.** Both the men, X and Y, do equal amount of work against gravity because irrespective of whether they reach the top of building by using a spiral staircase or a slanting ladder, the vertical distance moved by them against gravity is the same **79.** Yes, the kinetic energy of a ball thrown inside a moving bus depends on the speed of the bus. This is because the speed of bus adds up to the speed with which the ball is thrown inside the moving bus **80.** 1200 J ; 6×10^4 N ; Kinetic energy is converted mainly into heat energy (by friction)

POWER

Suppose an old man takes 10 minutes to do a particular "work" whereas a young man takes only 5 minutes to do the same work. It is obvious that the "rate of doing work" of the young man is more than that of the old man. The rate of doing work is known as power, so we can say that the power of young man is more than that of the old man. Thus, **power is defined as the rate of doing work.** We can obtain power by dividing the '**Work done**' by '**Time taken**' for doing the work. That is,

(*a*) An old man

(*b*) A young man

Figure 38. The rate of doing work (or power) of a young man is more than that of an old man.

$$\textbf{Power} = \frac{\textbf{Work done}}{\textbf{Time taken}}$$

or $$P = \frac{W}{t}$$

where P = power

W = work done

and t = time taken

In other words, **power is the work done per unit time** or power is the work done per second. Please note that the value which we get by dividing 'Work done' by 'Time taken' actually gives us 'Average power'.

We know that **when work is done, an equal amount of energy is consumed**. So, we can also define power by using the term 'energy' in place of 'work'. Thus, **power is also defined as the rate at which energy is consumed** (or utilised). We can also obtain power by dividing '**Energy consumed**' by '**Time taken**' for consuming the energy. That is,

$$\textbf{Power} = \frac{\textbf{Energy consumed}}{\textbf{Time taken}}$$

or $$P = \frac{E}{t}$$

where P = power

E = energy consumed

and t = time taken

We can now say that : **Power is the rate at which work is done or energy is consumed**. It is clear from the above discussion that we can write the formula for calculating power in terms of 'work done' or in terms of 'energy consumed'. **Power is a scalar quantity** which has only magnitude but no direction.

Units of Power

Power is obtained by dividing 'work done' by 'time taken' to do the work. Now, work is measured in the unit of 'joule' and the time is measured in the unit of 'second', so the unit of power is 'joules per second'. This unit of power is called 'watt'. Thus, **the SI unit of power is watt** which is denoted by the symbol **W**. We can now define the unit of power 'watt' as follows : **1 watt is the power of an appliance which does work at the rate of 1 joule per second.** We can also define watt by using the term 'energy' as follows : **1 watt is the power of an appliance which consumes energy at the rate of 1 joule per second.** We can write an expression for watt as follows :

$$1 \text{ watt} = \frac{1 \text{ joule}}{1 \text{ second}}$$

or $1\text{ W} = \frac{1\text{ J}}{1\text{ s}}$

So **1 watt = 1 joule per second**

Figure 39. James Watt : The scientist after whom the unit of power called 'watt' is named.

Figure 40. This electric bulb consumes electric energy at the rate of 60 joules per second, so its power is 60 watts.

Watt is an important unit of power since it is used in electrical work. **The power of an electrical appliance tells us the rate at which electrical energy is consumed by it.** For example, a bulb of 60 watts power consumes electrical energy at the rate of 60 joules per second (60 J/s or 60 J s^{-1}). Different electrical appliances have different power ratings. The greater the power of an appliance, and the longer it is switched on for, the more electrical energy it consumes. The unit of power called 'watt' is named after a Scottish inventor, engineer and designer James Watt who became famous for improving the design of steam engine.

Watt is a small unit of power. Sometimes bigger units of power called kilowatt (kW) and megawatt (MW) are also used.

1 kilowatt = 1000 watts

or 1 kW = 1000 W

And 1 megawatt = 1000,000 watts

or 1 MW = 1000,000 W

or 1 MW = 10^6 W

A yet another unit of power is called 'horse power' (h.p.) which is equal to 746 watts. Thus,

1 horse power = 746 watts

or 1 h.p. = 746 W

This means that 1 horse power is equal to about 0.75 kilowatt (0.75 kW).

Figure 41. This electric train engine can provide 2 megawatts (2 MW) of power to drive the train at full speed. This power is more than 2680 b.h.p.

Figure 42. The power of the engine of this Skoda Yeti car is 138 b.h.p.

The unit called 'horse power' originated long back when steam engines first replaced 'horses' as a source of power. These days the powers of engines (of cars, and other vehicles, etc.) are expressed in the unit called 'brake horse power' (b.h.p.). Brake horse power is the unit of power equal to one horse power which is used in expressing power available at the shaft of an engine. The b.h.p. of Maruti-800 car is 37 whereas that of Maruti Zen is 60. **The more powerful a car is, the quicker it can accelerate or climb a hill, that is, more rapidly it does work.** We will now solve some problems based on power.

Sample Problem 1. A body does 20 joules of work in 5 seconds. What is its power ?

Solution. Power is calculated by using the formula :

$$\text{Power} = \frac{\text{Work done}}{\text{Time taken}}$$

Here, Work done = 20 J

And, Time taken = 5 s

So, putting these values in the above formula, we get :

$$\text{Power} = \frac{20\ \text{J}}{5\ \text{s}}$$

$$= 4\ \text{J/s}$$

Thus, Power = 4 W (because 1 J/s = 1 W)

Thus, the power of this body is 4 watts.

Sample Problem 2. What is the power of a pump which takes 10 seconds to lift 100 kg of water to a water tank situated at a height of 20 m ? (g = 10 m s^{-2})

Solution. In this problem first of all we have to calculate the work done by the pump in lifting the water against the force of gravity. We know that the work done against gravity is given by the formula :

Figure 43. A pump (or water pump).

$$W = m \times g \times h$$

Here, Mass of water, m = 100 kg

Acceleration due to gravity, g = 10 m s^{-2}

And, Height, h = 20 m

So, putting these values in the above formula, we get :

$$\text{Work done, } W = 100 \times 10 \times 20$$

$$= 20000\ \text{J}$$

And, Time taken, t = 10 s

Now, we know that :

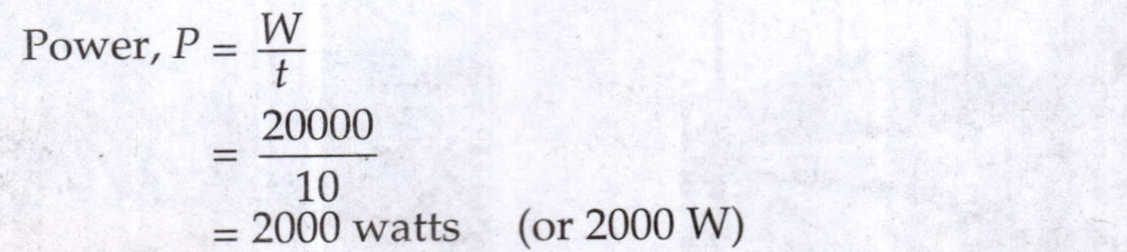

$$\text{Power, } P = \frac{W}{t}$$

$$= \frac{20000}{10}$$

$$= 2000\ \text{watts} \quad (\text{or } 2000\ \text{W})$$

Thus, the power of this pump is 2000 watts. This power can be converted from watts into kilowatts by dividing it by 1000.

So, $$\text{Power} = \frac{2000}{1000}\ \text{kilowatts}$$

$$= 2\ \text{kilowatts} \quad (\text{or } 2\ \text{kW})$$

Sample Problem 3. An electric bulb consumes 7.2 kJ of electrical energy in 2 minutes. What is the power of the electric bulb ?

Solution. We know that :

$$\text{Power} = \frac{\text{Energy consumed}}{\text{Time taken}}$$

Here, Energy consumed = 7.2 kJ

$$= 7.2 \times 1000\ \text{J}$$

$$= 7200\ \text{J}$$

And, Time taken = 2 minutes

$$= 2 \times 60 \text{ seconds}$$

$$= 120 \text{ s}$$

Now, putting these values of 'energy consumed' and 'time taken' in the above formula, we get :

$$\text{Power} = \frac{7200 \text{ J}}{120 \text{ s}}$$

$$= 60 \text{ J/s}$$

$$= 60 \text{ W}$$

Thus, the power of this electric bulb is 60 watts.

Figure 44. This is the traditional filament-type electric lamp (or electric bulb). The glowing filament of this electric lamp produces light but also wastes a lot of electrical energy in the form of heat. Filament-type electric lamps consume a lot of electricity, so they are not energy efficient.

Figure 45. These are Compact Fluorescent Lamps (which are called CFL in short). CFLs do not have filaments like traditional electric lamps, so they do not waste much electrical energy as heat. CFLs consume much less electrical energy for producing the same amount of light (as filament-type lamps), so they are much more energy efficient. We should use only CFLs and tube-lights in our homes, schools, shops and offices to save electricity.

COMMERCIAL UNIT OF ENERGY

The commercial unit (or trade unit) of energy is kilowatt-hour which is written in short form as **kWh**. Kilowatt-hour is usually used as a commercial unit of **electrical energy**. This is discussed below.

The SI unit of electrical energy is joule and we know that *"A joule is the amount of electrical energy consumed when an appliance of 1 watt power is used for one second"*. Actually, **joule represents a very small quantity of energy and, therefore, it is inconvenient to use where a large quantity of energy is involved.** So, for commercial purposes we use a bigger unit of electrical energy which is called "kilowatt-hour". **One kilowatt-hour is the amount of electrical energy consumed when an electrical appliance having a power rating of 1 kilowatt is used for 1 hour.** Since a kilowatt means 1000 watts, so we can also say that *one kilowatt-hour is the amount of electrical energy consumed when an electrical appliance of 1000 watts is used for 1 hour.*

Relation Between Kilowatt-Hour and Joule

1 kilowatt-hour is the amount of energy consumed at the rate of 1 kilowatt for 1 hour. That is,

1 kilowatt-hour = 1 kilowatt for 1 hour

or 1 kilowatt-hour = 1000 watts for 1 hour ...(1)

$$\text{But : 1 watt} = \frac{1 \text{ joule}}{1 \text{ second}}$$

So, equation (1) can be rewritten as :

$$1 \text{ kilowatt-hour} = 1000 \ \frac{\text{joules}}{\text{seconds}} \ \text{for 1 hour}$$

And, 1 hour = 60 × 60 seconds

$$\text{So,} \quad 1 \text{ kilowatt-hour} = 1000 \ \frac{\text{joules}}{\text{seconds}} \times 60 \times 60 \text{ seconds}$$

or **1 kilowatt-hour = 36,00,000 joules** **(or 3.6×10^6 J)**

From this discussion we conclude that **1 kilowatt-hour is equal to 3.6×10^6 joules of electrical energy.** It should be noted that **watt or kilowatt is the unit of electrical power but kilowatt-hour is the unit of electrical energy.**

Figure 46. This is a domestic electricity meter. The reading in this meter shows the number of kilowatt-hours (or units) that have been used. The reading from this electricity meter is used to prepare our monthly electricity bill.

The electrical energy used in homes, shops, and industries is measured in kilowatt-hours (kWh). The electricity meter installed in our home records the electrical energy consumed by us in kilowatt-hours.

1 kilowatt-hour (or 1 kWh) of electrical energy is commonly known as '1 unit' of electricity. Our electricity bill shows the electrical energy consumed by our household in a month in 'kilowatt-hours' or 'units' of electricity. One unit of electricity (or 1 kWh) may cost anything from ₹ 3 to ₹ 5 (or even more). The rates of electrical energy vary from place to place and keep on changing from time to time. We will now solve some problems based on commercial unit of energy.

Sample Problem 1. A radio set of 60 watts runs for 50 hours. How many 'units' (kWh) of electrical energy are consumed ?

Solution. We want to calculate the electrical energy in kilowatt-hours, so first we should convert the power of 60 watts into kilowatts by dividing it by 1000. That is :

$$\text{Power, } P = 60 \text{ watts}$$

$$= \frac{60}{1000} \text{ kilowatts}$$

$$= 0.06 \text{ kW}$$

And, $\quad$ Time, $t = 50$ h

Now, putting $P = 0.06$ kW and $t = 50$ h in the formula :

$$\text{Power} = \frac{\text{Energy consumed}}{\text{Time taken}}$$

We get :

$$0.06 \text{ kW} = \frac{\text{Energy consumed}}{50 \text{ h}}$$

So,

$$\text{Energy consumed} = 0.06 \text{ kW} \times 50 \text{ h}$$

$$= 3 \text{ kWh}$$

Thus, the electrical energy consumed is 3 kWh or 3 units.

Sample Problem 2. A family uses 250 units of electrical energy during a month. Calculate this electrical energy in joules.

Solution. 250 units of electrical energy means 250 kWh of electrical energy. Now, we know that :

$$1 \text{ kWh of energy} = 3.6 \times 10^6 \text{ J}$$

So, $$250 \text{ kWh of energy} = 3.6 \times 10^6 \times 250 \text{ J}$$

$$= 9 \times 10^8 \text{ J}$$

Thus, 250 units of electrical energy is equal to 9×10^8 joules.

TRANSFORMATION OF ENERGY

Energy exists in many different forms. One form of energy can be changed into another form. **The change of one form of energy into another form of energy is known as transformation of energy.** We will now take some examples to show how the transformation of energy takes place. Suppose a stone is lying on the roof of a house. In this position, all the energy of the stone is in the form of potential energy. When the stone is dropped from the roof, it starts moving downwards towards the ground and the potential energy of stone starts changing into kinetic energy. As the stone continues falling downwards, its potential energy goes on decreasing (because its height goes on decreasing) but its kinetic energy goes on increasing (because its velocity goes on increasing). In other words, the potential energy of the stone gradually gets transformed into kinetic energy. And by the time stone reaches the ground, its potential energy becomes zero and entire energy will be in the form of kinetic energy. From this we conclude that **when a body is released from a height then the potential energy of the body is gradually transformed (or changed) into kinetic energy.**

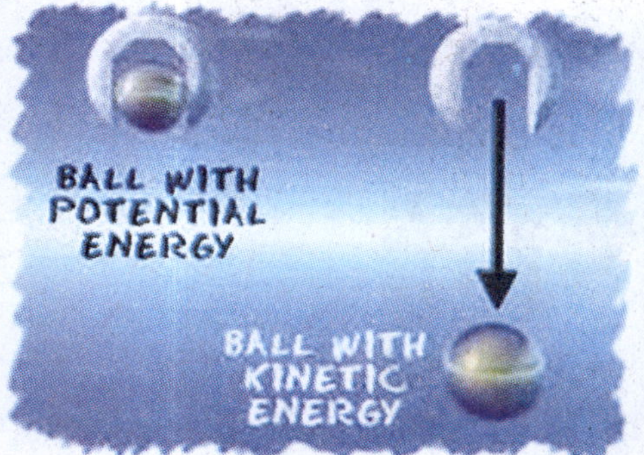

Figure 47. A ball held at a height has only potential energy. When the ball is released from a height, then the potential energy of the ball is gradually transformed (or changed) into kinetic energy.

Figure 48. In this fun-fair ride called 'Pirate Ship', kinetic energy is changed into potential energy and back into kinetic energy (as in a simple pendulum).

Figure 49. A high dive is an example of transferring (or converting) potential energy of the diver into kinetic energy.

The reverse happens when a piece of stone is thrown upwards. When we throw a piece of stone upwards, the initial kinetic energy of the stone starts changing into potential energy. As the stone moves up, its kinetic energy goes on decreasing (because its velocity goes on decreasing) but its potential energy goes on increasing (because its height goes on increasing). In other words, the kinetic energy of stone gradually gets transformed into potential energy. And when the stone reaches at the highest point of its path, its kinetic energy becomes zero and its potential energy becomes maximum. Thus, at the highest point, the total energy of the stone will be in the form of potential energy. From this we conclude that **when a body is thrown upwards, the kinetic energy of body is gradually transformed (or changed) into potential energy.**

Energy Transformations at a Hydroelectric Power House

We will now describe the energy transformations which take place at a hydroelectric power house. At a hydroelectric power house, a dam is built on a river. The river water collects behind the dam to form a 'reservoir' (see Figure 50). Water stored behind the dam has a lot of potential energy but as such this potential energy is of no use to us. If, however, this water is allowed to fall from its great height, the potential energy of water changes into kinetic energy. This kinetic energy of the falling water is used to

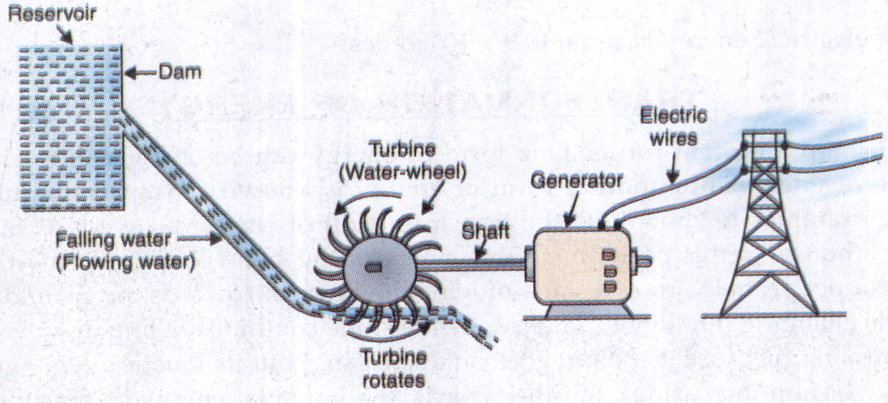

Figure 50. Arrangement at a hydroelectric power house.

drive huge water-wheels or turbines which are connected to electricity generators for producing electricity. Thus, **at a hydroelectric power house, the potential energy of water is transformed into kinetic energy and then into electrical energy.** The transformations of energy taking place at a hydroelectric power house can be written as :

$$\text{Potential energy} \rightarrow \text{Kinetic energy} \rightarrow \text{Electrical energy}$$

Figure 51. This photograph shows a number of turbines in a hydroelectric power house (or hydroelectric power station). The fast flowing water coming from the dam reservoir, rotates these turbines rapidly. The rotating turbines then rotate the electromagnet of the electric generator (called alternator). When the electromagnet turns rapidly inside the huge fixed coil of generator, then electric current (or electricity) is produced by the process of electromagnetic induction.

Energy Transformations at a Thermal Power House

At a thermal power house, coal is used to produce electricity. When coal is burnt, the chemical energy of coal is changed into heat energy. This heat energy converts water into steam. The high pressure steam turns the steam turbines changing the heat energy into kinetic energy. The turbines run electricity generators which convert kinetic energy into electrical energy. Thus, **at a thermal power house, chemical energy of coal is changed into heat energy, which is further converted into kinetic energy and electrical energy.**

This can be written as :

Chemical energy → Heat energy → Kinetic energy → Electrical energy

Figure 52. This is a thermal power house (or thermal power station). At a thermal power house, coal (or natural gas) is burnt to obtain heat which then boils water to form steam. The high pressure steam turns the steam turbines. The steam turbines then drive generators (or alternators) to produce electricity.

Figure 53. This is the steam-turbine assembly for a thermal power house generator. We can see the large number of turbine blades in this photograph. The superheated, high pressure steam is used to turn this turbine which is connected to the electric generator for producing electricity. All of us should save on electricity so as to conserve our precious fossil fuels like coal and natural gas.

From the above discussion we conclude that **one of the important characteristics of energy is that it can be transformed (or changed) from one form to another**. We will now discuss some of the important transformations of energy and the appliances which bring about these transformations. Please note that the appliances (machines or devices) which bring about the transformation of energy are called 'energy converters'.

USING ENERGY CONVERTERS

Energy is like money, it is useful because it can be changed into so many different forms. **In our everyday life we make use of many appliances (or machines) which convert (or transform) one form of energy into another form.** Some examples of the energy converters which make our life more comfortable are : Electric motor, Electric generator, Electric iron, Electric bulb, Radio, Steam engine, Car engine, Cell (or Battery), Gas stove, Solar water heater and Solar cell. These are discussed below.

1. Electric Motor. Electric energy spins the motor in various electrical appliances which do various types of work for us. For example, electric energy spins the motor in a fan, causing the fan to turn and cool our room. **A motor converts electrical energy into mechanical energy.** That is :

Electrical energy → Mechanical energy

Electric motor is used in electric fans, washing machines, refrigerators, mixer and grinder, hair dryer,

Figure 54. Electric motor.

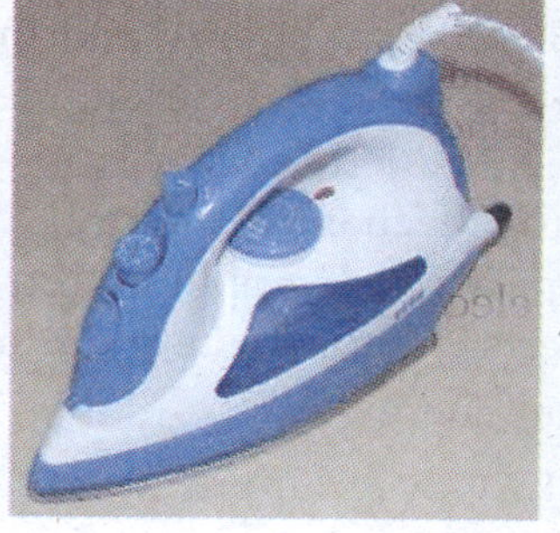

Figure 55. Electric iron.

Figure 56. Electric bulb.

Figure 57. Radio.

and many other appliances. A generator is the reverse case of an electric motor. **A generator converts mechanical energy into electrical energy.**

2. Electric Iron. When we switch on an electric iron, it becomes hot. So, **an electric iron converts electrical energy into heat energy**. That is :

Electrical energy → Heat energy

An electric heater also converts electrical energy mainly into heat energy.

3. Electric Bulb. An electric bulb (or electric lamp) converts electrical energy into light energy. This happens as follows : Electrical energy causes the filament in the bulb to become white-hot and give out light. So, **in an electric bulb, electrical energy is first converted into heat energy and then into light energy**. The energy transformations taking place in an electric bulb can be written as follows :

Electrical energy → Heat energy → Light energy

Please note that it is not always possible to convert the whole of one kind of energy to any other kind. Usually, one kind of energy gets converted into many kinds of energy. For example, an electric bulb (or lamp) converts electrical energy into light energy but at the same time a lot of heat energy is also produced (which does not get converted to light energy and goes waste).

4. Radio. A radio converts electrical energy into sound energy. This happens as follows : In a radio set, electrical energy causes the diaphragm in the speaker to vibrate and produce sound. So, **a radio first converts electrical energy into kinetic energy and then into sound energy.** The energy transformations taking place in a radio set can be written as :

Electrical energy → Kinetic energy → Sound energy

5. Steam Engine. In a steam engine, heat is used to boil water and obtain steam under high pressure to turn the shaft and drive the wheels. So, **a steam engine converts heat energy into kinetic energy (or mechanical energy)**. That is :

Heat energy → Kinetic energy
(or Mechanical energy)

Figure 58. Steam engine.

Figure 59. Car engine.

Figure 60. Cell (or Battery).

6. Car Engine. A car burns fuel (like petrol) to get energy and drive its engine. This happens as follows : **The car engine converts the chemical energy of petrol into heat energy and then into kinetic energy (or mechanical energy)**. The transformations of energy taking place in a car engine can be written as :

Chemical energy → Heat energy → Kinetic energy
(or Mechanical energy)

7. Cell (or Battery). A cell (or battery) contains chemicals and supplies electrical energy required to run various types of appliances. So, **a cell (or battery) converts chemical energy into electrical energy.** That is :

Chemical energy → Electrical energy

8. Gas Stove . When cooking gas (LPG) is burnt in a gas stove, then mainly heat energy is produced. So, **a gas stove converts the chemical energy of cooking gas into heat energy.** That is :

Chemical energy $\rightarrow$ Heat energy

Please note that during the burning of cooking gas in a gas stove some light energy is also produced.

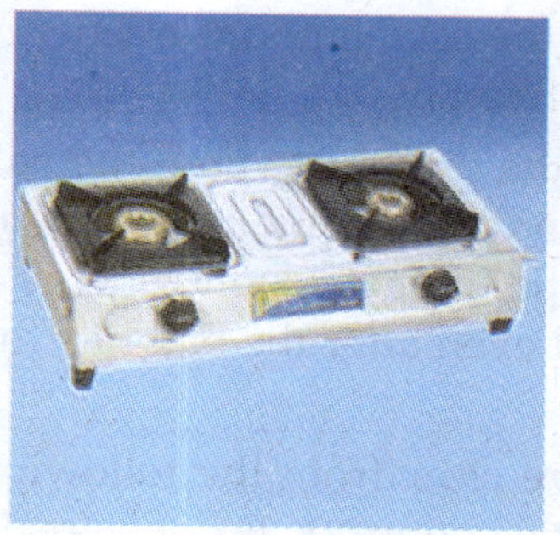

Figure 61. Gas stove.

Figure 62. Solar water heater.

Figure 63. Solar cells.

9. Solar Water Heater. A solar water heater traps sun's light and produces heat. So, **a solar water heater converts light energy into heat energy.** That is :

Light energy $\rightarrow$ Heat energy

10. Solar Cell. A solar cell traps sun's light and produces electricity. So, **a solar cell converts light energy into electrical energy**. That is :

Light energy $\rightarrow$ Electrical energy

LAW OF CONSERVATION OF ENERGY

Energy can be transformed (or changed) from one form to another. According to the law of conservation of energy : **Whenever energy changes from one form to another, the total amount of energy remains constant.** In other words, when energy changes from one form to another, there is no loss or gain of energy. The total energy before and after transformation remains the same. Another definition of the law of conservation of energy is that : **Energy can neither be created nor destroyed.**

During the conversion of energy from one form to another, some energy may be wasted. For example, when electrical energy is converted into light energy in an electric bulb, then some electrical energy is wasted in the form of heat. **Although some energy may be wasted during conversion, but the total energy of the system remains the same.** We will now take an example to understand the conservation of energy more clearly.

Figure 64. A ball of mass m has been dropped from a height h above the ground. As the ball falls downwards, its height h above the ground decreases gradually but its velocity v goes on increasing gradually.

Conservation of Energy During the Free Fall of a Body

Suppose we have a ball of mass m and we raise it to a height h above the ground. The work done in raising the ball gives it a potential energy equal to $m \times g \times h$. Let us allow the ball to fall downwards. As the ball falls, its height h above the ground decreases and thus the potential energy also decreases. But as the ball falls, its velocity v constantly increases and, therefore, its kinetic energy $\frac{1}{2}mv^2$ also increases. As the ball falls more and more, its potential energy is gradually converted into an equal amount of kinetic energy. But **the sum of potential energy and kinetic energy of the ball remains the same at every point during its fall.** When the ball just reaches the ground, its potential energy becomes zero (because h becomes zero) and its kinetic energy becomes the maximum (because v becomes the maximum). At this stage, all the potential energy has been converted into kinetic energy. From this we conclude that the potential energy of ball has been changed into an equal amount of kinetic energy. There is no destruction of energy, and the total amount of energy remains constant. This is an example of the conservation of energy during the free fall of a body.

When a falling ball hits the ground, a sound (of hitting) is produced and the ground (where the ball hits) also gets heated slightly. This means that when a falling ball hits the ground, then some of its kinetic energy is converted into sound energy and heat energy. But the total energy (kinetic energy + sound energy + heat energy) remains the same. Thus, the law of conservation of energy is valid even after the ball hits the ground.

The conservation of energy during the free fall of a body will become more clear from the following data obtained in an experiment in which the potential energy (P.E.) and kinetic energy (K.E.) of a freely falling ball were calculated at different positions of its downward journey :

	Ball		P.E. of Ball	K.E. of Ball	Total Energy of Ball (P.E. + K.E.)
Ball at rest		A	20 J	0 J	20 + 0 = 20 J
Falling ball		B	15 J	5 J	15 + 5 = 20 J
Falling ball		C	10 J	10 J	10 + 10 = 20 J
Falling ball		D	5 J	15 J	5 + 15 = 20 J
Just before hitting the ground		E	0 J	20 J	0 + 20 = 20 J

Figure 65. Conservation of energy during the free fall of a ball.

We can see from the data given in Figure 65 that :

(*i*) At position *A*, when the ball is at rest, it has 20 J of potential energy but zero kinetic energy. So, the total energy of the ball at position *A* is 20 + 0 = 20 J.

(*ii*) At position *B* when the ball is falling, it has 15 J of potential energy and 5 J of kinetic energy. So, the total energy of the ball at position *B* is 15 + 5 = 20 J.

(*iii*) At position C when the ball has fallen by half the distance, it has 10 J of potential energy and 10 J of kinetic energy. So, the total energy of the ball at position C is 10 + 10 = 20 J.

(*iv*) At position *D* when the ball has fallen by more than half the distance, it has 5 J of potential energy and 15 J of kinetic energy. So, the total energy of the ball at position *D* is 5 + 15 = 20 J.

(*v*) At position *E* when the ball is about to hit the ground, it has 0 J of potential energy and 20 J of kinetic energy. So, the total energy of the ball at position *E* is 0 + 20 = 20 J.

It is clear from the above observations that as the ball falls downwards, its potential energy goes on decreasing but its kinetic energy goes on increasing. **The decrease in potential energy of the freely falling ball at any point in its path appears as an equal increase in its kinetic energy.** So, the total energy (potential energy + kinetic energy) of the ball remains the same (20 joules) at every point during its free fall. Thus, **the energy of a freely falling ball is conserved.**

If, however, a ball is thrown upwards, then its kinetic energy goes on decreasing and its potential energy goes on increasing. The decrease in kinetic energy of the upward going ball at any point during its flight appears as an equal increase in its potential energy. But the total energy (kinetic energy + potential energy) of a ball thrown upwards remains constant at every stage of its flight. In this way, **the energy of a ball thrown upwards is also conserved**. We will now discuss the case of a simple pendulum.

Conservation of Energy in a Simple Pendulum

A swinging simple pendulum is an example of conservation of energy. This is because a swinging simple pendulum is a body whose energy can either be potential or kinetic, or a mixture of potential and kinetic, but its total energy at any instant of time remains the same. Thus, **a very simple illustration of the transformation of potential energy into kinetic energy, and of kinetic energy back into potential energy is given by a swinging simple pendulum (or an oscillating simple pendulum).** This will become more clear from the following discussion.

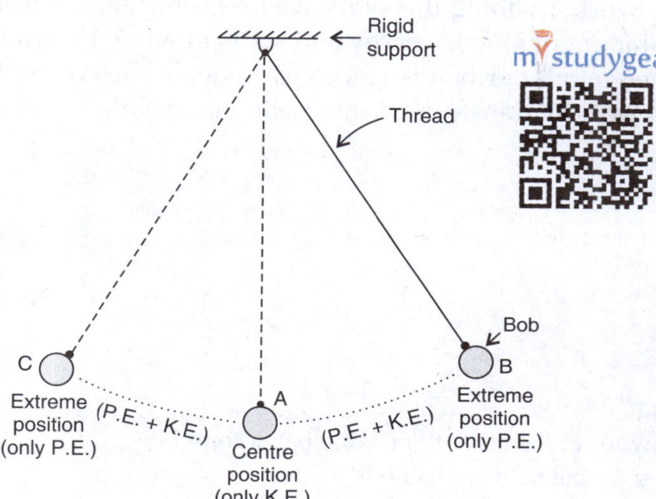

Figure 66. A swinging (or oscillating) simple pendulum. Its energy is continuously transformed (or converted) from potential energy to kinetic energy and vice-versa.

Figure 67. This is a pendulum clock. It keeps time by the oscillations (or vibrations) of a long metal pendulum.

A simple pendulum consists of a small metal ball (called bob) suspended by a long thread from a rigid support, such that the bob is free to swing back and forth when displaced (see Figure 66). Initially, the simple pendulum is at rest with its bob in the centre position (or mean position) *A*. When the pendulum bob is pulled to one side to position *B* (to give it potential energy because of higher position of *B* with respect to position *A*), and then released, the bob starts swinging (moving back and forth) between positions *B* and *C* (see Figure 66).

(*i*) When the pendulum bob is at position *B* (see Figure 66), it has only potential energy (but no kinetic energy).

(*ii*) As the bob starts moving down from position *B* to position *A*, its potential energy goes on decreasing but its kinetic energy goes on increasing.

(*iii*) When the bob reaches the centre position *A*, it has only kinetic energy (but no potential energy).

(*iv*) As the bob goes from position *A* towards position *C*, its kinetic energy goes on decreasing but its potential energy goes on increasing.

(*v*) On reaching the extreme position *C*, the bob stops for a very small instant of time. So at position *C*, the bob has only potential energy (but no kinetic energy).

From the above discussion we conclude that at the extreme positions *B* and *C* of a swinging pendulum, all the energy of pendulum bob is potential, and at the centre position *A*, all the energy of the pendulum bob is kinetic. At all other intermediate positions, the energy of pendulum bob is partly potential and partly kinetic. But **the total energy of the swinging pendulum at any instant of time remains the same (or conserved).**

The pendulum bob keeps on oscillating (or swinging) for a considerable time but ultimately the oscillations die down and the pendulum stops oscillating. It comes to rest. This is because the friction at the point of support of the pendulum and friction of air acting on the swinging bob converts the mechanical energy of the oscillating pendulum into heat energy gradually. This heat energy goes into the environment.

It should be noted that **the body which does work loses energy and the body on which work is done, gains energy**. For example, when we lift a stone from the ground and raise it to a height, we have to do some work on the stone. As a result of doing this work, we lose some energy from our body. On the other hand, the stone which we raised, gains an equal amount of potential energy. Thus, the total energy remains the same. Now, when we kick a ball, we do some work. In doing this work we lose some energy from our body. On the other hand, the ball gains an equal amount of kinetic energy and starts moving. Here also, the total energy of the system is conserved. And when we rub our hands vigorously against each other, we do work. The energy lost by our body in doing this work is transformed into heat energy. We are now in a position to **answer the following questions :**

Very Short Answer Type Questions

1. Name the commercial unit of measurement of energy.
2. Define kilowatt-hour.
3. Name two units of power bigger than watt.
4. Define the term 'watt'.
5. How many watts equal one horse power ?
6. Name the physical quantity whose unit is watt.
7. What is the power of a body which is doing work at the rate of one joule per second ?
8. A body does 1200 joules of work in 2 minutes. Calculate its power.
9. How many joules are there in one kilowatt-hour ?
10. Name the quantity whose unit is :
    (*a*) kilowatt
    (*b*) kilowatt-hour
11. What is the common name of '1 kWh' of electrical energy ?
12. A cell converts one form of energy into another form. Name the two forms.
13. Name the device which converts electrical energy into mechanical energy.
14. Name the devices or machines which convert :
    (*a*) Mechanical energy into electrical energy.
    (*b*) Chemical energy into electrical energy.
    (*c*) Electrical energy into heat energy.
    (*d*) Light energy into electrical energy.
    (*e*) Electrical energy into light energy.
15. Name the devices or machines which convert :
    (*i*) Electrical energy into sound energy.
    (*ii*) Heat energy into kinetic energy (or mechanical energy).
    (*iii*) Chemical energy into kinetic energy (or mechanical energy).
    (*iv*) Chemical energy into heat energy.
    (*v*) Light energy into heat energy.
16. Fill in the following blanks with suitable words :
    (*a*) Power is the rate of doing ....
    (*b*) 1 watt is a rate of working of one .... per ....

(*c*) The electricity meter installed in our home measures electric energy in the units of ....

(*d*) The principle of .... of energy says that energy can be...............from one form to another, but it cannot be....................or..................

(*e*) When a ball is thrown upwards,............... energy is transformed into.................energy.

Short Answer Type Questions

17. A trolley is pushed along a road with a force of 400 N through a distance of 60 m in 1 minute. Calculate the power developed.

18. What kind of energy transformations take place at a hydroelectric power station ?

19. What kind of energy transformations take place at a coal-based thermal power station ?

20. A man weighing 500 N carried a load of 100 N up a flight of stairs 4 m high in 5 seconds. What is the power ?

21. The power output of an engine is 3 kW. How much work does the engine do in 20 s ?

22. An electric heater uses 600 kJ of electrical energy in 5 minutes. Calculate its power rating.

23. How much electrical energy in joules does a 100 watt lamp consume :

(*a*) in 1 second ?

(*b*) in 1 minute ?

24. Five electric fans of 120 watts each are used for 4 hours. Calculate the electrical energy consumed in kilowatt-hours.

25. Describe the energy changes which take place in a radio.

26. Write the energy transformations which take place in an electric bulb (or electric lamp).

27. Name five appliances or machines which use an electric motor.

28. A bulb lights up when connected to a battery. State the energy change which takes place :

(*i*) in the battery. (*ii*) in the bulb.

29. The hanging bob of a simple pendulum is displaced to one extreme position *B* and then released. It swings towards centre position *A* and then to the other extreme position *C*. In which position does the bob have :

(*i*) maximum potential energy ?

(*ii*) maximum kinetic energy ?

Give reasons for your answer.

30. A car of weight 20000 N climbs up a hill at a steady speed of 8 m/s, gaining a height of 120 m in 100 s. Calculate :

(*a*) work done by the car.

(*b*) power of engine of car.

Long Answer Type Questions

31. (*a*) What do you understand by the term "transformation of energy" ? Explain with an example.

(*b*) Explain the transformation of energy in the following cases :

(*i*) A ball thrown upwards.

(*ii*) A stone dropped from the roof of a building.

32. (*a*) State and explain the law of conservation of energy with an example.

(*b*) Explain how, the total energy a swinging pendulum at any instant of time remains conserved. Illustrate your answer with the help of a labelled diagram.

33. (*a*) What is the meaning of the symbol kWh ? What quantity does it represent ?

(*b*) How much electric energy in kWh is consumed by an electrical appliance of 1000 watts when it is switched on for 60 minutes ?

34. (*a*) Derive the relation between commercial unit of energy (kWh) and SI unit of energy (joule).

(*b*) A certain household consumes 650 units of electricity in a month. How much is this electricity in joules ?

35. (*a*) Define power. Give the SI unit of power.

(*b*) A boy weighing 40 kg carries a box weighing 20 kg to the top of a building 15 m high in 25 seconds. Calculate the power. ($g = 10\ m/s^2$)

Multiple Choice Questions (MCQs)

36. When an object falls freely towards the earth, then its total energy :
(*a*) increases (*b*) decreases
(*c*) remains constant (*d*) first increases and then decreases

37. Which one of the following is not the unit of energy ?
(*a*) joule (*b*) newton-metre (*c*) kilowatt (*d*) kilowatt-hour

38. Which of the following energy change involves frictional force ?
(*a*) chemical energy to heat energy (*b*) kinetic energy to heat energy
(*c*) potential energy to sound energy (*d*) chemical energy to kinetic energy

39. Which one of the following statements about power stations is not true ?
(*a*) hydroelectric power stations use water to drive turbines
(*b*) in a power station, turbines drive generators
(*c*) electricity from thermal power stations differs from that produced in hydroelectric power stations
(*d*) in hydroelectric power stations and thermal power stations, alternators produce electricity

40. An electric motor raises a load of 0.2 kg, at a constant speed, through a vertical distance of 3.0 m in 2 s. If the acceleration of free fall is 10 m/s^2, the power in W developed by the motor in raising the load is :
(*a*) 0.3 (*b*) 1.2 (*c*) 3.0 (*d*) 6.0

41. An object is falling freely from a height x. After it has fallen a height $\frac{x}{2}$, it will possess :
(*a*) only potential energy (*b*) only kinetic energy
(*c*) half potential and half kinetic energy (*d*) less potential and more kinetic energy

42. The commercial unit of energy is :
(*a*) watt (*b*) watt-hour (*c*) kilowatt-hour (*d*) kilowatt

43. How much energy does a 100 W electric bulb transfer in 1 minute ?
(*a*) 100 J (*b*) 600 J (*c*) 3600 J (*d*) 6000 J

44. The device which converts mechanical energy into energy which runs our microwave oven is :
(*a*) electric motor (*b*) alternator (*c*) turbine (*d*) electric heater

45. A microphone converts :
(*a*) electrical energy into sound energy in ordinary telephone
(*b*) microwave energy into sound energy in a mobile phone
(*c*) sound energy into mechanical energy in a stereo system
(*d*) sound energy into electrical energy in public address system

Questions Based on High Order Thinking Skills (HOTS)

46. The following data was obtained for a body of mass 1 kg dropped from a height of 5 metres :

Distance above ground	*Velocity*
5 m	0 m/s
3.2 m	6 m/s
0 m	10 m/s

Show by calculations that the above data verifies the law of conservation of energy (Neglect air resistance). (g = 10 m/s^2).

47. A ball falls to the ground as shown below :

A potential energy = 80 J
kinetic energy = 0

B kinetic energy = 48 J

C potential energy = 0

(*a*) What is the kinetic energy of ball when it hits the ground ?
(*b*) What is the potential energy of ball at B ?
(*c*) Which law you have made use of in answering this question ?

48. In an experiment to measure his power, a student records the time taken by him in running up a flight of steps on a staircase. Use the following data to calculate the power of the student :

Number of steps = 28
Height of each step = 20 cm
Time taken = 5.4 s
Mass of student = 55 kg
Acceleration due to gravity = 9.8 m s^{-2}

49. In loading a truck, a man lifts boxes of 100 N each through a height of 1.5 m.
(*a*) How much work does he do in lifting one box ?
(*b*) How much energy is transferred when one box is lifted ?
(*c*) If the man lifts 4 boxes per minute, at what power is he working ?
(g = 10 m s^{-2})

50. Name the energy transfers which occur when :
(*a*) an electric bell rings
(*b*) someone speaks into a microphone
(*c*) there is a picture on a television screen
(*d*) a torch is on

Name the energy transfer which occurs when someone speaks into a microphone

ANSWERS

3. Kilowatt (kW) and Megawatt (MW) **6.** Power **7.** 1 W **8.** 10 W **10.** (*a*) Power (*b*) Energy **11.** Unit of electricity **12.** Chemical energy into Electrical energy **13.** Electric motor **14.** (*a*) Electric generator (Alternator or Dynamo) (*b*) Cell (or Battery) (*c*) Electric iron (*d*) Solar cell (*e*) Electric bulb **15.** (*i*) Speaker (as in radio) (*ii*) Steam engine (*iii*) Car engine (*iv*) Gas stove (*v*) Solar water heater **16.** (*a*) work (*b*) joule ; second (*c*) kWh (*d*) conservation ; transformed ; created ; destroyed (*e*) kinetic ; potential **17.** 400 W **20.** 480 W **21.** 60 kJ **22.** 2 kW **23.** (*a*) 100 J (*b*) 6000 J **24.** 2.4 kWh **27.** Fan ; Washing machine ; Mixer and grinder ; Water pump ; Hair dryer **28.** (*i*) Chemical energy to Electrical energy (*b*) Electrical energy to Light energy (and Heat energy) **29.** (*i*) Maximum potential energy in position C ; Because at position C, the bob is at the maximum height (*ii*) Maximum kinetic energy in position A ; Because at position A, the bob has maximum speed (or velocity) **30.** (*a*) 2400 kJ (*b*) 24 kW **33.** (*b*) 1 kWh **34.** (*b*) 2.34 × 10^9 J **35.** (*b*) 360 W **36.** (*c*) **37.** (*c*) **38.** (*b*) **39.** (*c*) **40.** (*c*) **41.** (*c*) **42.** (*c*) **43.** (*d*) **44.** (*b*) **45.** (*d*) **46.** Total energy at 5 m above ground = P.E. 50 J + K.E. 0 J = 50 J ; Total energy at 3.2 m above ground = P.E. 32 J + K.E. 18 J = 50 J ; Total energy at 0 m above ground = P.E. 0 J + K.E. 50 J = 50 J ; Since the total energy (potential energy + kinetic energy) of the freely falling body at all the three positions during its fall remains the same (50 J), therefore, the given data verifies the law of conservation of energy **47.** (*a*) 80 J (*b*) 32 J (*c*) Law of conservation of energy **48.** 559 W **49.** (*a*) 150 J (*b*) 150 J (*c*) 10 W **50.** (*a*) Electrical energy to Sound energy (*b*) Sound energy to Electrical energy (c) Electrical energy to Light energy (and Heat energy) (*d*) Chemical energy to Electrical energy to Light energy (and Heat energy)

SOUND

The sensation felt by our ears is called sound. **Sound is a form of energy. Sound is that form of energy which makes us hear**. We hear many sounds around us in our everyday life. At home we hear the sounds of our parents talking to us. We also hear the sounds of telephone bell, radio, television, stereo-system, mixer-grinder and washing machine. At school we hear the sounds of our teachers, classmates and the school bell. We hear the sounds of scooters, motorcycles, cars, buses and trucks on the road. And the sound of a flying aeroplane is heard from the sky. At a music concert, we hear the sounds produced by various musical instruments like *sitar*, *veena*, violin, guitar, *tanpura*, piano, harmonium, flute, *shehnai*, *tabla* and cymbals, etc. And in a garden, we hear the sounds of chirping of birds.

SOUND TRAVELS IN THE FORM OF WAVES

A wave is a vibratory disturbance in a medium which carries energy from one point to another

Figure 1. If we throw a piece of stone in the still surface of water in a pond, then expanding circles called ripples (or water waves) are formed over the surface of water. When a water wave passes over the surface of water in a pond, there is no actual movement of water from the centre to the sides of the pond, only the water molecules vibrate up and down about their fixed positions (though the water appears to be moving to us).

Figure 2. Just like ripples or water waves on the surface of water, sound is also a kind of wave motion. When sound produced by any vibrating body (say, the vocal cords of a singer or the vibrating parts of a muscial instrument) comes to us through air, there is no actual movement of air from the sound producing body to our ears. Only sound energy travels through the vibrations of air molecules in the form of sound waves.

without there being a direct contact between the two points. A wave is produced by the vibrations of the particles of the medium through which it passes. When a wave passes through a medium, the medium itself does not move along the direction of the wave, only the particles of the medium vibrate about their fixed positions. For example, when sound waves produced by a ringing bell come to us through air, there is no actual movement of the air from the bell to our ears. Only the sound energy travels through the vibrations of the air molecules. Similarly, when a water wave passes over the surface of water in a pond, it does not drive water to one side of the pond, only the water molecules vibrate up and down about their fixed positions. **There are two types of waves : longitudinal waves and transverse waves.**

Sound Waves are Longitudinal Waves

A wave in which the particles of the medium vibrate back and forth in the 'same direction' in which the wave is moving, is called a longitudinal wave. A longitudinal wave has been illustrated in Figure 3. In Figure 3, the direction of wave has been shown from *A* to *B*, in the horizontal plane. The direction of

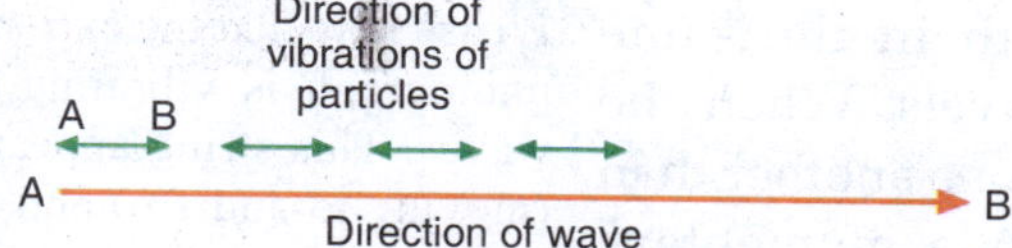

Figure 3. Diagram to explain the meaning of a longitudinal wave.

vibrations of the particles is also along *AB*, parallel to the direction of wave. That is, the particles of the medium vibrate back and forth in the horizontal direction. Please note that **longitudinal waves can be produced in all the three media : solids, liquids and gases.** We will now describe the formation of longitudinal waves on a spring or slinky. A long, flexible spring which can be compressed or extended easily is called slinky.

1. The waves which travel along a spring (or slinky) when it is pushed and pulled at one end, are longitudinal waves. Before we discuss this further, it is necessary to understand the words 'compression' and 'rarefaction' as applied to a spring. The normal position of a spring has been shown in Figure 4(*a*).

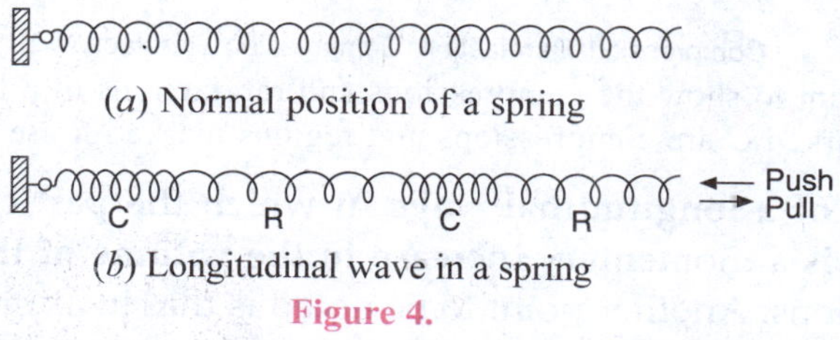

Figure 4.

(*a*) In a spring, a compression is that part in which the coils (or turns) are closer together than normal. In Figure 4(*b*), the regions marked *C* are compressions.

(*b*) In a spring, a rarefaction is that part in which the coils (or turns) are farther apart than normal. In Figure 4(*b*), the regions marked *R* are rarefactions.

We will now describe how longitudinal waves are formed on a spring. Figure 4(*a*) shows the normal position of a spring whose one end is fixed. Now, if the free end of the spring is moved to and fro continuously, then longitudinal waves consisting of alternate compressions and rarefactions travel along the spring [see Figure 4(*b*)].

When a wave travels along the spring, then each turn of the spring moves back and forth by only a small distance in the direction of the wave. Since the particles of the medium (turns of the spring) are moving back and forth in the direction of the wave, the waves which travel across the spring are longitudinal waves.

2. The sound waves in air are longitudinal waves. When a sound wave passes through air, the particles of air vibrate back and forth parallel to the direction of sound wave. Thus, when a sound wave travels in the horizontal direction, then the particles of the medium also vibrate back and forth in the horizontal direction. Please note that **the waves produced in air when a guitar wire (*sitar* wire, *tanpura* wire or violin wire) is plucked are longitudinal waves,** because they are sound waves.

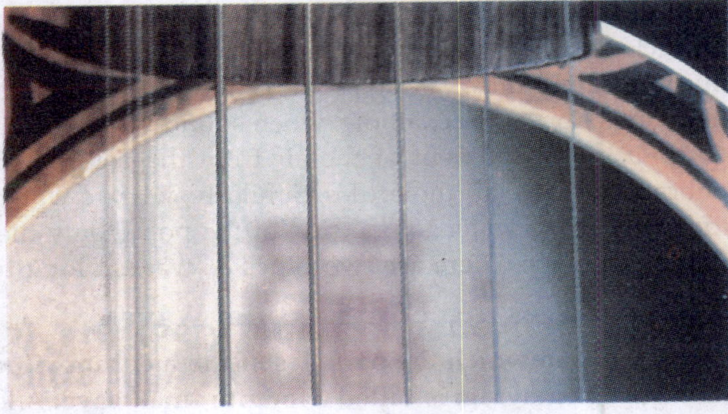

Figure 5. When a guitar wire or guitar string is plucked, it vibrates and produces longitudinal waves (sound waves) in air. Please note that the extreme left side string of guitar in the above photograph is vibrating at the moment and producing sound waves. This string appears to be blurred because it is vibrating (moving to-and-fro) and not stationary.

We know that when a longitudinal wave travels in a medium, then the particles of the medium vibrate back and forth in the same direction in which the wave travels. When the vibrating particles come closer to one another than they normally are, then there is a momentary reduction in volume and a compression is formed. On the other hand, when the vibrating particles move farther apart from one another than they normally are, then there is a momentary increase in volume and a rarefaction is formed.

A compression is that part of a longitudinal wave in which the particles of the medium are closer to one another than they normally are, and there is a momentary reduction in volume of the medium. Figure 6 shows a longitudinal sound wave in air. In Figure 6, all the regions marked *C* are compressions.

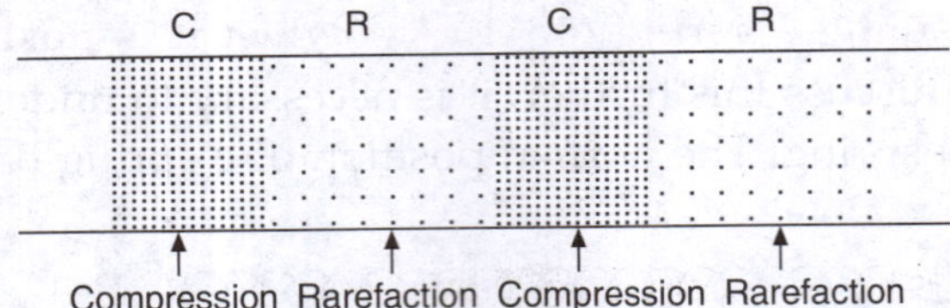

Figure 6. Diagram to show the compressions and rarefactions of a longitudinal wave. Regions marked *C* are compressions and regions marked *R* are rarefactions.

A rarefaction is that part of a longitudinal wave in which the particles of the medium are farther apart than normal, and there is a momentary increase in the volume of the medium. In Figure 6, all the regions marked *R* are rarefactions. Another point to be noted is that in a compression, there is a temporary increase in the density of the medium; and in a rarefaction, there is a temporary decrease in the density of the medium through which a longitudinal wave passes. When the density of the medium increases, its pressure also increases; and when the density of the medium decreases, then its pressure also decreases. So, we can also say that **compression is a region of high pressure** whereas **rarefaction is a region of low pressure.** From the above discussion we conclude that **a longitudinal wave consists of compressions and rarefactions travelling through a medium.**

There are also another type of waves called transverse waves. **A wave in which the particles of the medium vibrate up and down 'at right angles' to the direction in which the wave is moving, is called a transverse wave.** A transverse wave is illustrated in Figure 7. In Figure 7, the direction of wave is from *P* to

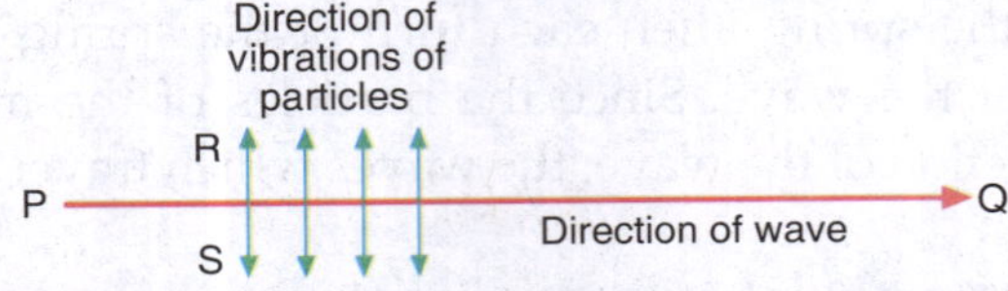

Figure 7. Diagram to explain the meaning of a transverse wave.

Q but the vibrations of the particles are along *RS* which is at right angles to the direction of wave *PQ*. So, this is a transverse wave. **Transverse waves can be produced only in solids and liquids but not in gases.** We will now describe the formation of transverse waves on a long spring or slinky.

1. The waves produced by moving one end of a long spring (or slinky) up and down rapidly, whose other end is fixed, are transverse waves. The transverse wave produced on a slinky is shown in Figure 8.

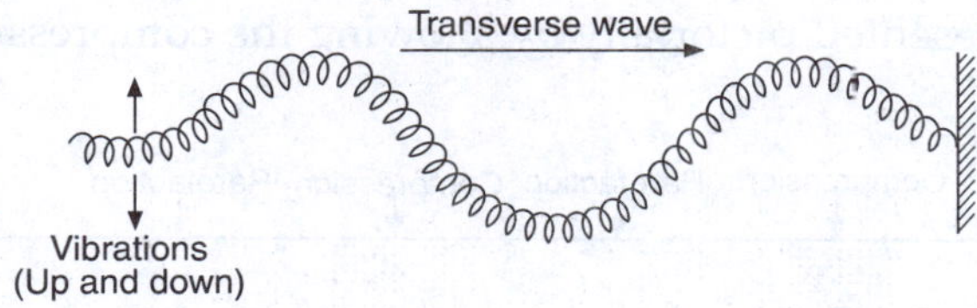

Figure 8. Transverse wave on a long spring (or slinky).

As the wave passes along the slinky in the horizontal direction, the particles of slinky vibrate 'up and down' at right angles to the direction of wave.

2. The water waves (or ripples) formed on the surface of water in a pond are also transverse waves. This is because of the fact that in a water wave, the molecules of water move up and down in the vertical direction when the wave travels in the horizontal direction along the water surface. Since the water molecules vibrate up and down at the same place, therefore, a cork or leaf placed on the surface of water moves up and down at the same place as water wave moves across the surface of the pond. The shape of transverse water waves produced on the surface of water is just like those formed on a slinky as shown in Figure 8. Thus, **when a stone is dropped in a pond of water, transverse water waves are produced on the surface of water.** Even the light waves and radio waves are transverse waves.

We know that when **a transverse wave travels horizontally in a medium, the particles of the medium vibrate up and down in the vertical direction**. When the vibrating particles move upward, above the line of zero disturbance, they form an 'elevation' or 'hump' and when the vibrating particles move downward, below the line of zero disturbance, they form a 'depression' or 'hollow' (see Figure 9).

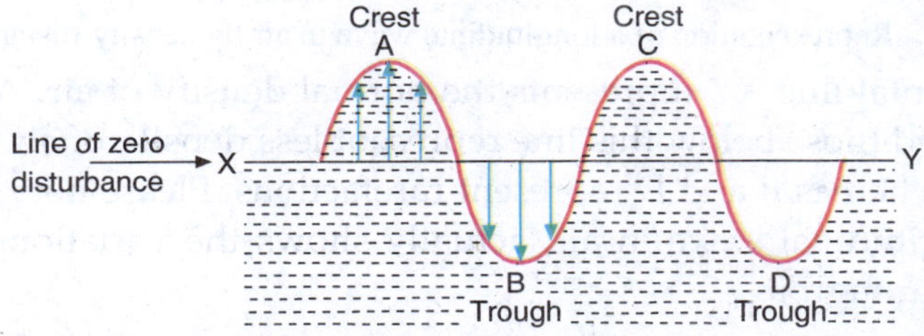

Figure 9. Diagram to show the crests and troughs of a transverse wave. Here, *A* and *C* are crests; *B* and *D* are troughs.

The 'elevation' or 'hump' in a transverse wave is called crest. In other words, **a crest is that part of the transverse wave which is above the line of zero disturbance of the medium.** In Figure 9, *XY* is the line of zero disturbance and *A* and *C* are the two crests of the transverse water waves.

The 'depression' or 'hollow' in a transverse wave is called trough. In other words, **a trough is that part of the transverse wave which is below the line of zero disturbance.** In Figure 9, *B* and *D* are the two troughs of the transverse water waves. These troughs are below the line of zero disturbance *XY*. When we look at the water waves moving on the surface of water in a pond, we find that at some places the water level is higher than the normal level whereas at other places the water level is lower than the normal level. The 'higher water level' points are 'crests' and the 'lower water level' points are 'troughs' of the water waves. From the above discussion we conclude that **a transverse wave consists of crests and troughs.**

When a wave passes through a medium, then some property of the medium like density or displacement etc., changes. So, **waves are represented graphically by showing how some property of the medium (like**

density, displacement, etc.,) changes when a wave passes through it. This point will become more clear from the following discussion.

Graphical Representation of Longitudinal Waves

When a longitudinal wave passes through a medium, say air, then some of the particles of air get crowded together and form compression, whereas other particles go farther apart and form a rarefaction. So, a longitudinal wave is represented pictorially by showing the compressions and rarefactions as follows (see Figure 10).

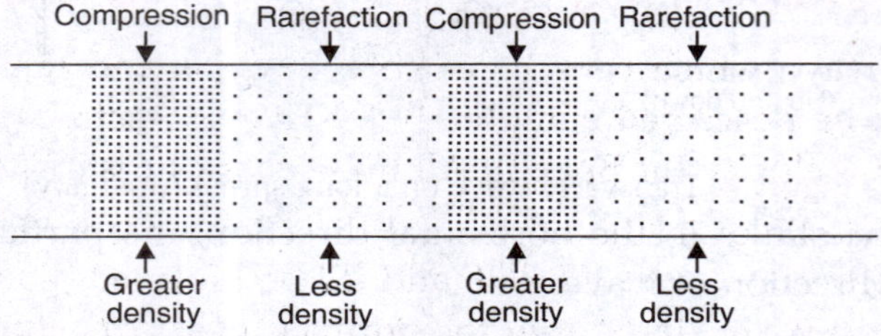

Figure 10. Pictorial representation of a longitudinal wave (in air).

In a compression, the density of air is high whereas in a rarefaction, the density of air is low. Thus, when a longitudinal wave passes through air, then the density of air changes continuously. So, **a longitudinal wave in air is represented graphically by plotting the density of air against distance from the source.** In other words, a longitudinal wave is represented by a *density-distance* graph. A longitudinal wave in air has been represented by means of a density-distance graph in Figure 11.

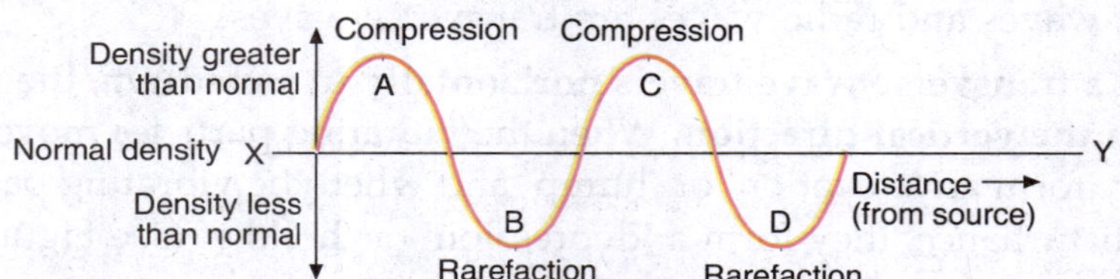

Figure 11. Representation of a longitudinal wave in air by density-distance graph.

In Figure 11, the horizontal line *XY* represents the normal density of air. All the points above this line represent greater density and those below this line represent less density of air than normal. So, here *A* and *C* represent compressions whereas *B* and *D* represent rarefactions. Please note that the wavy line in Figure 11 which represents a longitudinal wave in air, actually shows the variation of the density of air as the longitudinal wave passes through it.

We will now describe the graphical representation of transverse waves. When a transverse wave passes through a medium, then some particles of the medium are displaced above the line of zero disturbance whereas others are displaced below the line of zero disturbance. So, **a transverse wave is represented graphically by plotting the displacement of different particles of the medium from the line of zero disturbance against distance from the source.** In other words, a transverse wave is represented by a *displacement-distance* graph.

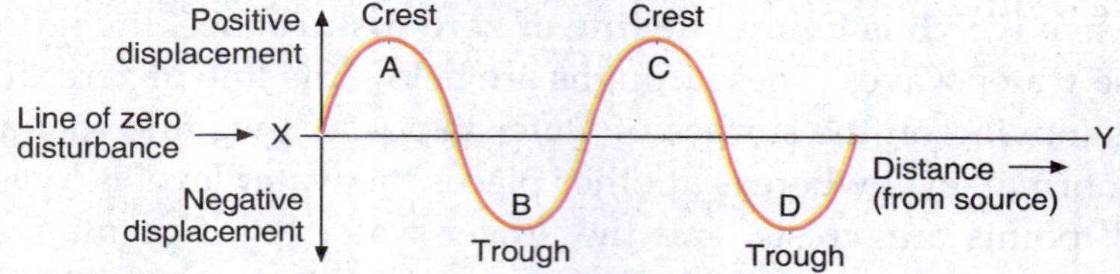

Figure 12. Representation of a transverse wave by a displacement-distance graph.

Figure 12 shows how a transverse wave is represented by a displacement-distance graph. In the above

Figure, the horizontal line *XY* represents the line of zero disturbance of the particles of the medium. All the particles above this line have positive displacements and those below it have negative displacements. In the above Figure, *A* and *C* represent two crests, and *B* and *D* represent two troughs of the transverse wave. Thus, the wavy line in Figure 12 which represents a transverse wave actually shows the variation of the displacements of the particles in the different parts of the wave. We will now describe the various characteristics of a sound wave.

CHARACTERISTICS OF A SOUND WAVE

Sound is a longitudinal wave which consists of compressions and rarefactions travelling through a medium. **A sound wave can be described completely by five characteristics : Wavelength, Amplitude, Time-period, Frequency and Velocity (or Speed).** All these characteristics of a sound wave are described below.

Consider the longitudinal sound waves *ABCDE* and *EFGHI* formed by the vibrations of a tuning fork (see Figure 13). The first sound wave starts from the normal density position *A* and after going through

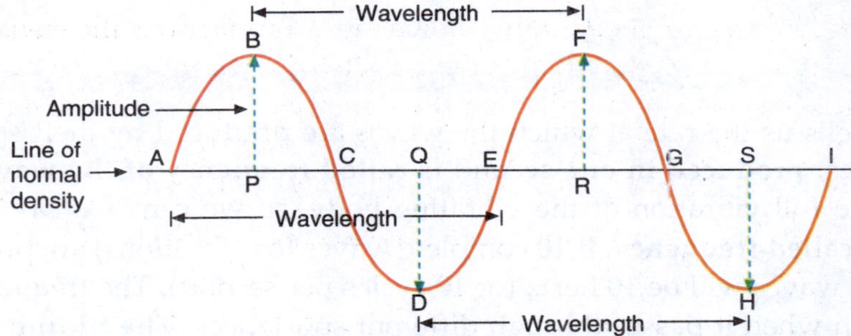

Figure 13. Characteristics of a sound wave.

compression along *ABC* and rarefaction along *CDE*, it returns to the normal density position *E*. Thus, the portion *ABCDE* represents one complete sound wave. The next sound wave starts from point *E* and goes up to point *I* (and so on). Thus, the above Figure shows two complete sound waves : from *A* to *E*, and from *E* to *I*. We will now describe the wavelength, amplitude, time-period, frequency and velocity (or speed) of the sound wave.

1. Wavelength

The minimum distance in which a sound wave repeats itself is called its wavelength. In most simple words, it is the length of one complete wave. The wavelength is denoted by the Greek letter lambda, λ. *In a sound wave, the combined length of a compression and an adjacent rarefaction is called its wavelength.* For example, in Figure 13, the length of compression is *AC* and that of the adjacent rarefaction is *CE*, so the combined length *AE* is equal to wavelength. *In a sound wave, the distance between the centres of two consecutive compressions (or two consecutive rarefactions) is also equal to its wavelength.* In Figure 13, the distance between the centres of two consecutive compressions is *PR*, so the distance *PR* represents wavelength of the sound wave. Similarly, the distance between the centres of two consecutive rarefactions is *QS*, so the distance *QS* also represents wavelength. Please note that *the distance between the centres of a compression and an adjacent rarefaction is equal to half the wavelength* $\left(\frac{\lambda}{2}\right)$. For example, the distance *PQ* in Figure 13 is half wavelength $\left(\frac{\lambda}{2}\right)$. **The SI unit for measuring wavelength is metre (m).** Sometimes, however, centimetre unit is also used for expressing wavelength.

2. Amplitude

When a wave passes through a medium, the particles of the medium get displaced temporarily from their original undisturbed positions. **The maximum displacement of the particles of the medium from their original undisturbed positions, when a wave passes through the medium, is called amplitude of the wave.** The term amplitude is, in fact, used to describe the size of the wave. In Figure 13, *PB* is the amplitude of the wave. The amplitude of a wave is usually denoted by the letter *A*. The SI unit of measurement of amplitude is metre (m) though sometimes it is also measured in centimetres. It should be noted that **the amplitude of a wave is the same as the amplitude of the vibrating body producing the wave.**

3. Time-Period

The time required to produce one complete wave (or cycle) is called time-period of the wave. Now, one complete wave is produced by one full vibration of the vibrating body. So, we can write another definition of time-period as follows : **The time taken to complete one vibration is called time-period.** Figure 13 shows two complete waves (one wave from *A* to *E* and another wave from *E* to *I*). Suppose these two waves are produced in 1 second. Then the time required to produce one wave will be $\frac{1}{2}$ second or 0.5 second. In other words, the time-period of this wave will be 0.5 second. The time-period of a wave is denoted by the letter *T*. The unit of measurement of time-period is second (s).

4. Frequency

The term frequency tells us the rate at which the waves are produced by their source. **The number of complete waves (or cycles) produced in one second is called frequency of the wave.** Since one complete wave is produced by one full vibration of the vibrating body, so we can also say that : **The number of vibrations per second is called frequency.** If 10 complete waves (or vibrations) are produced in one second, then the frequency of the waves will be 10 hertz (or 10 cycles per second). The frequency of a wave is fixed and does not change even when it passes through different substances. **The SI unit of frequency is hertz** (which is written as **Hz**). A vibrating body emitting 1 wave per second is said to have a frequency of 1 hertz. In other words, **1 hertz is equal to 1 vibration per second.** Sometimes, however, a bigger unit of frequency called kilohertz (kHz) is also used (1 kHz = 1000 Hz). The frequency of a wave is denoted by the letter *f*, though in some books, they use *ν* (nu) to denote frequency. The tuning forks are often marked with

Figure 14. Heinrich Hertz : The scientist after whom the unit of frequency called 'hertz' (Hz) is named.

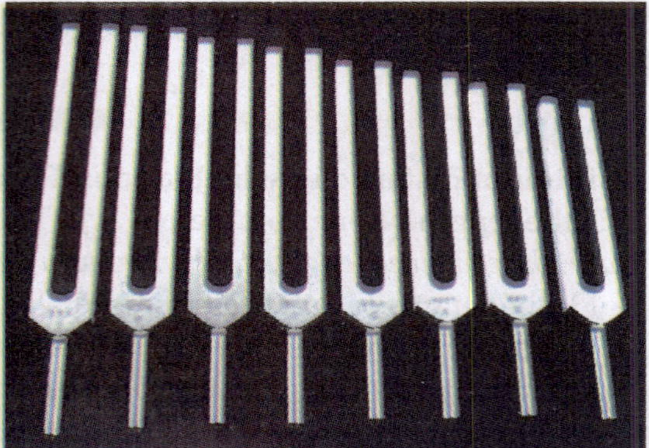

Figure 15. This is a set of tuning forks all having different frequencies. The frequency of a tuning fork is usually engraved on it. These tuning forks are used to produce sound waves in air having different frequencies for performing experiments based on sound.

numbers like 256, 384 or 512, etc. These numbers signify the frequency of vibration of the tuning forks. For example, a tuning fork of frequency 256 means that its prongs will make 256 vibrations per second and emit 256 complete sound waves per second when hit on a hard surface. It should be clear by now that **the frequency of a wave is the same as the frequency of the vibrating body which produces the wave.**

We will now give **the relation between time-period and frequency of a wave.** The time required to produce one complete wave is called time-period of the wave. Suppose the time-period of a wave is T seconds.

Now, In T seconds, number of waves produced = 1

So, In 1 second, number of waves produced will be $= \frac{1}{T}$

But the number of waves produced in 1 second is called its frequency. This means that the frequency of the wave of time-period T will be $\frac{1}{T}$. So, we can now say that **the frequency of a wave is the reciprocal of its time-period.** That is,

$$\textbf{Frequency} = \frac{\textbf{1}}{\textbf{Time period}}$$

or $$f = \frac{1}{T}$$

where f = frequency of the wave

and T = time-period of the wave

5. Velocity of Wave (or Speed of Wave)

The distance travelled by a wave in one second is called velocity of the wave (or speed of the wave). The velocity of a wave is represented by the letter v. **The SI unit for measuring the velocity of a wave is metres per second (m/s or m s^{-1}).**

Relationship Between Velocity, Frequency and Wavelength of a Wave

We know that, $$\text{Velocity} = \frac{\text{Distance travelled}}{\text{Time taken}}$$

Suppose a wave travels a distance lambda, λ, (which is its wavelength) in time T, then :

$$v = \frac{\lambda}{T}$$

Here T is the time taken by one wave. We know that $\frac{1}{T}$ becomes the number of waves per second and this is known as frequency (f) of the wave. So, we can write f in place of $\frac{1}{T}$ in the above relation. Thus,

$$v = f \times \lambda$$

where v = velocity of the wave

f = frequency

and lambda, λ = wavelength

In other words : **Velocity of a wave = Frequency × Wavelength**

Thus, **the velocity (or speed) of a wave in a medium is equal to the product of its frequency and wavelength.** The formula $v = f \times \lambda$ is called wave equation. It applies to all types of waves : transverse waves (like water waves), longitudinal waves (like sound waves) and electromagnetic waves (like light waves and radio waves). **The wave equation has three quantities in it, so if we know the values of any two quantities, then the value of third quantity can be calculated.** We will use this formula to solve numerical problems.

Sample Problem 1. If 25 sound waves are produced per second, what is the frequency in hertz ?

Solution. The frequency in hertz is equal to the number of waves produced per second. In this case, since 25 waves are being produced per second, so the frequency of the sound waves is 25 hertz (which is also written as 25 Hz).

Sample Problem 2. What is the frequency of a sound wave whose time-period is 0.05 s ?

Solution. The relationship between the frequency and time-period of a wave is :

$$f = \frac{1}{T}$$

Here, Frequency, f = ? (To be calculated)

And, Time-period, T = 0.05 s

Putting this value in the above relation, we get :

$$f = \frac{1}{0.05}$$

$$f = \frac{100}{5}$$

$$f = 20 \text{ Hz}$$

Thus, the frequency of the sound wave is 20 hertz.

Sample Problem 3. The wavelength of sound emitted by a source is 1.7×10^{-2} m. Calculate frequency of the sound, if its velocity is 343.4 m s^{-1}.

Solution. The relationship between velocity, frequency and wavelength of a wave is given by the formula :

$$v = f \times \lambda$$

Here, Velocity, v = 343.4 m s^{-1}

Frequency, f = ? (To be calculated)

And, Wavelength, $\lambda = 1.7 \times 10^{-2}$ m

So, putting these values in the above formula, we get :

$$343.4 = f \times 1.7 \times 10^{-2}$$

$$f = \frac{343.4}{1.7 \times 10^{-2}}$$

$$f = \frac{3434 \times 10^{2}}{17}$$

$$f = 2.02 \times 10^{4} \text{ Hz}$$

Thus, the frequency of sound is 2.02×10^4 hertz.

Sample Problem 4. Sound waves travel with a speed of about 330 m/s. What is the wavelength of sound whose frequency is 550 hertz ?

Solution. Here, Speed of waves, v = 330 m/s

Frequency of waves, f = 550 Hz

And, Wavelength, λ = ? (To be calculated)

Now, $v = f \times \lambda$

So, $330 = 550 \times \lambda$

$$\lambda = \frac{330}{550}$$

$$\lambda = 0.6 \text{ m}$$

Thus, the wavelength of sound waves is 0.6 metre.

Sample Problem 5. A source is producing 1500 sound waves in 3 seconds. If the distance covered by a compression and an adjacent rarefaction be 68 cm, find : (*a*) frequency, (*b*) wavelength, and (*c*) velocity, of the sound wave.

Solution. (*a*) **Frequency.** We know that frequency of a wave is the number of waves produced in 1 second.

Here, No. of waves produced in 3 seconds = 1500

So, No. of waves produced in 1 second $= \dfrac{1500}{3}$

$= 500$

So, the frequency of this sound wave is 500 hertz.

(*b*) **Wavelength.** In a sound wave, the distance covered by a compression and an adjacent rarefaction is equal to its wavelength. This distance has been given to be 68 cm. So, the wavelength (λ) of this sound wave is 68 cm.

(*c*) **Velocity.** The formula for calculating the velocity of a sound wave is :

$$v = f \times \lambda$$

Here, Frequency, f = 500 Hz (Calculated above)

And, Wavelength, λ = 68 cm (Calculated above)

$$= \frac{68}{100} \text{ m}$$

$$= 0.68 \text{ m}$$

Putting these values of f and λ in the above formula, we get :

$$v = 500 \times 0.68$$

$$= 340 \text{ m/s}$$

Thus, the velocity (or speed) of the sound waves is 340 m/s.

PRODUCTION OF SOUND

If we touch a silent bicycle bell, we do not find anything special in it. Let us now ring the bicycle bell and touch it gently again. We will find that a ringing bicycle bell (which is producing sound) is vibrating, that is, it is moving back and forth continuously through a very small distance. Now, if we hold this ringing bell tightly with our hand, it stops vibrating and the sound coming from it also stops. It is clear that when the bicycle bell is vibrating, it is producing sound, and when the bicycle bell stops vibrating, the sound also stops. From this discussion we conclude that **sound is produced when an object vibrates (moves back and forth rapidly).** In other words, **sound is produced by vibrating objects.** Whenever we hear a sound, then some material must be vibrating to produce that sound. A vibrating object, which produces sound, has a certain amount of energy which travels in the form of sound waves. **The energy required to make an object vibrate and produce sound is provided by some outside source (like our hand, wind, etc.).**

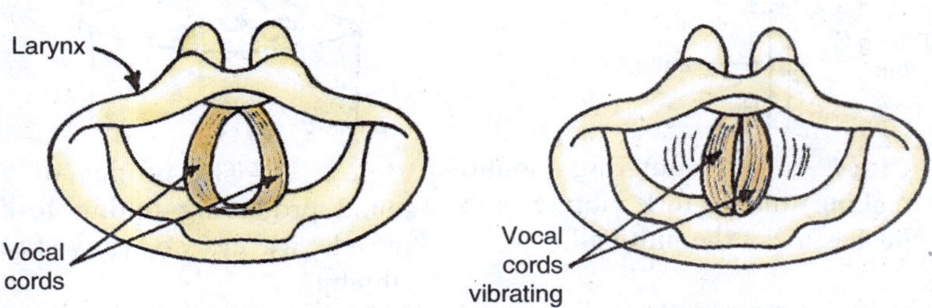

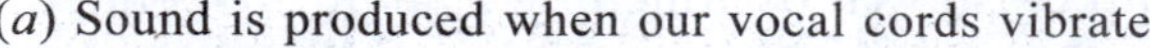
(*a*) Sound is produced when our vocal cords vibrate

(*b*) Sound is produced when the skin (or membrane) of a drum vibrates

Figure 16. Sound is produced by vibrating objects.

The buzzing sound of a bee or mosquito is produced by the vibrations of their wings; the sound in a *sitar*, *veena* or guitar is produced by the vibrations of stretched strings (stretched wires); **the sound of our voice is produced by the vibrations of two vocal cords in our throat** caused by air coming from the lungs; **the sound of a drum (or *tabla*) is produced by the vibrations of its skin (or membrane) when struck**; the sound of a flute (*bansuri*) is produced by the vibrations of air enclosed in the flute tube; the sound of school bell is produced by the vibrations of an iron or brass plate when it is hit by a hammer; and the sound in a

Figure 17. In a guitar, sound is produced by the vibrations of stretched strings (or stretched wires) when plucked.

Figure 18. In a flute, sound is produced by the vibrations of an air column enclosed inside it when wind is blown into it.

Figure 19. In a drum, sound is produced by the vibrations of its stretched skin (or stretched membrane) when struck.

radio (or television) is produced by the vibrations of the thin diaphragm of a speaker. **In most of the cases, a sound producing object vibrates so fast that we cannot see its vibrations with our eyes.**

In the laboratory experiments, sound is produced by vibrating tuning forks. A tuning fork has two hard steel prongs *A* and *B* connected at the lower end to a stem or handle *H* (see Figure 21). When the prongs of the tuning fork are struck on a hard rubber pad, the prongs vibrate and a sound is produced. If we look at the prongs of the sounding tuning fork, they appear to be blurred as if they were moving back

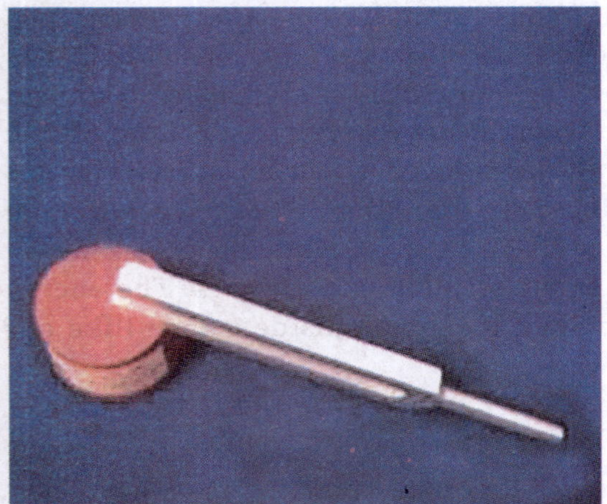

Figure 20. This photograph shows a tuning fork alongwith the hard rubber pad on which it is struck to produce sound.

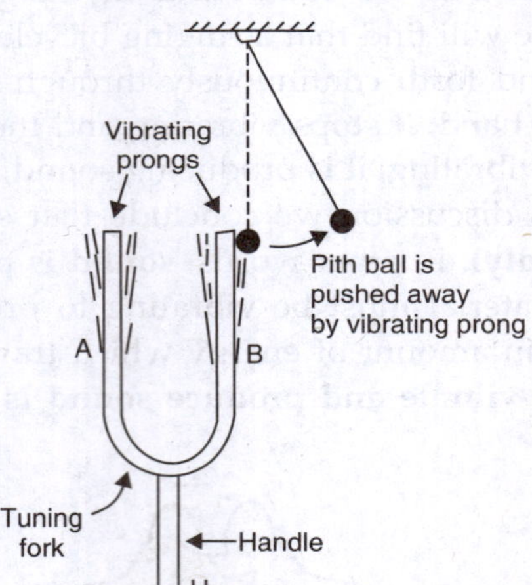

Figure 21. A sounding (sound making) tuning fork vibrates and pushes away the pith ball.

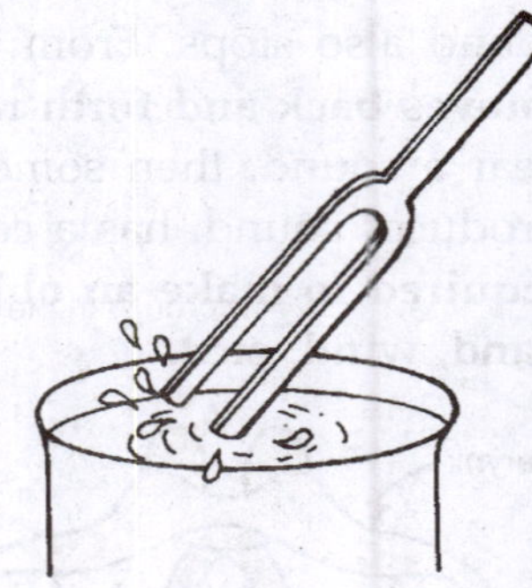

Figure 22. The prongs of a sound producing tuning fork splash water, so they are vibrating.

and forth rapidly. The vibrations of the tuning fork can be shown by touching a small suspended pith ball (cork ball) with a prong of the sounding tuning fork. The pith ball is pushed away with a great force (as shown in Figure 21). The pith ball can be pushed away only if the prong *B* moves to the right side (while vibrating) and strikes it hard. This experiment shows that the prongs of a sound producing tuning fork are vibrating.

We can also show the vibrations of the prongs of a sound making tuning fork by performing another simple experiment as follows : We fill water in a beaker up to its brim. Touch the surface of water with the prongs of a sound making tuning fork (which has been struck on a hard rubber pad). The prongs of sound making tuning fork splash water (see Figure 22). This shows that the prongs of a sound producing tuning fork are vibrating (moving forwards and backwards rapidly). Please note that we cannot see the ends of a tuning fork vibrating because the vibrations are too fast.

From the above discussion we conclude that **sound can be produced by the following methods :**

1. By vibrating strings (as in a *sitar*),
2. By vibrating air (as in a flute),

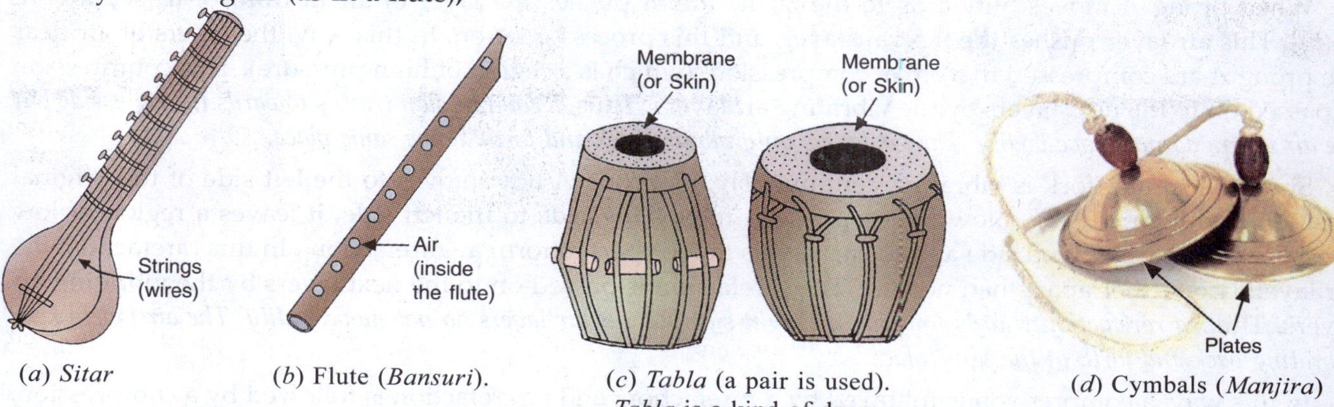

(*a*) *Sitar* (*b*) Flute (*Bansuri*). (*c*) *Tabla* (a pair is used). *Tabla* is a kind of drum. (*d*) Cymbals (*Manjira*)

Figure 23. Sound can be produced by vibrating stretched strings (as in a *sitar*), by vibrating air columns (as in a flute), by vibrating stretched membranes (as in a drum, *tabla*, etc.), and by vibrating plates (as in cymbals).

3. By vibrating membranes (as in a drum), and
4. By vibrating plates (as in cymbals)

We will now describe how sound waves are produced in air by the vibrating bodies and how sound is transmitted from the sound-producing body to our ears.

Sound Waves in Air

Sound waves in air consist of compressions and rarefactions of air. We will now describe how sound waves are set up in air by a vibrating body.

Suppose the original position of the air layers (when no sound is passing through it) is as shown in Figure 24(*a*). We now strike a tuning fork against a rubber pad so that both the prongs start vibrating back

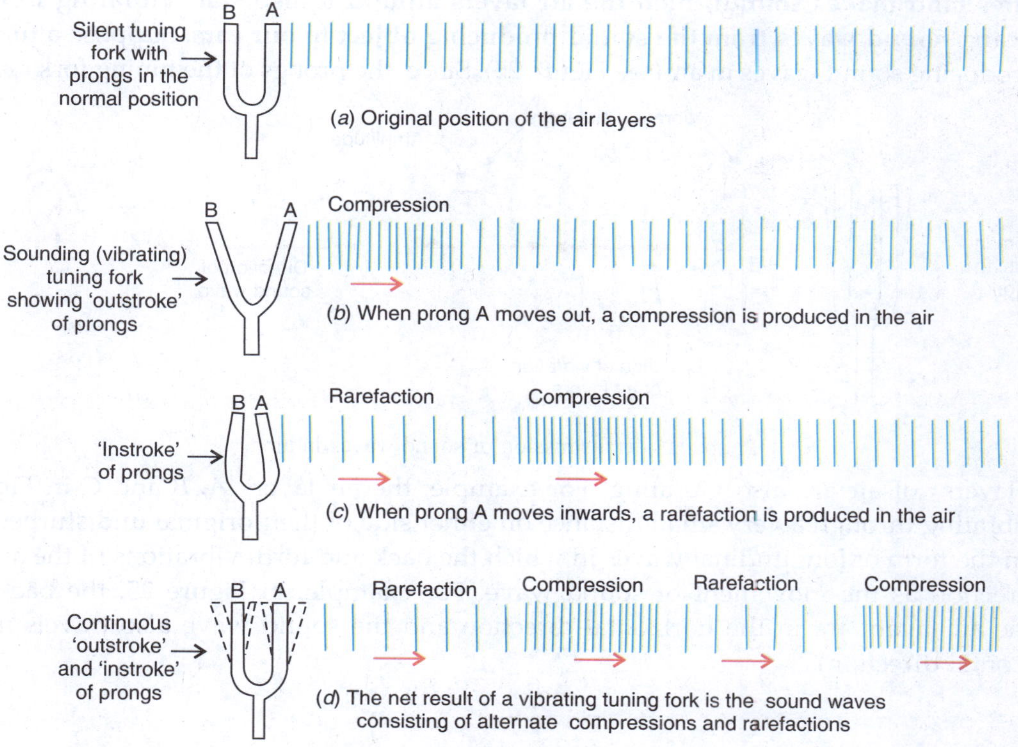

Figure 24. Production of sound waves in air.

and forth continuously and produce sound (To make things simple, we will consider only one prong *A* of the tuning fork).

When prong *A* moves outwards to the right side, it pushes the layer of air in front of it [see Figure 24(*b*)]. This air layer pushes the next air layer, and this process goes on. In this way, the layers of air near the prong *A* are compressed to form a 'compression' (which is a region of high pressure). This compression is passed on to the next layers by the vibrating air layers. Thus, *a compression travels towards the right side but the air layers do not move bodily. The air layers only vibrate back and forth at the same place.*

Since the tuning fork is vibrating continuously, its prong *A* now moves to the left side of the original position [see Figure 24(*c*)]. Now, when prong *A* moves inwards to the left side, it leaves a region of low pressure on the right hand side and the air layers move apart to form a 'rarefaction'. In this rarefaction, the air layers are farther apart than normal. The rarefaction is passed on to the next layers by the vibrating air layers. Thus, *a rarefaction travels towards the right side but the air layers do not move bodily. The air layers keep vibrating back and forth at the same place.*

In this way, a compression is followed by a rarefaction, and a rarefaction is followed by a compression, and so on. This process is repeated as long as the tuning fork is vibrating and producing sound. Thus, **the net result of a sound producing body (here a tuning fork) is that it sends the waves consisting of alternate compressions and rarefactions in air** [as shown in Figure 24(*d*)]. When these waves of compressions and rarefactions of air fall on our ears, the ear drums vibrate accordingly and reproduce the sound. And we can hear the sound being produced by the vibrating tuning fork.

The sound waves in air are longitudinal waves. When a sound wave passes through the air, the layers of air vibrate back and forth in the same direction in which the sound wave travels. Please note that the layers of air consist of molecules of gases of air. So, when we say that the air layers vibrate back and forth, we actually mean that the molecules in air layers vibrate back and forth by a small distance.

Propagation of Sound (or Transmission of Sound)

We will now describe how sound reaches from a vibrating body (source of sound) to our ears. **When an object vibrates (and makes sound), then the air layers around it also start vibrating in exactly the same way and carry sound waves from the sound producing object to our ears.** Suppose a tuning fork is vibrating and producing sound waves in air (see Figure 25). Since the prongs of the tuning fork are vibrating,

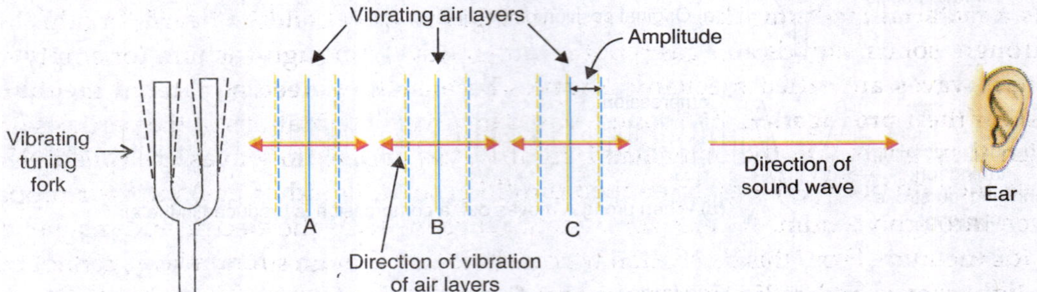

Figure 25. Transmission of sound waves in air.

the individual layers of air are also vibrating. For example, the air layers *A*, *B* and *C* in Figure 25 are continuously vibrating through a very small distance on either side of their original undisturbed positions. Sound travels in the form of longitudinal waves in which the back and forth vibrations of the air layers are in the same direction as the movement of sound wave. For example, in Figure 25, the back and forth vibrations of the air layers are in the horizontal direction and the sound wave also travels in the same direction (horizontal direction).

Please note that **in the transmission of sound through air, there is no actual movement of air from the sound-producing body to our ear. The air layers only vibrate back and forth, and transfer the sound energy from one layer to the next layer till it reaches our ear.** This point will become more clear from the following example.

If we turn on a gas tap for a few seconds, a person standing a few metres away will hear the sound of escaping gas first and the smell of gas reaches him afterwards. This can be explained as follows. The sound of gas travels through the vibrations of air layers so it reaches first, but the smell of gas reaches the person through the actual movement of the air layers, which takes more time. It is clear that the sound is not being transmitted by the actual movement of air from the gas tap to the person, otherwise he would hear and smell the gas at the same time. We will now discuss the amplitude and frequency of a sound wave.

The maximum distance moved by a vibrating air layer on either side of its original position is known as the amplitude of the sound wave (see Figure 25). The amplitude of a sound wave is usually a very, very small fraction of a centimetre.

The number of complete back and forth vibrations of an air layer in one second is known as the frequency of the sound wave. The frequency of a sound wave is the same as that of the vibrating body which produces the sound. Suppose the frequency of a tuning fork is 256 hertz. This means that when this tuning fork is vibrating and making sound, then the layers of air make 256 complete vibrations per second (as the sound wave passes through the air). So, the frequency of this sound wave will also be 256 hertz.

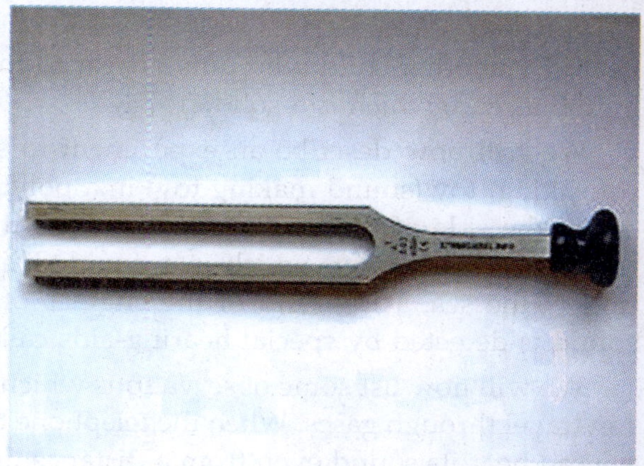

Figure 26. This is a tuning fork of frequency 256 Hz. When the prong of this tuning fork is struck on a hard rubber pad, it will vibrate with a frequency of 256 Hz and produce sound waves of frequency 256 Hz.

SOUND NEEDS A MATERIAL MEDIUM TO TRAVEL

The substance through which sound travels is called a medium. The medium can be a solid substance, a liquid or a gas. Solids, liquids and gases are called material media (media is the plural of medium). **Sound needs a material medium like solid, liquid or gas to travel and be heard.** In other words, sound can travel through solids, liquids and gases but it cannot travel through vacuum (or empty space). Please note that **sound waves are called mechanical waves because they need a material medium (like solid, liquid or gas) for their propagation.** The sound waves involve the vibrations of the particles of the medium through which they travel. On the other hand, light waves and radio waves are called electromagnetic waves because they do not need a material medium (like, solid, liquid or gas) for their propagation, they can travel even through vacuum. An electromagnetic wave involves the electric and magnetic fields of the empty space (or vacuum). From this discussion we conclude that **though sound waves cannot travel through vacuum but light waves and radio waves can travel even through vacuum.** We will now describe some experiments which will show that sound can travel through solids, liquids and gases, but not through vacuum.

Sound Can Travel Through Solids, Liquids and Gases

If a train is very far away from us, we cannot hear its sound through the air. But if we put our ear to the railway line, then we can hear the sound of the coming train even if it is quite far away. This shows that sound can travel through the railway line which is a solid substance made of steel. In fact, **sound travels about 15 times faster in steel than in air.** Let us take another example. The little children in our homes use the toy telephone in which two tins are connected by a thread. If a child speaks into one tin, he can be

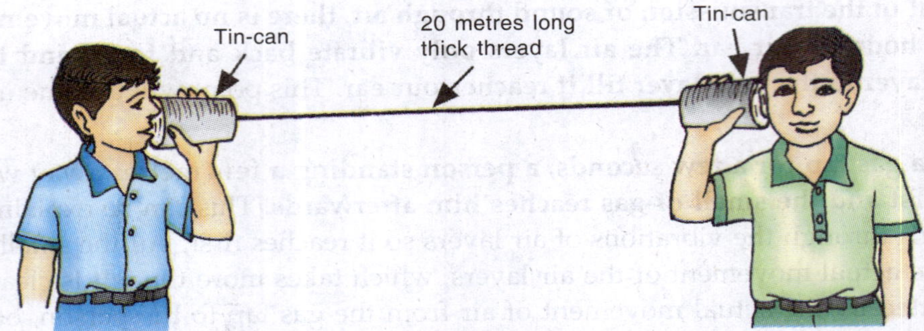

Figure 27. A toy telephone (Here sound travels through the thread, which is a solid substance).

heard by another child who puts his ear to the other tin. In this case the sound vibrations are transmitted by the thread, which is a solid.

We will now describe an experiment to show that sound can travel through liquids. Let us place a squeaking toy (sound making toy) in a polythene bag and hold it in a bucket full of water. We put our ear to the side of the bucket and squeeze the toy. We can hear the squeak. This shows that sound can travel through water, which is a liquid. This fact has been used in the detection of submarines hidden under the sea. The sound of the engines of submarines is transmitted through the sea-water and this sound is detected by special hearing-aids called hydrophones.

We will now list some observations which will show that sound can travel through gases. When the telephone bell rings in our home, we can hear its sound even from a distance. In this case, **the sound of ringing telephone bell travels to us through the air in the room which is a gas (or rather a mixture of gases).** When we talk to a person standing near us, then the sound of our talk travels to the other person through the air around us. The sounds of radio, television, motor cars, buses, trains, aeroplanes, and chirping of birds, all travel through the air and reach our ears. In fact, most of the sounds which we hear in our everyday life, reach us through the air. All these observations show that sound can travel through air, which is a gas.

Figure 28. The sound of ringing telephone bell travels to us through the air in the room which is a gas (or rather a mixture of gases). We can, however, not see this air.

From the above discussion we conclude that sound can travel through solids, liquids and gases. We will now describe an experiment to show that sound cannot travel through vacuum. The word 'vacuum' means 'empty space'. Even air is not present in vacuum. Thus, **when there is no air in something, we say there is vacuum.** A vacuum can be created in a glass vessel by removing all the air from it with the help of a suction pump, called vacuum pump. Let us describe the experiment now.

Sound Cannot Travel Through Vacuum

A material medium (like air) is necessary for the transmission of sound. Sound cannot travel through vacuum (or empty space). This can be shown by the following experiment.

1. A ringing electric bell is placed inside an airtight glass jar (called bell jar) containing air as shown in Figure 29(*a*). We can hear the sound of ringing bell clearly. Thus, when air is present as medium in the bell jar, sound can travel through it and reach our ears.

2. The bell jar containing ringing bell is placed over the plate of a vacuum pump [see Figure 29(*b*)]. Air is gradually removed from the bell jar by switching on the vacuum pump. As more and more air is removed from the bell jar, the sound of ringing bell becomes fainter and fainter. And when all the air is removed

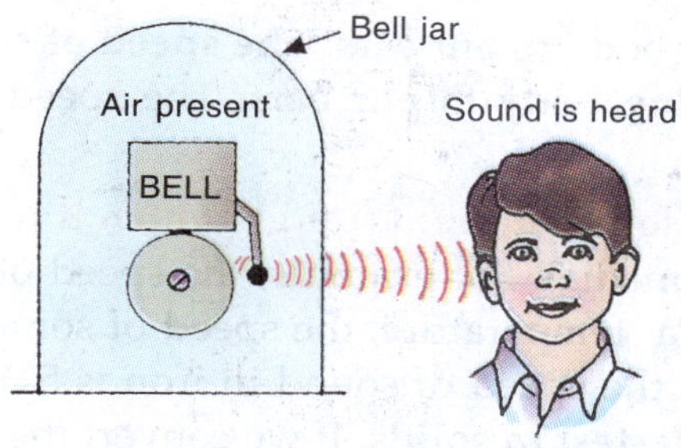

(*a*) Air present in bell jar : Sound of bell is heard

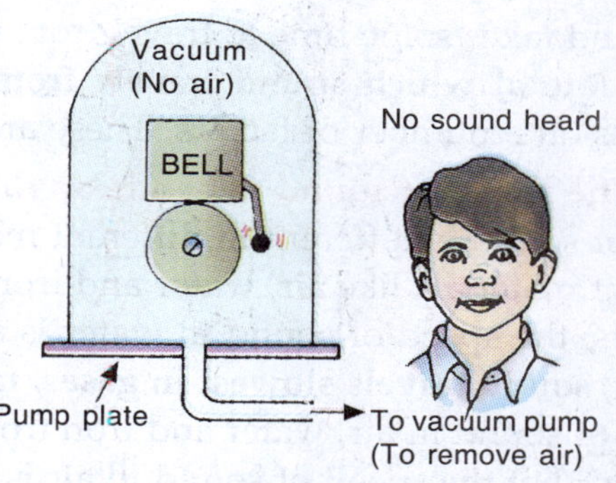

(*b*) Vacuum in bell jar : Sound of bell is not heard

Figure 29. Experiment to show that sound cannot travel through vacuum.

from the bell jar, no sound can be heard at all (though we can still see the clapper striking the bell) [see Figure 29(*b*)]. Thus, when vacuum is created in the bell jar, then the sound of ringing bell placed inside it cannot be heard. This shows that **sound cannot travel through vacuum** (and reach our ears).

3. If air is now put back into bell jar, the sound of ringing bell can be heard again. This shows that **air is necessary for the sound to travel from the ringing bell to our ears.** This happens as follows :

When clapper hits the bell, the bell vibrates (and makes sound). The vibrating bell makes the nearby air molecules to vibrate back and forth. These vibrating air molecules make the next layer of air molecules to vibrate, and so on. In this way, ultimately all the air molecules around the ringing bell start vibrating back and forth. The vibrations of air molecules present inside the bell jar are transmitted to the outside air molecules by the glass wall of the bell jar. Due to this, the air molecules outside the bell jar also start vibrating in the same way. When these vibrating air molecules fall on our ears, we can hear the sound of ringing bell. If, however, there is no air in the bell jar, then the vibrations of the ringing bell cannot reach our ears and hence we cannot hear the sound of ringing bell. So, **when there is vacuum in glass jar, there are no air molecules to carry sound vibrations.**

Please note that **sound can travel through solids, liquids and gases because the molecules of solids, liquids and gases carry the sound waves from one place to another through their vibrations.** Sound cannot travel through vacuum because vacuum has no molecules which can vibrate and carry sound waves. So, a material medium like air, water, wood, etc., is necessary for the transmission of sound from the 'source of sound' to our 'ear'.

The Case of Moon and Outer Space

The moon has no air or atmosphere at all. It is all vacuum (or empty space) on the surface of moon. **Sound cannot be heard directly on the surface of moon because there is no air on the moon to carry the sound waves (or sound vibrations).** So, we cannot talk to one another directly on the moon as we do on earth, even though we may be very close. Similarly, there is no air (or any other gas) in outer space to carry sound waves. It is all vacuum in outer space due to which sound cannot be heard in outer space. Thus, the astronauts who land on moon (or walk in outer space) are not able to talk directly to one another. **The astronauts who land on moon (or walk in outer space) talk to one another through wireless sets using radio waves.** This is because radio waves can travel even through vacuum (though sound waves cannot travel through vacuum).

Figure 30. The astronauts cannot talk directly to one another on moon because there is no air on moon to carry the sound waves.

THE SPEED OF SOUND

Sound takes some time to travel from the sound producing body to our ears. **The speed of sound tells us the rate at which sound travels from the sound producing body to our ears.** The speed of sound depends on a number of factors. These are given below :

1. The speed of sound depends on the nature of material (or medium) through which it travels. The speed of sound is different in different materials (or different media). For example, the speed of sound in different materials like air, water and iron is different. At room temperature, the speed of sound in air is 344 m/s; the speed of sound in water is about 1500 m/s; and the speed of sound in iron is 5130 m/s. In general, **sound travels slowest in gases, faster in liquids and fastest in solids.** If we convert the just given speeds of sound in air, water and iron from metres per second (m/s) into kilometres per hour (km/h), we will find that the speed of sound in air is 1238 km/h ; the speed of sound in water is 5400 km/h; and the speed of sound in iron is 18468 km/h.

2. The speed of sound depends on the temperature. For example, the speed of sound in air at a temperature of 0°C is 332 m/s but the speed of sound in air at a temperature of 20°C is 344 m/s. In fact, **as the temperature of air rises, the speed of sound in it increases.** Thus, the speed of sound in air will be more on a hot day than on a cold day.

3. The speed of sound depends on the humidity of air. For example, the speed of sound is less in dry air but more in humid air. In other words, sound travels slower in dry air but faster in humid air. In fact, **as the humidity of air increases, the speed of sound through it also increases.**

The speeds of sound in some common materials at different temperatures are given below.

Speed of Sound in Various Materials (or Media)

Material (or Medium)		*Speed of sound (or Velocity of sound)*
1. Dry Air	(at 0°C)	332 m/s
2. Dry Air	(at 20°C)	344 m/s
3. Hydrogen	(at 0°C)	1284 m/s
4. Water (Distilled)	(at 20°C)	1498 m/s
5. Sea-Water	(at 0°C)	1531 m/s
6. Blood	(at 37°C)	1570 m/s
7. Copper	(at 20°C)	3750 m/s
8. Aluminium	(at 20°C)	5100 m/s
9. Iron (or Steel)	(at 20°C)	5130 m/s
10. Glass	(at 20°C)	5170 m/s

From the above table we can see that the speed of sound in air at room temperature is 344 metres per second (which is written as 344 m/s). This means that **sound travels a distance of 344 metres in 1 second through air at the room temperature.** Sound travels faster through water than through air. For example, the speed of sound in water is about 1500 metres per second (1500 m/s). Thus, **sound travels about 5 times faster in water than in air.** This means that sound can be heard very fast inside water. The fact that sound can be heard very fast inside water is used by creatures living in the sea-water to communicate with one another (even when they are far away). For example, two whales which are even hundreds of kilometres away from each other under the sea can talk to each other very easily through sea-water. The sound of their talk is carried by sea-water very rapidly (due to high speed of sound in water).

Figure 31. Sound travels about 5 times faster in water than in air. Since the speed of sound in sea water is very large (being about 1530 m/s which is more than 5500 km/h), two whales in the sea which are even hundreds of kilometres away from each other can talk to each other very easily through the sea water (because the sound of their talk is carried away very quickly by sea water).

Figure 32. Sound travels about 15 times faster in iron (or steel) than in air. Since the speed of sound in steel is very, very large (being about 5130 m/s which is more than 18000 km/h), we can hear the sound of an approaching train by putting our ear to the railway line made of steel even when the train is far away (because the sound produced by the motion of train's wheels over the railway line is carried away quickly by the steel rails).

Sound travels faster in solids than in liquids. For example, sound travels at a speed of 5130 metres per second through iron (or steel). This is more than 3 times the speed of sound in water and about 15 times the speed of sound in air. Thus, **sound travels about 15 times faster in iron (or steel) than in air.** Here is an interesting consequence of the very high speed of sound in iron or steel. If a train is very far away from us, we cannot hear the sound of approaching train through the air. But if we put our ear to the railway line made of steel, then we can hear the sound of the coming train easily even if it is quite far away. This is due to the fact that sound travels much more fast through the railway line made of steel than through air.

Sonic Boom

Many objects such as some aircrafts, bullets and rockets, etc., travel at speeds which are greater than the speed of sound in air. They are said to have 'supersonic speed'. Thus, **the term supersonic refers to the speed of an object which is greater than the speed of sound.** For example, when an aircraft flies with a speed greater than the speed of sound, it is said to have supersonic speed. Due to its very high speed, a supersonic aircraft produces extremely loud sound waves called 'shock waves' in air. The shock waves produced by a supersonic aircraft carry a great amount of energy. The tremendous air pressure variations caused by the shock waves produce a loud burst of sound called 'sonic boom'. We can now define sonic boom as follows : **Sonic boom is an explosive noise caused by the shock waves from an aircraft (or any other object) which is travelling faster than the speed of sound.** The sonic boom produces intolerable loud noise which causes pain in our ears. The tremendous sound

Figure 33. This jet aircraft flies at supersonic speed. Its speed (2650 km/h) is more than twice the speed of sound (which is about 1200 km/h). This jet aircraft produces sonic boom in the area where it flies.

energy emitted by sonic boom can even shatter the glass panes of a building if the supersonic aircraft flies low over it. As long as an aircraft flies at the supersonic speed, it continues to emit unpleasant sonic boom in the surrounding area. The first supersonic jet aircraft was made in 1948.

The Race Between Sound and Light

The speed of sound in air is about 344 m/s and the speed of light in air is 300,000,000 m/s. It is clear that **the speed of light is very great as compared to the speed of sound.** So, though sound may take a few seconds to travel a distance of a few hundred metres, light will take practically no time to reach a distance of even a few kilometres. Some of the everyday observations based on the low speed of sound in air but very high speed of light are given below :

(*i*) It is a common observation that **in the rainy season, the flash of lightning is seen first and the sound of thunder is heard a little later** (though both are produced at the same time in clouds). It is due to the very high speed of light that we see the flash of lightning first and it is due to comparatively low speed of sound that the thunder is heard a little later.

(*ii*) **In the game of cricket, the ball is seen to hit the bat first and the sound of hitting is heard a little later.** It is due to the very high speed of light that we see the ball hitting the bat first. And it is due to comparatively low speed of sound that the sound of hitting is heard a little later.

Figure 34. Light travels much faster than sound. Due to this, the flash of lightning is seen first and the sound of thunder is heard a little later.

(*iii*) **If a gun is fired from a distance, we see the flash of gun first and the sound of gun shot is heard a little later.** It is due to the very high speed of light that we see the flash of gun first, and it is because of the comparatively low speed of sound that the sound of gun shot is heard a little later.

In all the above observations we notice that **the light reaches us from a distant object instantly (because of its great speed) but sound takes a little more time to reach us from the same object (due to its low speed).** Thus, it is light which wins the race between light and sound. We will now solve one problem based on the speed of sound (or velocity of sound).

Sample Problem. If a thunder is heard by a man 4 seconds after the lightning is seen, how far is the lightning from the man ? (Speed of sound in air = 330 m/s).

Solution. We know that light travels at a great speed as compared to that of sound, therefore, the flash of light of 'lightning' will reach the man in no time but sound takes 4 seconds to reach the man. Now :

$$\text{Speed of sound} = 330 \text{ m/s}$$

$$\text{Distance} = ? \quad \text{(To be calculated)}$$

And $$\text{Time} = 4 \text{ s}$$

We know that : $$\text{Speed} = \frac{\text{Distance}}{\text{Time}}$$

So, $$330 = \frac{\text{Distance}}{4}$$

And, $$\text{Distance} = 330 \times 4 \text{ m}$$

$$= 1320 \text{ m}$$

Thus, the lightning is at a distance of 1320 metres from the man.

Before we go further and discuss the reflection of sound, **please answer the following questions :**

Very Short Answer Type Questions

1. Can sound travel through *(a)* iron, and *(b)* water ?
2. Can sound travel through vacuum ?
3. Name the type of waves which are used by astronauts to communicate with one another on moon (or in outer space).
4. Name one solid, one liquid and one gas through which sound can travel.
5. Which of the following cannot transmit sound ?
   Water, Vacuum, Aluminium, Oxygen gas
6. Name the physical quantity whose SI unit is 'hertz'.
7. What is the SI unit of frequency ?
8. What type of wave is represented :
   (a) by density-distance graph ?
   (b) by displacement-distance graph ?
9. Is the speed of sound more in water or in steel ?
10. In which medium sound travels faster : air or iron ?
11. In which medium sound travels fastest : air, water or steel ?
12. Out of solids, liquids and gases :
    (a) in which medium sound travels slowest ?
    (b) in which medium sound travels fastest ?
13. Which of the following is the speed of sound in copper and which in aluminium ?
    (a) 5100 m/s   *(b)* 1500 m/s   *(c)* 3750 m/s
14. If you want to hear a train approaching from far away, why is it more convenient to put the ear to the track ?
15. What is the speed of sound :
    (a) in air ?   *(b)* in water ?   *(c)* in iron ?
16. What name is given to those aircrafts which fly at speeds greater than the speed of sound ?
17. A jet aircraft flies at a speed of 410 m/s. What is this speed known as ?
18. What is meant by supersonic speed ?
19. State one observation from everyday life which shows that sound travels much more slow than light.
20. Name the two types of waves which can be generated in a long flexible spring (or slinky).
21. A stone is dropped on the surface of water in a pond. Name the type of waves produced.
22. Name the type of waves produced when a tuning fork is struck in air.
23. What is the general name of the waves consisting of :
    (a) compressions and rarefactions ?
    (b) crests and troughs ?
24. State the general name of the waves in which the particles of the medium vibrate :
    (i) in the same direction as wave.
    (ii) at right angles to the direction of wave.
25. What type of waves are illustrated by the movement of a rope whose one end is fixed to a pole and the other end is moved up and down ?
26. What should an object do to produce sound ?
27. What is the name of the strings which vibrate in our voice box when we talk ?
28. Name the device which is used to produce sound in laboratory experiments.
29. What is the nature of sound waves in air ?
30. What conclusion can be obtained from the observation that when the prongs of a sound making tuning fork touch the surface of water in a beaker, the water gets splashed ?

31. State whether the following statement is true or false :
Sound produced by a vibrating body travels to our ears by the actual movement of air.

32. Which of the following travels slowest in air and which one fastest ?
Supersonic aircraft, Light, Sound

33. Which term is used to denote a speed greater than the speed of sound ?

34. In which medium sound travels faster : air or hydrogen ?

35. A tuning fork has a number 256 marked on it. What does this number signify ?

36. What is the time-period of a tuning fork whose frequency is 200 Hz ?

37. Calculate the frequency of a wave whose time-period is 0.02 s.

38. What will be the change in the wavelength of a sound wave in air if its frequency is doubled ?

39. If 20 waves are produced per second, what is the frequency in hertz ?

40. Fill in the following blanks with suitable words :

(*a*) Sound is caused by ....

(*b*) A sound wave consists of places of higher pressure called .... and places of................pressure called................

(*c*) Wave speed in metres per second equals frequency in .... multiplied by .... in ....

(*d*) Sound cannot travel through ....

(*e*) The speed of sound in a solid is .... than the speed of sound in air.

(*f*) When the frequency of the sound is increased, the wavelength................

Short Answer Type Questions

41. What is vacuum ? Explain why, sound cannot travel through vacuum ?

42. Explain the term 'amplitude' of a wave. Draw the diagram of a wave and mark its amplitude on it.

43. (*a*) Distinguish between longitudinal and transverse waves.
(*b*) Are sound waves longitudinal or transverse ?

44. A cricket ball is seen to hit the bat first and the sound of hitting is heard a little later. Why ?

45. Explain why, the flash of lightning reaches us first and the sound of thunder is heard a little later.

46. Explain why, the flash of a gun shot reaches us before the sound of the gun shot.

47. Which of the following terms apply to sound waves in air and which to water waves ?
Transverse, Rarefaction, Trough, Crest, Compression, Longitudinal

48. (*a*) Name four ways in which sound can be produced.
(*b*) Calculate the speed of a sound wave whose frequency is 2 kHz and wavelength 65 cm.

49. If a ringing bicycle bell is held tightly by hand, it stops producing sound. Why ?

50. Which object is vibrating when the following sounds are produced ?
(*i*) The sound of a *sitar* (*ii*) The sound of a *tabla* (*iii*) The sound of a tuning fork
(*iv*) The buzzing of a bee or mosquito (*v*) The sound of a flute

51. Give reason for the following :
In most of the cases, we cannot see the vibrations of a sound producing object with our eyes.

52. Describe a simple experiment to show that the prongs of a sound producing tuning fork are vibrating.

53. When we open a gas tap for a few seconds, the sound of escaping gas is heard first but the smell of gas comes later. Why ?

54. A sound signal of 128 vibrations per second has a wavelength of 2.7 m. Calculate the speed with which the wave travels.

55. A wave is moving in air with a velocity of 340 m/s. Calculate the wavelength if its frequency is 512 vibrations/sec.

56. Define the 'frequency' and 'time-period' of a wave. What is the relation between the two ?

57. Explain why, a ringing bell suspended in a vacuum chamber cannot be heard outside.

58. The frequency of the sound emitted by the loudspeaker is 1020 Hz. Calculate the wavelength of the sound wave in air in cm where its velocity is 340 m/s.

59. What is the difference between a compression and a rarefaction in a sound wave ? Illustrate your answer with a sketch.

Long Answer Type Questions

60. (*a*) What is sound ? What type of waves are sound waves in air ?
(*b*) Describe an experiment to show that sound cannot pass through vacuum.

61. (*a*) How is sound produced ? Explain with the help of an example.
(*b*) How does sound from a sound producing body travel through air to reach our ears ? Illustrate your answer with the help of a labelled diagram.

62. (*a*) An electric bell is suspended by thin wires in a glass vessel and set ringing. Describe and explain what happens if the air is gradually pumped out of the glass vessel.
(*b*) Why cannot a sound be heard on the moon ? How do astronauts talk to one another on the surface of moon ?

63. (*a*) Define the terms 'frequency', 'wavelength' and 'velocity' of a sound wave. What is the relation between them ?
(*b*) A body vibrating with a time-period of $\frac{1}{256}$ s produces a sound wave which travels in air with a velocity of 350 m/s. Calculate the wavelength.

64. (*a*) What are longitudinal waves and transverse waves ? Explain with the help of labelled diagrams.
(*b*) Give two examples each of longitudinal waves and transverse waves.

65. (*a*) Explain the terms 'compressions' and 'rarefactions' of a wave. What type of waves consist of compressions and rarefactions ?
(*b*) A worker lives at a distance of 1.32 km from the factory. If the speed of sound in air be 330 m/s, how much time will the sound of factory siren take to reach the worker ?

66. (*a*) Explain the terms 'crests' and 'troughs' of a wave ? What type of waves consist of crests and troughs ?
(*b*) The flash of a gun is seen by a man 3 seconds before the sound is heard. Calculate the distance of the gun from the man (Speed of sound in air is 332 m/s).

67. (*a*) When we put our ear to a railway line, we can hear the sound of an approaching train even when the train is far off but its sound cannot be heard through the air. Why ?
(*b*) How could you convince a small child that when you speak, it is not necessary for air to travel from your mouth to the ear of a listener ?

Multiple Choice Questions (MCQs)

68. Which of the following statement best describes frequency ?
(*a*) the maximum disturbance caused by a wave
(*b*) the number of complete vibrations per second
(*c*) the distance between one crest of a wave and the next one
(*d*) the distance travelled by a wave per second

69. Which of the following vibrates when a musical note is produced by the cymbals in an orchestra ?
(*a*) stretched strings (*b*) stretched membranes (*c*) metal plates (*d*) air columns

70. If the speed of a wave is 340 m/s and its frequency is 1700 Hz, then λ for this wave in cm will be :
(*a*) 2 (*b*) 0.2 (*c*) 20 (*d*) 200

71. A musical instrument is producing a continuous note. This note cannot be heard by a person having a normal hearing range. This note must then be passing through :
(*a*) water (*b*) wax (*c*) vacuum (*d*) empty vessel

72. Which one of the following does not consist of transverse waves ?
(*a*) light emitted by a CFL
(*b*) TV signals from a satellite
(*c*) ripples on the surface of a pond
(*d*) musical notes of an orchestra

73. Sound travels in air :
(*a*) if particles of medium travel from one place to another
(*b*) if there is no moisture in the atmosphere
(*c*) if disturbance moves
(*d*) if both, particles as well as disturbance move from one place to another

74. In the sound wave produced by a vibrating turning fork shown in the diagram, half the wavelength is represented by :
(*a*) AB
(*b*) BD
(*c*) DE
(*d*) AE

75. The maximum speed of vibrations which produce audible sound will be in :
(*a*) dry air (*b*) sea water (*c*) ground glass (*d*) human blood

76. The sound waves travel fastest :
(*a*) in solids (*b*) in liquids (*c*) in gases (*d*) in vacuum

77. The speeds of sound in four different media are given below. Which of the following is the most likely speed in m/s with which the two under water whales in a sea talk to each other when separated by a large distance ?
(*a*) 340 (*b*) 5170 (*c*) 1280 (*d*) 1530

78. When the pitch of note produced by a harmonium is lowered, then the wavelength of the note :
(*a*) decreases
(*b*) first decreases and then increases
(*c*) increases
(*d*) remains the same

79. The velocities of sound waves in four media P, Q, R and S are 18,000 km/h, 900 km/h, 0 km/h, and 1200 km/h respectively. Which medium could be a liquid substance ?
(*a*) P (*b*) Q (*c*) R (*d*) S

80. Which of the following can produce longitudinal waves as well as transverse waves under different conditions ?
(*a*) water (*b*) TV transmitter (*c*) slinky (*d*) tuning fork

Questions Based on High Order Thinking Skills (HOTS)

81. Draw the sketches of two waves A and B such that wave A has twice the wavelength and half the amplitude of wave B.

82. A device called oscillator is used to send waves along a stretched string. The string is 20 cm long, and four complete waves fit along its length when the oscillator vibrates 30 times per second. For the waves on the string :
(*a*) what is their wavelength ?
(*b*) what is their frequency ?
(*c*) what is their speed ?

83. Through which of the following materials can sound travel ?
wood, air, water, steam, ice, hydrogen, steel, diamond.

84. A sound producing body is at considerable distance from a man. There can be four different media W, X, Y and Z between the sound producing body and the man. The medium X brings the sound to man most quickly whereas medium Z takes the maximum time. The time taken by medium W in bringing sound to man is less than that of X but more than that of Z. The medium Y, however, fails to bring the sound from the sound producing body to the man. Which medium could be the one :
(*a*) having no fixed shape and no fixed volume ?
(*b*) having a fixed volume but no fixed shape ?
(*c*) having the same composition as that on the moon ?
(*d*) having a fixed shape and a fixed volume ?

85. The longitudinal waves travel in a coiled spring at a rate of 4 m/s. The distance between two consecutive compressions is 20 cm. Find :
(*i*) Wavelength of the wave (*ii*) Frequency of the wave

ANSWERS

3. Radio waves **5.** Vacuum 6. Frequency **8.** (*a*) Longitudinal wave (*b*) Transverse wave **13.** In copper : 3750 m/s ; In aluminium : 5100 m/s **16.** Supersonic aircrafts **17.** Supersonic speed **20.** Transverse waves and Longitudinal waves **21.** Transverse (water) waves **22.** Longitudinal (sound) waves **23.** (*a*) Longitudinal waves (*b*) Transverse waves **24.** (*i*) Longitudinal waves (*ii*) Transverse waves **25.** Transverse waves **26.** Vibrate **27.** Vocal cords **28.** Tuning fork **30.** That the prongs of tuning fork are vibrating **31.** False **32.** Slowest : Sound ; Fastest : Light **33.** Supersonic **35.** Frequency (of vibration) of the tuning fork **36.** 5×10^{-3} s **37.** 50 Hz **38.** Wavelength is halved **39.** 20 Hz **40.** (*a*) vibrations (*b*) compressions ; lower; rarefactions (*c*) hertz ; wavelength ; metres (*d*) vacuum (*e*) greater (*f*) decreases **47.** Sound waves : Longitudinal, Compression, Rarefaction ; Water waves : Transverse, Crest, Trough **48.** (*b*) 1300 m/s **54.** 345.6 m/s **55.** 0.66 m **58.** 33.3 cm **63.** (*b*) 1.36 m **65.** (*b*) 4 s **66.** (*b*) 996 m **68.** (*b*) **69.** (*c*) **70.** (*c*) **71.** (*c*) **72.** (*d*) **73.** (*c*) **74.** (*b*) **75.** (*c*) **76.** (*a*) **77.** (*d*) **78.** (*c*) **79.** (*d*) **80.** (*c*)

81.

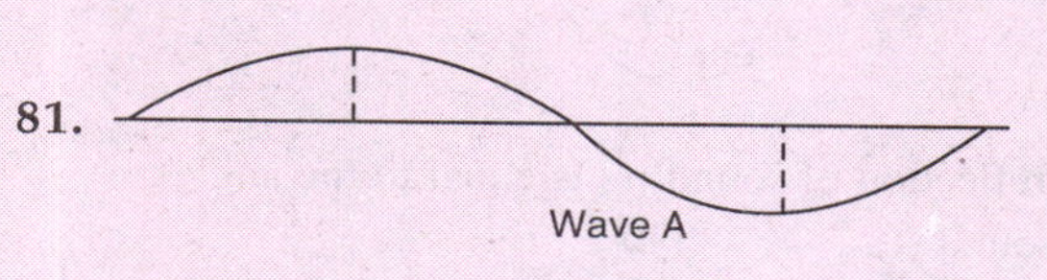

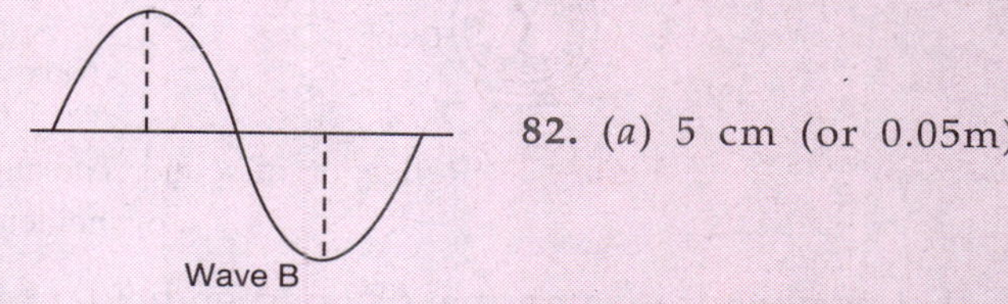

82. (*a*) 5 cm (or 0.05m) (*b*) 120 Hz (*c*) 6 m/s **83.** Sound can travel through all the given materials **84.** (*a*) Z (*b*) W (*c*) Y (*d*) X **85.** (*i*) 20 cm (*ii*) 20 Hz.

REFLECTION OF SOUND

We have studied the reflection of light in earlier classes. Just like light, sound can also be made to change its direction and bounce back when it falls on a hard surface. **The bouncing back of sound when it strikes a hard surface is called reflection of sound**. Hard, solid surfaces are the best for reflecting sound waves. For example, **sound is reflected well from hard surfaces like a wall, a metal sheet, hard wood and a cliff** (A cliff is a steep rock, especially at the edge of the sea). Soft surfaces are bad reflectors of sound. Soft surfaces absorb sound. The reflection of sound does not require a smooth and shining surface like that of a mirror. Sound can be reflected from any surface, whether smooth or rough. Sound waves are much longer than light waves, so they require a much larger area for reflection.

Sound is reflected in the same way as light. **The laws of reflection of light are obeyed during the reflection of sound**. We can write down the laws of reflection of sound as follows :

1. The incident sound wave, the reflected sound wave, and the normal at the point of incidence, all lie in the same plane.
2. The angle of reflection of sound is always equal to the angle of incidence of sound.

We will now describe an experiment to study the reflection of sound. We fix a drawing board *DD′* vertically on a table (see Figure 35). This drawing board acts as a reflecting surface for sound. Two cardboard tubes T_1 and T_2, about 50 cm long and 3 cm in diameter, are taken and kept in inclined positions with respect to the drawing board (as shown in Figure 35). The ends of cardboard tubes should not touch the drawing board, they should be at a distance of about 5 cm each from the drawing board.

We keep a clock near the outer end of the tube T_1 (see Figure 35). The clock makes a ticking sound. The sound waves of ticking of clock pass through the tube T_1, get reflected from the drawing board at point *O*, and then enter the other tube T_2. We put our ear to the outer end of tube T_2 and try to hear the ticking sound of the clock. We adjust the angle of tube T_2 with respect to the drawing board till the sound of ticking of clock heard by us becomes the loudest.

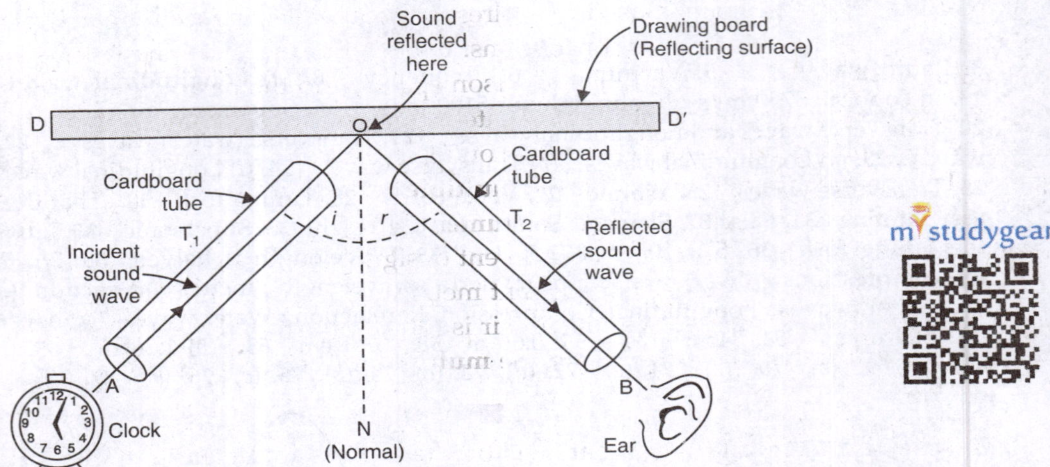

Figure 35. Reflection of sound. The angle of reflection of sound (r) is equal to the angle of incidence of sound (i).

Let us now draw a normal *ON* perpendicular to the reflecting surface (drawing board) and measure the angles *AON* and *NOB*. We will find that when the ticking sound of clock heard by our ear through the tube T_2 is the loudest, then the angle of reflection of sound (*NOB*) is equal to the angle of incidence of sound (*AON*). Moreover, the incident sound wave (*AO*), the reflected sound wave (*OB*) and the normal (*ON*) at the point of incidence, all lie in the same plane (which is the plane of the table). From this experiment we conclude that sound obeys the same laws of reflection as light.

Applications of Reflection of Sound

We will now discuss some of the applications of the reflection of sound. **The reflection of sound is utilised in the working of devices such as : Megaphone, Bulb horn, Stethoscope, and Soundboard.** All these devices involve multiple reflections of sound waves. We will describe all these devices in somewhat detail, one by one. Let us start with megaphone and bulb horn.

1. Megaphone and Bulb Horn

The devices like megaphone and bulb horn (and the musical instruments like trumpets and *shehnai*) are all designed to send sound in a particular direction, without spreading all around. All these devices and musical instruments have a funnel-shaped tube which reflects sound waves repeatedly so that most of the sound waves produced go in the forward direction (towards the audience). During successive reflections, the amplitude of sound waves adds up due to which the loudness of sound increases.

Figure 36. Megaphone.

Figure 37. Bulb horn.

A megaphone is a large, cone-shaped (or funnel-shaped) device for amplifying and directing the voice of a person who speaks into it (see Figure 36). A megaphone is also known as 'loud-hailer' or 'speaking-tube'. A megaphone is used to address a small gathering of people at places like tourist spots, fairs, market places and during demonstrations. One end of the megaphone tube is narrow and its other end is quite wide (see Figure 36). When a person speaks into the narrow end of the megaphone tube, the sound waves produced by his voice are prevented from spreading by successive reflections from the wider end of the megaphone tube. Due to this the sound of the voice of the person can be heard over a longer distance. Thus, **a megaphone works on the multiple reflection of sound.**

A bulb horn is a cone-shaped wind instrument which is used for signalling in bicycles, cars, buses, trucks and boats, etc. Bulb horns are of different designs. One design of bulb horn is shown in Figure 37. This bulb horn consists of a cone-shaped, bent metal-tube having a hollow rubber bulb at its narrow end. When the rubber bulb is pressed with hand, air is forced out from the tube making a loud sound. Just like a megaphone, **a bulb horn also works on the multiple reflection of sound.**

2. Stethoscope

Stethoscope is a medical instrument used by the doctors for listening to the sounds produced within the human body, mainly in the heart and the lungs (see Figure 38). A stethoscope consists of three parts :

(*i*) A chest piece (which carries a sensitive diaphragm at its bottom). The diaphragm amplifies the sound (of heartbeats, etc.).

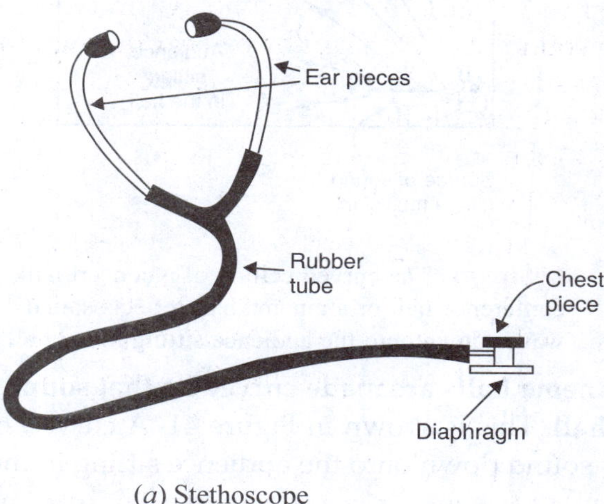

(*a*) Stethoscope

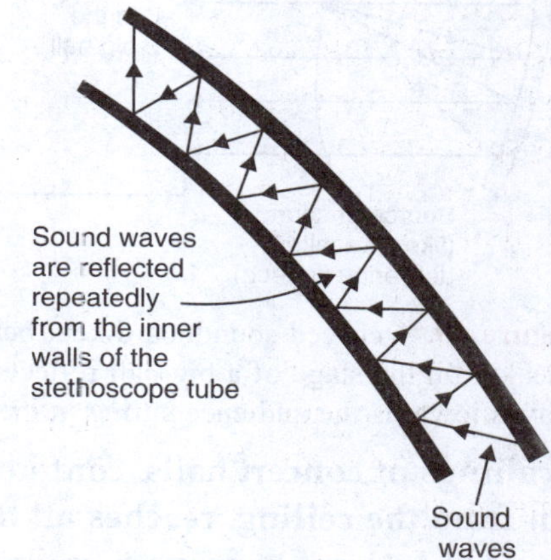

(*b*) Multiple reflections of sound waves in a part of stethoscope tube

Figure 38.

(*ii*) Two ear-pieces (which are made of metal tubes). These are put by the doctor into his ears.

(*iii*) A rubber tube which joins the chest piece to the ear pieces. The rubber tube transmits the sound from the chest piece to the ear pieces.

The doctor puts the ear-pieces of stethoscope into his ears and places the chest-piece above the part of the patient's body (such as heart, lungs, etc.) which is to be examined. The sound of heartbeats (or lungs) reaches the doctor's ears by the multiple reflections of sound waves through the stethoscope tube [as shown in Figure 38(*b*)]. Thus, **a stethoscope works on the principle of multiple reflection of sound.**

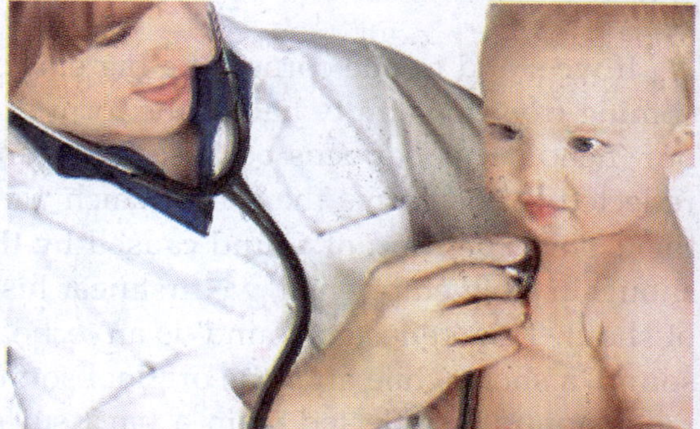

Figure 39. Doctor examining a baby with stethoscope.

3. Soundboard

In a big hall, sound can be absorbed by the walls, ceiling, floor, seats and even by the clothes of the people sitting inside. This leads to too much absorption of sound due to which the speech cannot be heard clearly. This problem is overcome by using a soundboard. The soundboard reflects sound and helps to spread sound evenly in the big hall.

The soundboard is a concave board (curved board) which is placed behind the speaker in large halls or auditoriums so that his speech can be heard easily even by the persons sitting at a considerable distance. The soundboard works as follows : The speaker is made to stand at the focus of the concave soundboard (see Figure 40). The concave surface of the soundboard reflects the sound waves of the speaker towards the audience (and hence prevents the spreading of sound in various directions). Due to this, sound is distributed uniformly throughout the hall and even the persons sitting at the back of the hall can hear his speech easily. It is obvious that **the soundboards work on the multiple reflection of sound.**

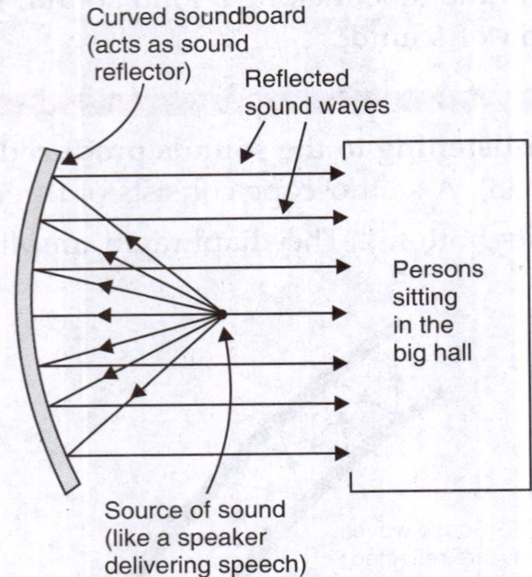

Figure 40. A curved soundboard kept behind the speaker on the stage of a big hall reflects sound waves towards the audience sitting in the hall.

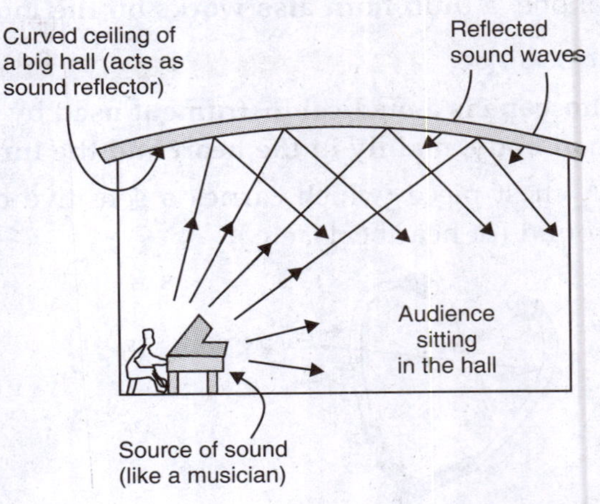

Figure 41. The curved ceiling of a concert hall, conference hall or a cinema hall reflects sound waves down onto the audience sitting in the hall.

The ceilings of concert halls, conference halls and cinema halls are made curved so that sound, after reflection from the ceiling, reaches all the parts of the hall. This is shown in Figure 41. A curved ceiling actually acts like a large concave soundboard and reflects sound down onto the audience sitting in the hall.

The reflection of sound produces echoes. Echo is called *'pratidhvani'* or *'goonj'* in Hindi. We will now discuss the formation of echoes.

ECHO

If we stand in one corner of a big empty hall and shout the word 'hello', we will hear the word 'hello' coming from the empty hall in the form of an echo a little while later. It appears as if the hall is repeating our 'hello'. This happens because the sound of our 'hello' is reflected from the walls of the hall and this reflected sound forms the echo (which we hear as 'hello' coming from the empty hall). We can now say that : **The repetition of sound caused by the reflection of sound waves is called an echo.** When a person shouts in a big empty hall, we first hear his original sound. After a little while, we hear the reflected sound of shout. This 'reflected sound' is an 'echo'. So, when we hear an echo, we are actually hearing a reflected sound, a short while after the original sound. Thus, **an echo is simply a reflected sound.** An echo is heard when sound is reflected from a hard surface such as a tall brick wall or a cliff. A soft surface tends to absorb sound, so there is no echo. We know that the speed of sound in air (at 20°C) is 344 metres per second. So, if we shout at a wall from 344 metres away, the sound takes 1 second to reach the wall. The sound reflects from the wall, and takes another 1 second to return to us. So, we hear the echo 2 seconds after we have shouted. We will now calculate the minimum distance from a sound reflecting surface (like a wall) which is necessary to hear an echo clearly.

Calculation of Minimum Distance to Hear an Echo

It has been estimated by scientists that if two sounds reach our ears within an interval of $\frac{1}{10}$th of a second, then we cannot hear them as separate sounds, they appear to be just one sound. The human ear can hear two sounds separately only if there is a time interval (or time gap) of $\frac{1}{10}$th of a second (or more) between the two sounds. This means that **we can hear the original sound and the reflected sound (echo) separately only if there is a time-interval (or time gap) of at least $\frac{1}{10}$th of a second (or 0.1 second) between them**. Now, knowing the minimum time interval required for an echo to be heard and the speed of sound in air, we can calculate the minimum distance from a sound reflecting surface (like a wall, etc.) which is necessary to hear an echo. These calculations are given below :

We know that : $\text{Speed} = \frac{\text{Distance travelled}}{\text{Time taken}}$

Here, Speed of sound = 344 m/s (at 20°C)

Distance travelled = ? (To be calculated)

And, $\text{Time taken} = \frac{1}{10}\text{ s}$

$= 0.1\text{ s}$

Now, putting these values in the above formula, we get :

$$344 = \frac{\text{Distance travelled}}{0.1}$$

So, Distance travelled = 344×0.1

= 34.4 metres

Thus, the distance travelled by sound in $\frac{1}{10}$th of a second is 34.4 metres. But this distance is travelled by sound in going from us (the source of sound) to the sound reflecting surface (like a wall), and then coming back to us. So, our distance from the sound reflecting surface (like a wall, etc.) to hear an echo should be half of 34.4 metres which is $\frac{34.4}{2} = 17.2$ metres. From this we conclude that **the minimum distance from a sound reflecting surface (wall, etc.) to hear an echo is 17.2 metres (at 20°C).** This means that in order to hear an echo of our shout, we should be at least 17.2 metres away from a sound reflecting surface like a wall. This has been shown clearly in Figure 42.

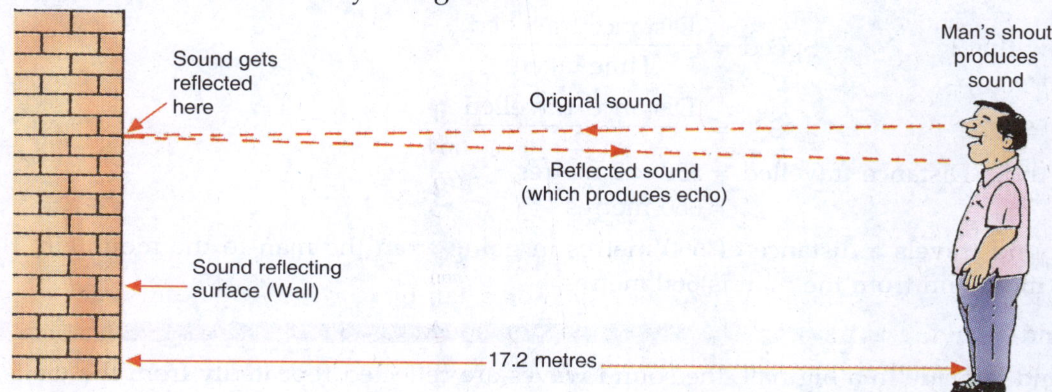

Figure 42. The minimum distance to hear an echo is 17.2 metres (at 20°C).

We can see from Figure 42 that though the sound reflecting surface (wall) is only 17.2 metres away from us, but the sound has to travel 17.2 + 17.2 = 34.4 metres to produce an echo (17.2 metres in going from us to the wall, and 17.2 metres in coming back from the wall to us, after reflection). **Please note that 17.2**

metres from a sound reflecting surface is the minimum distance to hear an echo in air at a temperature of 20°C. This distance will change with the temperature of air. Actually, the speed of sound in air increases with increasing temperature. So, the speed of sound in air will be more on a hot day (when the temperature is high) than on a cold day. **Since the speed of sound is more on a hot day, therefore, an echo is heard sooner on a hot day (than on a cold day).**

We have just said that 17.2 metres from a sound reflecting surface is the minimum distance to hear an echo. We will also hear an echo when the distance is more than 17.2 metres from a reflecting surface. But no echo can be heard when our distance from the sound reflecting surface is less than 17.2 metres. When we are at a distance of less than 17.2 metres from a sound reflecting surface, then we will hear the original sound and the reflected sound as one, and no echo will be produced.

If there are several reflecting surfaces, then multiple reflections of sound take place and hence several echoes may be heard. For example, **rolling of thunder is due to the multiple reflections of sound of thunder from a number of reflecting surfaces such as the clouds and the land.**

Please note that the minimum distance from a sound reflecting surface is 17.2 metres to hear an echo when the sound travels in air. But **when the sound travels in water, then the minimum distance for hearing an echo will be different (because the speed of sound in water is different).** If the speed of sound in water is taken as 1500 m/s, then the minimum distance to hear echo in water will be 75 metres. Thus, the minimum distance of a diver from an under-water rock to hear the echo of his own shout will be 75 metres.

The formation of echoes by the reflection of sound waves is used to measure the depth of sea (or ocean); to locate the under-water objects like the shoals of fish, shipwrecks, submarines, sea-rocks and hidden ice-bergs in the sea; and to investigate inside the human body. In all these applications of echoes, we do not use ordinary sound waves. We use high frequency sound waves called 'ultrasonic waves' or 'ultrasound'. We will discuss all this after a short while. At the moment we will solve a numerical problem based on echoes.

Sample Problem. A man claps his hands near a mountain and hears the echo after 4 seconds. If the speed of sound under these conditions be 330 m/s, calculate the distance of the mountain from the man.

Solution. Here the time taken by the sound (of clap) to go from the man to the mountain, and return to the man (as echo) is 4 seconds. So, the time taken by the sound to go from the man to the mountain only will be half of this time, which is $\frac{4}{2} = 2$ seconds. Now, knowing the speed of sound in air, we can calculate the distance travelled by sound in 2 seconds. This will give us the distance of the mountain from the man.

We know that : $\text{Speed} = \dfrac{\text{Distance travelled}}{\text{Time taken}}$

So, $330 = \dfrac{\text{Distance travelled}}{2}$

And, $\text{Distance travelled} = 330 \times 2 \text{ metres}$

$= 660 \text{ metres}$

Since sound travels a distance of 660 metres in going from the man to the mountain, therefore, the distance of mountain from the man is 660 metres.

Reverberation

If a sound is made in a big hall, the sound waves are reflected repeatedly from the walls, ceiling and floor of the hall, and produce many echoes. The echo time is, however, so short that the many echoes overlap with the original sound. Due to this the original sound seems to be prolonged and lasts for a longer time. In other words, a sound made in a big hall persists (or lasts) for a longer time. **The persistence of**

sound in a big hall due to repeated reflections from the walls, ceiling and floor of the hall is called reverberation. A short reverberation is desirable in a concert hall (where music is being played) because it gives 'life' to sound and boosts the sound level. But **if the reverberation is too long, then the sound becomes blurred, distorted and confusing due to overlapping of different sounds**. Modern concert halls are designed for the optimum amount of reverberation.

The excessive reverberations in big halls and auditoriums are reduced (or controlled) by using various types of sound-absorbing materials. Some of **the methods used for reducing excessive reverberation in big halls and auditoriums** are as follows :

(*i*) Panels made of sound-absorbing materials (like compressed fibreboard or felt) are put on the walls and ceiling of big halls and auditoriums to reduce reverberations.

(*ii*) Carpets are put on the floor to absorb sound and reduce reverberations.

(*iii*) Heavy curtains are put on doors and windows to absorb sound and reduce reverberations.

(*iv*) The material having sound-absorbing properties is used for making the seats in a big hall or auditorium to reduce reverberations.

Figure 43. The 'mushroom' like panels on the ceiling of this Concert Hall are sound absorbers to reduce the reverberations (unwanted echoes).

The soft and porous materials are bad reflectors of sound. The soft and porous materials are actually good absorbers of sound. For example, the materials like curtains (fabrics) and carpets, etc., are bad reflectors of sound but they are good absorbers of sound. The bad reflectors of sound do not give good echo of the sound falling on them. They absorb the sound and hence muffle (or silence) the sound falling on them. **We can hear more clearly in a room having curtains because curtains are bad reflectors of sound. The curtains absorb most of the sound falling on them, and hence do not produce echoes**. On the other hand, in a room without curtains, there is a greater reflection of sound due to which some echoes are produced. These echoes cause a hindrance to hearing. **In addition to curtains, carpets and sofa-sets in our rooms also reduce the formation of echoes by absorbing sound waves**. From this discussion we conclude that some of the sound-absorbing materials (or objects) which make our big rooms less echoey are curtains, carpets and sofa-sets.

THE FREQUENCY RANGE OF HEARING IN HUMANS

The sounds produced in our environment have many different frequencies. The sounds of all the frequencies cannot be heard by the human beings. For example, if the frequency of a sound is less than 20 hertz, it cannot be heard by human beings. And if the frequency of a sound is greater than 20,000 hertz, even then it cannot be heard by human beings. Thus, a human ear cannot hear sounds of frequencies less than 20 hertz and more than 20,000 hertz. The human ear can hear sounds having frequencies of 20 hertz to 20,000 hertz. **The range of frequency from 20 Hz to 20,000 Hz is known as the frequency range of hearing in humans.** The sound which we are able to hear is called 'audible' sound. So, we can also say that : The audible range of sound frequencies for human ear is from 20 Hz to 20,000 Hz.

Figure 44. The human beings can hear sounds having frequencies of 20 Hz to 20,000 Hz. They can neither hear sounds of frequencies less than 20 Hz nor hear sounds of frequences more than 20,000 Hz.

The sounds of frequencies lower than 20 hertz are known as 'infrasonic sounds' (or just 'infrasound'). Thus, infrasonic sounds are very low-frequency sounds. **Infrasonic sounds cannot be heard by human beings**. Infrasonic sounds are produced by those objects which vibrate very slowly. For example, **a vibrating simple pendulum produces infrasonic sound**. We cannot hear the sound of a vibrating simple pendulum because it vibrates with a frequency less than 20 hertz. **Earthquakes, and some animals like whales, elephants and rhinoceroses also produce infrasonic sounds**. Rhinoceroses communicate with one another by using infrasonic sound having a frequency as low as 5 hertz. It is observed that some animals get disturbed and start running here and there just before the earthquakes occur. This is because, before the main shock waves, the earthquakes produce low-frequency infrasonic sounds which some animals can hear and get disturbed.

Figure 45. Rhinoceros can produce infrasonic sounds having frequencies less than 20 Hz. They can also hear infrasonic sounds.

Figure 46. Dogs are used for detective work by police because they can hear ultrasonic sounds and also because they have an excellent sense of smell.

Figure 47. Bats can produce ultrasonic sounds having frequencies much beyond 20,000 Hz while screaming. They can hear ultrasonic sounds having frequencies of up to 1,20,000 Hz.

The sounds of frequencies higher than 20,000 hertz are known as 'ultrasonic sounds' (or just 'ultrasound'). Thus, ultrasonic sounds are very high frequency sounds. **Ultrasonic sounds cannot be heard by human beings**. Though human beings cannot hear ultrasonic sounds but dogs can hear ultrasonic sounds of frequency up to 50,000 hertz. This is the reason why dogs are used for detective work by the police. Bats, monkeys, deer, cats, dolphins, porpoises and leopard can also hear ultrasonic sounds. Bats can hear ultrasonic sounds having frequencies up to 1,20,000 hertz. In fact, bats can also produce ultrasonic sounds while screaming. **We cannot hear the screams of a bat because its screams consist of ultrasonic sound having a frequency much higher than 20,000 hertz (which is beyond our limit of hearing).** In addition to bats, dolphins, porpoises and rats can also produce ultrasonic sounds as well as hear ultrasonic sounds. Children under the age of five years can hear ultrasonic sounds of frequency up to 25,000 hertz. As people grow older, their ears become less sensitive to sounds of higher frequencies. Ultrasonic sound cannot be produced by ordinary vibrators like tuning forks. They are produced by special vibrators which can vibrate very, very rapidly. We will discuss this in detail in higher classes.

ULTRASOUND

The sounds having too high frequency which cannot be heard by human beings are called ultrasonic sound or ultrasound. In other words, the sounds having frequency greater than 20,000 hertz are called ultrasound. For example, a sound of frequency 100,000 hertz is an ultrasound. **The ultrasound is reflected just like ordinary sound waves and produces echoes.** But the echoes produced by ultrasound cannot be heard by our ears, they can only be detected by special equipment. **Due to its very high frequency, ultrasound has a much greater penetrating power than ordinary sound.** So, it can be used to detect objects under the sea, and organs inside the human body. These days ultrasound is used for a large number of purposes. These are discussed below.

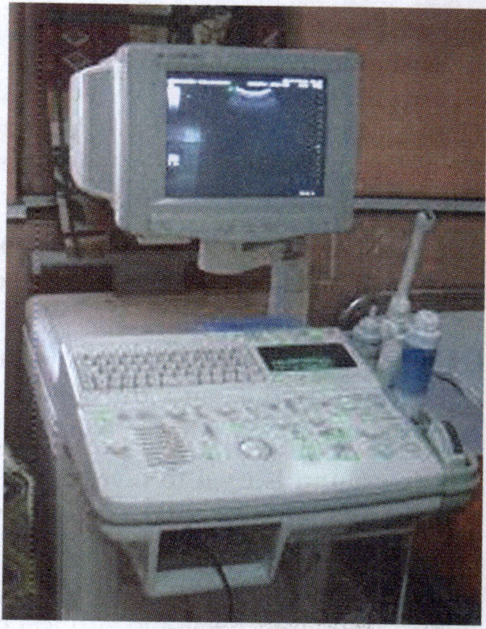

Figure 48. This is an ultrasound machine which is used in hospitals. It produces ultrasound scans of the inner organs of human body such as liver, gall bladder, pancreas, kidneys, uterus and heart, etc.

Applications of Ultrasound

Ultrasound waves are high-energy sound waves. They travel in straight lines without bending around the corners. **Ultrasound waves have a very-high frequency (and very short wavelength) due to which they can penetrate into 'matter' to a large extent.** Because of all these properties, ultrasound is used extensively in industry, and in hospitals for medical purposes. Some of the important applications (or uses) of ultrasound are given below :

1. Ultrasound is used in industry for detecting flaws (cracks, etc.) in metal blocks without damaging them

Metal blocks are used in the construction of big structures like buildings, bridges, machines, and scientific equipment, etc. There may be some flaws or defects (such as cracks or holes, etc.) inside the metal blocks which are invisible from outside. These flaws weaken the metal blocks. The use of such metal blocks having internal cracks (or other defects) reduces the strength of the structure to be constructed. **The flaws like internal cracks, etc., in the metal blocks are detected by using ultrasound.** This is based on the fact that an internal crack (or hole, etc.) does not allow ultrasound to pass through it. It reflects the ultrasound. This will become more clear from the following discussion.

Ultrasound waves are made to pass through one face of the metal block (to be tested), and ultrasound detectors are placed on the opposite face of the metal block to detect the transmitted ultrasound waves (see Figure 49).

(*a*) If the ultrasound waves pass uninterrupted through all the parts of the metal block, then the metal block is flawless (or defect-free) having no internal cracks, etc.

(*b*) If, however, ultrasound waves are not able to pass through a part of the metal block and get reflected back, then there is a flaw or defect in the metal block (like a crack or a hole).

In Figure 49(*a*) ultrasound waves are passing through all the parts of the metal block, so the metal block shown in Figure 49(*a*) is flawless or defect-free (having no cracks, etc.). On the other hand, in

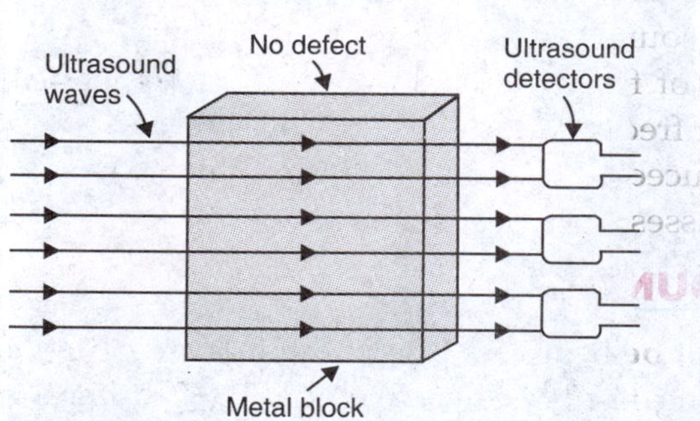

(*a*) No ultrasound reflected. So this is a flawless (defect-free) metal block.

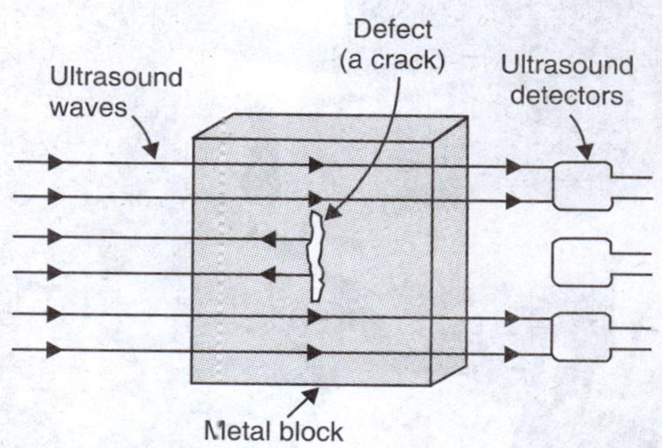

(*b*) Ultrasound reflected from a part of block. So this metal block has a flaw or defect (like a crack) inside it.

Figure 49.

Figure 49(*b*) the ultrasound waves falling on the centre part of the metal block are not able to pass through it (as shown by ultrasound detector), they are reflected back. This shows that there is a crack, etc., in the centre part of the metal block which does not allow ultrasound to pass through it. So, the block shown in Figure 49(*b*) is defective (having a crack inside it). Please note that ordinary sound waves cannot be used for detecting the flaws in metal blocks because they will bend around the corners of the defective location (crack, etc.) and hence enter the detector.

2. Ultrasound is used in industry to clean 'hard to reach' parts of objects such as spiral tubes, odd-shaped machines and electronic components, etc.

The object to be cleaned is placed in a cleaning solution and ultrasound waves are passed into the solution. Due to their high frequency, the ultrasound waves stir up the cleaning solution. Because of stirring, the particles of dust and grease sticking to the dirty object vibrate too much, become loose, get detached from the object and fall into solution. The object gets cleaned thoroughly.

3. Ultrasound is used to investigate the internal organs of the human body such as liver, gall bladder, pancreas, kidneys, uterus and heart, etc.

Ultrasound waves can penetrate the human body and different types of tissues (like bones, fat, and muscle) reflect the ultrasound waves in different ways. Due to these properties, ultrasound is being used increasingly in medical and surgical diagnosis in hospitals. **Ultrasound waves are used to investigate the organs which are inside the human body.** In a way, ultrasound helps us to 'see' inside the human body by giving pictures of the inner organs. This happens as follows :

The source of ultrasound waves is placed above the human body organ to be investigated. The ultrasound waves given out by this source enter the human body and are reflected from the organ. The reflected ultrasound waves are fed into a computer which builds up a picture of the organ concerned which the doctors can see on a television-type screen (called monitor). This picture of the organ helps in the diagnosis of ailment. The picture can also be obtained on a photographic film. **The technique of obtaining pictures of internal organs of the body by using echoes of ultrasound pulses is called ultrasonography.** And such pictures are called ultrasound scans. A machine which uses ultrasonic waves for obtaining images of the internal organs of human body is called 'ultrasound scanner'.

A doctor can take the ultrasound scans of a person's organs like liver, gall bladder, kidney, pancreas, uterus and heart, etc. It helps the doctors in the detection of stones in gall bladder and kidney, tumors in different organs and many other ailments. Ultrasound is also used for diagnosing heart diseases by detecting the motion of the heart wall, and even scanning the heart from inside. **The use of ultrasound waves to investigate the action of the heart is called 'echocardiography'.**

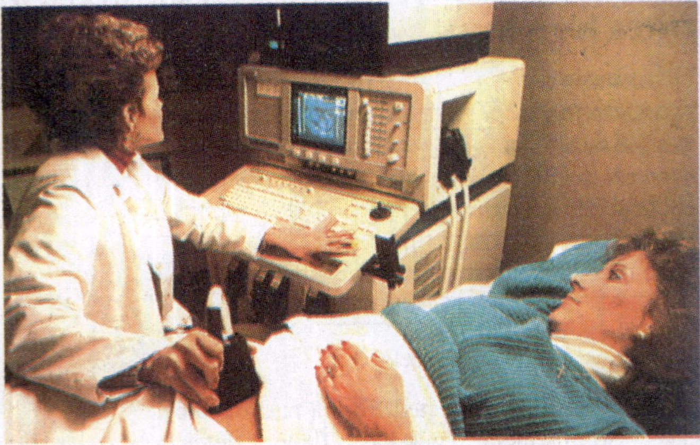

Figure 50. An ultrasound scanner builds up a picture of fetus (unborn baby) in the mother's uterus. This helps the doctor to keep a track of the developing baby.

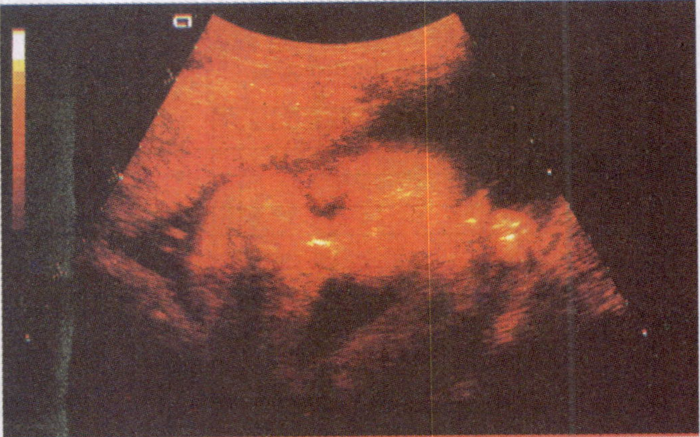

Figure 51. This photograph shows the ultrasound scan image of the face of a fully developed fetus in the mother's uterus.

4. Ultrasound scans are used to monitor the development of fetus (unborn baby) inside the mother's uterus

The ultrasound scanner transmits ultrasound into the mother's body and receives echoes formed by the reflection of ultrasound from inside. The ultrasound echoes form a picture of the developing baby on a monitor which helps the doctor to keep a track of the developing baby. Thus, ultrasonography is used for the examination of fetus (unborn baby) during pregnancy to detect any growth abnormalities. This helps in taking the necessary action to rectify the abnormalities. The ultrasound method is a safer way of checking whether the baby is developing normally or not than using X-rays (because X-rays can damage the delicate body cells of the unborn baby).

5. Ultrasound is used to break kidney stones into fine grains (which then get flushed out with urine)

Sometimes tiny stones develop in the kidneys of patients which are very painful. Such patients can be treated with ultrasound. When high-frequency ultrasound waves are directed on the stones in the kidney, the strong ultrasound vibrations shake the stones so much that they ultimately break into fine grains. These fine grains of stone are so small that they pass out from the kidney alongwith urine. And the patient gets relief from pain.

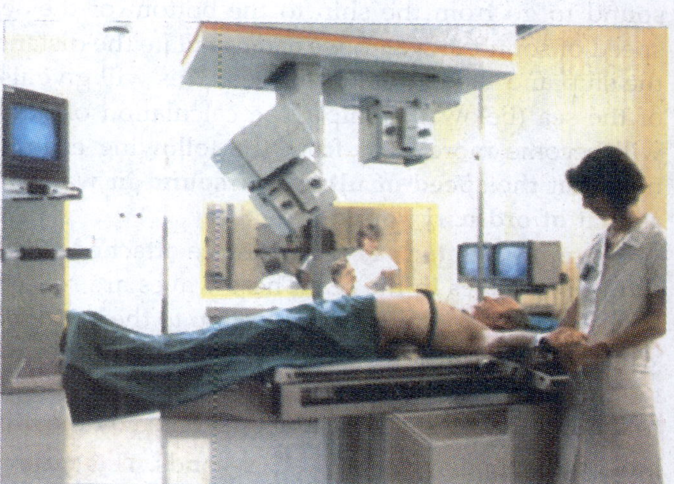

Figure 52. This photo shows a high-energy shock-wave of ultrasound being used to smash the stones present in the kidney of a patient into tiny pieces. These tiny pieces of stones can then come out with the urine.

6. Ultrasound is used in 'sonar' apparatus to measure the depth of sea (or ocean); and to locate under-sea objects like shoal of fish, shipwrecks, submarines, sea-rocks and hidden ice-bergs in the sea

Before we discuss 'sonar' in detail, please note that whether we use the word 'ultrasound', 'ultrasonic sound' or 'ultrasonic waves', it means the same thing. Another point to be noted is that the ultrasonic sound can penetrate water to great distances (because of their very high frequency and very short wavelength), but ordinary sound waves cannot penetrate water to such great distances. We will now discuss 'sound ranging'. **Sound ranging is the process of finding the distance (or range) of distant objects by using the property of reflection of ultrasonic sound.** This is done by using 'sonar' as described below.

SONAR

The word **'SONAR'** stands for **'SO**und **N**avigation **A**nd **R**anging'. **Sonar is an apparatus (or device) which is used to find the depth of a sea or to locate the under-water things like shoals of fish, shipwrecks, and enemy submarines.** Sonar works by sending short bursts of ultrasonic sound from a ship down into sea-water and then picking up the echo produced by the reflection of ultrasonic sound from under-water objects like bottom of sea, shoal of fish, shipwreck or a submarine. The time taken for the echo to return to the ship is measured by the sonar apparatus. The distance (or range) of the under-water object is then calculated from the time taken by the echo to return. Thus, **the time it takes for an echo to return is used to find out how far away something is.** This will become more clear from the following discussion.

A sonar apparatus consists of two parts : (*i*) a transmitter (for emitting ultrasonic waves), and (*ii*) a receiver (for detecting ultrasonic waves) (see Figure 53). Now, suppose a sonar device is attached to the under-side of a ship and we want to measure the depth of sea (below the ship). To do this, the transmitter of sonar is made to emit a pulse of ultrasonic sound with a very high frequency of about 50,000 hertz. This pulse of ultrasonic sound travels down the sea-water towards the bottom of the sea. When the ultrasonic sound pulse strikes the bottom of the sea, it is reflected back to the ship in the form of an echo. This echo produces an electrical signal in the receiver part of the sonar device. **The sonar device measures the time taken by the ultrasonic sound pulse to travel from the ship to the bottom of the sea, and back to the ship.** In other words, the sonar measures the time taken by the echo to return to the ship. **Half of this time gives the time taken by the ultrasonic sound to travel from the ship to the bottom of the sea.** Knowing the time taken by the ultrasonic sound to go from the ship to the bottom of the sea, and the speed of sound in water, we can calculate the distance between the ship and the bottom of the sea. This will give us the depth of the sea (below the ship). The calculation of depth of a sea will become more clear from the following example. Please note that **the speed of ultrasonic sound in water is the same as that of ordinary sound.**

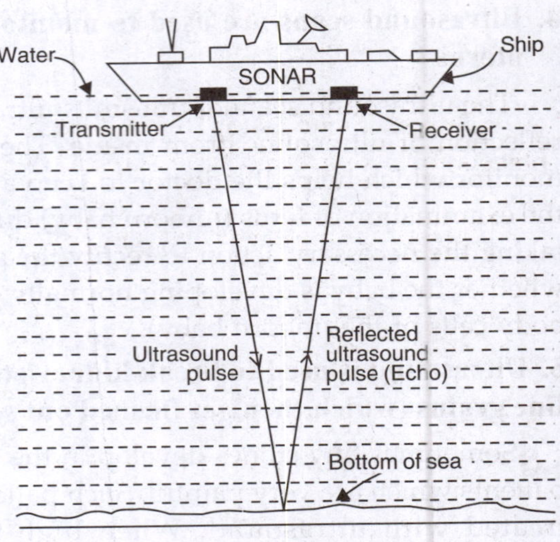

Figure 53. To measure the depth of a sea by using sonar.

Sample Problem. A sonar device attached to a ship sends ultrasonic waves in the sea. These waves are reflected from the bottom of the sea. If the ultrasonic waves take 4 seconds to travel from the ship to the bottom of the sea and back to the ship (in the form of an echo), what is the depth of the sea ? (Speed of sound in water = 1500 m/s).

Solution. The time taken by the ultrasonic sound waves to travel from the ship to the sea-bed, and back to the ship is 4 seconds. So, the time taken by the ultrasonic sound to travel from the ship to sea-bed will be half of this time, which is $\frac{4}{2} = 2$ seconds. This means that the sound takes 2 seconds to travel from the ship to the bottom of the sea.

Now, $$\text{Speed} = \frac{\text{Distance}}{\text{Time}}$$

So, $$1500 = \frac{\text{Distance}}{2}$$

And, $$\text{Distance} = 1500 \times 2 \text{ m} = 3000 \text{ m}$$

Thus, the depth of this sea below the ship is 3000 metres.

Figure 54. The shoal of fish (like the one shown in this photograph) is located in the sea by using 'sonar'. This makes it easy to catch a lot of fish from the sea. The 'sonar' device is attached to the fishing boat.

Figure 55. When a ship drowns in the sea due to an accident, the shipwreck (like the one shown in this photograph) is located in the deep sea by using 'sonar'.

Sonar is also used to locate the shoal of fish, a shipwreck or a submarine in the sea. This happens as follows : A ship's sonar sends out ultrasonic sound waves into the sea-water. The shoal of fish, the shipwreck or the submarine in the sea reflects these ultrasonic sound waves back to the ship (in the form of echoes). These reflected ultrasonic sound waves (or echoes) are used by a computer to build up pictures of submerged objects on a television-type screen. We will now explain why only ultrasonic sound waves are used in sonar.

Ultrasonic sound waves are used in sonar because of the following advantages it has over the ordinary sound waves :

(*i*) Ultrasonic sound waves have a very high frequency (and very short wavelength) due to which they can penetrate into sea-water to a large extent.

(*ii*) Ultrasonic sound waves cannot be confused with engine noises or other sounds made by the ship (because they cannot be heard by human beings).

7. Bats use ultrasound to fly at night (without colliding with other objects) and to search their prey (like flying insects)

In nature, the principle of sonar is used by bats for avoiding obstacles in their path and locating prey (food) while flying at night (Bats are nearly blind). **The method used by some animals (like bats, porpoises and dolphins) to locate the objects by hearing the echoes of their ultrasonic squeaks is called 'echolocation'.**

(*a*) Bats fly in the darkness of night without colliding with other objects (or obstacles) by the method of echolocation. This happens as follows : Bats emit high-frequency ultrasonic squeaks while flying and listen to the echoes produced by the reflection of their squeaks from the objects (or obstacles) in their path. From the time taken by the echo to be heard, bats can judge the distance of the object (or obstacle) in their path and hence avoid it by changing the direction.

(*b*) Bats search their prey (like flying insects) at night by the method of echolocation. This happens as follows : Bats emit high-frequency ultrasonic squeaks while flying and listen to the echoes produced by the reflection of their squeaks from the prey like a flying insect (see Figure 56). From the time taken by the echo to be heard, bats can judge the distance of the insect and hence catch it. Certain moths can, however, hear the high-frequency ultrasonic squeaks of a bat. So, these moths can know when the bat is flying nearby, and are able to escape being captured.

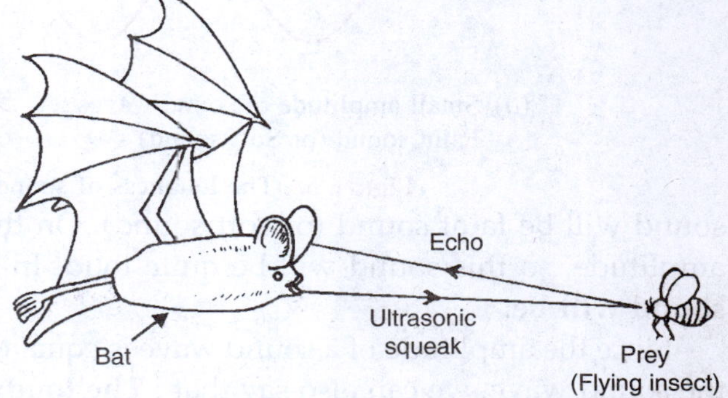

Figure 56. Bats search their prey in the darkness of night by the method of 'echolocation'.

The porpoises (which are mammals with a round snout) and dolphins also use the method of 'echolocation' involving ultrasonic waves for under-water navigation and location of prey. We will now discuss the characteristics of sound.

CHARACTERISTICS OF SOUND

A sound has three characteristics : loudness, pitch and quality (or timbre). In other words, sounds are recognised by three characteristics : loudness, pitch and quality (or timbre). Two musical sounds may differ from one another in one or more of these characteristics. We will now discuss all the characteristics of sound in detail, one by one. Let us start with loudness.

1. Loudness

Sounds are produced by vibrating objects. If less energy is supplied to an object by hitting it lightly (or by stretching it lightly), then the object vibrates with a smaller amplitude and produces a faint sound (or feeble sound) [see Figure 57(*a*)]. On the other hand, if more energy is supplied to an object by hitting it

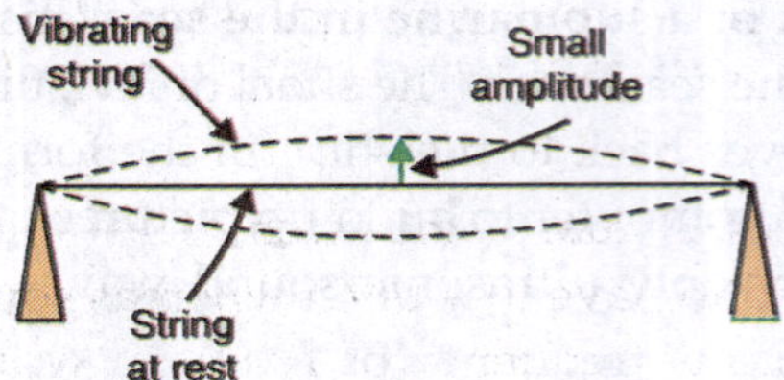

(*a*) The string shown in this diagram has been plucked lightly due to which it vibrates with a small amplitude and produces a faint sound (or feeble sound)

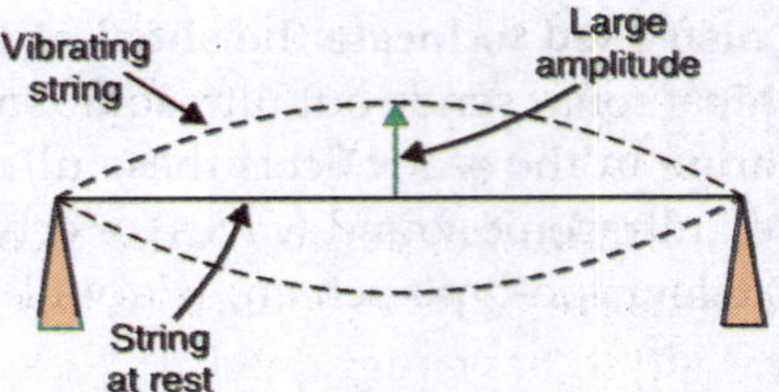

(*b*) When the string is plucked hard (or strongly), then it vibrates with a large amplitude and produces a loud sound

Figure 57. Loudness of sound produced depends on the amplitude of vibrations of the stretched string.

more strongly (or by stretching it more strongly), then the object will vibrate with a greater amplitude and produce a louder sound [see Figure 57(*b*)]. **The loudness of sound is a measure of the sound energy reaching the ear per second**. Greater the sound energy reaching our ears per second, louder the sound will appear to be.

The loudness of sound depends on the amplitude of sound waves. If the sound waves have a small amplitude, then the sound will be faint (or soft). On the other hand, if the sound waves have a large amplitude, then the sound will be loud. Figure 58(*a*) shows a sound wave of small amplitude, so this

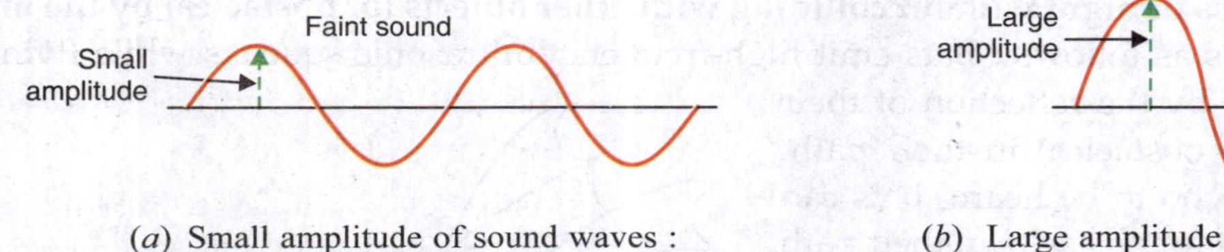

(*a*) Small amplitude of sound waves : Faint sound (or Soft sound)

(*b*) Large amplitude of sound waves : Loud sound

Figure 58. The loudness of sound depends on the amplitude of sound waves.

sound will be faint sound (or soft sound). On the other hand, Figure 58(*b*) shows a sound wave of large amplitude, so this sound will be quite loud. In fact, **greater the amplitude of sound waves, louder the sound will be.**

Since the amplitude of a sound wave is equal to the amplitude of vibrations of the source which produces the sound wave, we can also say that : **The loudness of sound depends on the amplitude of vibration of the source producing the sound waves**. This point will become clear from the following example. When we strike a table lightly, then due to less energy supplied, the table top vibrates with a small amplitude and hence a faint sound (or soft sound) is produced. If, however, we hit the table hard, then due to greater energy supplied, the table top vibrates with a large amplitude and hence produces a loud sound. Thus, the amplitude of sound waves depends on the force with which an object is made to vibrate.

The loudness of sound is measured in 'decibel', written as **dB**. The softest sound which human ears can hear is said to have a loudness of 0 dB (zero decibel). The loudness of sound of people talking quietly is about 65 dB, the loudness of sound in a very noisy factory is about 100 dB and the sound of a jet aircraft 50 metres away is said to have a loudness of about 130 dB.

2. Pitch

We can distinguish between a man's voice and a woman's voice of the same loudness even without seeing them. This is because a man's voice and a woman's voice

(*a*) Beating a drum

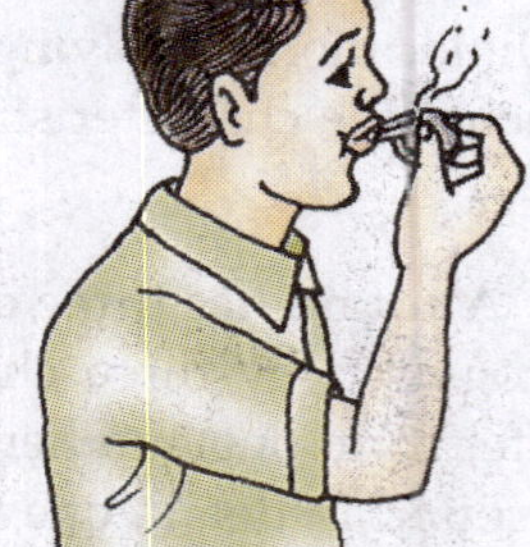

(*b*) Blowing a whistle

Figure 59. The beating of drum produces a low-pitched sound (having low frequency) but the blowing of whistle produces a high pitched sound (having high frequency).

differ in pitch. A man's voice is flat having a low pitch, whereas a woman's voice is shrill having a high pitch. We can now say that : **Pitch is that characteristic of sound by which we can distinguish between different sounds of the same loudness.**

The pitch of a sound depends on the frequency of vibration. Actually, **the pitch of a sound is directly proportional to its frequency**. Sounds of low frequency are said to have low pitch whereas sounds of high frequency are said to have high pitch. For example, a sound of low frequency of 100 hertz will have a low pitch whereas a sound of high frequency of 1000 hertz will have a high pitch. Figure 60(*a*) shows sound

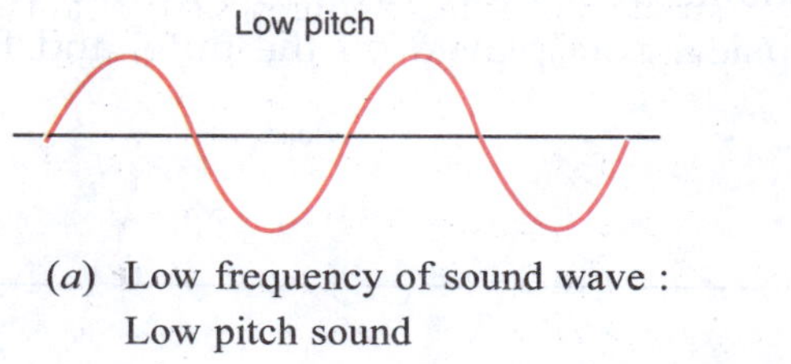

(*a*) Low frequency of sound wave : Low pitch sound

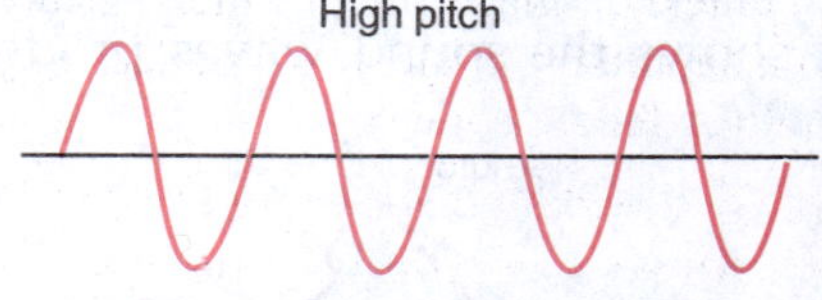

(*b*) High frequency of sound wave : High pitch sound

Figure 60. The pitch of sound depends on the frequency of vibration.

wave of low frequency and hence low pitch. On the other hand, the sound wave shown in Figure 60(*b*) has a high frequency and hence a high pitch. In fact, **greater the frequency of a sound, the higher will be its pitch**. Please note that both the sound waves shown above have the same amplitude and hence they have the same loudness. They differ only in their pitch.

Since the frequency of a sound wave is equal to the frequency of vibration of the source which produces the sound wave, **faster the vibrations of the sound producing source, the higher is the frequency and higher is the pitch**. This point will become more clear from the following experiment.

We put a bicycle on its 'stand' so that its rear wheel (back wheel) is free to rotate. We rotate the bicycle wheel by using pedals and touch its spokes with the edge of a cardboard piece. We will hear a sound as the cardboard touches the spoke after spoke. As we go on increasing the speed of rotation of the wheel, the shrillness of sound produced increases or the pitch of sound increases. These observations can be explained as follows : The cardboard piece is made to vibrate by the spokes of the bicycle wheel, and the frequency of vibration depends on the speed of rotation of wheel. When the wheel is rotated rapidly, the frequency of vibration of cardboard piece increases, due to which the pitch of the sound produced also increases. From this experiment we conclude that *the pitch of the sound is determined by the frequency of vibration of the object which produces sound.*

3. Quality (or Timbre)

We can distinguish between the sounds (or notes) produced by a flute and a violin even without seeing these instruments. This is because the sounds produced by a flute and a violin differ in quality (or

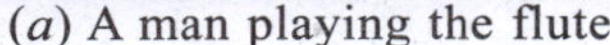

(*a*) A man playing the flute

(*b*) A man playing the violin

Figure 61. The sounds (or notes) produced by the two musical instruments flute and violin differ in quality (or timbre)

timbre). It is the difference in the quality of sound which enables us to tell at once which instrument played the musical sound (or musical note). We can now say that : **Quality (or timbre) is that characteristic of musical sound which enables us to distinguish between the sounds of same pitch and loudness produced by different musical instruments (and different singers).**

The quality (or timbre) of a musical sound depends on the shape of sound wave (or waveform) produced by it. The quality (or timbre) of sound varies from one musical instrument to another musical instrument. The difference in the quality (or timbre) of two musical sounds produced by two musical instruments is due to the difference in the shapes of sound waves (or waveforms) produced by them. Figure 62(*a*) shows the sound waves produced by a musical note played on the flute, and Figure 62(*b*)

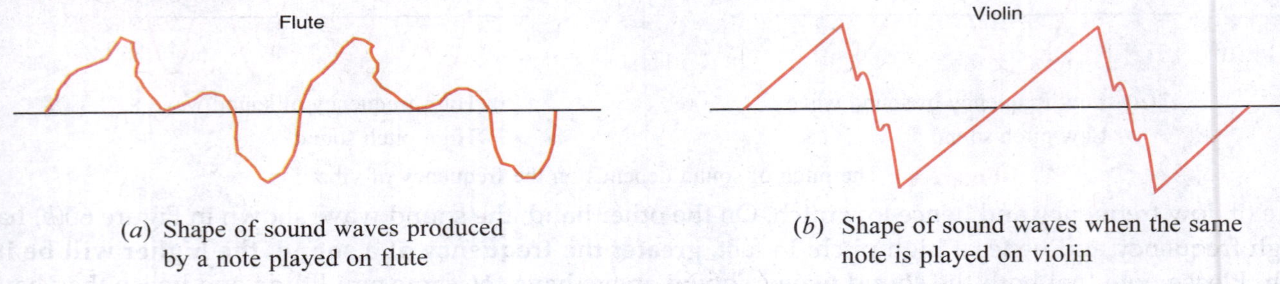

(*a*) Shape of sound waves produced by a note played on flute

(*b*) Shape of sound waves when the same note is played on violin

Figure 62. The quality (or timbre) of a musical sound depends on its waveform.

shows the sound waves produced when the same musical note is played on the violin. Both these sound waves have the same pitch and loudness but different shapes and hence different quality (or different timbre).

It should be clear by now that the sounds (or notes) produced by different musical instruments like flute, violin, piano, harmonium, clarinet, *sitar*, *tanpura*, and trumpet, etc., can be distinguished from one another by their quality (or timbre) even if they are of the same pitch and loudness. Similarly, the sounds (or notes) produced by different 'singers' such as Mohammad Rafi, Kishore Kumar, Kumar Sanu, Udit

Figure 63. The sounds (or notes) produced by different singers (when they sing) can be distinguished from one another on the basis of their quality (or timbre).

Narayan, Daler Mehndi, Lata Mangeshkar, Asha Bhonsle, Ila Arun, Usha Uthup and Sunidhi Chauhan can be distinguished from one another on the basis of their quality or timbre. We can even recognise a person from his voice (even without seeing him) on the basis of the unique quality or timbre of his voice.

The musical sounds have complex waveforms (wave-shapes) because they consist of a 'fundamental frequency' mixed with different 'higher frequencies.' So, we can also say that : **The quality (or timbre) of a musical sound depends on the mixture of frequencies present in it.** We will study this in detail in higher classes. At the moment we will learn the construction and working of human ear.

THE HUMAN EAR

The ears are the sense organs which help us in hearing sound. We will now describe the construction and working of a human ear. A highly simplified diagram of human ear is shown in Figure 65.

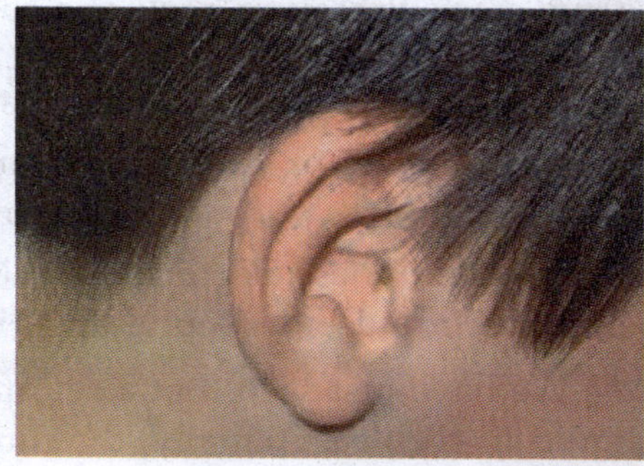

Figure 64. This is how the human ear looks like from outside.

Construction of Human Ear

The ear consists of three compartments : outer ear, middle ear and inner ear (see Figure 65). The part of ear which we see outside the head is called outer ear. The outer ear consists of a broad part called pinna and about 2 to 3 centimetres long passage called ear canal. At the end of ear canal is a thin, elastic and circular membrane called ear-drum (see Figure 65). The ear-drum is also called tympanum. The outer ear contains air.

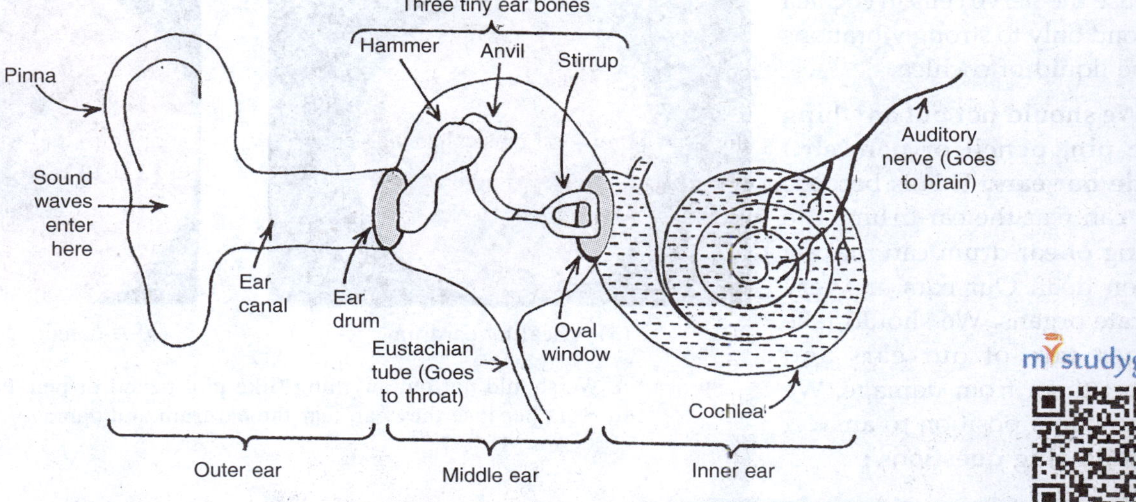

Figure 65. Structure of human ear.

The middle ear contains three small and delicate bones called hammer, anvil and stirrup. These ear-bones are linked to one another. One end of the bone called hammer is touching the ear-drum and its other end is connected to the second bone called anvil (see Figure 65). The other end of anvil is connected to the third bone called stirrup. And the free end of stirrup is held against the membrane over the oval window of inner ear (see Figure 65). The middle ear also contains air. The lower part of middle ear has a narrow tube called 'eustachian tube' going to the throat. Eustachian tube connects the middle ear to throat and ensures that the air pressure inside the middle ear is the same as that on the outside.

The inner ear has a coiled tube called cochlea. One side of cochlea is connected to the middle ear through the elastic membrane over the oval window. The cochlea is filled with a liquid. The liquid present in cochlea contains nerve cells which are sensitive to sound. The other side of cochlea is connected to auditory nerve which goes into the brain (see Figure 65). We will now describe the working of ear.

Working of Human Ear

The sound waves (coming from a sound producing body) are collected by the pinna of outer ear (see Figure 65). These sound waves pass through the ear canal and fall on the ear-drum. Sound waves consist of compressions (high pressure regions) and rarefactions (low pressure regions). When the compression of sound wave strikes the ear-drum, the pressure on the outside of ear-drum increases and pushes the ear-drum inwards. And when the rarefaction of sound wave falls on the ear-drum, the pressure on the outside of ear-drum decreases and it moves outward. Thus, **when the sound waves fall on the ear-drum, the ear-drum starts vibrating back and forth rapidly**.

The vibrating ear-drum causes a small bone hammer to vibrate. From hammer, vibrations are passed on to the second bone anvil and finally to the third bone stirrup. The vibrating stirrup strikes on the membrane of the oval window and passes its vibrations to the liquid in the cochlea. Due to this, the liquid in the cochlea begins to vibrate. The vibrating liquid of cochlea sets up electrical impulses in the nerve cells present in it. These electrical impulses are carried by auditory nerve to the brain. The brain interprets these electrical impulses as sound and we get the sensation of hearing.

We have just seen that a set of three tiny bones passes on sound vibrations from the ear-drum to the liquid in cochlea. Actually, the three ear-bones, hammer, anvil and stirrup, act as a system of levers and amplify (make stronger) the vibrations of ear-drum by more than 20 times. Thus, **the function of three tiny bones in the middle ear is to increase the strength of vibrations coming from the ear-drum before passing them on to the inner ear.** Please note that it is necessary to make the sound vibrations stronger (or amplified) because the nerve cells in cochlea respond only to strong vibrations in the liquid of cochlea.

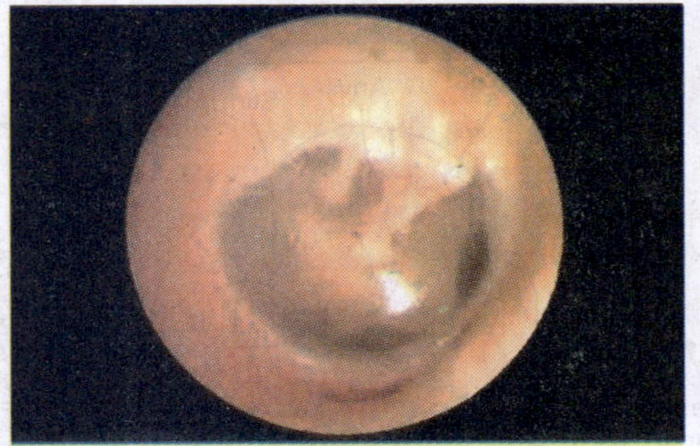

(*a*) A healthy eardrum

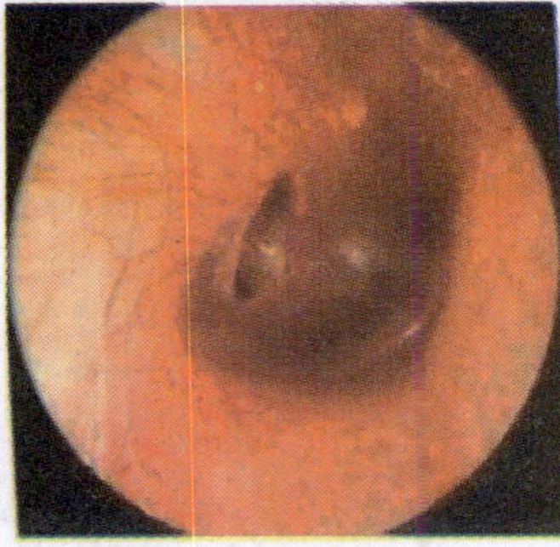

(*b*) A damaged eardrum

Figure 66. We should not put anything (like pin, pencil or pen, etc., inside our ears because they can tear the eardrum and damage it.

We should not put anything (like pin, pencil or pen, etc.) inside our ears. This is because they can tear the ear-drum. The tearing of ear-drum can make a person deaf. Our ears are very delicate organs. We should take proper care of our ears and protect them from damage. We are now in a position to **answer the following questions :**

Very Short Answer Type Questions

1. Which property of sound leads of the formation of echoes ?
2. What name is given to the repetition of sound caused by the reflection of sound waves ?
3. What name is given to the persistence of sound in a big hall or auditorium ?
4. Name three devices which work on the reflection of sound.
5. What is the other name of a loud-hailer ?
6. Name the three characteristics of sound.
7. Name the unit used to measure the loudness of sound. Also write its symbol.
8. Name the characteristic which helps us distinguish between a man's voice and a woman's voice, even without seeing them.
9. How does the pitch of a sound depend on frequency ?
10. Name the characteristic of sound which depends on (*a*) amplitude (*b*) frequency, and (*c*) waveform.
11. Name the characteristic of sound which can distinguish between the 'notes' (musical sounds) played on a flute and a *sitar* (both the notes having the same pitch and loudness).
12. Name the organs of hearing in our body.
13. Name that part of ear which vibrates when outside sound falls on it.
14. Name the three tiny bones present in the middle part of ear.
15. There are three small bones in the middle ear — anvil, hammer and stirrup :
    (*a*) Which of these bones is in touch with ear-drum ?
    (*b*) Which of these bones is in touch with oval window ?
16. What is the function of three tiny bones in the ear ?

17. Name the tube which connects the middle ear to throat.
18. Name the nerve which carries electrical impulses from the cochlea of ear to the brain.
19. What is the name of passage in outer ear which carries sound waves to the ear-drum ?
20. Why should we not put a pin or pencil in our ears ?
21. What type of scans are used these days to monitor the growth of developing baby in the uterus of the mother ?
22. How is an ultrasound scan for fetus (unborn baby) better than X-ray ?
23. What is the name of the device which is used to find the depth of sea (or ocean) by using ultrasonic sound waves ?
24. Write the full name of 'SONAR'.
25. Name the principle on which a soundboard works.
26. Name the device which is used to address a small gathering of people.
27. Name the device used by doctors to listen to our heartbeats.
28. What is the shape of a soundboard kept behind the speaker on the stage of a big hall ?
29. Name two sound absorbing materials (or objects) which can make our big room less echoey.
30. Can we hear (*a*) infrasonic waves (*b*) ultrasonic waves ?
31. What name is given to the sound waves of frequency too low for humans to hear ?
32. What name is given to the sound waves of frequency too high for humans to hear ?
33. What type of sound waves are produced by a vibrating simple pendulum ?
34. What happens to the pitch of a sound if its frequency increases ?
35. What happens to the loudness of a sound if its amplitude decreases ?
36. What name is given to sound waves of frequencies higher than 20 kHz ?
37. Fill in the following blanks with suitable words :
    (*a*) An echo is simply a .... sound.
    (*b*) Pitch of sound depends on ....
    (*c*) Loudness of sound depends on ....
    (*d*) Quality of sound depends on ....
    (*e*) Echoes are caused by the .... of sound.

Short Answer Type Questions

38. On which day, a hot day or a cold day, an echo is heard sooner ? Give reason for your answer.
39. In which medium, air or water, an echo is heard much sooner ? Why ?
40. What is reverberation ? What will happen if the reverberation time in a big hall is too long ?
41. How can reverberations in a big hall or auditorium be reduced ?
42. Why do we hear more clearly in a room with curtains than in a room without curtains ?
43. What is a megaphone ? Name the principle on which a megaphone works.

Megaphone

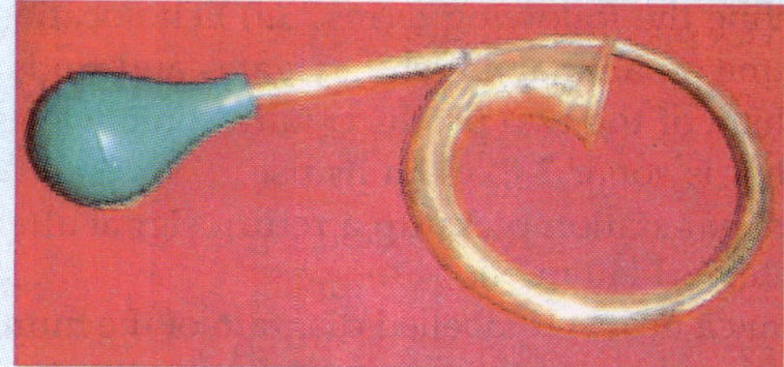
Bulb horn

44. What is a bulb horn ? Name the principle on which a bulb horn works.
45. What is a stethoscope ? Name the principle on which a stethoscope works.
46. What is a soundboard ? Explain the working of a soundboard with the help of a labelled diagram.
47. (*a*) What is meant by the 'loudness' of sound ? On what factor does the loudness of a sound depend ?
    (*b*) Draw labelled diagrams to represent (*a*) soft sound, and (*b*) loud sound, of the same frequency.
48. (*a*) Explain the term 'pitch' of a sound. On what factor does the 'pitch' of a sound depend ?
    (*b*) Draw labelled diagrams to represent sound of (*a*) low pitch, and (*b*) high pitch, of the same loudness.

49. What is meant by the quality (or timbre) of sound ? On what factor does the quality (or timbre) of a sound depend ?

50. Explain why, if we strike a table lightly, we hear a soft sound but if we hit the table hard, a loud sound is heard.

51. Give one use of ultrasound in industry and one in hospitals.

52. How is it that bats are able to fly at night without colliding with other objects ?

53. Explain how, bats use ultrasound to catch the prey.

54. Explain how, flaws (or defects) in a metal block can be detected by using ultrasound.

55. Why are the ceilings of concert halls made curved ? Draw a labelled diagram to illustrate your answer.

56. Draw a labelled diagram to show the multiple reflections of sound in a part of the stethoscope tube.

57. What is the range of frequencies associated with (*a*) infrasound (*b*) audible sound, and (*c*) ultrasound ?

58. (*a*) What is the difference between infrasonic waves and ultrasonic waves ?

(*b*) Choose the infrasonic waves and ultrasonic waves from the following frequencies :

(*i*) 10,000 Hz (*ii*) 30,000 Hz (*iii*) 18 Hz (*iv*) 50,000 Hz (*v*) 10 Hz

59. (*a*) What is the frequency range of hearing in humans ?

(*b*) Which of the following sound frequencies cannot be heard by a human ear ?

(*i*) 10 Hz (*ii*) 100 Hz (*iii*) 10,000 Hz (*iv*) 15 Hz (*v*) 40,000 Hz

60. The echo of a sound is heard after 5 seconds. If the speed of sound in air be 342 m/s, calculate the distance of the reflecting surface.

61. The speed of sound in water is 1500 metres per second. How far away from an under-sea rock should a deep sea diver be so that he can hear his own echo ?

Long Answer Type Questions

62. (*a*) What is meant by 'reflection of sound' ? What type of surfaces are the best for reflecting sound ?

(*b*) Name any two objects which are good reflectors of sound.

(*c*) State the laws of reflection of sound.

63. (*a*) What is an echo ? How is echo formed ?

(*b*) What is the minimum distance in air required from a sound reflecting surface to hear an echo (at 20°C) ?

(*c*) A man standing 825 metres away from a cliff (steep rock) fires a gun. After how long will he hear its echo ? Speed of sound in air is 330 m/s.

64. (*a*) What is ultrasound ? What is the difference between ordinary sound and ultrasound ?

(*b*) Write any three applications (or uses) of ultrasound.

65. (*a*) What are infrasonic waves ? Name two animals which produce infrasonic waves.

(*b*) What are ultrasonic waves ? Name two animals which can produce ultrasonic waves

(*c*) The audible range of frequencies of an average human ear is from 20 Hz to 20 kHz. Calculate the corresponding wavelengths. (Speed of sound in air is 344 m s^{-1}).

66. (*a*) Define the following terms : (*a*) Echolocation (*b*) Echocardiography, and (*c*) Ultrasonography.

(*b*) Name an animal which navigates and finds food by ecolocation.

(*c*) Which of the two produces ultrasonic waves : porpoise or whale ?

67. (*a*) What is sonar ? Explain its use.

(*b*) A sonar station picks up a return signal after 3 seconds. How far away is the object ? (Speed of sound in water = 1440 m/s).

68. Draw a neat and labelled diagram of the human ear. With the help of this diagram, explain the construction and working of the human ear.

Multiple Choice Questions (MCQs)

69. In SONAR we use :

(*a*) ultrasonic waves (*b*) infrasonic waves (*c*) radio waves (*d*) audible sound waves

70. When we change a feeble sound to a loud sound, we increase its :

(*a*) frequency (*b*) amplitude (*c*) velocity (*d*) wavelength

71. Which kind of sound is produced in an earthquake before the main shock wave begins ?

(*a*) ultrasound (*b*) infrasound (*c*) audible sound (*d*) none of the above

72. Before playing the orchestra in a musical concert, a *sitarist* tries to adjust the tension and pluck the strings suitably. By doing so he is adjusting :

(*a*) intensity of sound only

(*b*) amplitude of sound only

(*c*) frequency of the *sitar* string with the frequency of other musical instruments

(*d*) loudness of sound

73. 'Note' is a sound :

(*a*) of a mixture of several frequencies (*b*) of mixture of only two frequencies

(*c*) of a single frequency (*d*) always unpleasant to listen to

74. A key of mechanical piano is first struck gently and then struck again but much harder this time. In the second case :

(*a*) sound will be louder but pitch will not be different

(*b*) sound will be louder and the pitch will also be higher

(*c*) sound will be louder but pitch will be lower

(*d*) both loudness and pitch will remain unaffected

75. One of the following can hear infrasound. This one is :

(*a*) dog (*b*) bat (*c*) rhinoceros (*d*) humans

76. An echo-sounder in a trawler (fishing boat) receives an echo from a shoal of fish 0.4 s after it was sent. If the speed of sound in water is 1500 m/s, how deep is the shoal ?

(*a*) 150 m (*b*) 300 m (*c*) 600 m (*d*) 7500 m

77. The speed of highly penetrating ultrasonic waves is :

(*a*) lower than those of audible sound waves (*b*) higher than those of audible sound waves

(*c*) much higher than those of audible sound waves (*d*) same as those of audible sound waves

78. The ultrasound waves can penetrate into matter to a large extent because they have :

(*a*) very high speed (*b*) very high frequency (*c*) very high wavelength (*d*) very high amplitude

79. The frequencies of four sound waves are given below. Which of these sound waves can be used to measure the depth of sea by the echo method ?

(*a*) 15,000 Hz (*b*) 10 kHz (*c*) 50 kHz (*d*) 10,000 Hz

80. Which of the following frequency of sound can be generated by a vibrating simple pendulum as well as by the vibrating vocal cords of a rhinoceros ?

(*a*) 5 kHz (*b*) 25 Hz (*c*) 10 Hz (*d*) 15,000 Hz

81. Which of the following device does not work on the multiple reflections of sound waves ?

(*a*) stethoscope (*b*) hydrophone (*c*) soundboard (*d*) megaphone

82. What type of waves are generated by SONAR device fixed to a fishing ship ?

(*a*) water waves (*b*) radio waves (*c*) sound waves (*d*) infrared waves

83. We can distinguish between the musical sounds produced by different singers on the basis of the characteristic of sound called :

(*a*) frequency (*b*) timbre (*c*) pitch (*d*) loudness

84. At 20°C, the minimum distance of a person from a sound reflecting surface to hear an echo is :

(*a*) 12.2 m (*b*) 17.2 m (*c*) 15.2 m (*d*) 34.4 m

Questions Based on High Order Thinking Skills (HOTS)

85. The drawing shows a ship 800 m from a cliff. A gun is fired on the ship. After 5 seconds the people at the front of the ship hear the sound of the gun again.

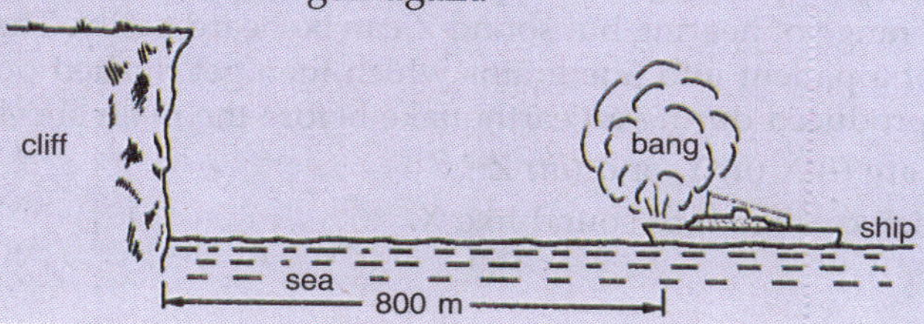

(*a*) What is the name of this effect ?

(*b*) What happens to the sound at the cliff ?

(*c*) How far does the sound travel in 5 seconds ?

(*d*) Calculate the speed of sound.

86. Consider the following sound waves marked A, B, C and D :

(*a*) Which two waves represent sounds of the same loudness but different pitch ?

(*b*) Which two waves represent sounds of the same frequency but different loudness ?

(*c*) State whether all these sound waves have been produced by the same vibrating body or different vibrating bodies ?

(*d*) Which vibrating body/bodies could have generated the sound waves shown here ?

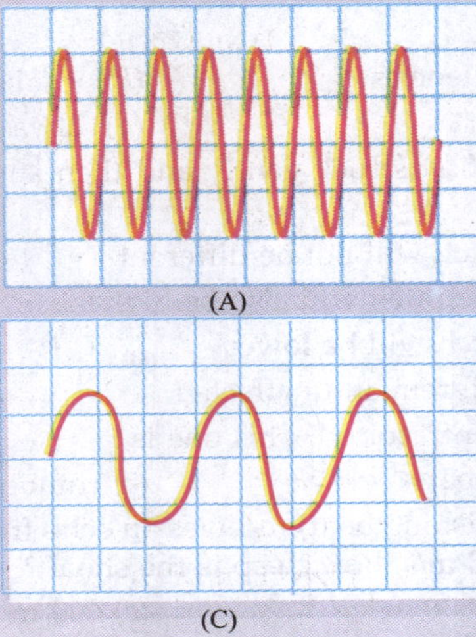
(A)
(C)

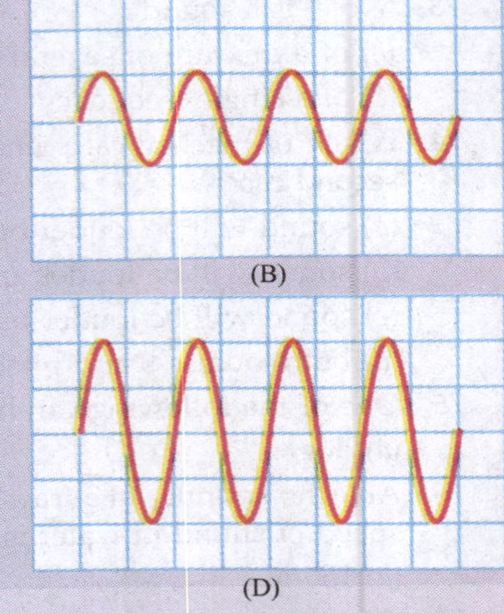
(B)
(D)

87. In an experiment, Anhad studies sound waves. He sets up a loudspeaker to produce sound as shown below :

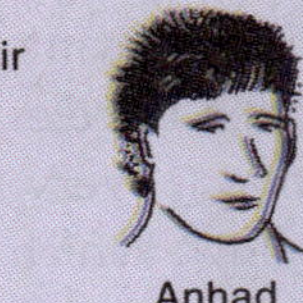

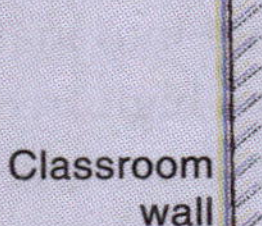

Anhad adjusts the signal to the loudspeaker to give a sound of frequency 200 Hz.

(*a*) What happens to the air in-between Anhad and the loudspeaker ?

(*b*) Explain how Anhad receives sound in both ears.

88. Figure X shows a trace of a sound wave produced by a particular tuning fork :

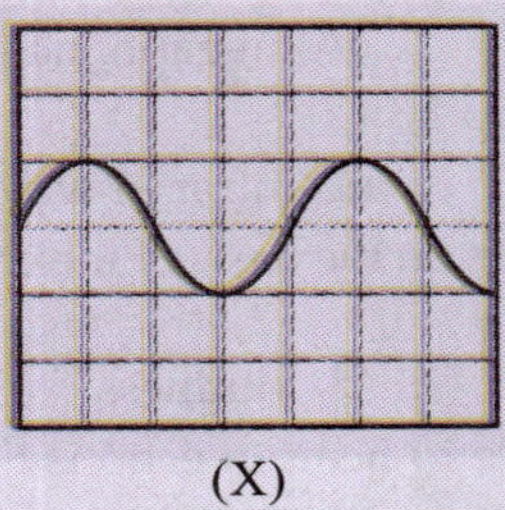
(X)

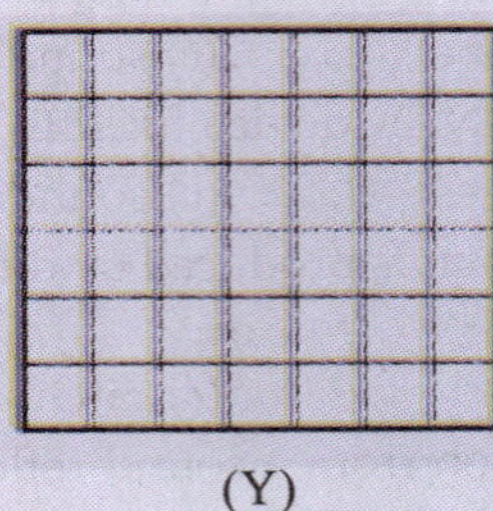
(Y)

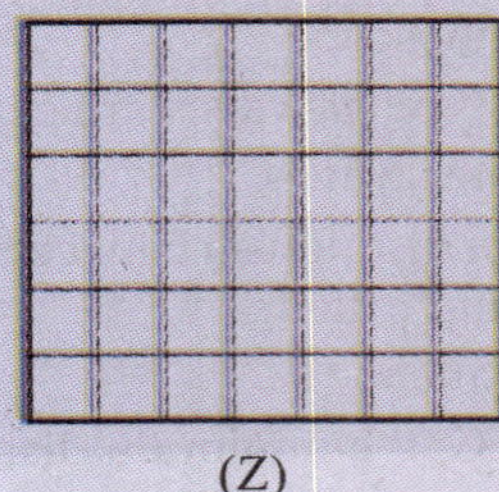
(Z)

(*a*) On the graph paper given in Figure Y, draw a trace of the sound wave which has a higher frequency than that shown in Figure X.

(*b*) On the graph paper shown in Figure Z, draw a trace of the sound wave which has a larger amplitude than that shown in Figure X.

89. Three different vibrating objects produce three types of sounds X, Y and Z. Sounds X and Y cannot be heard by a man having normal range of hearing but sound Z can be heard easily. The sound X is used in hospitals to break kidney stones of a patient into fine grains which then get flushed out with urine. The sound Y is similar to that which is produced during an earthquake before the main shock wave is generated.

(*a*) What type of sounds are (*i*) X (*ii*) Y, and (*iii*) Z ?

(*b*) Name one device which can produce sound like X.

(*c*) Name one device in a science laboratory which can produce sound like Y.
(*d*) Name one device in our homes which can produce sound like Z.
(*e*) What is the frequency range of sounds like Z ?

90. A man is kidnapped, blindfolded and imprisoned in a big room. How could the man tell if he was in : (*a*) a city (*b*) a village (*c*) a bare room (*d*) a furnished room ?

ANSWERS

1. Reflection of sound **2.** Echo **3.** Reverberation **5.** Megaphone **8.** Pitch **11.** Timbre **21.** Ultrasound scans **25.** Reflection of sound **33.** Infrasonic sound waves **36.** Ultrasonic sound waves **37.** (*a*) reflected (*b*) frequency (*c*) amplitude (*d*) waveform (*e*) reflection **58.** (*b*) Infrasonic waves : 18 Hz, 10 Hz; Ultrasonic waves : 30,000 Hz, 50,000 Hz **59.** (*b*) 10 Hz; 15 Hz; 40,000 Hz **60.** 855 m **61.** 75 m **63.** (*c*) 5 seconds **65.** (*c*) 17.2 m to 0.0172 m **67.** (*b*) 2160 m **69.** (*a*) **70.** (*b*) **71.** (*b*) **72.** (*c*) **73.** (*c*) 74. (*a*) **75.** (*c*) **76.** (*b*) **77.** (*d*) **78.**(*b*) **79.** (*c*) **80.** (*c*) **81.** (*b*) **82.** (*c*) **83.** (*c*) **84.** (*b*) **85.** (*a*) Echo (*b*) Sound gets reflected (*c*) 1600 m (*d*) 320 m/s **86.** (*a*) A and D (*b*) B and D (*c*) Same vibrating body (*d*) Tuning forks **87.** (*a*) The air in-between Anhad and the loudspeaker vibrates with the frequency of 200 Hz (*b*) Anhad receives sound in the right ear by the sound waves coming directly from the loudspeaker (through air); Anhad receives sound in the left ear from sound waves reflected from the wall of classroom.

88. (*a*)

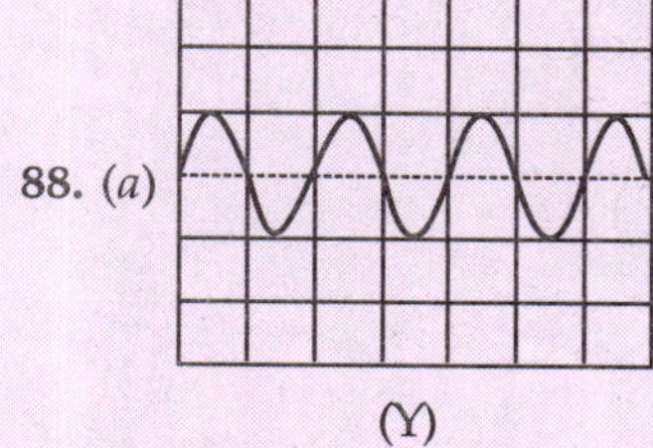

(Y)

(*b*)

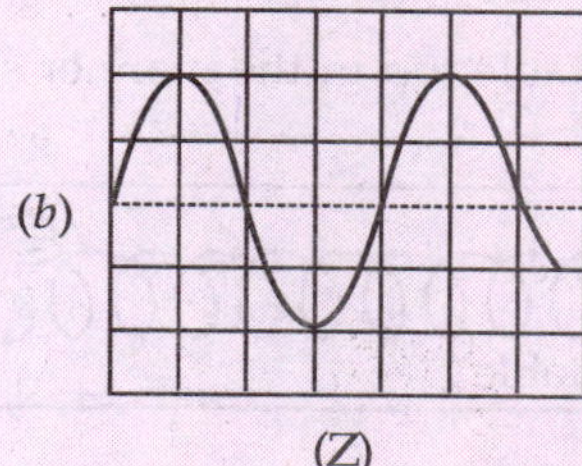

(Z)

89. (*a*) (*i*) Ultrasonic sound (*ii*) Infrasonic sound (*iii*) Audible sound (Ordinary sound) (*b*) Ultrasound machine in hospitals (*c*) Simple pendulum (*d*) Radio (*e*) 20 Hz to 20000 Hz **90.** (*a*) Lot of noise of heavy traffic in a city (*b*) Very little noise of traffic in a village (*c*) Echoes of persons talking in a bare room (*d*) Furnished room is less echoey

Multiple Choice Questions (MCQs)
(Based on Practical Skills in Science)

1. While performing an experiment on verifying the laws of reflection of sound, a student is to choose between (*i*) a narrow or a wide tube, and (*ii*) a strong or a faint source of sound.
The observed experimental difference, between the values of angle of incidence and angle of reflection, is likely to be minimum when he chooses a :
(1) narrow tube and a faint source (2) wide tube and a faint source
(3) narrow tube and a strong source (4) wide tube and a strong source

2. For verifying the laws of reflection of sound, a student has to choose from :
(*i*) a black polished metal sheet or a white thermocole sheet.
(*ii*) a 0.5 m long tube of diameter 3 cm or a 1.5 m long tube of diameter 20 cm
He should prefer to choose the :
(1) metal sheet and the 0.5 m long tube (2) metal sheet and the 1.5 m long tube
(3) thermocole sheet and the 0.5 m long tube (4) thermocole sheet and the 1.5 m long tube

3. A student sets up a slinky on a smooth table top in the manner shown here.

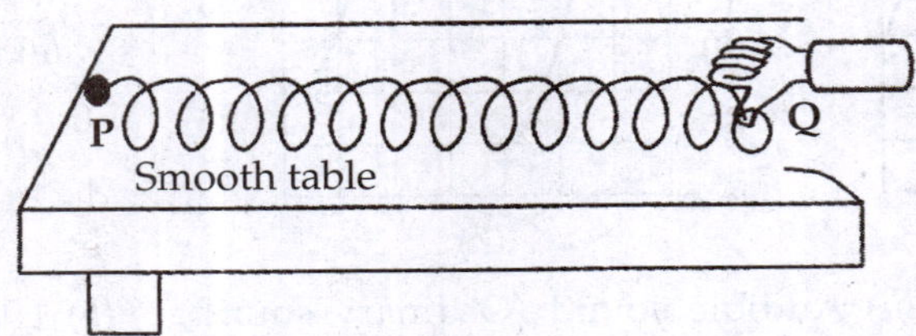

How can he produce transverse waves in the slinky by moving its free end Q ?
(1) at an angle of 45° with the table top (2) backward and forward along the length of the slinky
(3) up and down (4) left and right

4. A student lists the following precautions for the experiment on determining the velocity of a pulse propagated through a stretched string :
(A) The string should not be stretched too tight.
(B) The counting of the pulse journeys must start from zero and not from one.
(C) The string should be stretched straight in contact with the table.
(D) The amplitude of the pulse should be kept appreciably high.
The incorrect entry, in this list of precautions, is the precaution listed as :
(1) A (2) B (3) C (4) D

5. For plotting temperature-time graph for a hot body, as it cools to room temperature, a student is to choose one each from each of the following pairs.
A : Calorimeter
(*i*) blackened from outside (*ii*) polished from outside
B : Base for keeping the calorimeter
(*i*) insulated (*ii*) metallic
In order to get the correct graph he should prefer to choose :
(1) A (*i*), B (*ii*) (2) A (*ii*), B (*ii*) (3) A (*i*), B (*i*) (4) A (*ii*), B (*i*)

6. The magnitude of zero error of the spring balance and least count of the measuring cylinder, shown here, are, respectively :

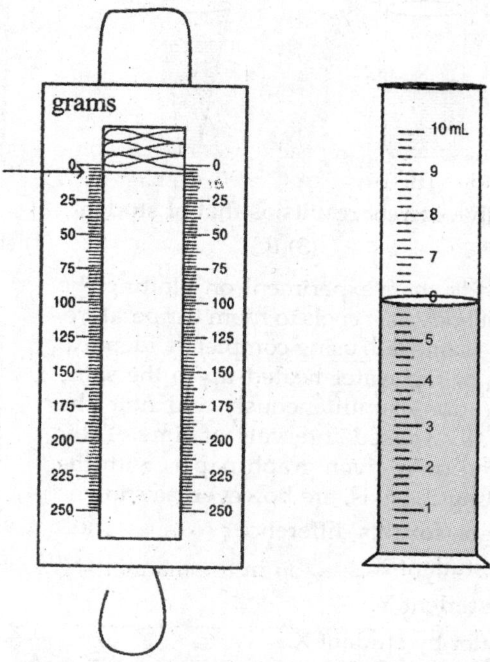

(1) 2.5 g and 0.1 mL (2) 5.0 g and 0.1 mL (3) 2.5 g and 0.2 mL (4) 5.0 g and 0.2 mL

7. A student takes some water in a beaker and heats it over a flame for determining its boiling point. He keeps on taking its temperature readings. He would observe that the temperature of water :
   (1) keeps on increasing regularly
   (2) keeps on increasing irregularly
   (3) first increases slowly, then decreases rapidly and eventually becomes constant
   (4) first increases gradually and then becomes constant.

8. The zero-error in the spring balance shown and the correct weight of the solid, suspended from it, are equal, respectively, to :

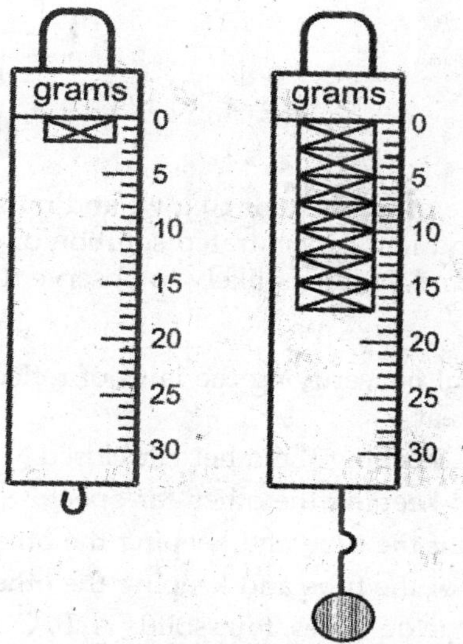

(1) + 2 g wt ; 19 g wt (2) + 2 g wt ; 15 g wt (3) – 2 g wt ; 19 g wt (4) – 2 g wt ; 15 g wt

9. Four students A, B, C and D while performing an experiment on establishing the relation between the loss of weight of a small solid when fully immersed in tap water, and the weight of water displaced by it, used

four different shapes of overflow cans containing water as shown.

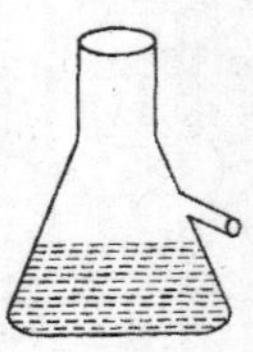

(A)

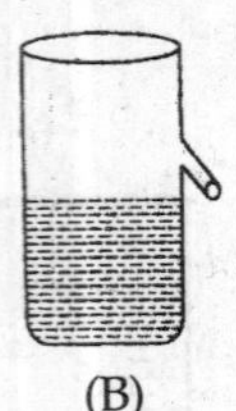

(B)

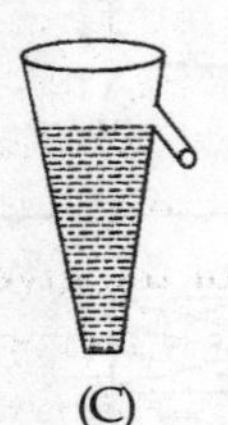

(C)

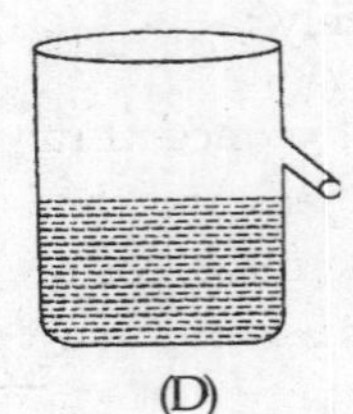

(D)

The arrangement, that would give correct results, is that of student :

(1) (A) (2) (B) (3) (C) (4) (D)

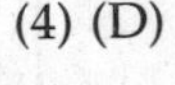

10. Two students X and Y have to do their experiment on plotting the temperature-time graph for a hot body as it cools to room temperature. They do their experiments in the same lab, using completely identical apparatus, take equal amounts of tap water heated up to the same temperature, start their observations simultaneously and note the temperature values at identically spaced intervals of time. Their temperature-time graphs, plotted on a given graph paper, with the same given choices of scales along the axis, are however, as shown :

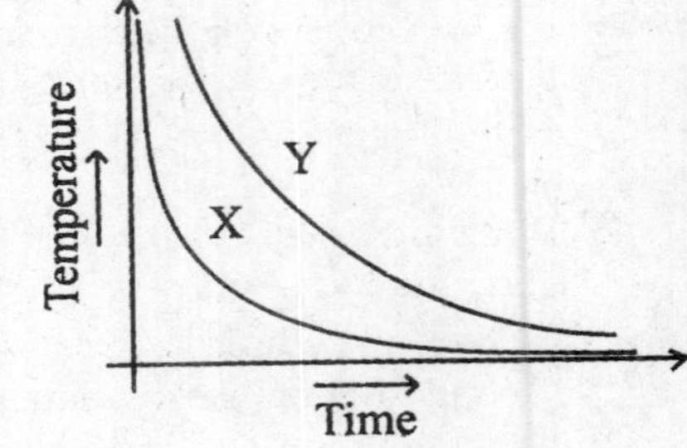

The following could be the reason for this difference :

(A) Use of an overhead fan by student X.

(B) Use of an overhead fan by student Y.

(C) Less frequent stirring of water by student X.

(D) Less frequent stirring of water by student Y.

The most likely reason is :

(1) A (2) B (3) C (4) D

11. In the set up shown the weight of the body was measured in air and in water. The reading of mark X in the spring balance would be :

(1) 36 g wt

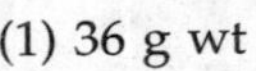

(2) 30 g wt

(3) 24 g wt

(4) 6 g wt

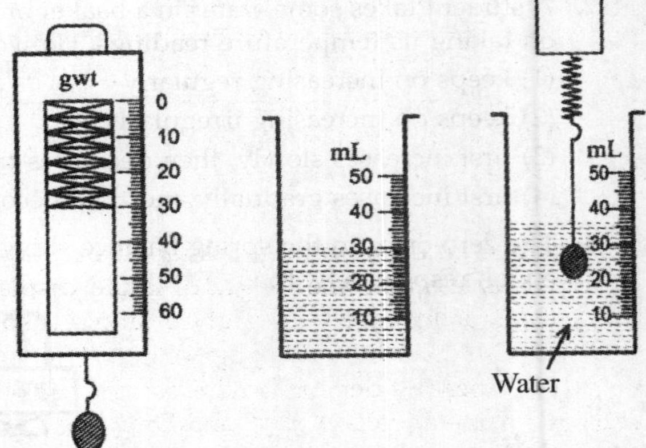

12. A student uses a spring balance of least count 10 g wt and range 500 g wt. He records the weight of small iron cube in air, in tap water and in a concentrated solution of common salt in water. If his three readings taken in this order are W_1, W_2 and W_3, he is likely to observe that :

(1) $W_1 > W_2 > W_3$ (2) $W_3 > W_2 > W_1$ (3) $W_1 > W_3 > W_2$ (4) $W_2 > W_1 > W_3$

13. While performing an experiment on verifying the laws of reflection of sound, the 'reflected sound' can be detected better by keeping one ear :

(1) near the end of the tube and keeping the other ear closed

(2) near the end of the tube and keeping the other ear open

(3) at about 5 cm from the end of the tube and keeping the other ear closed

(4) at about 5 cm from the end of the tube and keeping the other ear open

14. In an experiment to determine the densities, four solids A, B, C and D are immersed in a liquid contained in a measuring cylinder, one by one. The volumes of water displaced by the solids A, B, C and D are 100 cm^3, 100 cm^3, 80 cm^3 and 80 cm^3, respectively. When weighed in air, the masses of solids A, B, C and D were

found to be 80 g, 100 g, 100 g and 80 g, respectively. The two solids having identical densities are :
(1) A and C (2) B and D (3) C and D (4) A and D

15. A student is given an iron cube of side 1 cm, a measuring cylinder of range 100 mL and least count 1 mL, and a spring balance of range 100 g wt and least count 1 g wt. He can use these to measure :
(1) both the mass and the volume of the given iron cube
(2) neither the mass nor the volume of the given iron cube
(3) only the mass of the given iron cube but not its volume
(4) only the volume of the given iron cube but not its mass

16. Four beakers are labelled as P, Q, R and S. A student puts salt solutions of different concentrations in the four beakers without noting which beaker contains solution of which concentration. A solid suspended from the hook of a spring balance gives a reading of 150 g in air. When this solid, while still suspended from the hook of spring balance, is fully immersed in beakers P, Q, R and S, the readings shown by the spring balance in the four beakers P, Q, R and S are 110 g, 130 g, 140 g and 120 g respectively. The most concentrated solution is contained in the beaker labelled as :
(1) P (2) Q (3) R (4) S

17. While doing an experiment on plotting the temperature-time graph of hot water as it cools, we can get a good graph :
(1) only by noting the temperature of hot water every 30 seconds throughout
(2) only by noting the temperature of hot water every 1 minute throughout
(3) by noting the temperature of hot water every 1 minute to start with and every 2 minutes later on
(4) by noting the temperature of hot water every 2 minutes to start with and every 1 minute later on

18. A student heats some amount of tap water in a calorimeter to a temperature of nearly 50°C above the room temperature. He then records the temperature of this water as it is cooling down at regular intervals of 2 minutes each. He tabulates his observations as follows :

Time (in minutes) →	0	2	4	6	8	10
Temperature (in °C) →	t_1	t_2	t_3	t_4	t_5	t_6

He is likely to observe that :
(1) $(t_1 - t_2) > (t_3 - t_4) > (t_5 - t_6)$ (2) $(t_1 - t_2) = (t_3 - t_4) = (t_5 - t_6)$
(3) $(t_1 - t_2) < (t_3 - t_4) < (t_5 - t_6)$ (4) $(t_1 - t_2) < (t_3 - t_4) > (t_5 - t_6)$

19. When an object is fully immersed in a liquid, the apparent loss in weight :
(1) is less than the weight of liquid displaced by it
(2) is more than the weight of liquid displaced by it
(3) is equal to the weight of liquid displaced by it
(4) does not depend on the density of the liquid displaced by it

20. Four metal balls A, B, C and D having radius of 2.5 cm each are made of copper, aluminium, gold and iron respectively. The densities of copper, aluminium, gold and iron are 8.9 g/cm^3, 2.7 g/cm^3, 19.3 g/cm^3 and 7.8 g/cm^3 respectively. When the balls A, B, C and D are tied to threads, suspended from the hook of a spring balance and immersed completely in strong salty water, one by one, the apparent loss in weight will be :
(1) maximum in ball B (2) maximum in ball C
(3) minimum in ball B (4) same in all the balls

21. A glass ball hanging from the hook of a sensitive spring balance is completely submerged in highly salty water and tap water, one by one. If the readings of spring balance when the ball is in highly salty water and tap water are x and y respectively, then :
(1) $x < y$ (2) $x > y$ (3) $x = y$ (4) $x = 2y$

22. You are given four salt solutions W, X, Y and Z of different concentrations. W is a 20% salt solution, X is a 35% salt solution, Y is a 10% salt solution whereas Z is a 50% salt solution. When a solid suspended from the hook of a spring balance is fully submerged in all these salt solutions, one by one, then the spring balance will show the minimum reading when the solid is immersed in :
(1) solution W (2) solution X (3) solution Y (4) solution Z

23. An aluminium ball is fully immersed in distilled water, well water, sea water and inland lake water, one by one. The aluminium ball will appear to suffer the maximum loss in weight when immersed in :
(1) distilled water (2) sea water (3) well water (4) lake water

24. When an object is fully submerged in strong salty water, it undergoes an apparent :
(1) loss in mass (2) loss in volume (3) loss in density (4) loss in weight

25. If a body tied to a spring balance is fully immersed in a liquid, the apparent loss in its weight :
(1) is more in a denser liquid
(2) is less in a denser liquid
(3) does not depend on density of liquid
(4) is equal to apparent gain in weight of liquid

26. In an experiment on determining the velocity of a pulse propagating through a stretched string, the stopwatch should be started and stopped at instants corresponding to the ones shown in :
(1) Fig. 1 and Fig. 2 (2) Fig. 1 and Fig. 3
(3) Fig. 2 and Fig. 1 (4) Fig. 2 and Fig. 3

Fig. 1

Fig. 2

Fig. 3

27. When a fresh egg is put into a beaker filled with water, it sinks. When the same egg is put in a strong salty water, then it floats. Which of the following is the incorrect statement in this context ?
(1) salt water enters into egg by osmosis and makes it lighter
(2) salt water exerts more buoyant force
(3) salt water is denser than tap water
(4) upthrust exerted by a liquid depends on its density

28. When two balls, one of iron and the other of aluminium, are completely immersed in strong salty water, they undergo an equal loss in weight. This shows that iron and aluminium balls have :
(1) the same densities (2) the same masses (3) the same volumes (4) the same weights

29. When two solids are put in two pans of a beam balance, they exactly balance each other in air. When the two solids are completely immersed in water alongwith pans of balance, then they no longer balance each other. Which of the following is the incorrect statement about these balls ?
(1) they have equal masses in air (2) they have equal weights in air
(3) they have equal volumes in air (4) they have unequal densities

30. The temperature-time graph obtained when hot water is allowed to cool resembles the graph given in one of the following figures. The correct figure is :

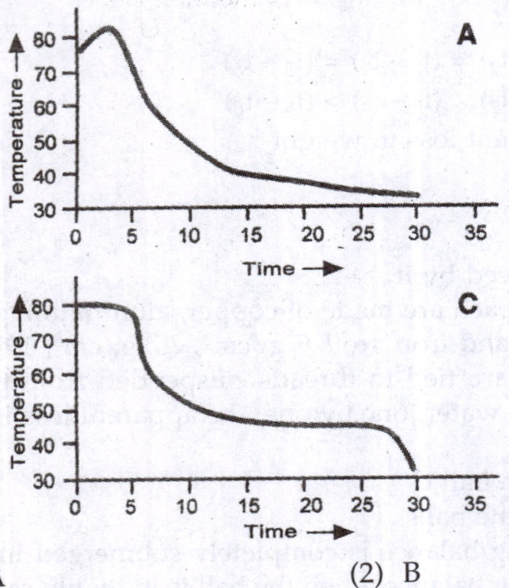

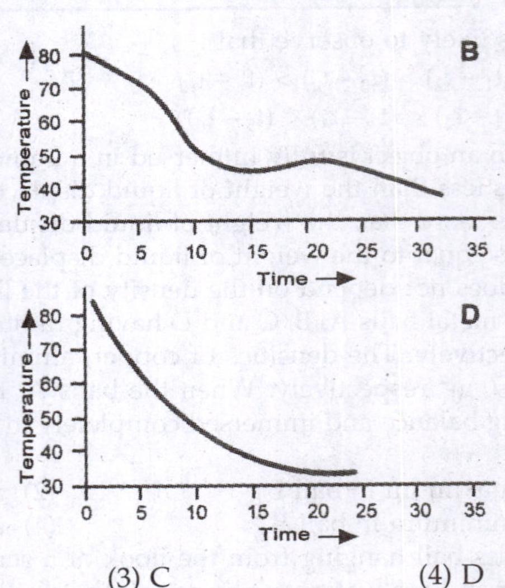

(1) A (2) B (3) C (4) D

ANSWERS

1. 3	2. 1	3. 3	4. 3	5. 3
6. 4	7. 4	8. 2	9. 3	10. 1
11. 3	12. 1	13. 1	14. 2	15. 1
16. 1	17. 3	18. 1	19. 3	20. 4
21. 1	22. 4	23. 2	24. 4	25. 1
26. 2	27. 1	28. 3	29. 3	30. 4

NCERT BOOK QUESTIONS AND EXERCISES (with answers)

Chapter : MOTION

NCERT Book, Page 100

Q.1. An object has moved through a distance. Can it have zero displacement ? If yes, support your answer with an example.

Ans. Yes, even if an object has moved through a distance, it can have zero displacement. This can happen if, after moving through a certain distance, the moving object comes back to its starting position. For example, if an athlete runs along a circular track and after completing one round, comes back to his starting position, then the distance moved by the athlete will be equal to the circumference of circular track but his displacement will be zero (because the straight line distance between his initial and final positions will be zero).

Q.2. A farmer moves along the boundary of a square field of side 10 m in 40 s. What will be the magnitude of displacement of the farmer at the end of 2 minutes 20 seconds from his initial position ?

Ans. First of all we will convert the total time of 2 minutes 20 seconds into seconds.

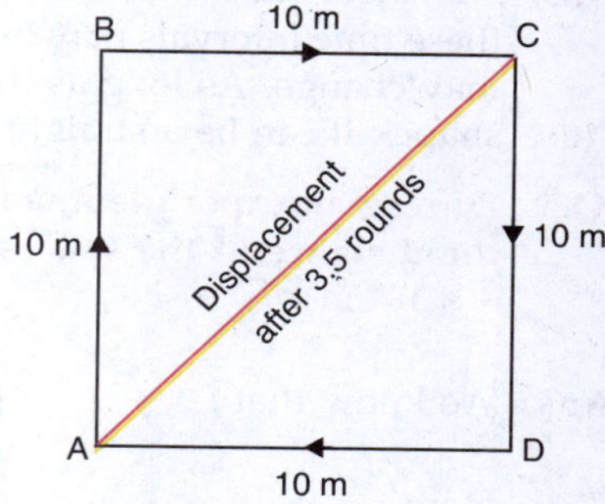

$$\begin{aligned}\text{Total time} &= 2 \text{ minutes } 20 \text{ seconds}\\ &= 2 \times 60 \text{ seconds} + 20 \text{ seconds}\\ &= 120 \text{ seconds} + 20 \text{ seconds}\\ &= 140 \text{ seconds}\end{aligned}$$

Now, In 40 s, number of rounds made = 1

So, In 140 s, number of rounds made $= \frac{1}{40} \times 140$

$= 3.5$

Thus, the farmer will make three and a half rounds (3.5 rounds) of the square field. If the farmer starts from position A (see Figure), then after three complete rounds, he will reach at starting position A. But in the next half round, the farmer will move from A to B, and B to C, so that his final position will be at C. Thus, the net displacement of the farmer will be AC. Now, ABC is a right angled triangle in which AC is the hypotenuse. So,

$$\begin{aligned}(AC)^2 &= (AB)^2 + (BC)^2\\ (AC)^2 &= (10)^2 + (10)^2\\ (AC)^2 &= 100 + 100\\ (AC)^2 &= 200\\ AC &= \sqrt{200}\\ AC &= 14.143 \text{ m}\end{aligned}$$

Thus, the magnitude of displacement of the farmer at the end of 2 minutes and 20 seconds will be 14.143 metres.

Q.3. Which of the following is true for displacement ?

(a) It cannot be zero.

(b) Its magnitude is greater than the distance travelled by the object.

Ans. (a) The displacement can be zero. So, the first statement is not true.

(b) The magnitude of displacement can never be greater than the distance travelled by the object. So, the second statement is also not true.

NCERT Book, Page 102

Q.1. Distinguish between speed and velocity.

Ans.

Speed	*Velocity*
1. Speed of a body is the distance travelled by it per unit time 2. In speed, the direction of motion of the body is not specified 3. Speed has only magnitude, so speed is a scalar quantity	1. Velocity of a body is the distance travelled by it per unit time in a given direction 2. In velocity, the direction of motion of the body is specified 3. Velocity has both, magnitude as well as direction, so velocity is a vector quantity

Q.2. Under what condition(s) is the magnitude of average velocity of an object equal to its average speed ?

Ans. The magnitude of average velocity of an object is equal to its average speed only when the object moves along a straight line path.

Q.3. What does the odometer of an automobile measure ?

Ans. The odometer of an automobile measures the distance travelled by the automobile (or vehicle).

Q.4. What does the path of an object look like when it is in uniform motion ?

Ans. An object has a uniform motion if it travels equal distances in equal intervals of time, no matter how small these time intervals may be. This means that in uniform motion, speed is constant but the direction of motion may change. As long as the speed remains constant, the path of an object in uniform motion can have any shape : it can be a straight line path, a curved path, a circular path or even a zig-zag path.

Q.5. During an experiment, a signal from a spaceship reached the ground station in five minutes. What was the distance of the spaceship from the ground station ? The signal travels at the speed of light, that is, 3×10^8 m s^{-1}.

Ans. We know that : $\text{Speed} = \dfrac{\text{Distance travelled}}{\text{Time taken}}$

Here, Speed $= 3 \times 10^8$ m s^{-1}

Distance travelled = ? (To be calculated)

And, Time taken = 5 minutes

$= 5 \times 60$ seconds

$= 300$ s

Now, putting the values of speed and time in the above formula, we get :

$$3 \times 10^8 = \frac{\text{Distance travelled}}{300}$$

So, Distance travelled $= 3 \times 10^8 \times 300$ m

$= 9 \times 10^{10}$ m

Thus, the distance of spaceship from the ground station is 9×10^{10} metres.

NCERT Book, Page 103

Q.1. When will you say a body is in :

(*i*) uniform acceleration ?

(*ii*) non-uniform acceleration ?

Ans. (*i*) A body has a uniform acceleration if its velocity changes by equal amounts in equal intervals of time. The motion of a freely falling body is an example of uniform acceleration.

(*ii*) A body has a non-uniform acceleration if its velocity changes by unequal amounts in equal intervals of time. The motion of a car on a crowded city road is an example of non-uniform acceleration.

Q.2. A bus decreases its speed from 80 km h^{-1} to 60 km h^{-1} in 5 s. Find the acceleration of the bus.

Ans. In this problem, we will have to change the speeds of bus from km h^{-1} (kilometres per hour) to m s^{-1} (metres per second) because the time is given in seconds.

Now, Initial speed of bus, $u = 80 \text{ km h}^{-1}$

$$= \frac{80 \times 1000 \text{ m}}{60 \times 60 \text{ s}}$$

$$= 22.22 \text{ m s}^{-1} \quad \text{... (1)}$$

Final speed of bus, $v = 60 \text{ km h}^{-1}$

$$= \frac{60 \times 1000 \text{ m}}{60 \times 60 \text{ s}}$$

$$= 16.66 \text{ m s}^{-1} \quad \text{... (2)}$$

And, Time taken, $t = 5$ s ...(3)

Now, Acceleration, $a = \frac{v - u}{t}$

$$a = \frac{16.66 - 22.22}{5}$$

$$a = \frac{-5.56}{5}$$

$$a = -1.11 \text{ m s}^{-2}$$

Thus, the acceleration of the bus is, -1.11 m s^{-2}. The minus sign for acceleration shows that it is actually negative acceleration or retardation.

Q.3. A train starting from a railway station and moving with uniform acceleration attains a speed of 40 km h^{-1} in 10 minutes. Find its acceleration.

Ans. Here, Initial speed of train, $u = 0$ (Starts from rest)

Final speed of train, $v = 40 \text{ km h}^{-1}$

$$= \frac{40 \times 1000 \text{ m}}{60 \times 60 \text{ s}}$$

$$= 11.11 \text{ m s}^{-1}$$

And, Time taken, t = 10 minutes

= 10 × 60 seconds

= 600 s

Now, Acceleration, $a = \frac{v - u}{t}$

$$a = \frac{11.11 - 0}{600}$$

$$a = \frac{11.11}{600} \text{ m s}^{-2}$$

$$a = 0.0185 \text{ m s}^{-2} \quad (\text{or } 1.85 \times 10^{-2} \text{ m s}^{-2})$$

NCERT Book, Page 107

Q.1. What is the nature of the distance-time graphs for uniform and non-uniform motion of an object ?

Ans. (*i*) The distance-time graph for an object having uniform motion is a straight line with some slope [see Figure (*i*)]

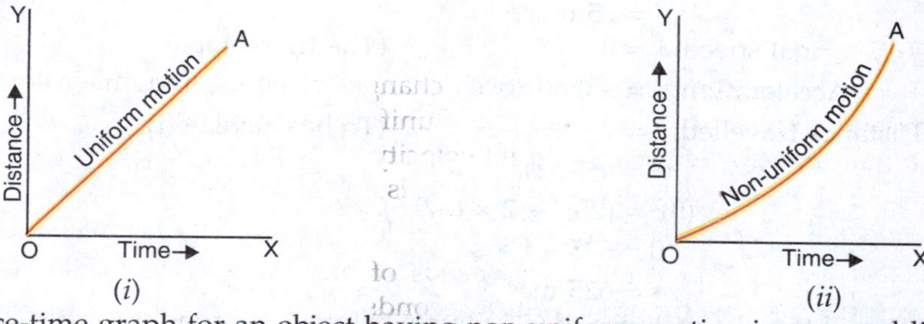

(*ii*) The distance-time graph for an object having non-uniform motion is a curved line [see Figure (*ii*)]

Q.2. What can you say about the motion of an object whose distance-time graph is a straight line parallel to the time-axis ?

Ans. If the distance-time graph of an object is a straight line parallel to the time axis, it shows that the distance of the object from its starting position is just the same at all times. Since the object remains at the same distance from the starting position, it is not moving. The object is stationary.

Q.3. What can you say about the motion of an object if its speed-time graph is a straight line parallel to the time axis ?

Ans. If the speed-time graph of an object is a straight line parallel to the time axis, then the speed of the object at every instant of time is just the same. So, the object is moving with constant speed (or uniform speed). There is no acceleration at all.

Q.4. What is the quantity which is measured by the area occupied below the velocity-time graph ?

Ans. Distance travelled by the object.

NCERT Book, Pages 109 and 110

Q.1. A bus starting from rest moves with a uniform acceleration of 0.1 m s^{-2} for 2 minutes. Find :

(a) the speed acquired.

(b) the distance travelled.

Ans. (a) *Calculation of speed acquired*

Here, Initial speed, $u = 0$ (Bus starts from rest)

Final speed, $v = ?$ (To be calculated)

Acceleration, $a = 0.1\ \text{m s}^{-2}$

And, Time, $t = 2$ minutes

$= 2 \times 60$ seconds

$= 120$ s

Now, Final velocity, $v = u + at$

So, $v = 0 + 0.1 \times 120$

$v = 12\ \text{m s}^{-1}$

Thus, the speed acquired by the bus is 12 metres per second.

(b) *Calculation of distance travelled*

Now, Distance travelled, $s = ut + \frac{1}{2}at^2$

So, $s = 0 \times 120 + \frac{1}{2} \times 0.1 \times (120)^2$

$s = 0 + \frac{1}{2} \times 0.1 \times 14400$

$s = 720$ m

Thus, the distance travelled by the bus is 720 metres.

Q.2. A train is travelling at a speed of 90 km h^{-1}. Brakes are applied so as to produce a uniform acceleration of, – 0.5 m s^{-2}. Find how far the train will go before it is brought to rest.

Ans. Here, Initial speed, $u = 90\ \text{km h}^{-1}$

$= \frac{90 \times 1000\ \text{m}}{60 \times 60\ \text{s}}$

$= 25\ \text{m s}^{-1}$

Final speed, $v = 0$ (The train stops)

Acceleration, $a = -0.5\ \text{m s}^{-2}$

And, Distance travelled, $s = ?$ (To be calculated)

Now, $v^2 = u^2 + 2as$

So, $(0)^2 = (25)^2 + 2 \times (-0.5) \times s$

$0 = 625 - 1 \times s$

$s = 625$ m

Thus, the train will travel a distance of 625 metres before it is brought to rest.

Q.3. A trolley, while going down an inclined plane, has an acceleration of 2 cm s^{-2}. What will be its velocity 3 s after the start ?

Ans. Here, Initial velocity, $u = 0$

Final velocity, $v = ?$ (To be calculated)

Acceleration, $a = 2$ cm s^{-2}

And, Time, $t = 3$ s

Now, $v = u + at$

So, $v = 0 + 2 \times 3$

or $v = 6$ cm s^{-1}

Thus, the velocity of trolley after 3 s will be 6 centimetres per second.

Q.4. A racing car has a uniform acceleration of 4 m s^{-2}. What distance will it cover in 10 s after start ?

Ans. Here, Distance covered, $s = ?$ (To be calculated)

Initial velocity, $u = 0$

Acceleration, $a = 4$ m s^{-2}

And, Time, $t = 10$ s

Now, $s = ut + \frac{1}{2}at^2$

So, $s = 0 \times 10 + \frac{1}{2} \times 4 \times (10)^2$

$s = 0 + 2 \times 100$

$s = 200$ m

Thus, the distance covered by the racing car in 10 s is 200 metres.

Q.5. A stone is thrown in vertically upward direction with a velocity of 5 m s^{-1}. If the acceleration of the stone during its motion is 10 m s^{-2} in the downward direction, what will be the height attained by the stone and how much time will it take to reach there ?

Ans. When the stone is thrown vertically upwards, then the velocity of stone goes on decreasing because of force of gravity of earth acting on it in the downward direction. So, the acceleration produced in the stone is negative and hence it is to be written with a minus sign (as, – 10 m s^{-2}).

Now, Initial velocity of stone, $u = 5$ m s^{-1}

Final velocity of stone, $v = 0$ (It stops at the top)

Acceleration, $a = -10$ m s^{-2}

And, Distance travelled, $s = ?$ (To be calculated)
(or Height attained)

Now, $v^2 = u^2 + 2as$

So, $(0)^2 = (5)^2 + 2 \times (-10) \times s$

$0 = 25 - 20\,s$

$20\,s = 25$

$s = \frac{25}{20}$

$s = 1.25$ m

Thus, the height attained by the stone will be 1.25 metres.

Let us find out the time now. We know that :

$v = u + at$

So, $0 = 5 + (-10) \times t$

$0 = 5 - 10t$

$10t = 5$

$t = \frac{5}{10}$

$t = 0.5$ s

Thus, the time taken by the stone to reach at the top will be 0.5 second.

NCERT Book, Pages 112 and 113

Q.1. An athlete completes one round of a circular track of diameter 200 m in 40 s. What will be the distance covered and the displacement at the end of 2 minutes 20 s ?

Ans. Here, Total time = 2 minutes 20 seconds

$= 2 \times 60$ seconds + 20 seconds

= 120 seconds + 20 seconds

= 140 s

Now, In 40 s, the number of rounds completed = 1

So, In 140 s, the number of rounds completed $= \frac{1}{40} \times 140$

$= 3.5$

(a) *Calculation of distance covered in 3.5 rounds*

The diameter of circular track is given to be 200 m, so the radius (r) of the circular track will be half of it, which is $\frac{200}{2} = 100$ m.

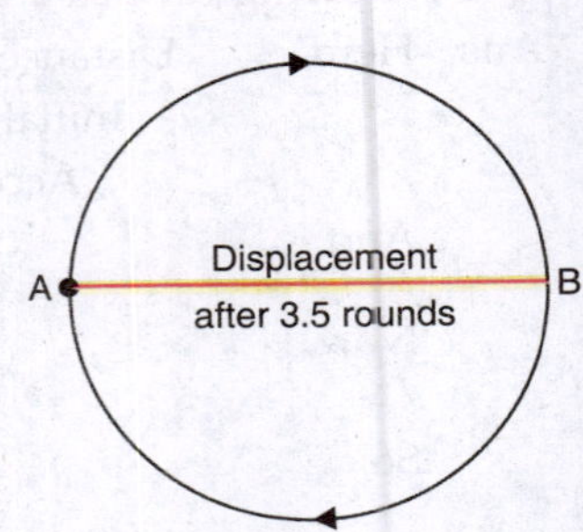

Now, Distance covered in 1 round = Circumference of circular track

$= 2\pi r$

$= 2 \times \frac{22}{7} \times 100$ m $\left(\text{Because } \pi = \frac{22}{7}\right)$

= 628.57 m

And, Distance covered in 3.5 rounds $= 628.57 \times 3.5$ m

= 2200 m

(b) *Calculation of displacement in 3.5 rounds*

The athlete makes three and a half rounds (3.5 rounds) of the circular track. Now, if the athlete starts from point A (see Figure), then after three complete rounds, he will reach at the same point A. And when the athlete again starts from point A and makes the remaining half round, he will reach point B (which is diametrically opposite to point A). So, the displacement of athlete will be equal to diameter of the circular track which is 200 m.

Q.2. Joseph jogs from one end A to the other end B of a straight 300 m road in 2 minutes 30 seconds and then turns around and jogs 100 m back to point C in another 1 minute. What are Joseph's average speeds and velocities in jogging :

(a) from A to B ?

(b) from A to C ?

Ans. We will first draw a line diagram to show the movement of Joseph during jogging. This is given below :

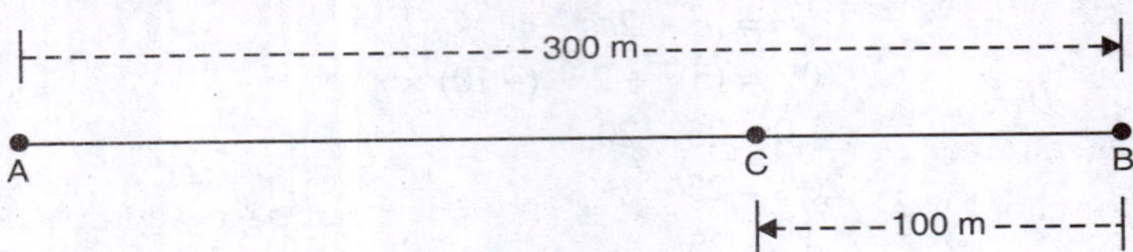

(a) *Calculation of average speed and average velocity from A to B*

Total distance from A to B = 300 m

Total time taken from A to B = 2 minutes 30 seconds

$= 2 \times 60$ seconds + 30 seconds

= 120 s + 30 s

= 150 s

Now, Average speed (from A to B) $= \frac{\text{Total distance}}{\text{Total time taken}}$

$= \frac{300 \text{ m}}{150 \text{ s}}$

= 2.0 m/s ...(1)

In going from A to B, the displacement of Joseph is also 300 m and the time taken is also 150 s.

Now, Average velocity (from A to B) $= \frac{\text{Displacement}}{\text{Total time taken}}$

$= \frac{300 \text{ m}}{150 \text{ s}}$

$= 2.0 \text{ m/s}$ ...(2)

Thus, when Joseph jogs from A to B, then the average speed and average velocity, both are equal in magnitude (each being 2.0 m/s).

(*b*) *Calculation of average speed and average velocity from A to C*

Now, Total distance from A to C (which is A to B to C) = 300 m + 100 m = 400 m

Total time from A to C (which is A to B to C) = 2 minutes 30 seconds + 1 minute = 150 s + 60 s = 210 s

So, Average speed (from A to C) $= \frac{\text{Total distance}}{\text{Total time taken}}$

$= \frac{400 \text{ m}}{210 \text{ s}}$

$= 1.90 \text{ m/s}$ ...(3)

Thus, the average speed of Joseph from A to C is 1.90 m/s

We will now calculate the average velocity of Joseph from A to C

Here, Displacement (from A to C) = 300 m – 100 m = 200 m

Total time (from A to C) = 210 s (Same as above)

Now, Average velocity (from A to C) $= \frac{\text{Displacement}}{\text{Total time taken}}$

$= \frac{200 \text{ m}}{210 \text{ s}}$

$= 0.95 \text{ m/s}$ ...(4)

Thus, the average velocity of Joseph from A to C is 0.95 m/s. This is different from his average speed (1.90 m/s) from A to C.

Q.3. Adbul, while driving to school, computes the average speed for his trip to be 20 km h^{-1}. On his return trip along the same route, there is less traffic and the average speed is 30 km h^{-1}. What is the average speed for Abdul's trip ?

Ans. Suppose the school is at a distance of *x* km.

(*i*) While driving to school, the average speed is 20 km h^{-1}. Suppose the time taken while driving to school is t_1.

Now, $\text{Speed} = \frac{\text{Distance}}{\text{Time taken}}$

So, $20 = \frac{x}{t_1}$

And, Time taken, $t_1 = \frac{x}{20}$ h ..(1)

(*ii*) On the return trip, the average speed is 30 km h^{-1}. Suppose the time taken for the return trip is t_2.

Now, $\text{Speed} = \frac{\text{Distance}}{\text{Time taken}}$

So, $30 = \frac{x}{t_2}$

And, Time taken, $t_2 = \frac{x}{30}$ h ...(2)

We will now consider the whole trip (going to school and coming back).

Total distance = $x + x$

(both ways) = $2x$ km ...(3)

And, Total time taken $= \frac{x}{20} + \frac{x}{30}$

$= \frac{3x+2x}{60}$

$= \frac{5x}{60}$

$= \frac{x}{12}$ h ...(4)

Now, Average speed $= \frac{\text{Total distance covered}}{\text{Total time taken}}$

(for whole trip) $= \frac{2x \times 12}{x}$

$= 24$ km h^{-1}

Thus, the average speed for Abdul's trip is 24 kilometres per hour.

Q.4. A motorboat starting from rest on a lake accelerates in a straight line at a constant rate of 3.0 m s^{-2} for 8.0 s. How far does the boat travel during this time ?

Ans. Here, Distance travelled, s = ? (To be calculated)

Initial speed, $u = 0$

Time, $t = 8.0$ s

And Acceleration, $a = 3.0$ m s^{-2}

Now, $s = ut + \frac{1}{2}at^2$

So, $s = 0 \times 8.0 + \frac{1}{2} \times 3 \times (8.0)^2$

$s = 0 + \frac{1}{2} \times 3 \times 64$

$s = 96$ m

Thus, the boat travels a distance of 96 metres.

Q.5. A driver of a car travelling at 52 km h^{-1} applies the brakes and accelerates uniformly in the opposite direction. The car stops in 5 s. Another driver going at 34 km h^{-1} in another car applies his brakes slowly and stops in 10 s. On the same graph paper, plot the speed versus time graphs for the two cars. Which of the two cars travelled farther after the brakes were applied ?

Ans. (*a*) *For first car :*

Initial speed, $u = 52$ km h^{-1}

$= \frac{52 \times 1000 \text{ m}}{60 \times 60 \text{ s}}$

$= 14.4$ m s^{-1} ... (1)

Final speed, $v = 0$ (The car stops) ...(2)

And, Time taken, $t = 5$ s ...(3)

(*b*) *For second car :*

Initial speed, $u = 34$ km h^{-1}

$= \frac{34 \times 1000 \text{ m}}{60 \times 60 \text{ s}}$

$= 9.4$ m s^{-1} ...(4)

Final speed, $v = 0$ (The car stops) ...(5)

And, Time taken, $t = 10$ s ...(6)

In order to plot the graph, we take time values on the *X*-axis and speed values on the *Y*-axis. Now, the

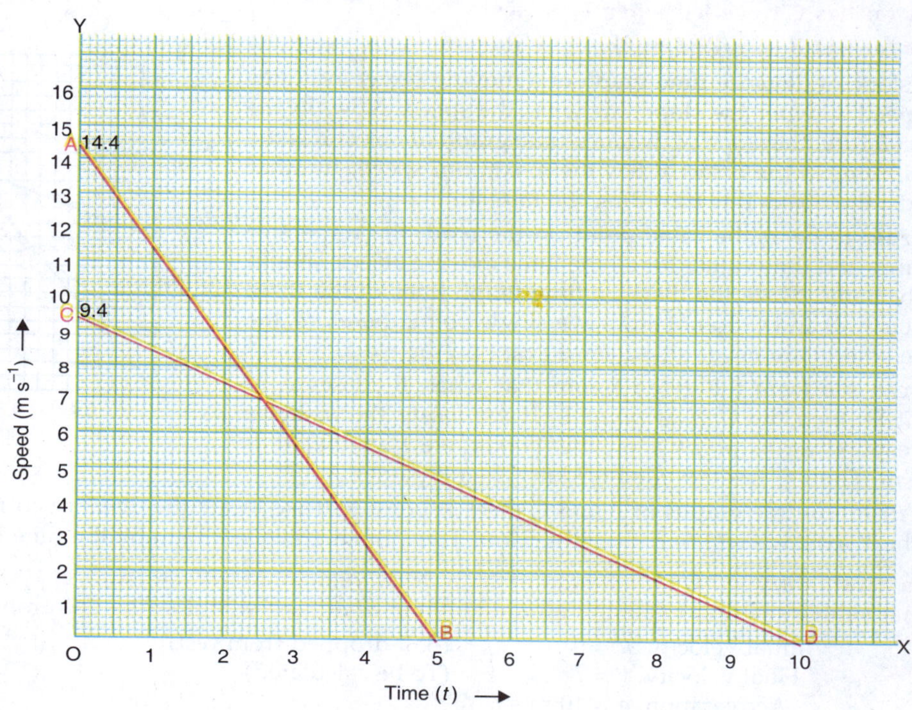

initial speed of first car is 14.4 m s^{-1} so, we take point A on the speed axis to represent a speed of 14.4 m s^{-1}. The first car stops in 5 seconds, so we take point B on the time axis to represent the time of 5 s. Let us join the points A and B. The sloping straight line AB is the speed-time graph for the first car. Now, the initial speed of second car is 9.4 m s^{-1}, so we take a point C on the speed axis to represent a speed of 9.4 m s^{-1}. The second car stops in 10 seconds, so we take a point D on time axis to represent the time of 10 s. Let us join the points C and D. The sloping straight line CD is the speed-time graph for second car. Now :

(*i*) Distance travelled by first car = Area under the graph line AB

= Area of triangle OAB

$$= \frac{1}{2} \times \text{base} \times \text{height}$$

$$= \frac{1}{2} \times 5 \times 14.4 \text{ m}$$

$$= 36 \text{ m} \qquad ...(7)$$

(*ii*) Distance travelled by second car = Area under the graph line CD

= Area of triangle OCD

$$= \frac{1}{2} \times \text{base} \times \text{height}$$

$$= \frac{1}{2} \times 10 \times 9.4 \text{ m}$$

$$= 47 \text{ m} \qquad ... (8)$$

From the above calculations we find that the first car travels a distance of 36 metres before coming to a stop whereas the second car travels a distance of 47 metres before coming to a stop. Thus, the second car travelled farther after the brakes were applied.

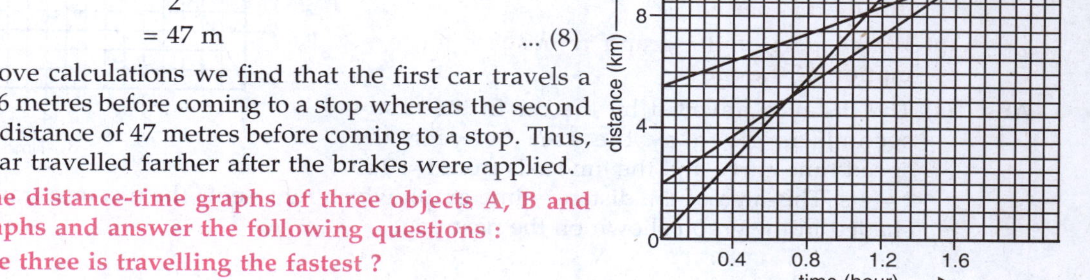

Q.6. Figure shows the distance-time graphs of three objects A, B and C. Study the graphs and answer the following questions :

(*a*) Which of the three is travelling the fastest ?

(b) Are all three ever at the same point on the road ?

(c) How far has C travelled when B passes A ?

(d) How far has B travelled by the time it passes C ?

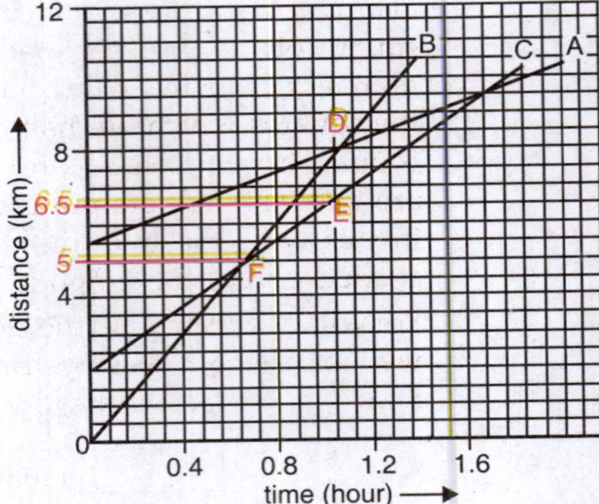

Ans. (a) The slope of distance-time graph of a moving object indicates its speed. Greater the slope, higher is the speed. Now, in the given figure, the slope of distance-time graph of object B is the maximum, so the object B has the maximum speed. In other words, the object B is travelling the fastest.

(b) In order to be at the same point on the road, the respective distance and time values for all the three moving objects should be the same. Since the distance-time graph lines of the three objects A, B and C do not cross at a single point, therefore, the three objects are never at the same point on the road.

(c) We can see from the given figure that when B passes A at point D, then the C is at point E. If we locate the distance corresponding to point E on the Y-axis, we find that it is 6.5 km. Thus, C has travelled 6.5 km when B passes A.

(d) The distance-time graphs of B and C meet at point F. If we locate the distance corresponding to point F on the Y-axis, we will find that it is 5 km. Thus, B has travelled 5 km by the time it passes C.

Q.7. A ball is gently dropped from a height of 20 m. If its velocity increases uniformly at the rate of 10 m s^{-2}, with what velocity will it strike the ground ? After what time will it strike the ground ?

Ans. Here,

Initial velocity, $u = 0$ (Ball dropped from rest)

Final velocity, $v = ?$ (To be calculated)

Acceleration, $a = 10$ m s^{-2}

And, Distance, $s = 20$ m (or Height)

Now,

$$v^2 = u^2 + 2as$$
$$v^2 = (0)^2 + 2 \times 10 \times 20$$
$$v^2 = 0 + 400$$
$$v^2 = 400$$
$$v = \sqrt{400}$$
$$v = 20 \text{ m s}^{-1}$$

Thus, the ball will strike the ground with a velocity of 20 metres per second. Let us calculate the time now.

We know that :
$$v = u + at$$
So,
$$20 = 0 + 10 \times t$$
$$10t = 20$$
$$t = \frac{20}{10}$$
$$t = 2 \text{ s}$$

Thus, the ball will strike the ground after 2 seconds.

Q.8. The speed-time graph for a car is shown here.

(a) Find how far does the car travel in the first 4 seconds. Shade the area on the graph that represents the distance travelled by the car during this period.

(b) Which part of the graph represents uniform motion of the car ?

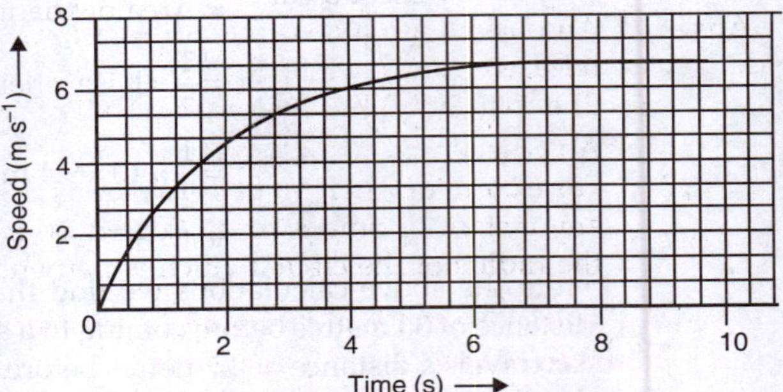

Ans. (a) The distance travelled by the car in the first 4 seconds is given by the area between the speed-time curve and the time axis from $t = 0$ to $t = 4$ s. This area of the distance-time graph which represents the distance travelled by the car has been shaded in the graph shown on the next page.

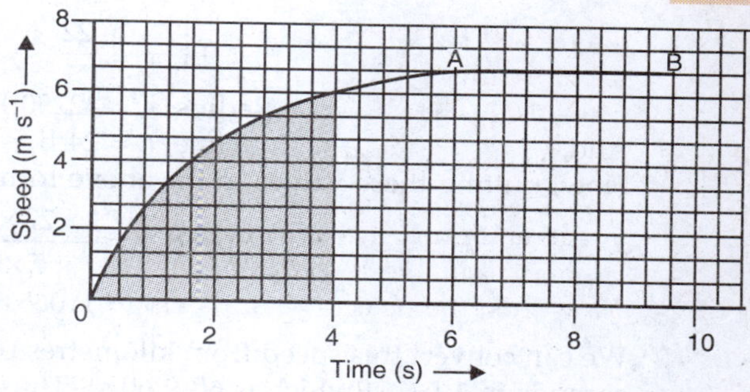

In order to find the distance travelled by the car in the first 4 seconds, we have to count the number of squares in the shaded part of the graph and also calculate the distance represented by one square of the graph paper. While counting the number of squares in the shaded part of the graph, the squares which are half or more than half are counted as complete squares but the squares which are less than half are not counted. When counted in this way, the total number of squares in the shaded part of the graph is found to be 63.

We will now calculate the distance represented by 1 square of the graph. This can be done as follows : If we look at the *X*-axis, we find that 5 squares on *X*-axis represent a time of 2 seconds.

Now, 5 squares on *X*-axis = 2 s

So, 1 square on *X*-axis $= \frac{2}{5}$ s ...(1)

Again, if we look at the *Y*-axis, we find that 3 squares on *Y*-axis represent a speed of 2 m s^{-1}.

Now, 3 squares on *Y*-axis = 2 m s^{-1}

So, 1 square on *Y*-axis $= \frac{2}{3}$ m s^{-1} ...(2)

Since 1 square on *X*-axis represents $\frac{2}{5}$ s and 1 square on *Y*-axis represents $\frac{2}{3}$ m s^{-1}, therefore :

Area of 1 square on graph represents a distance $= \frac{2}{5}\text{ s} \times \frac{2}{3}\text{ m s}^{-1}$

$= \frac{4}{15}$ m

Now, 1 square represents distance $= \frac{4}{15}$ m

So, 63 squares represent distance $= \frac{4}{15} \times 63$ m

= 16.8 m

Thus, the car travels a distance of 16.8 metres in the first 4 seconds.

(*b*) In uniform motion, the speed of car becomes constant. The constant speed is represented by a speed-time graph line which is parallel to the time axis. In the given figure, the straight line graph from t = 6 s to t = 10 s represents the uniform motion of the car. The part of graph representing uniform motion has been labelled AB.

Q.9. State which of the following situations are possible and give an example for each of these :

(*a*) an object with a constant acceleration but zero velocity.

(*b*) an object moving in a certain direction with an acceleration in the perpendicular direction.

Ans. (*a*) An object with a constant acceleration but zero velocity is possible. For example, when an object is just released from a height, then it is being acted upon by a constant acceleration of 9.8 m/s^2 (called acceleration due to gravity) but its initial velocity is zero.

(*b*) An object moving in a certain direction with an acceleration in the perpendicular direction is possible. For example, when an object is moving with uniform motion in a circle, then the motion of the object at any instant of time is along tangent to the circle at that instant but the (centripetal) acceleration is along the radius of the circle (which is perpendicular to the direction of motion along the tangent).

Q.10. An artificial satellite is moving in a circular orbit of radius 42250 km. Calculate its speed if it takes 24 hours to revolve around the earth.

Ans. The speed of an object moving in a circular orbit (or circular path) is given by the formula :

$$v = \frac{2\pi r}{t}$$

Here, Speed, v = ? (To be calculated)

$$\text{Pi, } \pi = \frac{22}{7} \quad \text{(It is a constant)}$$

$$\text{Radius, } r = 42250 \text{ km}$$

And, $\text{Time, } t = 24 \text{ h}$

Now, putting these values in the above formula, we get :

$$\text{Speed, } v = \frac{2 \times 22 \times 42250}{7 \times 24}$$

$$v = 11065.4 \text{ km h}^{-1}$$

We can convert this speed from kilometres per hour to kilometres per second by dividing it by the number of seconds in 1 hour (which is 60 × 60 s). Thus :

$$v = \frac{11065.4}{60 \times 60} \text{ km s}^{-1}$$

$$v = 3.07 \text{ km s}^{-1}$$

Chapter : FORCE AND LAWS OF MOTION

NCERT Book, Page 118

Q.1. Which of the following has more inertia ?
(a) a rubber ball and a stone of the same size.
(b) a bicycle and a train.
(c) a five-rupee coin and a one-rupee coin.

Ans. Mass is a measure of the inertia of an object. If an object has more mass, it has more inertia.

(a) A stone has more inertia (than a rubber ball of the same size) because it has more mass than a rubber ball of the same size.

(b) A train has more inertia (than a bicycle) because it has more mass than a bicycle.

(c) A five-rupee coin has more inertia (than a one-rupee coin) because it has more mass than a one rupee coin.

Q.2. In the following example, try to identify the number of times the velocity of the ball changes :
"A football player kicks a football to another player of his team who kicks the football towards the goal. The goalkeeper of the opposite team collects the football and kicks it towards a player of his own team".
Also identify the agent supplying the force in each case.

Ans. (i) The velocity of football changes for the 1st time when a football player kicks the football to another player of his team. The agent supplying the force in this case is the kick applied by the player.

(ii) The velocity of football changes for the 2nd time when another player of the same team kicks the football towards the goal. Here the force is supplied by the kick of another player.

(iii) The velocity of football changes for the 3rd time when the goalkeeper of opposite team collects the football (or stops the football). In this case the force is applied by the hands of the goalkeeper.

(iv) The velocity of football changes for the 4th time when the goalkeeper kicks the stationary football towards a player of his own team. Here the force is supplied by the kick of goalkeeper.

Thus, the velocity of football changes four times.

Q.3. Explain why, some of the leaves may get detached from a tree if we vigorously shake its branch.

Ans. If we shake the branch of a tree vigorously, then the branch of tree comes in motion but the leaves tend to remain at rest (or stationary) due to their inertia and hence detach from the branch and fall down.

Q.4. Why do you fall in the forward direction when a moving bus brakes to a stop and fall backwards when it accelerates from rest ?

Ans. (a) When a moving bus brakes suddenly to a stop, we fall in the forward direction because though the lower part of our body comes to a stop when the bus stops but the upper part of our body continues to move forward due to its inertia (making us fall in the forward direction).

(b) When a bus accelerates from rest, we tend to fall backwards because though the lower part of our body starts moving with the moving bus but the upper part of our body tries to remain at rest due to its inertia (making us fall backwards).

NCERT Book, Pages 126 and 127

Q.1. If action is always equal to the reaction, explain how a horse can pull a cart.

Ans. According to the Newton's third law of motion, the horse exerts some force on the cart, and the cart exerts an equal and opposite force on the horse. So, at first glance it seems that the action and reaction forces being equal and opposite cancel out and hence the cart would not move. But it should be noted that it is only the force on the cart which determines whether the cart will move or not, and that the force exerted by the cart on the horse affects the horse alone. Thus, if the horse is able to apply enough force to overcome the frictional forces present, the cart will move. So, to make the cart move, the horse bends forward and pushes the ground with its feet. When the forward reaction to the backward push of the horse is greater than the opposing frictional forces of the wheels, the cart moves.

Q.2. Explain why it is difficult for a fireman to hold a hose which ejects large amounts of water at a high velocity ?

Ans. When a fire hose pipe ejects large amounts of water in the forward direction at a high velocity, then the forward going stream of water exerts a backward reaction force due to which the hose pipe tends to go backward and slips from the hands of fireman. This backward movement of hose pipe makes it difficult for a fireman to hold the hose pipe. And the fireman has to hold the hose pipe strongly.

Q.3. From a rifle of mass 4 kg, a bullet of mass 50 g is fired with an initial velocity of 35 m s^{-1}. Calculate the initial recoil velocity of the rifle.

Ans. We will first calculate the momentum of bullet and of the rifle separately and then apply the law of conservation of momentum.

(*i*) Momentum of bullet = Mass of bullet × Velocity of bullet

$$= \frac{50}{1000} \text{ kg} \times 35 \text{ m s}^{-1}$$
$$= 0.05 \text{ kg} \times 35 \text{ m s}^{-1}$$
$$= 1.75 \text{ kg m s}^{-1} \quad \text{... (1)}$$

(*ii*) Suppose the recoil velocity of the rifle is v m s^{-1}. So,

Momentum of rifle = Mass of rifle × Velocity of rifle

$$= 4 \text{ kg} \times v \text{ m s}^{-1}$$
$$= 4v \text{ kg m s}^{-1} \quad \text{...(2)}$$

Now, according to the law of conservation of momentum :

Momentum of bullet = Momentum of rifle

So, $1.75 = 4v$

And $v = \frac{1.75}{4}$

$v = 0.4375$ m s^{-1}

Thus, the recoil velocity of the rifle is 0.4375 metres per second.

Q.4. Two objects of masses 100 g and 200 g are moving along the same line and direction with velocities of 2 m s^{-1} and 1 m s^{-1}, respectively. They collide and after the collision, the first object moves at a velocity of 1.67 m s^{-1}. Determine the velocity of the second object.

Ans. In order to solve this problem, we will first calculate total momentum of both the objects before and after the collision.

(*a*) Momentum of first object (before collision) = Mass of first object × Velocity of first object

$$= \frac{100}{1000} \text{ kg} \times 2 \text{ m s}^{-1}$$
$$= 0.1 \text{ kg} \times 2 \text{ m s}^{-1}$$
$$= 0.2 \text{ kg m s}^{-1}$$

Momentum of second object (before collision) = Mass of second object × Velocity of second object

$$= \frac{200}{1000} \text{ kg} \times 1 \text{ m s}^{-1}$$
$$= 0.2 \text{ kg} \times 1 \text{ m s}^{-1}$$
$$= 0.2 \text{ kg m s}^{-1}$$

Total momentum (before collision) = 0.2 + 0.2 = 0.4 kg m s^{-1} ...(1)

(*b*) After collision, the velocity of first object of mass 100 g becomes 1.67 m s^{-1}. So,

Momentum of first object (after collision) $= \frac{100}{1000} \text{ kg} \times 1.67 \text{ m s}^{-1}$

$$= 0.1 \text{ kg} \times 1.67 \text{ m s}^{-1}$$
$$= 0.167 \text{ kg m s}^{-1}$$

After collision, suppose the velocity of second object of mass 200 g becomes v m s^{-1}. So,

$$\text{Momentum of second object (after collision)} = \frac{200}{1000} \text{ kg} \times v \text{ m s}^{-1}$$

$$= 0.2 \text{ kg} \times v \text{ m s}^{-1}$$

$$= 0.2v \text{ kg m s}^{-1}$$

$$\text{Total momentum (after collision)} = 0.167 + 0.2v \qquad ...(2)$$

Now, according to the law of conservation of momentum :

Total momentum before collision = Total momentum after collision

That is,

$$0.4 = 0.167 + 0.2v$$

$$0.2v = 0.4 - 0.167$$

$$0.2v = 0.233$$

$$v = \frac{0.233}{0.2}$$

$$v = 1.165 \text{ m s}^{-1}$$

Thus, the velocity of second object is 1.165 metres per second.

NCERT Book, Pages 128 and 129

Q.1. An object experiences a net zero external unbalanced force. Is it possible for the object to be travelling with a non-zero velocity ? If yes, state the conditions that must be placed on the magnitude and direction of the velocity. If no, provide a reason.

Ans. Yes, when an object experiences a net zero external unbalanced force, it is possible for the object to be travelling with a non-zero velocity. This can happen under the following conditions :

(*a*) The object should already be travelling with a uniform speed in a straight line path.
(*b*) There should be no change in the magnitude of speed.
(*c*) There should be no change in the direction of motion.
(*d*) The friction between the object and the ground must be zero.
(*e*) The air resistance on the moving object must also be zero.

Q.2. When a carpet is beaten with a stick, dust comes out of it. Explain.

Ans. When a hanging carpet is beaten with a stick then the force of stick makes the carpet move to and fro slightly but the dust particles in it tend to remain at rest (or stationary) due to their inertia and hence come out of it.

Q.3. Why is it advised to tie any luggage kept on the roof of a bus, with a rope ?

Ans. It is advised to tie any luggage kept on the roof of a bus with a rope because :

(*a*) if the bus starts moving suddenly, then due to its inertia of rest, the luggage kept on the roof of the bus tends to remain at rest and hence may fall down from the roof of the bus.
(*b*) if the moving bus stops suddenly, then due to its inertia of motion, the luggage kept on the roof of the bus tends to remain in motion and hence may fall down from the roof of the bus.

If, however, the luggage items kept on the roof of a bus are tied with a rope, they cannot fall down when the bus starts suddenly or stops suddenly.

Q.4. A batsman hits a cricket ball which then rolls on a level ground. After covering a short distance, the ball comes to rest. The ball slows to a stop because :

(*a*) the batsman did not hit the ball hard enough.
(*b*) velocity is proportional to the force exerted on the ball.
(*c*) there is a force on the ball opposing the motion.
(*d*) there is no unbalanced force on the ball, so the ball would want to come to rest.

Ans. (*c*) there is a force on the ball opposing the motion.

Q.5. A truck starts from rest and rolls down a hill with a constant acceleration. It travels a distance of 400 m in 20 s. Find its acceleration. Find the force acting on it if its mass is 7 metric tonnes (Hint. 1 metric tonne = 1000 kg).

Ans. (*a*) *Calculation of acceleration*

Here, Initial velocity, $u = 0$

Distance travelled, $s = 400$ m

Time, $t = 20$ s

And, Acceleration, $a = ?$ (To be calculated)

Now, $$s = ut + \frac{1}{2}at^2$$

So, $$400 = 0 \times 20 + \frac{1}{2} \times a \times (20)^2$$

$$400 = 0 + \frac{1}{2} \times a \times 400$$

$$400 = a \times 200$$

$$a = \frac{400}{200}$$

$$a = 2 \text{ m/s}^2.$$

Thus, the acceleration of the truck is 2 m/s^2.

(*b*) *Calculation of force*

Force, $F = m \times a$

So, $$F = 7 \times 1000 \times 2$$

$$F = 14000 \text{ N}$$

Thus, the force acting on the truck is of 14000 newtons.

Q.6. A stone of 1 kg is thrown with a velocity of 20 m s^{-1} across the frozen surface of a lake and comes to rest after travelling a distance of 50 m. What is the force of friction between the stone and the ice ?

Ans. Here, Initial velocity, $u = 20$ m s^{-1}

Final velocity, $v = 0$ (The stone stops)

Acceleration, $a = ?$ (To be calculated)

And, Distance travelled, $s = 50$ m

Now, $$v^2 = u^2 + 2as$$

So, $$(0)^2 = (20)^2 + 2 \times a \times 50$$

$$0 = 400 + 100\, a$$

$$100\, a = -\, 400$$

$$a = -\frac{400}{100}$$

$$a = -\, 4 \text{ m s}^{-2}$$

Now, Force, $F = m \times a$

$$F = 1 \times (-\, 4) \text{ N}$$

$$F = -\, 4 \text{ N}$$

Thus, the force of friction between the stone and the ice is 4 newtons. The negative sign shows that this force opposes the motion of stone.

Q.7. A 8000 kg engine pulls a train of 5 wagons, each of 2000 kg, along a horizontal track. If the engine exerts a force of 40000 N and the track offers a friction force of 5000 N, then calculate :

(*a*) the net accelerating force,

(*b*) the acceleration of the train, and

(*c*) the force of wagon 1 on wagon 2.

Ans. (*a*) *Calculation of the net accelerating force*

Here, the force exerted by the engine is 40000 N and the opposing force of friction offered by the track is 5000 N. So,

Net accelerating force, F = Force of engine – Force of friction

= 40000 – 5000

= 35000 N

Thus, the net accelerating force (F) exerted by the engine is 35000 newtons. This force will be used in further calculations.

(*b*) *Calculation of the acceleration of train*

We have just calculated that the net force exerted by the engine on the train is 35000 N. Now, the mass of 1 wagon of train is 2000 kg, so the mass of 5 wagons of train will be 2000 × 5 = 10000 kg. In other words, the mass of whole train is 10000 kg.

Now, Net force = mass of train × acceleration

$$F = m \times a$$

So, $35000 = 10000 \times a$

And, $$a = \frac{35000}{10000} \text{ m s}^{-2}$$

$$a = 3.5 \text{ m s}^{-2}$$

Thus, the acceleration of the train is 3.5 m s^{-2}.

(*c*) *Calculation of force of wagon 1 on wagon 2*

There are 5 wagons behind the engine (which have been marked 1, 2, 3, 4 and 5 in the Figure given

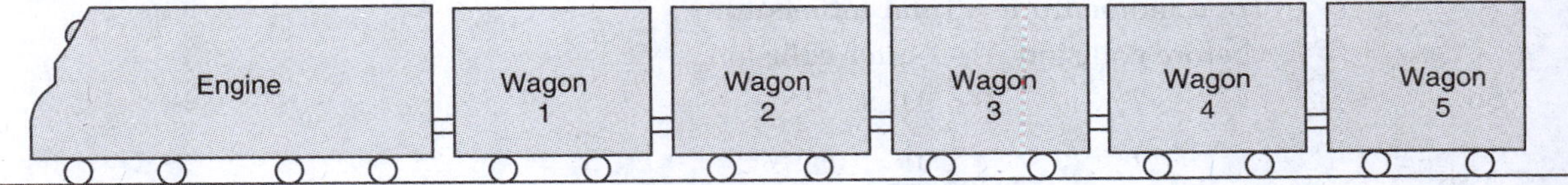

above) but there are only 4 wagons behind wagon 1. Now,

Force of wagon 1 on wagon 2 = mass of 4 wagons (behind wagon 1) × acceleration of train

= 2000 × 4 × 3.5

= 28000 N

Thus, the force of wagon 1 on wagon 2 is of 28000 newtons.

Q.8. An automobile vehicle has a mass of 1500 kg. What must be the force between the vehicle and road if the vehicle is to be stopped with a negative acceleration of 1.7 m s^{-2} ?

Ans. Here, Mass of vehicle, m = 1500 kg

And, Acceleration, a = – 1.7 m s^{-2}

Now, Force, $F = m \times a$

$F = 1500 \times (-1.7)$ N

$F = -2550$ N

Thus, the force between the vehicle and the road is 2550 newtons. The negative sign of force shows that the force acts in a direction opposite to the direction of motion of the vehicle.

Q.9. What is the momentum of an object of mass *m* moving with a velocity *v* ?

(*a*) $(mv)^2$ (*b*) mv^2 (*c*) 1/2 mv^2 (*d*) *mv*

Ans. (*d*) *mv*

Q.10. Using a horizontal force of 200 N, we intend to move a wooden cabinet across a floor at constant velocity. What is the frictional force that will be exerted on the cabinet ?

Ans. Since the wooden cabinet is to be moved at constant velocity, this means that the whole force of 200 N will be used to overcome the force of friction (because no force is spent on producing acceleration in the cabinet). Thus, the force of friction exerted on the cabinet will be equal to the force applied, which is 200 N.

Q.11. Two objects, each of mass 1.5 kg, are moving in the same straight line but in opposite directions. The velocity of each object is 2.5 m s^{-1} before the collision during which they stick together. What will be the velocity of the combined objects after collision ?

Ans. Mass of first object, m_1 = 1.5 kg

Velocity of first object, v_1 = 2.5 m s^{-1}

So, Momentum of first object = $m_1 \times v_1$

= 1.5 × 2.5

= 3.75 kg m s^{-1}

Mass of second object, $m_2 = 1.5$ kg

Velocity of second object, $v_2 = -2.5$ m s^{-1} (In opposite direction)

So, Momentum of second object $= m_2 \times v_2$

$= 1.5 \times (-2.5)$

$= -3.75$ kg m s^{-1}

Total momentum before collision $= 3.75 + (-3.75)$

$= 3.75 - 3.75$

$= 0$ kg m s^{-1} ... (1)

The mass of combined objects will be $m_1 + m_2 = 1.5$ kg $+ 1.5$ kg $= 3.0$ kg. Now, suppose the velocity of combined objects after collision is v m s^{-1}. So,

Total momentum after collision $= (m_1 + m_2) \times v$

$= 3.0 \times v$ ...(2)

Now, according to the principle of conservation of momentum :

Total momentum before collision = Total momentum after collision

So, $0 = 3.0 \times v$

And, $v = \frac{0}{3.0}$

or, $v = 0$ m s^{-1}

Thus, the velocity of the combined objects after the collision will be zero metres per second which means that the combined objects will come to a stop after the collision.

Q.12. According to the third law of motion when we push on an object, the object pushes back on us with an equal and opposite force. If the object is a massive truck parked along the roadside, it will probably not move. A student justifies this by answering that the two opposite and equal forces cancel each other. Comment on this logic and explain why the truck does not move.

Ans. The justification given by the student that the two opposite and equal forces cancel each other (and hence the truck does not move) is wrong. This is because the forces of action and reaction do not act on the same body (they act on two different bodies). So, there is no question of their cancellation. Actually, the massive truck does not move in this case because push (or force) applied to it is much smaller than the force of friction between the wheels of the truck and the road. Since the force of push is not able to overcome the force of friction, therefore, the truck does not move.

Q.13. A hockey ball of mass 200 g travelling at 10 m s^{-1} is struck by a hockey stick so as to return it along its original path with a velocity of 5 m s^{-1}. Calculate the change of momentum occurred in the motion of the hockey ball by the force applied by the hockey stick.

Ans. (*a*) *Calculation of initial momentum*

Mass of hockey ball, $m_1 = 200$ g

$= \frac{200}{1000}$ kg

$= 0.2$ kg

And, Initial velocity, $v_1 = 10$ m s^{-1}

So, Initial momentum $= m_1 \times v_1$

$= 0.2 \times 10$

$= 2$ kg m s^{-1} ...(1)

(*b*) *Calculation of final momentum*

Mass of hockey ball, $m_2 = 200$ g (Same as above)

$= 0.2$ kg

And, Final velocity, $v_2 = -5$ m s^{-1} (Reverse direction)

So, Final momentum $= m_2 \times v_2$

$= 0.2 \times (-5)$

$= -1$ kg m s^{-1} ...(2)

Now, Change in momentum = Final momentum – Initial momentum

$= -1 - 2$

$= -3 \text{ kg m s}^{-1}$

Thus, the change in momentum of the hockey ball is 3 kg m s^{-1}.

Q.14. A bullet of mass 10 g travelling horizontally with a velocity of 150 m s^{-1} strikes a stationary wooden block and comes to rest in 0.03 s. Calculate the distance of penetration of the bullet into the block. Also calculate the magnitude of the force exerted by the wooden block on the bullet.

Ans. We will first calculate the acceleration (or rather retardation) of the bullet.

Now, Initial velocity, $u = 150 \text{ m s}^{-1}$

Final velocity, $v = 0$

And, Time, $t = 0.03$ s

Now, $v = u + at$

So, $0 = 150 + a \times 0.03$

$0.03\,a = -150$

$$a = -\frac{150}{0.03}$$

$a = -5000 \text{ m s}^{-2}$

Let us calculate the distance of penetration of bullet now.

We know that : $v^2 = u^2 + 2as$

So, $(0)^2 = (150)^2 + 2 \times (-5000) \times s$

$0 = 22500 - 10000 \times s$

$10000\text{ s} = 22500$

So, $$s = \frac{22500}{10000}$$

$s = 2.25$ m

Thus, the distance of penetration of the bullet into the block of wood will be 2.25 metres.

We will now calculate the magnitude of force. Now :

Force, $F = m \times a$

$$F = \frac{10}{1000} \text{ kg} \times (-5000) \text{ m s}^{-2}$$

$F = 50$ N

Thus, the magnitude of force exerted by the wooden block on the bullet is 50 newtons.

Q.15. An object of mass 1 kg travelling in a straight line with a velocity of 10 m s^{-1} collides with, and sticks to, a stationary wooden block of mass 5 kg. Then they both move off together in the same straight line. Calculate the total momentum just before the impact and just after the impact. Also, calculate the velocity of the combined objects.

Ans. Here, Mass of object, $m_1 = 1$ kg

And, Velocity of object, $v_1 = 10 \text{ m s}^{-1}$

So, Momentum of object $= m_1 \times v_1$

$= 1 \times 10 \text{ kg m s}^{-1}$

$= 10 \text{ kg m s}^{-1}$ ...(1)

Now, Mass of wooden block, $m_2 = 5$ kg

And, Velocity of wooden block, $v_2 = 0$ (It is stationary)

So, Momentum of wooden block $= m_2 \times v_2$

$= 5 \times 0$

$= 0 \text{ kg m s}^{-1}$ ...(2)

Total momentum before impact $= 10 + 0$

$= 10 \text{ kg m s}^{-1}$ ...(3)

Now, according to the law of conservation of momentum, the total momentum just after the impact will be the same as the total momentum just before the impact. This means that the total momentum just after the impact will also be 10 kg m s^{-1}.

Now, Total momentum = 10 kg m s^{-1}

Total mass of object and wooden block = 1 kg + 5 kg = 6 kg

And Velocity of object and wooden block = v m s^{-1} (Supposed)

So, $10 = 6 \times v$

And, $v = \frac{10}{6}$

$v = 1.67$ m s^{-1}

Thus, the velocity of the object and wooden block together is 1.67 metres per second.

Q.16. An object of mass 100 kg is accelerated uniformly from a velocity of 5 m s^{-1} to 8 m s^{-1} in 6 s. Calculate the initial and final momentum of the object. Also find the magnitude of the force exerted on the object.

Ans. (*i*) Initial momentum = mass × initial velocity

= 100 × 5

= 500 kg m s^{-1} ...(1)

(*ii*) Final momentum = mass × final velocity

= 100 × 8

= 800 kg m s^{-1} ...(2)

(*iii*) $$\text{Force} = \frac{\text{Change in momentum}}{\text{Time taken}}$$

$$= \frac{800 - 500}{6}$$

$$= \frac{300}{6}$$

= 50 N

Q.17. Akhtar, Kiran and Rahul were riding in a motorcar that was moving with a high velocity on an expressway when an insect hit the windshield and got stuck on the windscreen. Akhtar and Kiran started pondering over the situation. Kiran suggested that the insect suffered a greater change in momentum as compared to the change in momentum of the motorcar (because the change in the velocity of the insect was much more than that of the motorcar). Akhtar said that since the motorcar was moving with a larger velocity, it exerted a large force on the insect. And as a result the insect died. Rahul while putting an entirely new explanation said that both the motorcar and the insect experienced the same force and a change in their momentum. Comment on these suggestions.

Ans. (*a*) Kiran's suggestion that the insect suffered a greater change in momentum as compared to the change in momentum of the motorcar is wrong.

(*b*) Akhtar's suggestion that since the motorcar was moving with a larger velocity, it exerted a larger force on the insect, is also wrong.

(*c*) Rahul's explanation that both the motorcar and the insect experienced the same force and same change in their momentum is correct. Both experience the same force because the action (force) and reaction (force) are always equal and opposite. Moreover, the magnitude of change in their momenta is also the same (though the change in momenta occur in opposite directions).

Q.18. How much momentum will a dumb-bell of mass 10 kg transfer to the floor if it falls from a height of 80 cm ? Take its downward acceleration to be 10 m s^{-2}.

Ans. We will first calculate the final velocity of falling dumb-bell (just before touching the floor).

Here, Initial velocity, $u = 0$ (Falls from rest)

Final velocity, v = ? (To be calculated)

Acceleration, a = 10 m s^{-2}

And, Distance, s = 80 cm

$$\text{(or Height)} = \frac{80}{100}\text{ m}$$
$$= 0.8\text{ m}$$

Now, $v^2 = u^2 + 2as$

So, $v^2 = (0)^2 + 2 \times 10 \times 0.8$

$v^2 = 16$

$v = \sqrt{16}$

$v = 4\text{ m s}^{-1}$

Momentum = mass × velocity

$= 10\text{ kg} \times 4\text{ m s}^{-1}$

$= 40\text{ kg m s}^{-1}$

Now, the momentum of falling dumb-bell just before touching the floor is 40 kg m s^{-1}. So, the dumb-bell will transfer an equal amount of momentum (40 kg m s^{-1}) to the floor.

NCERT Book, Page 130

Q.1. The following is the distance-time table of an object in motion :

Time in seconds	Distance in metres
0	0
1	1
2	8
3	27
4	64
5	125
6	216
7	343

(a) What conclusion can you draw about the acceleration ? Is it constant, increasing, decreasing or zero ?

(b) What do you infer about the forces acting on the object ?

Ans. (*a*) We can see from the given time (t) values and the distance (s) values that at time (t) = 0 s, distance (s) = 0 m, and at time (t) = 1 s, distance (s) = 1 m.

But, when time (t) = 2 s, then distance (s) = 8 m

We know that : $(2)^3 = 2 \times 2 \times 2 = 8$

Again, when time (t) = 3 s, then distance (s) = 27 m

So, $(3)^3 = 3 \times 3 \times 3 = 27$, and so on.

Thus, from the given distance and time values, we conclude that :

$$\text{distance} \propto (\text{time})^3$$

or $$s \propto t^3$$

So, in this question, the 'distance' travelled by the object is proportional to the 'cube of time'. Now :

(*i*) when the distance travelled is proportional to time ($s \propto t$), then the object has constant velocity (or uniform velocity) and hence acceleration in that case would be zero (This is because $s = ut + \frac{1}{2}at^2$, so when $a = 0$, then $s = ut$ or $s \propto t$). But since in this question, $s \propto t^3$, so the acceleration in this case cannot be zero).

(*ii*) when the distance travelled is proportional to the square of time ($s \propto t^2$), then the object has constant acceleration (This is because $s = ut + \frac{1}{2}at^2$, that is, $s \propto t^2$). But since in this question, $s \propto t^3$, so the acceleration in this case cannot be constant.

(*iii*) The data given in this question shows that the distance travelled is proportional to the cube of time ($s \propto t^3$), therefore, the conclusion drawn is that the acceleration is increasing uniformly with time.

(*b*) We know that Force = mass × acceleration or $F = m \times a$. In other words $F \propto a$ or acceleration is proportional to the force applied. Now, since the acceleration of the object in this case is increasing uniformly with time, therefore, the forces acting on the object must also be increasing uniformly with time.

Q.2. Two persons manage to push a motorcar of mass 1200 kg at a uniform velocity along a level road. The same motorcar can be pushed by three persons to produce an acceleration of 0.2 m s^{-2}. With what force does each person push the motorcar ? (Assume that all persons push the motorcar with the same muscular effort).

Ans. Suppose each person applies a force F to push the motorcar.

So, Total force applied by two persons $= F + F$

$$= 2F \quad ...(1)$$

Since this force ($2F$) gives a uniform velocity to the motorcar along a level road (where work is done only against the force of friction), so the force $2F$ can be taken as being equal to the force of friction f between the motorcar and the road. That is,

$$\text{Force of friction, } f = 2F \quad ...(2)$$

Now, when three persons apply force to push the motorcar, then :

$$\text{Total force applied by three persons} = F + F + F$$

$$= 3F \quad ...(3)$$

Now, the total force applied by three persons is $3F$ whereas the opposing force of friction is f. So,

$$\text{Force that produces acceleration} = 3F - f \quad ...(4)$$

But from equation (2), we have $f = 2F$. So,

$$\text{Force that produces acceleration} = 3F - 2F$$

or $$\text{Force that produces acceleration} = F$$

Now, $$\text{Force} = \text{mass} \times \text{acceleration}$$

or, $$F = m \times a$$

$$F = 1200 \times 0.2 \text{ N}$$

$$F = 240 \text{ N}$$

Thus, each person pushes the motorcar with a force of 240 newtons.

Q.3. A hammer of mass 500 g, moving at 50 m s^{-1}, strikes a nail. The nail stops the hammer in a very short time of 0.01 s. What is the force of the nail on the hammer ?

Ans. Here, $$\text{Mass, } m = 500 \text{ g}$$

$$= \frac{500}{1000} \text{ kg}$$

$$= 0.5 \text{ kg}$$

We will now calculate the acceleration.

Now, Initial velocity, $u = 50$ m s^{-1}

Final velocity, $v = 0$ (The hammer stops)

Acceleration, $a = ?$ (To be calculated)

And, Time, $t = 0.01$ s

Now, $$v = u + at$$

So, $$0 = 50 + a \times 0.01$$

$$0.01\, a = -50$$

$$a = -\frac{50}{0.01}$$

$$a = -5000 \text{ m s}^{-2}$$

We know that : Force, $F = m \times a$

So, $$F = 0.5 \times (-5000) \text{ N}$$

$$F = -2500 \text{ N}$$

Thus, the force of the nail on the hammer is 2500 newtons. The negative sign indicates that this force is opposing motion.

Q.4. A motorcar of mass 1200 kg is moving along a straight line with a uniform velocity of 90 km/h. Its velocity is slowed down to 18 km/h in 4 s by an unbalanced external force. Calculate the acceleration and change in momentum. Also calculate the magnitude of the force required.

Ans. (*a*) *Calculation of acceleration*

Here, Initial velocity, $u = 90 \text{ km/h}$

$$= \frac{90 \times 1000 \text{ m}}{60 \times 60 \text{ s}}$$

$$= 25 \text{ m/s}$$

Final velocity, $v = 18 \text{ km/h}$

$$= \frac{18 \times 1000 \text{ m}}{60 \times 60 \text{ s}}$$

$$= 5 \text{ m/s}$$

Acceleration, $a = ?$ (To be calculated)

And, Time, $t = 4 \text{ s}$

Now,

$$v = u + at$$

$$5 = 25 + a \times 4$$

$$4a = 5 - 25$$

$$4a = -20$$

$$a = -\frac{20}{4}$$

$$a = -5 \text{ m/s}^2$$

Thus, the acceleration of the motorcar is, -5 m/s^2. It is actually negative acceleration or retardation.

(*b*) *Calculation of change in momentum*

$$\text{Change in momentum} = mv - mu$$

$$= 1200 \times 5 - 1200 \times 25$$

$$= 6000 - 30000$$

$$= -24000 \text{ kg. m/s}$$

Thus, the change in momentum is 24000 kg. m/s

(*c*) *Calculation of magnitude of force*

$$\text{Force, } F = m \times a$$

$$F = 1200 \times (-5)$$

$$F = -6000 \text{ N}$$

Thus, the magnitude of force required is 6000 newtons. The negative sign shows that this force is opposing the motion.

Q.5. A large truck and a car, both moving with a velocity of magnitude *v*, have a head-on collision and both of them come to a halt after that. If the collision lasts for 1 s :

(*a*) which vehicle experiences the greater force of impact ?

(*b*) which vehicle experiences the greater change in momentum ?

(*c*) which vehicle experiences the greater acceleration ?

(*d*) why is the car likely to suffer more damage than the truck ?

Ans. (*a*) As the action (force) and reaction (force) are equal and opposite, both the vehicles experience the same force on collision.

(*b*) Since the change in momentum of truck is equal and opposite to the change in momentum of car, both the vehicles experience equal change in momentum.

(*c*) As the force on each vehicle is the same but the mass of car is smaller than the truck, therefore, the car experiences the greater acceleration (or greater retardation) $\left(\text{because } a = \frac{F}{m}\right)$.

(*d*) Since the car is much lighter than the truck, therefore, the car is likely to suffer more damage during the collision than the truck (The car has greater retardation than the truck).

Chapter : GRAVITATION

NCERT Book, Page 134

Q.1. State the universal law of gravitation.

Ans. According to the universal law of gravitation, every body in the universe attracts every other body with a force which is directly proportional to the product of their masses and inversely proportional to the square of the distance between them. The direction of force is along the line joining the centres of the two bodies.

Q.2. Write the formula to find the magnitude of the gravitational force between the earth and an object on the surface of the earth.

Ans. Gravitational force, $F = G \times \frac{M \times m}{R^2}$

where G = Gravitational constant

M = Mass of the earth

m = mass of the object

and R = Radius of the earth

NCERT Book, Page 136

Q.1. What do you mean by free fall ?

Ans. The falling of a body (or object) from a height towards the earth under the gravitational force of the earth (with no other forces acting on it) is called free fall.

Q. 2. What do you mean by acceleration due to gravity ?

Ans. When an object is dropped from some height, its velocity increases at a constant rate. In other words, when an object is dropped from some height, a uniform acceleration is produced in it by the gravitational pull of the earth and this acceleration does not depend on the mass of the falling object. The uniform acceleration produced in a freely falling object due to the gravitational force of the earth is known as acceleration due to gravity (g). The value of acceleration due to gravity (g) changes slightly from place to place but for most of the purposes it is taken to be 9.8 m/s^2.

NCERT Book, Page 138

Q.1. What are the differences between the mass of an object and its weight.

Ans. See Table on page 100 of this book.

Q.2. Why is the weight of an object on the moon $\frac{1}{6}$th of its weight on the earth ?

Ans. The mass and radius of moon are less than that of earth due to which the moon exerts a lesser gravitational force on objects (which is $\frac{1}{6}$th of that exerted by the earth). Since the gravitational force of the moon is $\frac{1}{6}$th that of the earth, therefore, the weight of an object on the moon is $\frac{1}{6}$th of its weight on the earth.

NCERT Book, Page 141

Q.1. Why is it difficult to hold a school bag having a strap made of a thin and strong string ?

Ans. We know that : Pressure = $\frac{\text{Force}}{\text{Area}}$. Now, when a school bag has a strap made of a thin string, then because of this thin string, the weight of a school bag (or force of school bag) will fall on a very small area of the shoulder (or hand) of the child. This will produce a large pressure on the shoulder (or hand) of the child. The large pressure makes it very painful to carry the heavy school bag.

Q.2. What do you mean by buoyancy ?

Ans. Whenever an object is immersed in a liquid (fully or partially), it experiences an upward force. The upward force is called buoyant force (or upthrust). The tendency of a liquid to exert an upward force on an object placed in it, is called buoyancy. Even the gases exhibit the property of buoyancy.

Q.3. Why does an object float or sink when placed on the surface of water ?

Ans. When an object is put in water, then two forces act on it :

(*i*) weight of the object acting downwards (which tends to pull down the object), and

(*ii*) buoyant force (or upthrust) acting upwards (which tends to push up the object).

Now, whether an object will float or sink in water will depend on the relative magnitudes of these two forces (weight and buoyant force) acting on the object in opposite directions.

(*a*) If the buoyant force (or upthrust) exerted by water is equal to or greater than the weight of the object, the object will float in water.

(*b*) If the buoyant force (or upthrust) exerted by water is less than the weight of the object, the object will sink.

NCERT Book, Page 142

Q.1. You find your mass to be 42 kg on a weighing machine. Is your mass more or less than 42 kg ?

Ans. Even gases (like air) exert an upward force (or buoyant force) on the objects placed in them. Now, when we stand on a weighing machine, then the air exerts an upward force (buoyant force or upthrust) on our body and makes us slightly lighter than we actually are. So, if a weighing machine shows our mass to be 42 kg, then our actual mass will be slightly more than 42 kg.

Q.2. You have a bag of cotton and an iron bar, each indicating a mass of 100 kg when measured on a weighing machine. In reality, one is heavier than the other. Can you say which one is heavier and why ?

Ans. We know that the density of cotton is must less than the density of iron. Due to this, 100 kg of cotton has a much bigger volume than the same mass (100 kg) of iron. Now, due to its bigger volume, 100 kg of cotton will displace much more weight of air (than 100 kg of iron). Due to this, the upward force (or buoyant force) on 100 kg of cotton will be much more than on 100 kg of iron. This means that due to greater upward buoyant force of air acting on cotton bag, the weighing machine will show a much lesser mass of cotton (than that of iron). So, in reality, 100 kg of cotton weighed in air will be heavier than 100 kg of iron weighed in air.

NCERT Book, Pages 143, 144 and 145

Q.1. How does the force of gravitation between two objects change when the distance between them is reduced to half ?

Ans. The force of gravitation between two objects is inversely proportional to the square of distance between them. That is, $F \propto \frac{1}{r^2}$. Now, when the distance between two objects is reduced to half, that is, made $\frac{1}{2}$, then the force between them will become 4 times $\left[\text{because} \left(\frac{1}{\frac{1}{2}}\right)^2 = 4\right]$.

Q.2. Gravitational force acts on all objects in proportion to their masses. Why then, a heavy object does not fall faster than a light object ?

Ans. We know that : Force = mass × acceleration. Now, it is given to us that gravitational force acts on all objects in proportion to their masses, that is, Force ∝ mass. This is possible only if the acceleration (due to gravity) is constant for a heavy object as well as a light object. Since the acceleration is constant, therefore, all the objects (heavy or light) fall at the same speed.

Q.3. What is the magnitude of the gravitational force between the earth and a 1 kg object on its surface ? (Mass of the earth is 6×10^{24} kg and radius of the earth is 6.4×10^6 m).

Ans. The magnitude of gravitational force is calculated by using the formula :

$$F = G \times \frac{m_1 \times m_2}{r^2}$$

Now, Gravitational constant, $G = 6.7 \times 10^{-11}\ \text{Nm}^2/\text{kg}^2$

Mass of earth, $m_1 = 6 \times 10^{24}$ kg

Mass of object, $m_2 = 1$ kg

And, Distance between centre of earth and object, r = Radius of earth

$= 6.4 \times 10^6$ m

Now, putting these values in the above formula, we get :

$$F = \frac{6.7 \times 10^{-11} \times 6 \times 10^{24} \times 1}{(6.4 \times 10^{6})^2}$$

or $$F = 9.8 \text{ N}$$

Thus, the magnitude of gravitational force between the earth and a 1 kg object on its surface is 9.8 newtons.

Q.4. The earth and the moon are attracted to each other by gravitational force. Does the earth attract the moon with a force that is greater or smaller or the same as the force with which the moon attracts the earth ? Why ?

Ans. The earth attracts the moon with the same force with which the moon attracts the earth. This is because according to Newton's third law of motion, the forces of action and reaction are always equal and opposite. So, when earth attracts the moon with a certain gravitational force, then the moon attracts the earth with an equal and opposite gravitational force.

Q.5. If the moon attracts the earth, why does the earth not move towards the moon ?

Ans. From Newton's second law of motion, it can be concluded that the acceleration produced in a body is inversely proportional to the mass of the body $\left(\text{because } a = \frac{F}{m}\right)$. Now, due to the very large mass (m) of the earth, the gravitational force (F) between the moon and the earth produces very small acceleration (a) in the earth. Actually, the acceleration produced in the earth (by the attraction of moon) is so small that it cannot be observed. And hence we do not see the earth move towards the moon.

Q.6. What happens to the force between two objects, if :

(i) the mass of one object is doubled ?

(ii) the distance between the objects is (a) doubled, and (b) tripled ?

(iii) the masses of both objects are doubled ?

Ans. (*i*) The gravitational force between two objects is directly proportional to the product of masses of the two objects. So, if the mass of one of the objects is doubled, then the force also gets doubled (it becomes 2 times).

(*ii*) The gravitational force between two objects is inversely proportional to the square of distance between them.

(*a*) If the distance between the objects is doubled (made 2 times), the force between them becomes $\left(\frac{1}{2}\right)^2$ or $\frac{1}{4}$ (one-fourth).

(*b*) If the distance between the objects is tripled (made 3 times), the force between them will become $\left(\frac{1}{3}\right)^2$ or $\frac{1}{9}$ (one-ninth).

(*iii*) The gravitational force between two objects is directly proportional to the product of their masses. So, if the masses of both the objects are doubled (made 2 times each), the force between them will become $2 \times 2 = 4$ times.

Q.7. What is the importance of the universal law of gravitation ?

Ans. The importance of universal law of gravitation is that it explains the motion of planets around the sun; the motion of moon around the earth; and the motion of artificial satellites around the earth. It also explains the phenomena of rainfall, snowfall, and flow of water in rivers on the earth.

Q.8. What is the acceleration of free fall ?

Ans. The falling of an object from a height towards the earth under the gravitational force of earth (with no other forces acting on it) is called free fall. The gravitational force of earth produces a uniform acceleration in the freely falling object due to which its speed goes on increasing. This is called the acceleration of free fall (which is commonly known as acceleration due to gravity). The value of acceleration of free fall is 9.8 m/s^2.

Q.9. What do we call the gravitational force between the earth and an object ?

Ans. The gravitational force between the earth and an object is called 'earth's gravity'.

Q.10. Amit buys few grams of gold at the poles as per the instructions of one of his friends. He hands over the

same when he meets him at the equator. Will his friend agree with the weight of gold bought ? If not, why ? (*Hint*. The value of g is greater at the poles than at the equator).

Ans. No, the friend at equator will not agree with the weight of gold bought at the poles. This can be explained as follows : We know that weight, $W = m \times g$. Now, since the value of g is greater at the poles, so the weight of a certain mass of gold will be greater at the poles (where it is bought). When the same mass of gold is brought to equator, then its weight will be found to be less because the value of g is less at the equator. Thus, a certain mass of gold bought at the poles will have lesser weight at the equator.

Q.11. Why will a sheet of paper fall slower than one that is crumpled into a ball ?

Ans. A sheet of paper has a larger area. Due to its large area, when a sheet of paper is dropped from a height, it experiences more resistance from air, its speed decreases and it falls at a slower rate. On the other hand, a sheet of paper crumpled into a ball has a smaller area. Due to its smaller area, when a ball made from crumpled sheet of paper is dropped from a height, it experiences less resistance from air, its speed increases and it falls at a faster rate.

Q.12. Gravitational force on the surface of moon is only $\frac{1}{6}$ as strong as gravitational force on the earth. What is the weight in newtons of a 10 kg object on the moon and on the earth ?

Ans. We know that the acceleration due to gravity on the surface of earth is 9.8 m/s². So, the acceleration due to gravity on the surface of moon will be $\frac{1}{6}$ of this value, that is, $9.8 \times \frac{1}{6}\ \text{m/s}^2$.

(*i*) *Calculation of weight on the moon*

Mass of object, $m = 10$ kg

Acceleration due to gravity on moon, $g = 9.8 \times \frac{1}{6}\ \text{m/s}^2$

Now, Weight of object (on moon), $W = m \times g$

$= 10 \times 9.8 \times \frac{1}{6}$

$= 16.3$ N (or 16.3 newtons)

(*ii*) *Calculation of weight on the earth*

Mass of object, $m = 10$ kg

Acceleration due to gravity on earth, $g = 9.8\ \text{m/s}^2$

Now, Weight of object (on earth), $W = m \times g$

$= 10 \times 9.8$

$= 98$ N (or 98 newtons)

Q.13. A ball is thrown vertically upwards with a velocity of 49 m/s. Calculate :

(*i*) the maximum height to which it rises.

(*ii*) the total time it takes to return to the surface of the earth.

Ans. (*i*) Please note that here the ball is going up against the gravity, so the value of acceleration due to gravity g is to be taken as negative (with a minus sign).

Here, Initial velocity of ball, $u = 49$ m/s

Final velocity of ball, $v = 0$ (The ball stops at top)

Acceleration due to gravity, $g = -9.8\ \text{m/s}^2$ (The ball goes up)

And, Height, $h = ?$ (To be calculated)

Now, putting all these values in the formula :

$$v^2 = u^2 + 2gh$$

we get :

$$(0)^2 = (49)^2 + 2 \times (-9.8) \times h$$

$$0 = 2401 - 19.6\,h$$

$$19.6\,h = 2401$$

So,

$$h = \frac{2401}{19.6}$$

$$h = 122.5\ \text{m}$$

Thus, the maximum height to which the ball rises is 122.5 metres.

(*ii*) We will first calculate the time taken by the ball to reach the highest point by using the formula :

$$v = u + gt$$

Here, Final velocity, $v = 0$ (The ball stops at top)

Initial velocity, $u = 49$ m/s

Acceleration due to gravity, $g = -9.8$ m/s^2 (The ball goes up)

And, Time taken, $t = ?$ (To be calculated)

So, putting these values in the above formula, we get :

$$0 = 49 + (-9.8) \times t$$
$$0 = 49 - 9.8\,t$$
$$9.8\,t = 49$$
$$t = \frac{49}{9.8}$$
$$t = 5 \text{ s}$$

Thus, the ball takes 5 seconds to reach the highest point of its upward journey. Please note that this ball will take an equal time, that is, 5 seconds to return to the surface of the earth. In other words, the ball will take a total time of 5 + 5 = 10 seconds to return to the surface of the earth.

Q.14. A stone is released from the top of a tower of height 19.6 m. Calculate its final velocity just before touching the ground.

Ans. Here, Initial velocity, $u = 0$

Final velocity, $v = ?$ (To be calculated)

Acceleration due to gravity, $g = 9.8$ m/s^2 (Stone comes down)

And, Height, $h = 19.6$ m

Now, we know that for a freely falling body :

$$v^2 = u^2 + 2gh$$

So,

$$v^2 = (0)^2 + 2 \times 9.8 \times 19.6$$
$$v^2 = 19.6 \times 19.6$$
$$v^2 = (19.6)^2$$

And,

$$v = 19.6 \text{ m/s}$$

Thus, the velocity of stone just before hitting the ground will be 19.6 metres per second.

Q.15. A stone is thrown vertically upward with an initial velocity of 40 m/s. Taking g = 10 m/s^2, find the maximum height reached by the stone. What is the net displacement and the total distance covered by the stone when it falls back to the ground ?

Ans. (*i*) Here, Initial velocity, $u = 40$ m/s

Final velocity, $v = 0$ (The stone stops)

Acceleration due to gravity, $g = -10$ m/s^2 (The stone goes up)

And, Height, $h = ?$ (To be calculated)

Now,

$$v^2 = u^2 + 2gh$$

So,

$$(0)^2 = (40)^2 + 2 \times (-10) \times h$$
$$0 = 1600 - 20\,h$$
$$20\,h = 1600$$
$$h = \frac{1600}{20}$$
$$h = 80 \text{ m}$$

Thus, the maximum height reached by the stone is 80 metres.

(*ii*) The stone is thrown up from the ground and after reaching the maximum height, falls back to the ground. As the final position of stone coincides with the initial position of stone, the net displacement of the stone is 'zero' (0).

(*iii*) The distance covered by the stone in reaching the maximum height is 80 metres. The stone will cover the same distance of 80 metres in coming back to ground. So, the total distance covered by the stone is 80 + 80 = 160 metres.

Q.16. Calculate the force of gravitation between the earth and the sun, given that the mass of the earth = 6 × 10^{24} kg and of the sun = 2 × 10^{30} kg. The average distance between the two is 1.5 × 10^{11} m.

Ans. The force exerted by one body on another body is given by the Newton's formula :

$$F = G \times \frac{m_1 \times m_2}{r^2}$$

Here, Gravitational constant, $G = 6.7 \times 10^{-11}$ Nm^2 kg^{-2}

Mass of the earth, $m_1 = 6 \times 10^{24}$ kg

Mass of the sun, $m_2 = 2 \times 10^{30}$ kg

And, Distance between the earth and sun, $r = 1.5 \times 10^{11}$ m

Putting these values in the above formula, we get :

$$F = \frac{6.7 \times 10^{-11} \times 6 \times 10^{24} \times 2 \times 10^{30}}{(1.5 \times 10^{11})^2}$$

$$F = 3.57 \times 10^{22} \text{ N}$$

Thus, the force of gravitation between the earth and the sun is 3.57×10^{22} newtons.

Q.17. A stone is allowed to fall from the top of a tower 100 m high and at the same time another stone is projected vertically upwards from the ground with a velocity of 25 m/s. Calculate when and where the two stones will meet.

Ans. Here, height of the tower is 100 m. Now, suppose the two stones meet at a point P which is at a height x above the ground as shown in the figure, so that the distance of point P from the top of the tower is $100 - x$.

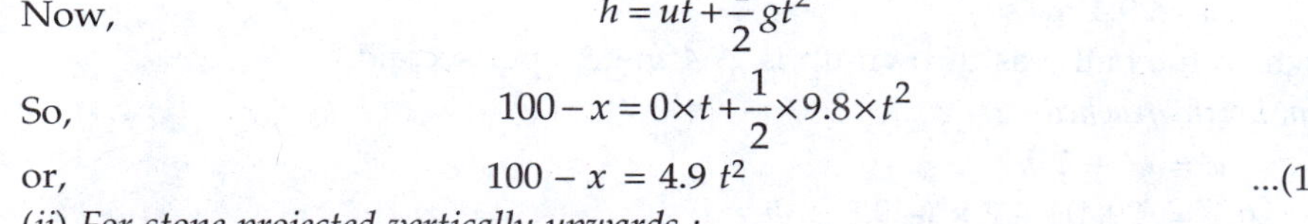

(i) For the stone falling from top of tower :

Height, $h = (100 - x)$ m

Initial velocity, $u = 0$

Time, $t = ?$

And, Acceleration due to gravity, $g = 9.8$ m/s^2 (Stone falls down)

Now, $$h = ut + \frac{1}{2}gt^2$$

So, $$100 - x = 0 \times t + \frac{1}{2} \times 9.8 \times t^2$$

or, $$100 - x = 4.9\, t^2 \quad \text{...(1)}$$

(ii) For stone projected vertically upwards :

Height, $h = x$ m

Initial velocity, $u = 25$ m/s

Time, $t = ?$

And, Acceleration due to gravity, $g = -9.8$ m/s^2 (Stone goes up)

Now, $$s = ut + \frac{1}{2}gt^2$$

So, $$x = 25 \times t + \frac{1}{2} \times (-9.8) \times t^2$$

or, $$x = 25\, t - 4.9\, t^2 \quad \text{...(2)}$$

On adding equations (1) and (2), we get :

$$100 - x + x = 4.9\, t^2 + 25\, t - 4.9\, t^2$$

or $$100 = 25\, t$$

$$t = \frac{100}{25}$$

$$t = 4 \text{ s}$$

Thus, the two stones will meet after a time of 4 seconds.

Now, from equation (1) we have :

$$100 - x = 4.9\, t^2$$

Putting $t = 4$ in this equation, we get :

$$100 - x = 4.9 \times (4)^2$$

$$100 - x = 4.9 \times 16$$

$$100 - x = 78.4$$
$$100 - 78.4 = x$$
$$21.6 \text{ m} = x$$
or $$x = 21.6 \text{ m}$$

Thus, the two stones will meet at a height of 21.6 metres from the ground.

Q.18. A ball thrown up vertically returns to the thrower after 6 s. Find :
(a) the velocity with which it was thrown up,
(b) the maximum height it reaches, and
(c) its position after 4 s.

Ans. Since the ball thrown up vertically returns to the thrower in 6 seconds, this means that the ball will take half of this time, that is, $\frac{6}{2} = 3$ seconds to go from the thrower to its maximum height and the remaining 3 seconds to fall down from the maximum height and return to the thrower.

(a) *Calculation of velocity with which ball was thrown up*

Here, Final velocity, $v = 0$ (The ball stops)
Initial velocity, $u = ?$ (To be calculated)
Acceleration due to gravity, $g = -9.8 \text{ m/s}^2$ (Ball goes up)
And, Time taken to reach the top, $t = 3$ s

Now, $$v = u + gt$$
So, $$0 = u + (-9.8) \times 3$$
$$0 = u - 29.4$$
$$u = 29.4 \text{ m/s}$$

Thus, the velocity with which the ball was thrown up is 29.4 metres per second.

(b) *Calculation of the maximum height reached*

We know that : $$v^2 = u^2 + 2gh$$
So, $$(0)^2 = (29.4)^2 + 2 \times (-9.8) \times h$$
$$0 = 864.36 - 19.6\,h$$
$$19.6\,h = 864.36$$
$$h = \frac{864.36}{19.6}$$
$$h = 44.1 \text{ m}$$

Thus, the maximum height reached by the ball is 44.1 metres.

(c) *Calculation of position of ball after 4 s*

We have seen above that the ball reaches the maximum height in 3 seconds. So, all that we have to do is to find the height (or distance) by which the freely falling ball comes down from the top in 1 second (because 3 s + 1 s = 4 s).

Now, $$h = ut + \frac{1}{2}gt^2$$
So, $$h = 0 \times 1 + \frac{1}{2} \times 9.8 \times (1)^2 \quad \text{(Because } t = 1 \text{ s)}$$
$$h = 0 + 4.9 \times 1$$
$$h = 4.9 \text{ m}$$

Thus, the position of the ball after 4 seconds of throwing is 4.9 metres below the maximum height reached.

Q.19. In what direction does the buoyant force on an object immersed in a liquid act ?

Ans. The buoyant force on an object immersed in a liquid acts in the vertically upward direction. In other words, buoyant force acts in a direction opposite to the direction in which weight of the object acts.

Q.20. Why does a block of plastic released under water come up to the surface of water ?

Ans. A block of plastic released under water comes up to the surface of water because the buoyant force (or upthrust) acting on the block of plastic due to water is greater than its weight. The buoyant force is greater because the density of water is greater than the density of plastic.

Q.21. The volume of 50 g of a substance is 20 cm^3. If the density of water is 1 g cm^{-3}, will the substance float or sink ?

Ans. We know that : $$\text{Density of substance} = \frac{\text{Mass of substance}}{\text{Volume of substance}}$$

Here, Mass of substance = 50 g

And, Volume of substance = 20 cm^3

So, $$\text{Density of substance} = \frac{50\ g}{20\ cm^3}$$

$$= 2.5\ g\ cm^{-3}$$

Since the density of substance (2.5 g cm^{-3}) is greater than the density of water (1 g cm^{-3}), therefore, the substance will sink in water.

Q.22. The volume of a 500 g sealed packet is 350 cm^3. Will the packet float or sink in water if the density of water is 1 g cm^{-3} ? What will be the mass of water displaced by this packet ?

Ans. Here, Mass of packet = 500 g

And, Volume of packet = 350 cm^3

Now, $$\text{Density of packet} = \frac{\text{Mass of packet}}{\text{Volume of packet}}$$

$$= \frac{500\ g}{350\ cm^3}$$

$$= 1.42\ g\ cm^{-3}$$

Since the density of packet (1.42 g cm^{-3}) is more than the density of water (1 g cm^{-3}), therefore, the packet will sink in water.

The packet which sinks in water will displace water equal to its own volume. Since the volume of packet is 350 cm^3, so it will displace 350 cm^3 of water. We have now to calculate the mass of 350 cm^3 of water.

Now, $$\text{Density of water} = \frac{\text{Mass of water}}{\text{Volume of water}}$$

So, $$1\ g\ cm^{-3} = \frac{\text{Mass of water}}{350\ cm^3}$$

And, $$\text{Mass of water} = 1\ g\ cm^{-3} \times 350\ cm^3$$

$$= 350\ g$$

Thus, the mass of water displaced by the packet is 350 grams.

Chapter : WORK AND ENERGY

NCERT Book, Page 148

Q.1. A force of 7 N acts on an object. The displacement is, say 8 m, in the direction of the force (see Figure below). Let us take it that the force acts on the object through the displacement. What is the work done in this case ?

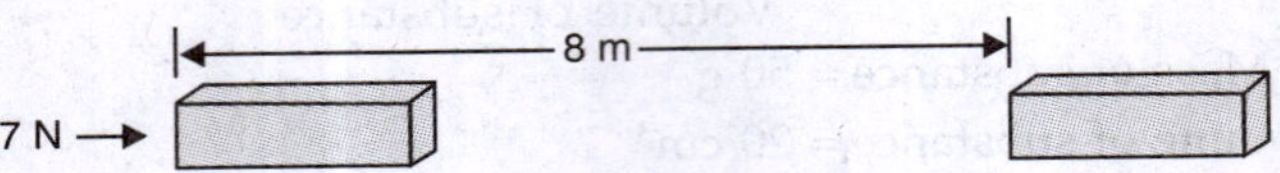

Ans. We know that : Work done = Force × Displacement

or $W = F \times s$

Here Force, $F = 7$ N

And Displacement, $s = 8$ m

So, $W = 7 \times 8$ J

or $W = 56$ J

Thus, the work done in this case is 56 joules.

NCERT Book, Page 149

Q.1. When do we say that work is done ?

Ans. Work is said to be done when a force produces motion in an object.

Q.2. Write an expression for the work done when a force is acting on an object in the direction of its displacement ?

Ans. If a force F acts on an object and s is the displacement of the object in the direction of force, then :

Work done = Force × Displacement

or $W = F \times s$

Q.3. Define 1 J of work.

Ans. When a force of 1 N moves an object through a distance of 1 m in its own direction, then the work done is known as 1 J.

Q.4. A pair of bullocks exerts a force of 140 N on a plough. The field being ploughed is 15 m long. How much work is done in ploughing the length of the field ?

Ans. Here, Work done, $W = ?$ (To be calculated)

Force, $F = 140$ N

And Distance, $s = 15$ m

Now, $W = F \times s$

So, $W = 140 \times 15$

$W = 2100$ J

Thus, the work done in ploughing the length of field is 2100 joules.

NCERT Book, Page 152

Q.1. What is the kinetic energy of an object ?

Ans. The energy of an object due to its motion is called kinetic energy. The kinetic energy of a moving object is measured by the amount of work it can do before coming to rest.

Q.2. Write an expression for the kinetic energy of an object.

Ans. Kinetic energy of an object $= \frac{1}{2}mv^2$

where m = mass of the object

and v = velocity of the object (or speed of the object)

Q.3. The kinetic energy of an object of mass 'm' moving with a velocity of 5 m s⁻¹ is 25 J. What will be its kinetic energy when its velocity is doubled ? What will be its kinetic energy when its velocity is increased three times ?

Ans. First of all we will calculate the mass '*m*' of the object.

Now, $$\text{Kinetic energy} = \frac{1}{2}mv^2$$

So, $$25 = \frac{1}{2} \times m \times (5)^2$$

$$25 = \frac{1}{2} \times m \times 25$$

$$m = \frac{25 \times 2}{25}$$

So, Mass, $m = 2$ kg

(*i*) In the first case, the velocity of 5 m s^{-1} is doubled, so the velocity becomes 5 × 2 = 10 m s^{-1}.

Now, $$\text{Kinetic energy} = \frac{1}{2}mv^2$$

$$= \frac{1}{2} \times 2 \times (10)^2$$

$$= \frac{1}{2} \times 2 \times 100$$

$$= 100 \text{ J}$$

Thus, when the velocity of object is doubled, then its kinetic energy becomes 100 J.

(*ii*) In the second case, the velocity of 5 m s^{-1} is increased three times so the velocity becomes 5 × 3 = 15 m s^{-1}.

Now, $$\text{Kinetic energy} = \frac{1}{2}mv^2$$

$$= \frac{1}{2} \times 2 \times (15)^2$$

$$= \frac{1}{2} \times 2 \times 225$$

$$= 225 \text{ J}$$

Thus, when the velocity of object is increased three times, then its kinetic energy becomes 225 J.

NCERT Book, Page 156

Q.1. What is power ?

Ans. Power is defined as the rate of doing work.

$$\text{Power} = \frac{\text{Work done}}{\text{Time taken}}$$

or $$P = \frac{W}{t}$$

where P = Power

W = Work done

and t = Time taken

Power is also defined as the rate at which energy is consumed (or utilised).

Q.2. Define 1 watt of power.

Ans. 1 watt is the power of an appliance which does work at the rate of 1 joule per second (or which consumes energy at the rate of 1 joule per second). That is :

$$1 \text{ watt} = \frac{1 \text{ joule}}{1 \text{ second}}$$

Q.3. A lamp consumes 1000 J of electrical energy in 10 s. What is its power ?

Ans. $$\text{Power} = \frac{\text{Energy consumed}}{\text{Time taken}}$$

$$\text{Power} = \frac{1000 \text{ J}}{10 \text{ s}}$$

$$= 100 \text{ J/s}$$

$$= 100 \text{ W} \qquad \text{(or 100 watts)}$$

Q.4. Define average power.

Ans. $$\text{Average power} = \frac{\text{Total work done (or Total energy consumed)}}{\text{Total time taken}}$$

The term 'average power' is used when an agent (or appliance) does work (or consumes energy) at different rates during different intervals of time.

NCERT Book, Pages 158 and 159

Q.1 Look at the activities listed below. Reason out whether or not work is done in the light of your understanding of the term 'work' :

(a) Suma is swimming in a pond.
(b) A donkey is carrying load on its back.
(c) A wind-mill is lifting water from a well.
(d) A green plant is carrying out photosynthesis.
(e) An engine is pulling a train.
(f) Food-grains are getting dried in the sun.
(g) A sailboat is moving due to wind energy.

Ans. (a) Suma is doing work. This is because Suma is moving herself in water of the swimming pool by applying force.

(b) A donkey is not doing work against gravity. This is because it is carrying load (weight) at right angles to the force of gravity. A donkey, however, does work against friction and air resistance.

(c) A wind-mill is doing work. This is because it is lifting up water from the well against the force of gravity.

(d) A green plant does no work during photosynthesis. This is because in this case both, the force as well as the distance moved are zero.

(e) An engine does work in pulling a train. This is because an engine applies force due to which the train moves.

(f) No work is done when food-grains are dried in the sun. This is because no force is applied and no motion takes place.

(g) Work is done when sailboat moves. This is because wind is applying force which produces motion in the sailboat.

Q.2. An object thrown at a certain angle to the ground moves in a curved path and falls back to the ground. The initial and the final points of the path of the object lie on the same horizontal line. What is the work done by the force of gravity on the object ?

Ans. Since the initial and final points of the path of an object thrown at an angle to the ground lie on the same

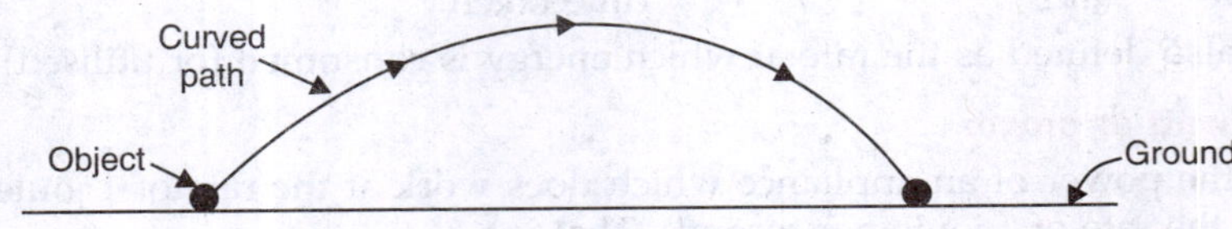

horizontal line, the displacement of the object is only in the horizontal direction. Since there is no net displacement of the object in the vertical direction (in which the force of gravity acts), therefore, no work is done by the force of gravity on the object.

Q.3. A battery lights a bulb. Describe the energy changes involved in the process.

Ans. A battery contains chemicals and supplies electrical energy. So, a battery converts chemical energy into electrical energy. In an electric bulb, the electrical energy is first converted into heat energy. This heat energy causes the filament of bulb to become white-hot and produce light energy. So, the energy changes involved when a battery lights up a bulb are :

Chemical energy → Electrical energy → Heat energy → Light energy

Q.4. Certain force acting on a 20 kg mass changes its velocity from 5 m s^{-1} to 2 m s^{-1}. Calculate the work done by the force.

Ans. The work done by the force will be equal to the change in kinetic energy when the velocity changes from 5 m s^{-1} to 2 m s^{-1}.

(*i*) *In the first case :*

Mass, m = 20 kg

And Velocity, v = 5 m s^{-1}

$$\text{K.E.} = \frac{1}{2}mv^2$$

$$= \frac{1}{2} \times 20 \times (5)^2$$

$$= \frac{1}{2} \times 20 \times 25$$

$$= 250 \text{ J} \quad ...(1)$$

(*ii*) *In the second case :*

Mass, m = 20 kg

And Velocity, v = 2 m s^{-1}

So,

$$\text{K.E.} = \frac{1}{2}mv^2$$

$$= \frac{1}{2} \times 20 \times (2)^2$$

$$= \frac{1}{2} \times 20 \times 4$$

$$= 40 \text{ J} \quad ...(2)$$

Work done by force = Change in kinetic energy
= 250 – 40 J
= 210 J

Q.5. An object of mass 10 kg is at a point A on a table. It is moved to a point B. If the line joining A and B is horizontal, what is the work done on the object by the gravitational force ? Explain your answer.

Ans. The work done on the object by the gravitational force is zero. This is because the motion of object is in the

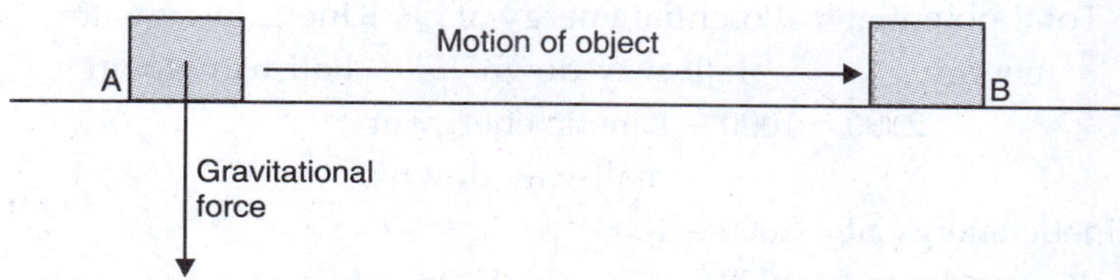

horizontal direction whereas the gravitational force (acting vertically downwards) is at right angles (90° angle) to the direction of motion of object. $W = F \cos 90° \times s = F \times 0 \times s = 0$ (because cos 90° = 0)

Q.6. The potential energy of a freely falling object decreases progressively. Does this violate the law of conservation of energy ? Why ?

Ans. When a freely falling object comes downwards, its height above the ground decreases due to which its potential energy decreases progressively. Now, as the freely falling object comes down, its speed (or velocity) goes on increasing due to which its kinetic energy also goes on increasing. At any point of time during the free fall, the sum of potential energy and kinetic energy of the falling object remains the same (or conserved). So, there is no violation of the law of conservation of energy in this case.

Q.7. What are the various energy transformations that occur when you are riding a bicycle ?

Ans. The chemical energy of food is transformed in our body into muscular energy of muscles. When we pedal a bicycle, the muscular energy of legs is transformed into kinetic energy which rotates the pedals. The rotational kinetic energy of pedals is transferred by bicycle chain to rotational kinetic energy of bicycle wheels. Due to this the bicycle wheels move forward. When the bicycle is moving, then the bicycle as well as the person riding the bicycle, both have kinetic energy.

Q.8. Does the transfer of energy take place when you push a huge rock with all your might and fail to move it ? Where is the energy you spend going ?

Ans. Yes, the transfer of energy takes place when we push a huge rock and fail to move it. The energy spent by us gets stored in the rock as potential energy of configuration due to the deformation of rock. The deformation in rock is so small that it cannot be observed by us. Some of the energy is also used up in stretching the muscles of our arms while pushing the rock and rapid displacement of blood to the stretched muscles.

Q.9. A certain household has consumed 250 units of energy during a month. How much energy is this in joules ?

Ans. Energy consumed = 250 units

= 250 kWh (or 250 kilowatt-hours)

Now, 1 kilowatt-hour = 3.6×10^6 joules

So, 250 kilowatt-hours = $3.6 \times 10^6 \times 250$ joules

= 9×10^8 joules

Q.10. An object of mass 40 kg is raised to a height of 5 m above the ground. What is its potential energy ? If the object is allowed to fall, find its kinetic energy when it is half way down (g = 10 m/s^2)

Ans. Here, Mass, m = 40 kg

Acceleration due to gravity, g = 10 m/s^2

And Height, h = 5 m

So, Potential energy = $m \times g \times h$

(at 5 m height) = $40 \times 10 \times 5$ J

= 2000 J (or 2000 joules)

Initially, the object is at a height of 5 m (and has a potential energy of 2000 J). When this object is allowed to fall and it is half way down, its height above the ground will be half of 5 m which is $\frac{5}{2} = 2.5\text{ m}$. Now, the potential energy of this object of 40 kg when it is at a height of 2.5 m will be :

Potential energy = $m \times g \times h$

(at 2.5 m height) = $40 \times 10 \times 2.5$ J

= 1000 J (or 1000 joules)

Now, according to the law of conservation of energy :

Total potential energy = Potential energy at half way down + Kinetic energy at half way down

or 2000 = 1000 + Kinetic energy at half way down

So, Kinetic energy at half way down = 2000 – 1000

= 1000 J (or 1000 joules)

Q.11. What is the work done by the force of gravity on a satellite moving round the earth ? Justify your answer.

Ans. When a satellite moves around the earth in a circular path, its displacement in any short interval of time is along the tangent to the circular path of the satellite. The force of gravity acting on the satellite is along the radius of the earth at that point. Since a tangent is always at right angles to the radius, therefore, the motion of a satellite and force of gravity are at right angles (90° angle) to each other. Now, work done $W = F \cos 90° \times s$. Since $\cos 90° = 0$, therefore, work done $W = F \times 0 \times s = 0$. Thus, the work done by the force of gravity on a satellite moving round the earth is zero.

Q.12. Can there be displacement of an object in the absence of any force acting on it ? Think. Discuss this question with your friends and teacher.

Ans. Yes, there can be displacement of an object in the absence of any force acting on it. We know that $F = m \times a$. Now, when force $F = 0$, then $m \times a = 0$. Since mass 'm' cannot be zero, therefore, when force $F = 0$, then acceleration 'a' = 0. In such a situation, either the object is at rest (not moving) or it is in uniform motion in a straight line. In the latter case, there is a displacement of the object without any force acting on it.

Q.13. A person holds a bundle of hay over his head for 30 minutes and gets tired. Has he done some work or not ? Justify your answer.

Ans. A person holding a bundle of hay over his head for 30 minutes has done no work because he has not moved the bundle over some distance ($s = 0$). The person gets tired due to muscular fatigue. This is because his muscles are stretched and blood is displaced to the strained muscles more rapidly. These changes consume energy and he feels tired.

Q.14. An electric heater is rated 1500 W. How much energy does it use in 10 hours ?

Ans. Here,

$$\text{Power, } P = 1500 \text{ W} = \frac{1500}{1000} \text{ kW} = 1.5 \text{ kW}$$

And,

$$\text{Time, } t = 10 \text{ h}$$

Now,

$$\text{Power} = \frac{\text{Energy used}}{\text{Time taken}}$$

So,

$$1.5 \text{ kW} = \frac{\text{Energy used}}{10 \text{ h}}$$

And

$$\text{Energy used} = 1.5 \text{ kW} \times 10 \text{ h} = 15 \text{ kWh} \quad \text{(or 15 units)}$$

Thus, the energy consumed is 15 kWh or 15 units.

Q.15. Illustrate the law of conservation of energy by discussing the energy changes which occur when we draw a pendulum bob to one side and allow it to oscillate. Why does the bob eventually come to rest ?

Ans. Initially, the simple pendulum is at rest with its bob in the centre position (or mean position) A. When the pendulum bob is pulled to one side to position B (to give it potential energy because of higher position of B with respect to position A), and then released, the bob starts swinging (moving back and forth) between positions B and C (see Figure).

(*i*) When the pendulum bob is at position B, it has only potential energy (but no kinetic energy).

(*ii*) As the bob starts moving down from position B to position A, its potential energy goes on decreasing but its kinetic energy goes on increasing.

(*iii*) When the bob reaches the centre position A, it has only kinetic energy (but no potential energy).

(*iv*) As the bob goes from position A towards position C, its kinetic energy goes on decreasing but its potential energy goes on increasing.

(*v*) On reaching the extreme position C, the bob stops for a very small instant of time. So at position C, the bob has only potential energy (but no kinetic energy).

From the above discussion we conclude that at the extreme positions B and C of a swinging pendulum, all the energy of pendulum bob is potential, and at the centre position A, all the energy of the pendulum bob is kinetic. At all other intermediate positions, the energy of pendulum bob is partly potential and partly kinetic. But the total energy of the swinging pendulum at any instant of time remains the same (or conserved).

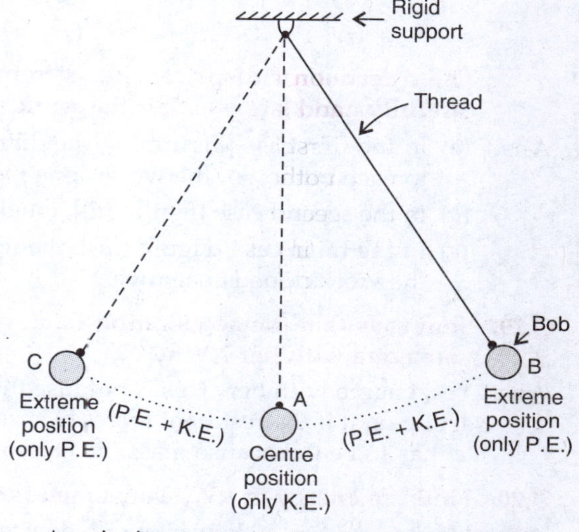

A swinging (or oscillating) simple pendulum

The swinging pendulum bob eventually comes to rest because it loses energy due to the friction at the point of support of the pendulum and friction of air (or air resistance) acting on the swinging pendulum bob. This energy is converted into heat energy and sound energy which go into the environment.

Q.16. An object of mass 'm' is moving with a constant velocity 'v'. How much work should be done on the object in order to bring the object to rest ?

Ans. An object of mass m moving with a constant velocity v has a kinetic energy equal to $\frac{1}{2}mv^2$. An equal amount of work $\left(\text{that is, } \frac{1}{2}mv^2 \text{ work}\right)$ should be done on this moving object to make its kinetic energy zero and bring it to rest.

Q.17. Calculate the work required to be done to stop a car of 1500 kg moving at a velocity of 60 km/h ?

Ans. When a moving car stops, its kinetic energy becomes zero. So, the work required to be done to stop the moving car will be equal to the kinetic energy possessed by the moving car. This can be calculated as follows.

Mass of car, $m = 1500$ kg

Velocity of car, $v = 60$ km/h

$$= \frac{60 \times 1000}{60 \times 60} \text{ m/s}$$

$$= \frac{50}{3} \text{ m/s}$$

Now, Kinetic energy $= \frac{1}{2}mv^2$

$$= \frac{1}{2} \times 1500 \times \left(\frac{50}{3}\right)^2$$

$$= \frac{1500 \times 2500}{2 \times 9}$$

$$= 208333.3 \text{ J}$$

Thus, 208333.3 joules of work has to be done to stop this moving car.

Q.18. In each of the following a force F is acting on an object of mass m.

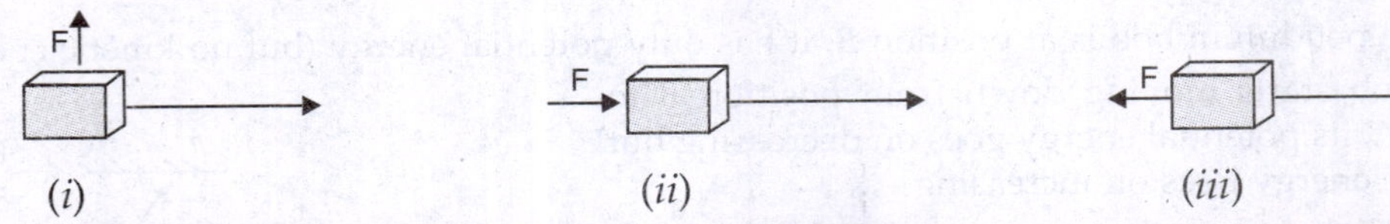

The direction of displacement is from west to east shown by the longer arrow. Observe the diagrams carefully and state whether the work done by the force is negative, positive or zero.

Ans. (*a*) In the first case [Figure (*i*)], the direction of force F and the direction of displacement are at right angles to each other. So, the work done in the first case is zero.

(*b*) In the second case [Figure (*ii*)], the displacement is in the direction of force F, so the work done is positive.

(*c*) In the third case [Figure (*iii*)], the force F acts in a direction opposite to the direction of displacement, so the work done is negative.

Q.19. Soni says that the acceleration in an object could be zero even when several forces are acting on it. Do you agree with her ? Why ?

Ans. Yes, I agree with her. This is because the acceleration in an object could be zero even when several forces are acting on it if the resultant force (F) is zero. We know that $F = m \times a$. Now, when force $F = 0$, then acceleration 'a' has to be 0 (because mass 'm' cannot be 0).

Q.20. Find the energy in kWh consumed in 10 hours by four devices of power 500 W each.

Ans. Here, Power of one device = 500 W

So, Power of four devices = 500 × 4 W

$$= 2000 \text{ W}$$

$$= \frac{2000}{1000} \text{ kW}$$

$$= 2 \text{ kW}$$

And, Time = 10 h

Now, $$\text{Power} = \frac{\text{Energy consumed}}{\text{Time taken}}$$

So, $$2 \text{ kW} = \frac{\text{Energy consumed}}{10 \text{ h}}$$

And, Energy consumed = 2 kW × 10 h

= 20 kWh (or 20 units)

Q.21. A freely falling object eventually stops on reaching the ground. What happens to its kinetic energy ?

Ans. When a freely falling object having kinetic energy hits the ground and eventually stops, then :

(*i*) Some of the kinetic energy is converted into sound energy (due to which a sound is produced when the falling object hits the ground).

(*ii*) Some of the kinetic energy is changed into heat energy (due to which the falling object and the ground where it falls become slightly warm).

(*iii*) Some of the kinetic energy is transformed into potential energy of configuration of the object and the ground (because the object and the ground get deformed a little bit at the point of their collision).

Chapter : SOUND

NCERT Book, Page 162

Q.1. How does the sound produced by a vibrating object in a medium reach your ear ?

Ans. The sound produced by a vibrating object reaches our ear through sound waves which travel in the medium as a series of compressions and rarefactions caused by the vibrations of the particles of the medium.

NCERT Book, Page 163

Q.1. Explain how, sound is produced by your school bell ?

Ans. When the school bell is struck with a hammer, it starts vibrating (or moving back and forth rapidly through a very small distance). The vibrating school bell produces sound.

Q.2. Why are sound waves called mechanical waves ?

Ans. The sound waves are called mechanical waves because they need a material medium (like solid, liquid or gas) for their propagation. The sound waves involve the vibrations of the particles of the medium through which they travel.

Q.3. Suppose you and your friend are on the moon. Will you be able to hear any sound produced by your friend ?

Ans. No, I will not be able to hear any sound produced by my friend while on the moon. This can be explained as follows : The moon has no air (or atmosphere). It is all vacuum (or empty space) on the surface of moon. Since there is no air (or atmosphere) on the moon to carry the sound waves (or sound vibrations), therefore, sound cannot be heard directly on the surface of moon.

NCERT Book, Page 166

Q.1. Which wave property determines (*a*) loudness (*b*) pitch ?

Ans. (*a*) The loudness of sound is determined by the amplitude of sound waves.

(*b*) The pitch of sound is determined by the frequency of vibration of the sound producing source.

Q.2. Guess which sound has a higher pitch : guitar or a car horn ?

Ans. A guitar has a higher pitch than a car horn.

NCERT Book, Page 166

Q.1. What are wavelength, frequency, time-period and amplitude of a sound wave ?

Ans. (*i*) The minimum distance in which a sound wave repeats itself is called its wavelength. In most simple words, it is the length of one complete wave.

(*ii*) The number of complete sound waves (or cycles) produced in one second is called frequency of the sound wave.

(*iii*) The time required to produce one complete sound wave (or cycle) is called time-period of the sound wave.

(*iv*) The maximum displacement of the particles of the medium from their original undisturbed positions, when a sound wave passes through the medium, is called amplitude of the sound wave.

Q.2. How are the wavelength and frequency of a sound wave related to its speed ?

Ans. Speed of sound wave = Frequency × Wavelength

$$v = f \times \lambda$$

Q.3. Calculate the wavelength of a sound wave whose frequency is 220 Hz and speed is 440 m/s in a given medium.

Ans. We know that : $v = f \times \lambda$

Here, Speed, v = 440 m/s

Frequency, f = 220 Hz

And, Wavelength, λ = ? (To be calculated)

Putting these values in the above formula, we get :

$$440 = 220 \times \lambda$$

And, $$\lambda = \frac{440}{220} \text{ m}$$

Wavelength, $\lambda = 2$ m

Q.4. A person is listening to a tone of 500 Hz sitting at a distance of 450 m from the source of the sound. What is the time interval between successive compressions from the source ?

Ans. Here, Frequency, $f = 500$ Hz

Now, Time period, $T = \frac{1}{f}$

$$= \frac{1}{500} \text{ s}$$

$$= 0.002 \text{ s}$$

The time interval between successive compressions from the source of sound is equal to the time-period of sound waves which is 0.002 second (The distance of 450 m has been given in this question just to confuse the students).

NCERT Book, Page 166

Q.1. Distinguish between loudness and intensity of sound.

Ans. The main differences between loudness and intensity of sound are given below.

Loudness of sound	*Intensity of sound*
1. The sensation produced in the ears which enables us to distinguish between a faint sound (feeble sound) and a loud sound is called loudness of sound.	**1.** The average energy transported by a sound wave per second per unit area (perpendicular to the direction of propagation) is called intensity of sound.
2. Loudness of sound is measured in the unit of decibel (dB)	**2.** Intensity of sound is measured in the unit of watts per square metre (W/m^2)
3. Loudness of sound depends on the sensitivity of ears	**3.** Intensity of sound does not depend on the sensitivity of ears.

NCERT Book, Page 167

Q.1. In which of the three media, air, water or iron, does sound travel the fastest at a particular temperature ?

Ans. The sound travels the fastest in a solid medium. Out of air, water and iron, iron is a solid, therefore, sound travels fastest in iron.

NCERT Book, Page 168

Q.1. An echo returned in 3 s. What is the distance of the reflecting surface from the source, given that the speed of sound is 342 m s^{-1} ?

Ans. In this case the time taken by sound to travel from the source to the reflecting surface, and back to the source (in the form of an echo) is 3 seconds. So, the time taken by sound to travel from the source to the reflecting surface will be half of this time, which is $\frac{3}{2} = 1.5$ seconds. This means that sound takes 1.5 seconds to travel from the source to the reflecting surface.

Now, $$\text{Speed} = \frac{\text{Distance}}{\text{Time}}$$

So, $$342 = \frac{\text{Distance}}{1.5}$$

And, $$\text{Distance} = 342 \times 1.5 \text{ m}$$

$$= 513 \text{ m}$$

NCERT Book, Page 169

Q.1. Why are the ceilings of concert halls curved ?

Ans. The ceilings of concert halls are made curved so that sound, after reflection from the curved ceiling, reaches all the parts of the hall. A curved ceiling actually acts like a large concave soundboard and reflects sound down onto the audience sitting in the hall.

NCERT Book, Page 170

Q.1. What is the audible range of the average human ear ?

Ans. The range of frequencies from 20 Hz to 20,000 Hz.

Q.2. What is the range of frequencies associated with :

(*a*) infrasound ?

(*b*) ultrasound ?

Ans. (*a*) Range of frequencies associated with infrasound is less than 20 Hz.

(*b*) Range of frequencies associated with ultrasound is higher than 20,000 Hz.

NCERT Book, Page 172

Q.1. A submarine sends a sonar pulse, which returns from an underwater cliff in 1.02 s. If the speed of sound in salt water is 1531 m/s, how far away is the cliff ?

Ans. Here the time taken by the sonar pulse (or ultrasound) to go from the submarine to the underwater cliff and return to the submarine is 1.02 second. So, the time taken by the sonar pulse (or ultrasound) to go from the submarine to cliff will be half of this time, which is $\frac{1.02}{2} = 0.51$ second. Now, knowing the speed of sound in water, we can calculate the distance travelled by sound in 0.51 second. This will give us the distance of the cliff from the submarine.

We know that : $\text{Speed} = \frac{\text{Distance}}{\text{Time}}$

So, $1531 = \frac{\text{Distance}}{0.51}$

And, $\text{Distance} = 1531 \times 0.51$

$= 780.8 \text{ m}$

NCERT Book, Pages 174 and 175

Q.1. What is sound and how is it produced ?

Ans. Sound is a form of energy which makes us hear. Sound is produced when objects vibrate (move back and forth rapidly). For example, sound can be produced :

(*i*) by vibrating strings (as in a sitar)

(*ii*) by vibrating air (as in a flute)

(*iii*) by vibrating membranes (as in a drum), and

(*iv*) by vibrating plates (as in cymbals)

Q.2. Describe with the help of a diagram, how compressions and rarefactions are produced in air near a source of sound.

Ans. See page 177 of this book.

Q.3. Cite an experiment to show that sound needs a material medium for its propagation.

Ans. See pages 180 and 181 of this book.

Q.4. Why is sound wave called a longitudinal wave ?

Ans. The sound wave is called a longitudinal wave because in a sound wave the particles of the medium vibrate back and forth in the 'same direction' in which the wave is moving.

Q.5. Which characteristic of the sound helps you to identify your friend by his voice while sitting with others in a dark room ?

Ans. Quality (or Timbre) of sound.

Q.6. Flash and thunder are produced simultaneously. But thunder is heard a few seconds after the flash is seen. Why ?

Ans. It is due to the very high speed of light that the flash of lightning is seen first and it is due to comparatively low speed of sound that the thunder is heard a few seconds later (though they are produced at the same time).

Q.7. A person has a hearing range from 20 Hz to 20 kHz. What are the typical wavelengths of sound waves in air corresponding to these two frequencies ? Take the speed of sound in air as 344 m s^{-1}.

Ans. (*i*) *In the first case :*

Speed, $v = 344 \text{ m s}^{-1}$

Frequency, $f = 20$ Hz

And, Wavelength, $\lambda = ?$ (To be calculated)

Now, $v = f \times \lambda$

So, $344 = 20 \times \lambda$

$$\lambda = \frac{344}{20} \text{ m}$$

Wavelength, $\lambda = 17.2$ m ...(1)

(*ii*) *In the second case :*

Speed, $v = 344 \text{ m s}^{-1}$

Frequency, $f = 20$ kHz

$= 20 \times 1000$ Hz (Because 1 kHz = 1000 Hz)

$= 20000$ Hz

And, Wavelength, $\lambda = ?$ (To be calculated)

Now, $v = f \times \lambda$

So, $344 = 20000 \times \lambda$

$$\lambda = \frac{344}{20000}$$

Wavelength, $\lambda = 0.0172$ m ... (2)

Thus, the wavelengths of sound in air corresponding to the frequencies of 20 Hz and 20 kHz are 17.2 m and 0.0172 m respectively.

Q.8. Two children are at opposite ends of an aluminium rod. One strikes the end of rod with a stone. Find the ratio of times taken by sound wave in air and in aluminium to reach the second child (Given : Speed of sound in air = 346 m/s ; Speed of sound in aluminium = 6420 m/s).

Ans. Suppose the length of aluminium rod is l. Then the distance travelled by sound in aluminium as well as in air to reach the second child will be equal to l.

(*i*)
$$\text{Speed of sound (in air)} = \frac{\text{Distance travelled in air}}{\text{Time taken in air}}$$

or
$$346 = \frac{l}{\text{Time taken in air}}$$

And,
$$\text{Time taken in air} = \frac{l}{346} \quad ...(1)$$

(*ii*)
$$\text{Speed of sound (in aluminium)} = \frac{\text{Distance travelled in aluminium}}{\text{Time taken in aluminium}}$$

or
$$6420 = \frac{l}{\text{Time taken in aluminium}}$$

And,
$$\text{Time taken in aluminium} = \frac{l}{6420} \quad ...(2)$$

Now, dividing equation (1) by equation (2), we get :

$$\frac{\text{Time taken by sound in air}}{\text{Time taken by sound in aluminium}} = \frac{l}{346} \times \frac{6420}{l}$$

Cancelling l from the right side, we get :

$$\frac{\text{Time taken by sound in air}}{\text{Time taken by sound in aluminium}} = \frac{6420}{346}$$

$$= \frac{18.55}{1}$$

Thus, the ratio of times taken by the sound waves in air and in aluminum to reach the second child (by travelling the same distance) is 18.55 : 1.

Q.9. The frequency of a source of sound is 100 Hz. How many times does it vibrate in a minute ?

Ans. The frequency of 100 Hz means that the source of sound vibrates 100 times in 1 second. Also, 1 minute is equal to 60 seconds.

Now, No. of vibrations in 1 second = 100

So, No. of vibrations in 60 seconds = 100 × 60

(or 1 minute) = 6000

Thus, the source of sound vibrates 6000 times in a minute.

Q.10. Does sound follow the same laws of reflection as light does ? Explain.

Ans. Sound is reflected in the same way as light. So, the sound follows the same laws of reflection as light does. For example :

(*i*) The incident sound wave, the reflected sound wave, and the normal at the point of incidence, all lie in the same plane.

(*ii*) The angle of reflection of sound is always equal to the angle of incidence of sound.

Q.11. When a sound is reflected from a distant object, an echo is produced. Let the distance between the reflecting surface and the source of sound production remain the same. Do you hear echo sound on a hotter day ?

Ans. The speed of sound increases on a hotter day (when the temperature is high) and it requires a larger distance from the reflecting surface for the echo to be heard. Since the distance between the reflecting surface and the source of sound remains the same, no echo can be heard on a hotter day.

Q.12. Give two practical applications of reflection of sound waves.

Ans. (*i*) The reflection of sound waves is utilised in the working of megaphone (For details, see page 190 of this book).

(*ii*) The reflection of sound waves is utilised in the working of a stethoscope (For details, see page 191 of this book).

Q.13. A stone is dropped from the top of a tower 500 m high into a pond of water at the base of the tower. When is the splash heard at the top ? Given g = 10 m s^{-2} and speed of sound = 340 m s^{-1}.

Ans. Distance covered by stone, s = 500 m

Initial speed, u = 0

Time taken, t = ? (To be calculated)

And, Acceleration, g = 10 m s^{-2}

Now,

$$s = ut + \frac{1}{2}gt^2$$

$$500 = 0 \times t + \frac{1}{2} \times 10 \times t^2$$

$$500 = 5 \times t^2$$

$$t^2 = \frac{500}{5}$$

$$t^2 = 100$$

$$t = \sqrt{100}$$

Time, t = 10 s ... (1)

Thus, the stone takes 10 seconds to fall into pond of water and produce the sound of splash. This sound of splash has to travel a distance of 500 m to be heard at the top of the tower.

Now, $$\text{Speed of sound} = \frac{\text{Distance travelled by sound}}{\text{Time taken by sound}}$$

So, $$340 = \frac{500}{\text{Time taken by sound}}$$

And, $$\text{Time taken by sound} = \frac{500}{340}\text{ s}$$

$$= 1.47 \text{ s} \qquad ...(2)$$

Time after which splash is heard at the top of tower $= 10 \text{ s} + 1.47 \text{ s}$

$= 11.47 \text{ s}$

Q.14. A sound wave travels at a speed of 339 m s^{-1}. If its wavelength is 1.5 cm, what is the frequency of the wave ? Will it be audible ?

Ans. Here, Speed of sound, $v = 339 \text{ m s}^{-1}$

Frequency, $f = ?$ (To be calculated)

Wavelength, $\lambda = 1.5$ cm

$$= \frac{1.5}{100}\text{ m}$$

$$= 0.015 \text{ m}$$

Now, $$v = f \times \lambda$$

So, $$339 = f \times 0.015$$

And, $$f = \frac{339}{0.015}$$

$$\text{Frequency, } f = 22600 \text{ Hz}$$

Since the frequency of 22600 Hz of this sound wave is beyond the upper limit of hearing which is 20000 Hz, therefore, this sound will not be audible. It is actually ultrasonic sound.

Q.15. What is reverberation ? How can it be reduced ?

Ans. The persistence of sound in a big hall due to repeated reflections from the walls, ceiling and floor of the hall is called reverberation. If the reverberation is too long, then the sound becomes blurred, distorted and confusing due to overlapping of different sounds. Some of the methods used for reducing excessive reverberations in big halls and auditoriums are as follows :

(*i*) Panels made of sound-absorbing materials (like compressed fibreboard or felt) are put on the walls and ceiling of big halls and auditoriums to reduce reverberations.

(*ii*) Carpets are put on the floor to absorb sound and reduce reverberations.

(*iii*) Heavy curtains are put on doors and windows to absorb sound and reduce reverberations.

(*iv*) The material having sound-absorbing properties is used for making the seats in a big hall or auditorium to reduce reverberations.

Q.16. What is loudness of sound ? What factors does it depend on ?

Ans. The sensation produced in the ears which enables us to distinguish between a faint sound (feeble sound) and a loud sound is called loudness of sound. The loudness of sound depends on the amplitude of sound waves. Since the amplitude of a sound wave is equal to the amplitude of vibrations of the source which produces the sound wave, we can also say that : The loudness of sound depends on the amplitude of vibration of the source producing the sound waves. This point will become clear from the following example. When we strike a table lightly, then due to less energy supplied, the table top vibrates with a small amplitude and hence a faint sound (or soft sound) is produced. If, however, we hit the table hard, then due to greater energy supplied, the table top vibrates with a large amplitude and hence produces a loud sound. Thus, the loudness of sound depends on the force with which an object is made to vibrate.

Q.17. Explain how bats use ultrasound to catch a prey ?

Ans. Bats emit high-frequency ultrasound squeaks (or ultrasonic squeaks) while flying and listen to the echoes produced by the reflection of their squeaks from the prey like a flying insect. From the time taken by the echo to be heard, bats can judge the distance of the insect and hence catch it.

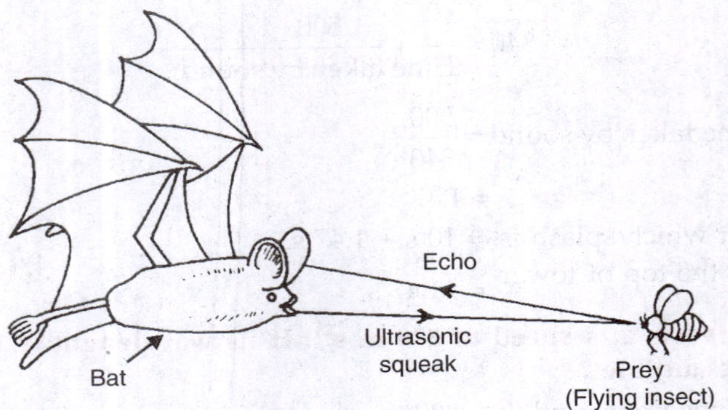

Q.18. How is ultrasound used for cleaning ?

Ans. Ultrasound is used in industry to clean 'hard to reach' parts of objects such as spiral tubes, odd-shaped machines and electronic components, etc. The object to be cleaned is placed in a cleaning solution and ultrasound waves are passed into the solution. Due to their high frequency, the ultrasound waves stir up the cleaning solution. Because of stirring, the particles of dust and grease sticking to the dirty object vibrate too much, become loose, get detached from the object and fall into solution. The object gets cleaned thoroughly.

Q.19. Explain the working and application of a sonar.

Ans. See page 199 of this book.

Q.20. A sonar device on a submarine sends out a signal and receives an echo 5 s later. Calculate the speed of sound in water if the distance of the object from the submarine is 3625 m.

Ans. The time taken by the ultrasound signal sent by sonar device to travel from the submarine to the object, and back to the submarine (in the form of an echo) is 5 seconds. So, the time taken by ultrasound signal to travel from the submarine to the object will be half of this time, which is $\frac{5}{2} = 2.5$ seconds. This means that the sound takes 2.5 seconds to travel from the submarine to the object in sea water.

Now,
$$\text{Speed} = \frac{\text{Distance}}{\text{Time}}$$

$$\text{Speed} = \frac{3625 \text{ m}}{2.5 \text{ s}}$$

$$\text{Speed} = 1450 \text{ m/s}$$

Thus, the speed of sound in sea water is 1450 m/s.

Q.21. Explain how defects in a metal block can be detected using ultrasound.

Ans. See page 197 of this book.

Q.22. Explain how the human ear works.

Ans. See page 205 of this book.

Q.4. Benny is a student of class IX in a city school but his brother John studies in class V. One day John was playing with his friends just outside the house. John had a balloon in his hands. John inflated the balloon by filling air into it. He did not tie the mouth of this air-filled balloon with a thread. John just held the mouth of the inflated balloon tightly in the downward direction (towards the ground) and released it. When the inflated balloon (containing compressed air) was released with its mouth in the downward direction, then the balloon moved upwards on its own. Benny was observing this incident very carefully. The upward going balloon reminded Benny of the principle of working of an important device. Benny also explained everything to his younger brother.

(*a*) Name the device whose principle of working is demonstrated by the inflated balloon released by John ?

(*b*) Name and state the principle (or law) on which the above device works.

(*c*) Explain the working of this device briefly.

(*d*) Which of the Newton's laws can also be said to be involved in the working of the above device ?

(*e*) Name another device which also works on the same principle as this device.

(*f*) What values are displayed by Benny in this episode ?

Ans. (*a*) The upward moving balloon demonstrates the principle of working of a rocket.

(*b*) The rocket works on the principle of conservation of momentum or law of conservation of momentum. According to the law of conservation of momentum : When two (or more) bodies act upon one another, their total momentum remains constant (or conserved) provided no external forces are acting.

(*c*) The chemicals inside the rocket burn and produce high velocity blast of hot gases. These hot gases rush out through the tail nozzle of the rocket in the downward direction with tremendous speed or velocity. Although the mass of gases emitted is comparatively small, but they have a very high velocity and hence a very large momentum. An equal momentum is imparted to the rocket in the opposite direction, so that inspite of its large mass, the rocket goes up with a high velocity (to balance the momentum of downward going gases).

(*d*) Newton's third law of motion (which says : To every action there is an equal and opposite reaction).

(*e*) Jet aeroplanes also work on the same principle as a rocket.

(*f*) The values displayed by Benny in this episode are (*i*) Keen observation of happenings around him (*ii*) knowledge of the working of rockets and jet aeroplanes, and (*iii*) Desire to impart knowledge to his younger brother.

Q.5. Mohan and Sohan are two friends. Both study in class IX in different schools. They have recently studied the chapter on force and motion in their class. Mohan plays cricket in the school team whereas Sohan learns karate. On the sports day celebrations in Sohan's school, there was also an item of karate competition. Sohan invited Mohan to attend the sports day function because he was also taking part in karate competition. For the karate competition, the sports teacher had placed a number of tiles one over the other and supported them at both ends. There were five karate contestants. All the contestants were of almost the same age, same built and same weight. They were supposed to break all the tiles with just one blow of their hand. Each contestant was to be given only one chance for doing this. The first four contesting boys could not break the tiles with a single blow of their hand. They rather got their hands hurt badly. It was now Sohan's turn. Sohan hit the pile of tiles in the middle with a blow of his hand in such a way that all the tiles broke into pieces. All the people standing around started clapping. Mohan was very happy to see his friend win the competition.

(*a*) Which physical quantity is involved in exerting force which breaks the pile of tiles in this competition ?

(*b*) Name two factors which multiply with each other to produce the above physical quantity.

(*c*) Explain why, Sohan was able to break the pile of tiles with a single blow of his hand.

(*d*) Why could the first four boys not break the pile of tiles with a single blow of their hand ?

(*e*) What values are displayed by Sohan in this episode ?

Ans. (*a*) Momentum (of the fast moving hand).

(*b*) Mass (of hand) and velocity (of hand) multiply together to produce momentum.

(*c*) Sohan strikes the pile of tiles with hand very, very fast. In doing so, the large momentum of the fast moving hand is reduced to zero in a very, very short time. This exerts a very large force on the pile of tiles which is sufficient to break them apart.

(*d*) The first four boys perhaps did not strike the pile of tiles with their hands very, very fast. Since the velocity of hands was comparatively less, so the momentum created was less (which could not exert sufficient force to break the pile of tiles).

(*e*) The values displayed by Sohan in this episode are (*i*) Awareness of the concept of momentum (*ii*) Knowledge that since the mass of hand is small, so to create a large momentum, the speed (or velocity) of moving hand has to be very, very large, and (*iii*) Desire to win karate competition.

Q.6. Ankit and Rehman are two friends who live in the same colony. Ankit studies in class IX whereas Rehman is a student of class VIII. One day, both Ankit and Rehman were playing cricket with other boys of the colony in the big ground just outside their colony. At the moment, Ankit and Rehman were standing at two different fielding positions. When batsman hit the ball hard, it went very fast towards Rehman. Rehman stopped and caught the fast moving cricket ball but his hands were hurt badly in stopping the ball. The severe pain in the hands of Rehman made him drop the catch. Next moment, the batsman again hit the ball hard. This time the fast moving ball went straight towards the direction of Ankit. Ankit stopped and caught the fast ball in a particular way without hurting his hands at all. While coming back home after playing cricket, Ankit explained the proper way of catching a fast cricket ball to Rehman without getting the hands hurt. Keeping this advice in mind, Rehman never hurt his hands again while playing cricket.

(*a*) Which physical quantity is very large in a fast moving cricket ball having high speed ?

(*b*) In what way do you think Rehman stopped and caught the fast cricket ball which hurt his hands ?

(*c*) Why were Rehman's hands hurt in stopping and catching the fast cricket ball in this way ?

(*d*) In what way do you think Ankit stopped and caught the fast cricket ball without hurting his hands ?

(*e*) Why were Ankit's hands not hurt in stopping and catching the fast cricket ball in this way ?

(*f*) Which law of motion is involved in catching a fast cricket ball ?

(*g*) What values are displayed by Ankit in this episode ?

Ans. (*a*) A fast moving cricket ball has a large 'momentum'.

(*b*) Rehman must have stopped (or caught) the fast moving cricket ball suddenly, keeping his hands stationary.

(*c*) When Rehman stopped (or caught) the fast moving cricket ball suddenly (keeping his hands stationary), then the large momentum of the fast ball was reduced to zero in a very short time. Due to this, the rate of change of momentum of cricket ball was very large and hence it exerted a large force on Rehman's hands. This large force hurt his hands.

(*d*) Ankit must have moved his hands backwards gradually (on catching the fast cricket ball).

(*e*) When Ankit moved back his hands gradually on catching a fast ball, then the time taken to reduce the large momentum of fast ball to zero was increased. Due to more time taken to stop the fast ball, the rate of change of momentum of ball was decreased and hence a small force was exerted on the hands of Ankit. This small force did not hurt Ankit's hands.

(*f*) Newton's second law of motion.

(*g*) The values displayed by Ankit in this episode are (*i*) Awareness (or knowledge) of Newton's second law of motion (*ii*) Application of knowledge in everyday situations, and (*iii*) Concern for the safety of his friend.

Q.7. Rohan is a student of class IX in a city school. Rohan visited his ancestral village alongwith his grandmother during the summer holidays. One day a *Baba* came to the village and told the villagers that he can perform a miracle by lying down on a bed of nails. So, a bed having thousands of nails was made for him. When all the village people had gathered, *Baba* recited a few *mantras* loudly and lay down on the bed of nails very, very carefully. The high point of this so called miracle was that *Baba* was not hurt at all by the large number of nails below his body. All the village people were highly impressed by this miracle of *Baba*. Even Rohan's grandmother was greatly impressed by this feat. But Rohan, who studies science, was not impressed at all. In fact, Rohan told the gathered village people that it was no miracle. This feat of *Baba* was based on a well known scientific principle. He told the people that any person can lie on a bed of nails unhurt, if there is a very large number of nails. Even he could lie on the same bed of nails without being hurt. He explained the underlying scientific principle to all the people. Even *Baba* was surprised by the knowledge of a school boy like Rohan.

(*a*) Which concept of science is involved in the show put up by *Baba* by lying down on a bed of nails ?

(*b*) Define and explain the above concept.

(*c*) What happens if we step barefooted on a nail accidently ? Explain.

(d) Why did *Baba* not get hurt by lying down on a bed of nails ? Explain.

(e) What values are displayed by Rohan ?

Ans. (a) The concept of science involved in the show put up by *Baba* is that of 'pressure'.

(b) Pressure is the force acting on a unit area of an object. The same force can produce different pressures depending on the size of the area over which it acts. For example :

(i) When a force acts on a small area of an object, it produces a large pressure.

(ii) But when the same force acts over a large area of the object, then it produces a small pressure.

(c) If we step barefooted on a nail accidently, then our foot gets hurt badly. This is because then the force of our entire body weight falls on the extremely small area of the tip of a single nail making the pressure extremely large. It is this extremely large pressure on a single nail which can pierce our foot and hurt the foot badly.

(d) The bed of nails has thousands of nails close to one another. When the *Baba* lies down on the bed of thousands of nails, then the force of his body weight gets distributed over the large area of thousands of nails. Due to this, the net pressure on a single nail becomes very small and hence the *Baba's* body does not get hurt at all.

(e) The various values displayed by Rohan are (i) Knowledge of the concept of pressure (ii) Application of knowledge in everyday situations, and (iii) Desire to remove the myth (false belief) of miracles from the minds of village people.

Q.8. Ravi is a student of class IX in a Delhi School. This year all the students of class IX were going to visit Kashmir during the winter holidays alongwith some of their teachers. All the students were asked to pack heavy woollen clothes with them because winter in Kashmir is very severe. Ravi had recently studied a particular chapter in science. Keeping that in mind, Ravi also purchased a pair of special type of shoes from the market and packed it alongwith his luggage. When the students reached Srinagar, it was extremely cold. When the students got up in the morning next day, they were told that heavy snowfall is going on in this area since last night and that there were thick layers of snow all around their hotel. Most of the students had not seen snowfall before. So, all the students and teachers decided to walk and play on fresh falling snow. Ravi put on his special shoes while walking on snow. It was noticed that the feet of all other students and teachers wearing ordinary shoes were sinking into soft snow making it very difficult for them to walk on soft snow. But this was not so with Ravi. Ravi could walk easily even on soft snow (without his feet sinking into it). All the students were very jealous of Ravi. But the teachers were all praise for Ravi.

(a) Which concept of science is involved in the incident which took place on soft snow ?

(b) Why do the feet of a student wearing ordinary shoes sink into soft snow ?

(c) What are the special shoes worn by Ravi called ? How do they differ from ordinary shoes ?

(d) Explain why, by wearing special shoes, Ravi could walk easily on soft snow (without his feet sinking into soft snow).

(e) What are a pair of long, narrow pieces of hard flexible material fastened under the feet for sliding very fast on the slopes of snow covered mountains called (which work on the same principle as snow shoes) ?

(f) What values are displayed by Ravi in this episode ?

Ans. (a) Pressure.

(b) The feet of a student wearing ordinary shoes sink into soft snow because due to the small size of the sole of the shoes, the weight of a student falls on a small area of soft snow producing a large pressure.

(c) The special shoes worn by Ravi are called 'snow shoes'. The area of sole of snow shoes (which comes in contact with snow) is much bigger than the area of sole of ordinary shoes worn by us in everyday life.

(d) By wearing snow shoes Ravi could walk easily on soft snow (without sinking into it) because due to large area of the sole of snow shoes, the weight of Ravi is spread over a large area of soft snow producing small pressure.

(e) Skis (*singular* : Ski).

(f) The values displayed by Ravi in this episode are (i) Knowledge of the concept of pressure (ii) Application of knowledge in real-life situations, and (iii) Foresight (in taking along snow shoes expecting snowfall in Kashmir during winter).

Q.9. Raman was waiting at a tyre puncture repair shop to get his bicycle tube repaired. There is a large pond of water a little distance away from this shop. Some children were playing near the pond. Raman saw a five year old child fall into the pond accidently while playing. The child was drowning in pond water and screaming for help. Raman took a big, inflated 'car rubber tube' which was lying in the shop and immediately threw it towards the drowning child in the pond. He shouted asking the child to cling to the inflated tube and hold on to it strongly till the help arrived. Raman then made a telephone call to Fire Brigade from his mobile phone. The Fire Brigade reached within ten minutes and the firemen brought the drowning child out of the pond safely. Everybody praised the efforts of Raman and firemen.

(*a*) What happens when an inflated car tube is thrown in water of the pond ? Why ?

(*b*) Why did Raman throw an inflated car rubber tube towards the drowning child and ask him to hold on to it ?

(*c*) Which principle is made use of by Raman in saving the drowning child ? State this principle.

(*d*) What values are displayed by Raman in this episode ?

Ans. (*a*) When an inflated car rubber tube is put in water, it floats in water. This can be explained as follows : The inflated rubber tube contains a lot of compressed air in it. Now, air is a very, very light substance. So, due to the presence of lot of air in it, the average density of inflated car tube is much less than the density of water. Since the average density of inflated car tube is less than that of water, therefore, the inflated car tube floats in water.

(*b*) Raman threw an inflated car rubber tube towards the drowning child and asked him to hold on to this inflated tube because the inflated rubber tube would remain floating in water and, alongwith it, the child would also remain floating in water and not get drowned. Actually, when the child clings to the inflated rubber tube, then (due to his weight) more portion of inflated rubber tube gets submerged in water, it displaces more water and hence the upward 'buoyant force' increases. This greater upward 'buoyant force' keeps the inflated rubber tube and the child holding it, both afloat on the surface of pond water (and prevents drowning).

(*c*) Raman made use of the principle of flotation. According to the principle of flotation : An object will float in a liquid if the weight of object is equal to the weight of liquid displaced by it.

(*d*) The various values displaced by Raman are (*i*) Knowledge of principle of flotation (*ii*) Application of knowledge in everyday situations (*iii*) Presence of mind (in throwing an inflated tube immediately towards the drowning child) (*iv*) Responsible citizen (in calling Fire Brigade to rescue the drowning child), and (*v*) Helping nature (in saving drowning child).

Q.10. Abhishek lives in society flats alongwith his parents. He is studying in class IX. For the last few days, his mother has been complaining that the milk being supplied by the milkman is not pure. When she talked to other neighbours, they told her that they are also facing the same problem. Abhishek thought over this problem for a while. He then went to the market and purchased a glass instrument to check the purity of milk being supplied by the milkman. When milkman brought milk the next day, Abhishek took this milk in a tall vessel and placed the instrument in it vertically. He explained to the milkman how this instrument indicated that the milk was not pure, it was adulterated. The milkman admitted his fault and promised to supply pure milk in future. Abhishek told about this incident to all his neighbours. Ultimately all the households in the society flats purchased the instrument to test the purity of milk.

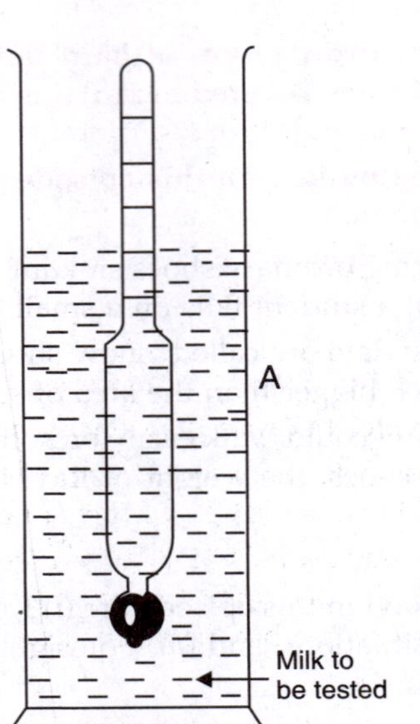

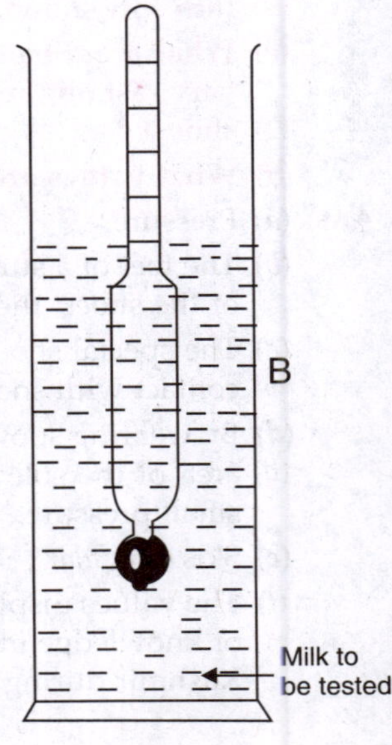

(*a*) Name the instrument which was purchased by Abhishek to check the purity of milk.

(*b*) Name the principle on which the above instrument works.

(*c*) **What substance is usually mixed with pure milk by the dishonest milkmen to adulterate it and increase their profit ?**

(*d*) **Which physical quantity of pure milk is used to detect the presence of the substance mixed in it (which is measured by the above instrument) ?**

(*e*) **How does the instrument purchased by Abhishek show the presence of the substance mixed in pure milk by the milkman ?**

(*f*) **Which position of the instrument placed in two containers of milk A and B (one by one) shows (*i*) pure milk, and (*ii*) adulterated milk ?**

(*g*) **What values are displayed by Abhishek in this episode ?**

Ans. (*a*) Lactometer (It is used to find out the amount of water mixed in pure milk).

(*b*) Lactometer works on the principle of flotation.

(*c*) Water is mixed with pure milk to adulterate it.

(*d*) Relative density (Relative density of pure milk is higher than that of impure milk containing water).

(*e*) (*i*) Since the relative density of pure milk is higher, therefore, pure milk will exert more upward (buoyant) force on the lactometer bulb due to which lactometer will float higher (with more of its calibrated tube above the milk level) when placed in a container of pure milk.

(*ii*) The relative density of water is lower than that of pure milk. So, when water is mixed with pure milk, then the relative density of adulterated milk becomes less than that of pure milk. Due to lower relative density, adulterated milk exerts less upward (buoyant) force on lactometer bulb due to which lactometer will sink more and float at lower level when placed in a container of adulterated milk.

(*f*) (*i*) Container B contains pure milk (*ii*) Container A contains adulterated milk (containing water mixed in it).

(*g*) The values displayed by Abhishek in this episode are (*i*) Awareness of the availability of lactometer to check the purity of milk (*ii*) Knowledge of principle of flotation and working of lactometer (*iii*) Idea of relative density of pure milk and water, and (*iv*) Desire to protect his family and neighbours from being cheated by dishonest milkman.

Q.11. One day all the students of class IX were performing physics experiments in the science laboratory. Just then, the physics teacher, Mr. Vinay, came to the laboratory with a sheet of tin weighing about half a kilogram. Mr. Vinay gathered all the students and in their presence put this sheet of tin in a big tub of water. The sheet of tin sank in water and settled at the bottom of tub. Mr. Vinay now turned to the students and asked who could transform this sheet into the simplest form (or shape) which would float in water. He allowed them to use any other required tools/materials from the laboratory for this purpose. Mohan offered to make an appropriate object from this tin sheet which could float in water and not sink. He took just half an hour to make this object. The teacher placed this object in the same tub of water. It started to float in water. The teacher was very happy. He appreciated the effort made by Mohan.

(*a*) **Why did the sheet of tin sink in water ?**

(*b*) **What do you think is the simplest form of object made by Mohan from this tin sheet which could float in water ?**

(*c*) **Why do you think the above object made from tin sheet floats in water ?**

(*d*) **Name two modes of transport used in rivers and seas which work on the same principle as the tin sheet object made by Mohan.**

(*e*) **The tin object made by Mohan was placed, turn by turn, in a tub of oil and glycerine. In which of these two liquids, the tin object will float with a greater part of it immersed inside the liquid than water and why ?**

(*f*) **What values are displayed by Mohan in this episode ?**

Ans. (*a*) The sheet of tin sinks in water because the density of tin is greater than that of water.

(*b*) Mohan may have made a water-proof box from the tin sheet (by using appropriate cutting tools and sealing materials). This hollow box made of the same tin sheet floats in water.

(*c*) The hollow tin box contains a lot of air in it. Air is a very, very light substance. Due to the presence of a lot of air in it, the average density of tin box becomes less than the density of water. And due to less average density than water, the hollow tin box floats in water.

(*d*) Boats and ships are the two modes of transport used in rivers and seas which float in water on the same principle as the hollow tin box made by Mohan.

(*e*) The tin box will float with its greater part immersed in oil (than in water) because oil has a lower density than water. Due to its lower density than water, oil exerts less upward (buoyant) force on tin box due to which it will sink more in oil (than water) and then float in it.

(*f*) The various values displayed by Mohan in this episode are (*i*) Awareness of Archimedes' principle (*ii*) Knowledge of factors affecting buoyant force (like volume of solid object immersed in a liquid and density of liquid) (*iii*) Application of knowledge in solving problems, and (*iv*) Accepting challenge (to do a job).

Q.12. Rajan went on a World Tour with his family during the summer holidays. Actually, it was a group tour consisting of 40 persons arranged by a leisure travel company 'Thomas Cook'. Today the whole group was taken to a sea that lies between Israel and Jordan, and has become a famous tourist spot. On reaching the seashore, everyone was surprised to see a person floating in this sea water in the sitting position and even reading a newspaper in this position. The Guide, Mr. Jose, who accompanied the group, asked if anyone could explain this strange observation. Rajan is a science student of class IX. Rajan took a little of sea water in his palm and put it into his mouth for a moment (and then spit it out). After thinking for a while, he could answer Mr. Jose's question. Rajan then explained everything very clearly to all the persons in the group. Everyone appreciated his knowledge of science.

(*a*) What is the name of the sea which lies between Israel and Jordan ?

(*b*) Why is this sea called by this name ?

(*c*) What did Rajan find when he put a little of water from this sea into his mouth for a moment ?

(*d*) Explain why, a person can float in this sea water in the sitting position.

(*e*) Why is it not possible to float in sitting position in the water of Indian sea ?

(*f*) What values are displayed by Rajan in this episode ?

Ans. (*a*) Dead sea.

(*b*) It is called 'Dead sea' because due to its very high salt content, no living things (plants and animals) can exist in it.

(*c*) When Rajan put a little of this sea water in his mouth, he found it to be extremely salty (having a lot of salts dissolved in it).

(*d*) The water of Dead sea has an extremely large amount of salts dissolved in it. Due to large amounts of dissolved salts, the density of this sea water is very, very high. Because of extremely high density, the water of Dead sea exerts a very, very large upward 'buoyant force' (or upthrust) that makes a person float in it sitting up.

(*e*) Indian sea water contains much less dissolved salts than the water of Dead sea. So, the salty water of Indian sea exerts much less upward 'buoyant force' (or upthrust) which is not able to support the weight of a person in sitting up position.

(*f*) The various values displayed by Rajan in this episode are (*i*) Awareness of buoyant force exerted by liquids (*ii*) Knowledge of factors affecting the magnitude of buoyant force (such as density of liquid) (*iii*) Application of knowledge in solving problems, and (*iv*) Analytical mind (in checking sea water).

Q.13. There is a four storeyed house in the neighbourhood of Rohan and Amit which has two types of staircases in it. One is a normal, slanting type staircase which is inside the house and the other one is a spiral type (vertical) staircase at the back side of the house. Both the staircases lead from the ground floor to the roof of the house. Rohan and Amit are both students of class IX in different schools. Incidently, they are both of the same weight. Rohan said that a person using slanting staircase inside the house would do more work against a certain 'natural force' in going from ground floor to the roof of the house (because the distance moved by the person in using the slanting staircase is more). Rohan also said that the work done by the same person against the same natural force in going from ground floor to roof of the house would be less by using the spiral type (vertical) staircase (because the distance moved by him in this case will be less). Amit, however, did not agree with Rohan. Amit said that whether this person uses slanting staircase or spiral type (vertical) staircase, work done by him against the natural force in going from ground floor to roof of the house would be the same. Rohan then decided to go from the ground floor to

the roof top by slanting staircase and took 90 seconds for doing this job. On the other hand, Amit went from ground floor to the roof top by spiral type (vertical) staircase and took 2 minutes for this job.

(a) Name the natural force against which work has to be done in going from ground floor to the roof top of the house.

(b) What supplies energy for doing work when Rohan and Amit climb up to the roof of the house ?

(c) Whose statement about the amount of work done against the natural force in going from ground floor to roof top is correct and why ?

(d) Who has more power in terms of physics in climbing to roof top : Rohan or Amit ? Why ?

(e) What values are displayed by Amit in this episode ?

Ans. (*a*) The force of gravity.

(*b*) Food supplies the chemical energy for doing work.

(*c*) Amit's statement about the amount of work done against gravity in going from ground floor to roof top is correct. This is because when the work is done against gravity, then the distance moved by the person is the 'vertical distance' through which the person lifts himself against gravity. And the vertical distance moved up by a person in going from ground floor to roof top of the house is the same whether he uses slanting staircase or spiral type staircase. Due to this, the work done by the person against gravity in both the cases is the same.

(*d*) Rohan does the work of going from ground floor to roof top in 90 seconds whereas Amit does the same amount of work in 2 minutes or $2 \times 60 = 120$ seconds. Since Rohan takes lesser time (of 90 seconds) to do the same work, so the rate of doing work (or power) of Rohan is more than that of Amit.

(*e*) The values displayed by Amit in this episode are (*i*) Awareness of the force of gravity (*ii*) Correct knowledge of the work done against gravity, and (*iii*) Application of knowledge in solving everyday problems.

Q.14. Jagdish is a student of class IX in a city where electricity supply comes from a thermal power house. The State Government has recently raised electricity tariff substantially due to which the electricity bill received by Jagdish's family this month is very high. Jagdish's family was worried about heavy electricity bills to be paid every month from now onwards. Jagdish was worried too. Jagdish thought over the problem and came out with some suggestions. He explained the various steps to be taken to reduce the electricity bill to some extent to his parents. His father and mother liked his ideas. Even his younger sister promised to cooperate in cost-cutting measures. When the suggestions made by Jagdish were put into practice, the next month's electricity bill was substantially lower than expected. Everyone in the family was happy. Because 'money saved' is 'money earned' !

(a) What is meant by a thermal power house ?

(b) What fuels are usually used in thermal power houses ?

(c) How is electricity produced at a thermal power house ?

(d) What energy transformations take place at a thermal power house ?

(e) What steps do you think were suggested by Jagdish to reduce the consumption of electricity in his house ?

(f) What values are displayed by Jagdish in this episode ?

Ans. (*a*) The term 'thermal' means 'of or related to heat'. A thermal power house is an installation where heat energy produced by the combustion of a fuel (or burning of a fuel) is used to generate electricity.

(*b*) The fuels used in thermal power houses are usually coal and natural gas.

(*c*) At a thermal power house, coal (or natural gas) is burnt to obtain heat energy. This heat then boils water to form steam. The high pressure steam turns the steam turbine. The steam turbine then drives (or rotates) the electric generator (or alternator) to produce electricity.

(*d*) At a thermal power house, when coal (or natural gas) is burnt, then the chemical energy of coal (or natural gas) is transformed into heat energy. This heat energy converts water into steam. The high pressure steam turns the steam turbine and transforms the heat energy into kinetic energy of turning turbine. The kinetic energy of turbine then rotates the electric generator. The electric generator transforms kinetic energy into electrical energy. These energy transformations can be written as :

$$\text{Chemical energy} \longrightarrow \text{Heat energy} \longrightarrow \text{Kinetic energy} \longrightarrow \text{Electrical energy}$$

(*e*) The various steps which could have been suggested by Jagdish to reduce the consumption of electricity in his house are :

(*i*) Switch off the lights, fans, TV and other electrical appliances when not required (to prevent wastage of electricity).

(*ii*) Replace all the traditional filament-type electric bulbs by CFLs (Compact Fluorescent Lamps) because CFLs consume much less electricity.

(*iii*) Use solar water heater (instead of electric geyser) to obtain hot water.

(*iv*) Use solar cooker to cook some types of foods, whenever possible.

(*v*) Get the household electric wiring checked properly by an electrician to prevent the leakage of electricity, if any.

(*f*) The various values displayed by Jagdish in this episode are (*i*) Awareness of various steps to save electricity (*ii*) Concern for the conservation of fossil fuels (coal and natural gas) which are used to generate electricity, and (*iii*) Desire to reduce electricity bill of his house.

Q.15. Ram is a college student in Delhi. Ram and his family are going by car to visit a hill station. Ram himself is driving the car. Ram drives the car very carefully. Before starting to drive, Ram has fastened the car seat belt himself properly. He has also made his father, mother and younger brother fasten their car seat belts. On the flat highway road, Ram is keeping the car speed within a range of 50 to 60 kmph (which is well within the prescribed speed limit on this highway). He does not accelerate the car unnecessarily. After driving for about five hours continuously on a flat road, there is a sight of hills in view. On approaching the hilly road, Ram increases the speed of his car. Ram's younger brother Anish, who is a student of class VI, is surprised to see his brother increasing the speed of car suddenly. Anish asks Ram why the speed of car has been increased. Ram explains the reason for increasing the speed of car to everyone.

(*a*) What type of energy is possessed by the car while running on the flat road ?

(*b*) What type of energy transformations take place in a car engine ?

(*c*) When the car is moving on the flat road, it has to do work to overcome mainly two types of forces. Name these two types of forces.

(*d*) When the car is moving on an uphill road, it has to do work to overcome three types of forces. Name these three types of forces.

(*e*) Why does Ram increase the speed of his car on approaching the hilly road ?

(*f*) What types of energy is possessed by the car going up on the hilly road ?

(*g*) What values are displayed by Ram in this episode ?

Ans. (*a*) The car running on a flat road possesses 'kinetic energy'.

(*b*) The car burns petrol as fuel. The car engine first converts the chemical energy of petrol into heat energy. This heat energy is then converted into kinetic energy (which drives the wheels of the car). The transformations of energy taking place in a car engine can be written as :

$$\underset{\text{(of petrol)}}{\text{Chemical energy}} \longrightarrow \text{Heat energy} \longrightarrow \text{Kinetic energy}$$

(*c*) When the car is moving on a flat road, it has to do work to overcome (*i*) friction of the road, and (*ii*) air resistance.

(*d*) When the car is moving on an uphill road, then it has to do work to overcome (*i*) friction of the road (*ii*) air resistance, and (*iii*) force of gravity.

(*e*) Ram increases the speed of car on approaching a hilly road to give more kinetic energy to the car so that it may go up the hill against gravity.

(*f*) The car going up on the hilly road possesses (*i*) kinetic energy, and (*ii*) gravitational potential energy.

(*g*) The various values displayed by Ram in this episode are (*i*) Concern for the safety of his family (as shown by the fastening of car seat belts and driving within speed limit) (*ii*) Conservation of fuel or petrol (by driving the car within a specified speed range and avoiding unnecessary accelerating) (*iii*) Awareness (that car needs more kinetic energy to go up on a hilly road), and (*iv*) Knowledge (that kinetic energy of car can be increased by increasing its speed).

Q.16. Saurabh is a student of class IX whereas his younger brother Ashu studies in class VI. During the summer holidays, Saurabh and Ashu went to visit their uncle who lives in a village. Their uncle has a big mango orchard near the village which has produced a bumper crop of mangoes this year. On the way to village, Saurabh purchased a catapult (*gulel*) from a shop because he enjoys felling ripe mangoes from the mango trees of orchard with the help of catapult. On reaching his uncle's mango orchard, Saurabh gave a tiny

piece of stone to Ashu and asked him to put it in the catapult and hit any mango on the tree. Ashu tried to throw away the stone with catapult without stretching the rubber strings of catapult. Due to this, the piece of stone fell down to the ground instead of reaching the mango on the tree. Saurabh then taught Ashu how to use the catapult properly. By using this catapult and tiny pieces of stones, Ashu was now able to fell many ripe mangoes from the orchard trees. Ashu then saw a beautiful bird sitting on the branch of a mango tree. When Ashu was aiming the catapult at the bird, Saurabh snatched the catapult from his hands quickly and scolded him. Meanwhile, Saurabh's uncle also reached the orchard. He was happy to see Saurabh and Ashu enjoying the mangoes which they had felled from the orchard trees.

(*a*) Which type of energy is possessed by the stretched rubber strings of a catapult ?.

(*b*) How do the catapult strings get this energy ?

(*c*) What energy transformation takes place when the stretched rubber strings of catapult throw away a piece of stone ?

(*d*) Why did the piece of stone just fall down when Ashu tried to throw it away without stretching the rubber strings of catapult ?

(*e*) When a mango attached to the tree is hit by a piece of stone thrown by catapult, the mango falls down. Which force causes mango to fall down ?

(*f*) Why did Saurabh prevent his brother Ashu from aiming catapult at the bird ?

(*g*) What values are displayed by Saurabh in this episode ?

Ans. (*a*) The stretched rubber strings of a catapult possess 'elastic potential energy'.

(*b*) When we do work in stretching the rubber strings of catapult, then the work done by us gets stored in the stretched rubber strings in the form of elastic potential energy.

(*c*) The stretched rubber strings possess elastic potential energy whereas the piece of stone thrown away by it possesses kinetic energy. So, the energy transformation taking place is :

$$\text{Elastic potential energy} \rightarrow \text{Kinetic energy}$$

(*d*) The unstretched rubber strings of catapult do not possess elastic potential energy due to which the piece of stone is not thrown away, it just falls to the ground by the action of gravity.

(*e*) The force of gravity causes mango to fall down.

(*f*) Saurabh prevented his brother Ashu from aiming catapult at the bird because he did not want the bird to get injured or killed.

(*g*) The values displayed by Saurabh in this episode are (*i*) Adventurous nature (because he went all the way to village to enjoy fresh orchard mangoes) (*ii*) Helping nature (because he taught his younger brother the proper use of catapult), and (*iii*) Protection of wildlife (because he prevents his brother from injuring or killing the bird).

Q.17. Veena's elder sister Rashmi, who is four months pregnant, has come to stay with them for a week. Veena's mother, Mrs. Nirmala, wanted to take Rashmi to a gynaecologist for a prenatal (before birth) medical check-up. Veena also accompanied them to the hospital. The gynaecologist carried out the required physical examination of Rashmi and then recommended a particular scan to be done. While going to the Imaging Department of the hospital, Mrs. Nirmala said that after the scan is done, she would ask the doctor doing the scan a specific question about the foetus. Veena is a student of class X who has studied the reproductive systems of humans in the class. She could make out what her mother was going to ask the doctor about the developing foetus. Veena asked her mother not to ask any irrelevant question based on the scan to be done and explained the reason for it. Mrs. Nirmala agreed to what Veena had said. After the required scan was done, all of them visited the gynaecologist again. The gynaecologist studied the scan carefully and said that everything was okay. Everyone was happy. While coming back home, Mrs. Nirmala said that instead of going to a far off hospital the same purpose could have been served by getting an X-ray done on Rashmi at the neighbourhood X-ray clinic. Veena did not agree with her mother. She said a firm 'No' to X-ray on Rashmi at this stage.

(*a*) What type of scan was recommended by gynaecologist for Rashmi ? Name the machine used for this purpose.

(*b*) Why was the above scan recommended ?

(*c*) Describe the principle of working of the scanning machine briefly. What is this technique known as ?

(*d*) What do you think was the irrelevant question which Mrs. Nirmala wanted to ask the doctor after the scan was done ?

(*e*) Why did Veena tell her mother not to ask such a question ?

(f) Why did Veena say 'No' to X-ray for Rashmi ?

(g) What values are displayed by Veena in this episode ?

Ans. (a) The gynaecologist recommended 'ultrasound scan' for Rashmi. An 'ultrasound scanner' machine is used for this purpose.

(b) The gynaecologist recommended ultrasound scan for Rashmi for the examination of foetus (unborn child) during pregnancy to detect any abnormality in the growth so that necessary steps could be taken to rectify the abnormality (if any) well in time.

(c) The ultrasound scanner works on the principle of reflection of sound (or rather principle of reflection of ultrasound). This happens as follows : The ultrasound scanner transmits ultrasound pulses into the pregnant woman's body and receives echoes formed by the reflection of ultrasound from the foetus inside the uterus. These ultrasound echoes form a picture of the developing baby on a computer screen which helps the doctor to keep a track of the developing baby and detect any growth abnormalities, etc. The technique of obtaining pictures of the internal organs of the body (having different densities) by using echoes of ultrasound pulses is called ultrasonography.

(d) Mrs. Nirmala wanted to ask about the sex (boy or girl) of the foetus (unborn child) of Rashmi.

(e) Veena knew that there is a law which prohibits doctors to tell the sex or gender of the unborn child.

(f) Veena said 'No' to X-ray for Rashmi because X-rays can damage the delicate body cells of the foetus. This is not so in using ultrasound for taking scans.

(g) The various values displayed by Veena in this episode are (i) Responsible citizen (in preventing her mother from knowing the sex of unborn child) (ii) Concern for the girl child (because sex determination of foetus can lead to female foeticide), and (iii) Concern for the healthy growth of her sister's unborn child (by not allowing Rashmi to be exposed to X-rays).

Q.18. Kunal has just appeared in class IX examination. All his examination papers are over. But Kunal's younger brother Rakesh, who is a student of class VII, is still preparing for his final examination. Yesterday, a man entered their colony in the afternoon. This man was a 'zip-repairer'. He was shouting through a large, cone-shaped, battery-less, amplifying device to make announcements for getting customers for his work. The hand-held device was making his voice too loud. As Rakesh was studying for his examination, he got disturbed by the loud announcements being made by this man. Rakesh told about this noise pollution problem to his elder brother Kunal because many other students living in the colony were also preparing for their examination and must be getting disturbed in their studies. Rakesh also asked Kunal about the amplifying device being used by this man. Kunal then went out of the house and talked to the man who was making announcements. The man immediately stopped using the device for making further announcements. Kunal also went to the security incharge at the entry gate of the colony and lodged a complaint regarding this incident.

(a) What do you think was the device being used by the man to amplify his voice ?

(b) State the principle on which this device works.

(c) Why did Rakesh get disturbed ?

(d) What do you think Kunal must have told the 'zip-repairer' man ?

(e) What complaint do you think Kunal must have lodged with the security incharge of the colony ?

(f) Name one very useful instrument which works on the same principle as the device discussed in this episode. For what purpose is it used ?

(g) What values are displayed by Kunal in this episode ?

Ans. (a) The device being used by the zip-repairing man to amplify his voice was megaphone. It is also known as loud-hailer.

(b) Megaphone works on the principle of 'multiple reflections of sound'.

(c) Rakesh got disturbed because due to the noise pollution caused by the use of megaphone, he could not concentrate on his studies.

(d) Kunal must have told the 'zip-repairer' man that since many students of the colony are preparing for their final examinations, he should not disturb their studies by using megaphone to make the announcements.

(e) Kunal must have complained to the security incharge of the colony that such unauthorised persons should not be allowed to enter the residential colony to create noise pollution and disturb their peace of mind.

(f) A stethoscope works on the same principle (multiple reflections of sound) as the megaphone. A stethoscope is used by doctors to listen to the sounds produced within the human body, mainly in the heart and lungs.

(*g*) The various values displayed by Kunal is this episode are (*i*) Awareness of megaphone and its working (*ii*) Helping nature (in helping his brother and other students study in peace without any disturbance), and (*iii*) Social responsibility (in asking for a ban on the entry of hawkers inside the residential colony who disturb their peace).

Q.19. Ramesh and Sandeep are two very close friends who study in classes IX and X respectively. One day Ramesh and Sandeep had to go to a neighbouring town on their bicycles for some work. They had to cross a railway line on the way to the neighbouring town. When Ramesh and Sandeep were going in the afternoon, the railway crossing barrier was open, so they did not have to wait for going across it. Their work in the neighbouring town kept Ramesh and Sandeep busy till late in the evening. On their way back home, when Ramesh and Sandeep reached the same railway crossing, it was quite dark in the night and the railway crossing barrier was down (or closed) indicating that some train was expected to pass through soon. Ramesh was in a hurry to go back home. Ramesh told Sandeep that since he could not hear the sound of approaching train, so they did not know when the train would pass through the crossing and barrier would open. He suggested that instead of keeping on waiting, they should cross the railway tracks by going below the closed barrier by tilting their bicycles and lowering their heads. Sandeep did not agree with Ramesh. Sandeep said that they would not cross the railway tracks as long as the barrier was closed. Suddenly, Ramesh slipped through the barrier and put his ear on the railway track. Sandeep pulled him away from the railway track quickly. As soon as Ramesh was pulled away from the railway track, a super-fast train passed through the same track in the darkness of night without blowing any horn. Sandeep was very angry with Ramesh and scolded him for the risk he had taken. After the train passed through the crossing, the barrier was opened by railway staff. Ramesh and Sandeep then crossed the railway track alongwith their bicycles and reached home safely.

(*a*) How many times more is the speed of sound in railway track than the speed of sound in air ?

(*b*) Why did Sandeep not allow Ramesh to cross the closed barrier of railway crossing ?

(*c*) Why did Ramesh put his ear to the railway track ?

(*d*) Why did Sandeep pull Ramesh away from the railway track ?

(*e*) What values are displayed by Sandeep in this episode ?

Ans. (*a*) Railway track is made of steel. The speed of sound in railway track (made of steel) is about 15 times more than the speed of sound in air.

(*b*) Sandeep did not allow Ramesh to pass through the closed barrier of railway crossing because it is very risky to do so. A closed barrier indicates that a train could pass through this crossing any time. And if a person is crossing the railway tracks at the time when a train is approaching very fast, it can lead to a train accident in which the person can get injured seriously or even killed (more especially in the darkness of night).

(*c*) Ramesh put his ear to the railway track to hear the sound of coming train through the railway track made of steel and get an idea of the distance of the incoming train (because the speed of sound in railway track made of steel is very high as compared to the speed of sound in air).

(*d*) Sandeep pulled Ramesh away from the railway track quickly because he did not want Ramesh to be involved in a train accident.

(*e*) The various values displayed by Sandeep in this episode are (*i*) Awareness that most of the train accidents are fatal (which cause death) (*ii*) Desire to prevent train accident (by not passing through

Life is short. Don't make it shorter.

closed railway crossing barrier), and (*iii*) Concern for the safety of his friend (in pulling him away from railway track).

Q.20. Radha is a student of class IX in a school in Ambala city in Haryana. Radha's father, Mr. Vijay Kumar, is the Deputy Commissioner of Police in Ambala zone. Radha's family including her father, mother and five year old brother Pulkit, were invited for the celebrations of Air Force Day at the Ambala Air Force Base. During these celebrations, the final item was a fly-past by the fighter jet planes of Indian Air Force. Suddenly there was a loud, explosive noise in the sky over the celebration venue. All the eyes turned up towards the sky. Everybody saw the Indian Air Force's fighter jet planes flying at tremendous speed in a special formation. All the people started clapping for this beautiful and daring fly-past by Indian Air Force pilots. The thunderous sound produced by the speeding fighter planes was so loud that all the birds sitting on the nearby trees flew away. Radha's brother Pulkit was already undergoing treatment for some ear ailment. So, Pulkit got too much pain in his ears due to this intolerable explosive sound. Pulkit was carrying two sharpened pencils with him at that time. He tried to put these pencils inside his ears to get relief from severe pain in the ears. Radha snatched the pencils from Pulkit and warned him not to do it again. Radha was carrying some cotton ear buds in her purse. So, she put cotton ear buds into the ears of Pulkit. These ear buds reduced Pulkit's pain so he enjoyed the remaining part of fly-past by fighter planes thoroughly. Everyone was praising Indian Air Force for putting up a great show. Jai Ho !

(*a*) What term is used for the extremely loud burst of sound produced by extremely fast, low flying fighter jet planes ?

(*b*) What can you say about the speed of fighter jet planes which produce loud bursts of sound (or explosive noise) when they fly ? What special name is given to this speed ?

(*c*) A fighter jet is flying low at a speed of 1100 km/h. State whether it will produce extremely loud burst of sound or not. Give reason for your answer.

(*d*) Why did Radha prevent Pulkit from putting sharpened pencils into his ears ?

(*e*) Why did Radha put cotton ear buds into Pulkit's ears ?

(*f*) Name one object which travels at a speed greater than that of a fighter jet plane producing loud burst of sound.

(*g*) What values are displayed by Radha in this episode ?

Ans. (*a*) Sonic boom.

(*b*) The fighter jet planes which produce loud bursts of sound (or explosive noise) like that of a thunder, are travelling at a speed faster than the speed of sound in air. The speed which is greater than the speed of sound in air is called 'supersonic speed'.

(*c*) A fighter jet flying low at a speed of 1100 km/h will not produce extremely loud burst of sound (or sonic boom) because this speed is less than the speed of sound in air (which is about 1200 km/h).

(*d*) Radha prevented Pulkit from putting sharpened pencils into his ears because sharp objects can tear the delicate ear drum. The tearing of ear drum can make a person deaf.

(*e*) Radha put cotton ear buds into Pulkit's ears to soften the effect of extremely loud sound waves emitted by supersonic fighter jet planes during sonic boom and reduce pain in his ears.

(*f*) Rocket.

(*g*) The various values displayed by Radha in this episode are (*i*) Awareness of the delicate nature of human ear (*ii*) Desire to prevent damage to the ear drum of her brother (by preventing him from putting pencils into ears), and (*iii*) Reduce the suffering of her brother (by putting cotton ear buds into his ears).